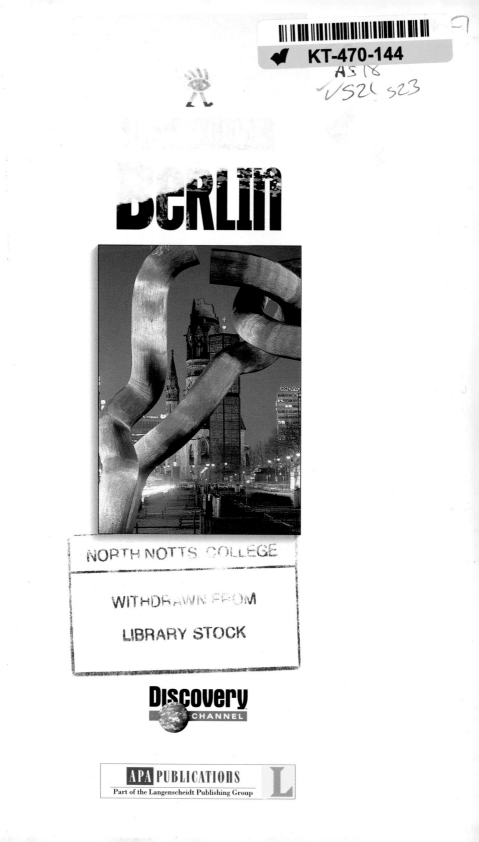

Berlin

Discovery CHANNEL

APA PUBLICATIONS L

Part of the Langenscheidt Publishing Group

ABOUT THIS BOOK

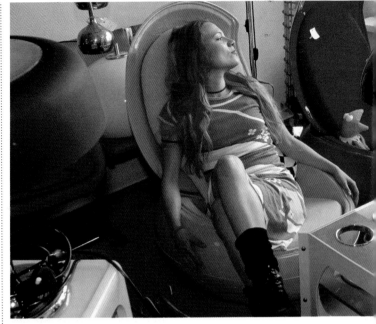

Editorial

Editor
Clare Griffiths
Editorial Director
Brian Bell

Distribution

UK & Ireland
GeoCenter International Ltd
The Viables Centre, Harrow Way
Basingstoke, Hants RG22 4BJ
Fax: (44) 1256-817988

United States
Langenscheidt Publishers, Inc.
46–35 54th Road, Maspeth, NY 11378
Fax: (1) 718 784-0640

Canada
Thomas Allen & Son Ltd
390 Steelcase Road East
Markham, Ontario L3R 1G2
Fax: (1) 905 475 6747

Australia
Universal Press
1 Waterloo Road
Macquarie Park, NSW 2113
Fax: (61) 2 9888 9074

New Zealand
Hema Maps New Zealand Ltd (HNZ)
Unit D, 24 Ra ORA Drive
East Tamaki, Auckland
Fax: (64) 9 273 6479

Worldwide
**Apa Publications GmbH & Co.
Verlag KG (Singapore branch)**
38 Joo Koon Road, Singapore 628990
Tel: (65) 865-1600. Fax: (65) 861-6438

Printing

Insight Print Services (Pte) Ltd
38 Joo Koon Road, Singapore 628990
Tel: (65) 865-1600. Fax: (65) 861-6438

©2001 Apa Publications GmbH & Co.
Verlag KG (Singapore branch)
All Rights Reserved
First Edition 1989
Sixth Edition 2001

CONTACTING THE EDITORS

We would appreciate it if readers would alert us to errors or outdated information by writing to:
**Insight Guides, P.O. Box 7910,
London SE1 1WE, England.**
Fax: (44) 20 7403-0290.
insight@apaguide.demon.co.uk

www.insightguides.com

This guidebook combines the interests and enthusiasms of two of the world's best-known information providers: Insight Guides, whose range of titles has set the standard for visual travel guides since 1970, and Discovery Channel, the world's premier source of non-fiction television programming. The editors of Insight Guides provide both practical advice and general understanding about a destination's history, culture, institutions and people. Discovery Channel and its website, www.discovery.com, help millions of viewers explore their world from the comfort of their own home and also encourage them to explore it firsthand.

This fully updated and expanded edition of *Insight Guide: Berlin* is carefully structured to convey an understanding Berlin and its culture as well as to guide readers through its sights and activities:

◆ The **Features** section, indicated by a yellow bar at the top of each page, covers the history and culture of the city in a series of informative essays.

◆ The main **Places** section, indicated by a blue bar, is a complete guide to all the sights and areas worth visiting. Places of special interest are coordinated by number with the maps.

◆ The **Travel Tips** listings section, with an orange bar, provides a handy point of reference for information on travel, hotels, shops, restaurants and more.

The contributors

This edition of *Insight Guide: Berlin* was commissioned and edited by **Clare Griffiths**. The book builds on the work of the original editors **Rolf Steinberg**, **Heinz Vestner** and **Wieland Giebel**. It has been carefully restructured and updated with the invaluable help of a team of people assembled by **Tim Reid** of the Berlin Information Group, an internet-based information provider on the city.

New essays commissioned for the this edition include a chapter on Berlin's Modern Architecture by travel writer **Michael Ivory**, and stories on multiculturalism and the gay and lesbian community written by **Jen Makin**. **Conor Hallahan** wrote the new chapter on Museum Island while **Tim Reid**, in addition to taking on the bulk of the updating work, contributed the one- page feature on

the history of Berlin's S- and U-Bahns. Many of the small tint box texts, which include pieces ranging from the impact of coffee bars on the drinking habits of Berliners to the architectural work of Karl Friedrich Schinkel, were written by **Dan Adler** and **Nathalie Ouriachi**. While much of the book's original text remains, it has been fully updated to reflect the city's recent changes. The contemporary history chapter, Modern Berlin, builds on an earlier essay by **Ute Frings** and **Petra Dubilski** and was bought up-to-date by **Stephanie Akin** who also wrote about the revival of Jewish culture and the city's alternative lifestyles. **Michael Ellsässer**'s original chapter on the people of Berlin was updated by **Izy Schoppe** who also found time to work on the chapter on the south and southwest outer districts. **Ken Ruesenberg** added to **Rita Unruh**'s essay on the Turkish Minority and also updated the chapter on Kreuzberg, originally written by **Arnold Seul**. Helping to update the original Places chapters written by, among others, **Sigrid Hoff**, **Arnold Seul**, **André Beck**, **Michael Bienert**, **Eva Schweitzer**, **Annette Leo** and **Anne Worst**, was **Simon Garnett** (southeast districts), **Nicola Varns** (Charlottenburg) and **Cordula Gdaniec** (Schöneberg and northwest districts). The Travel Tips section was updated and expanded by **Pan Tyndall**, **Carlos Silva**, **Stephanie Akin**, **Simon Garnett** and **Isabelle Claeys**. The main photographers who contributed to this edition include **Erhard Pansegrau**, **Frances Gransden**, **Günter Schneider** and **Blaine Harrington**. The text was proofread in London by **Susannah Wight** and indexed by **Isobel McLean**.

Map Legend

----	District Boundary
—•—	National Park/Reserve
Ⓢ	S–Bahn
Ⓤ	U–Bahn
✈ ✈	Airport: International/ Regional
🚌	Bus Station
❶	Tourist Information
✉	Post Office
🏛 † ⳨	Church/Ruins
†	Monastery
☾	Mosque
✡	Synagogue
🏰 ⌂	Castle/Ruins
⌂	Mansion/Stately home
∴	Archaeological Site
∩	Cave
👁	Statue/Monument
★	Place of Interest

The main places of interest in the Places section are coordinated by number with a full-colour map (e.g. ❶), and a symbol at the top of every right-hand page tells you where to find the map.

INSIGHT GUIDE
BERLIN

CONTENTS

Inside front cover:
Berlin
Inside back cover:
Berlin Transport.

The view over Nikolaiviertel (St Nicholas' Quarter), east of the centre, with the Fernsehturm (Television Tower) in the background

Travel Tips

Places

A MODERN MYTH

Berlin is reinventing itself yet again as it reassumes

its role as Germany's capital city

More history and more shock waves have reverberated through the world from Berlin than from virtually any other European metropolis. Ever since its foundation, and more especially since the beginning of the 20th century, Berlin has existed in a permanent state of transition. The seat of an imperial dynasty became a hotbed of revolution; the arena of the Roaring Twenties gave way to the headquarters of National Socialism; the scene of the greatest devastation in the German Reich was succeeded by a divided city dominated by two dialectically opposed hostile systems. West Berlin was a capitalist oasis, attached to an artificial life-support system and surrounded by a sea of socialism. East Berlin was the show capital, the shop window of socialist achievement. Berlin itself lived as the Siamese twin of two estranged and idealistically opposed parents.

The city still finds it hard to shake off its reputation. During the last century alone, Berlin became the capital from which two world wars were initiated. From here, too, the extermination of the Jewish race was planned. Berlin was the starting point for the student activism which was to spread across the West during the 1960s – whilst, across the Wall, huge parades were held in celebration of a Politburo which had lost much of its sense of direction.

Some view the city as a myth: a mere conglomeration of villages amalgamated into a city, an accumulation of Prussian conservatism whose significance has been artificially imposed. Instead of disregarding its status, one should ask why such importance has been imposed. After all, Berlin was intended as the standard bearer of a thousand-year Reich – praise indeed for a city that grew out of the marshes. Until now, however, no historical figure has managed to harness its almost mythic potential. Consensus will always be hard to break in a city grown from compromise rather than convenience.

It is said that history and legends are made here almost casually, out of events which only seem significant to politicians or a minority who cannot accept that they are merely a part of everyday life. For the citizens of Berlin, of whom now only half are native, history is only relevant at the moment of crisis; once that is over, they rapidly return to their daily routine. The destruction of the Wall? After a few weeks of jubilation, picnickers could be seen on what, until recently, had been a barrier of death.

A new European metropolis stands on the horizon but, while trying to form its new identity and embrace radical changes, Berlin finds itself not only looking forward but also glancing nervously behind at its confusing past. ❑

PRECEDING PAGES: statue of Victory crowning the Siegessäule in Tiergarten; Norman Foster's Reichstag dome; buildings in the business and finance district of Potsdamer Platz; *Molecule Man* sculpture by Jonathan Borofsky in Treptow. **LEFT:** partying at one of Berlin's many festivals.

Decisive Dates

EARLY SETTLEMENT

1244 Berlin, situated on the Spree on an adjacent island to the town of Cölln, is mentioned in contemporary records for the first time.

1307 Berlin and Cölln become the joint city of Berlin-Cölln under the Ascanian dynasty although both mint their own coinage until the 15th century.

1319 The death of the last Ascanian precipitates the collapse of the power of the margraves and consequently law and order in the province.

1369 Berlin and Cölln join the Hanseatic League.

1411 On the order of the Holy Roman Emperor, Burgrave Frederick of Nuremberg, a member of the Hohenzollern family, brings peace by becoming governor and subsequently Elector of the Marches.

1448 A citizens' rebellion is crushed by Frederick II after "The Berlin Indignation". Consolidation of Hohenzollern power is marked by a chain around the neck of Berlin's heraldic symbol, the bear.

1535 The first protestant elector, Joachim I Nestor, accedes to the throne, heralding the arrival of the Reformation to Berlin.

1540 The renaissance Schloss is completed and reflects the city's progress to stone buildings.

1617 Debut of Berlin's first weekly newspaper.

1618–48 Berlin's development is severely affected by the Thirty Years' War as it loses half its population of 12,000 and a third of its buildings. Plundering by Swedish and imperial troops adds to the misery. Accession to the throne of Friedrich Wilhelm, the Great Elector in 1640.

1668 The completion of the Oder-Spree canal provides a waterway between Beslau and Hamburg.

THE PRUSSIAN EMPIRE

1672 Jews and French Huguenot refugees are welcomed to Berlin. The city starts to benefit from their industry and culture. A mass influx of persecuted European Protestants is sparked.

1701 After the Hollenzollern's acquisition of Polish land up to the Russian frontier, the Great Elector's successor, Elector Friedrich II, declares himself King of Prussia. Berlin becomes a royal residence.

1713 Friedrich Wilhelm I, the Soldier King, ascends the throne and through a policy of "Army and Economy" tries to redress his predecessor's extravagances. The new conscription law is rewritten to exclude Berlin, which is now a garrison town, in order to stem the flow of skilled workers leaving the city.

1740 The ascension to the throne of Friedrich II (Friedrich the Great) means the start of military expansion and administrative reform. Berlin's status at the heart of Prussia is offset by its ongoing refinement and some of the city's finest-buildings, like those at the Gendarmemarkt and Unter den Linden, are constructed.

1791 The Brandenburg Gate, a monument to Prussian glory, is completed.

THE CITY EXPANDS

1806 During the Napoleonic Wars, Napoleon marches through the Brandenburg Gate marking the start of two years of French occupation. The *Quadriga* is removed and taken to France. Friedrich Wilhelm III flees to Königsberg.

1810 The Humboldt University is founded.

1813 Russia, Austria and Prussia defeat Napoleon at the Battle of Leipzig, and a year later the *Quadriga* is restored.

1837 The Borsig Werke is founded.

1838 The first railway line between Potsdam and Potsdamer Platz is completed. It is the third oldest line in Germany.

1840 Friedrich Wilhelm IV takes the throne and brings ageing cultural greats to Berlin but the poverty of the lower classes continues.

1844 The Berlin zoo (Zoologischer Garten) opens.

1848 Following revolutions in Paris and Vienna,

Berliners take to the streets in the "March Revolution". 200 lives are lost and the Kaiser is forced to pay tribute to the dead revolutionaries. The peace, however, is short-lived and, later in the year, General Wrangel occupies the city for the monarchy.
1861 Wilhelm I accedes to the throne.
1862 Otto von Bismarck becomes Prime Minister of Prussia. Four years later Berlin becomes the capital of the North-German Alliance.

THE SECOND GERMAN EMPIRE

1871 The German states' victory in the Franco-Prussian War is marked by the proclamation of the Second German Empire at Versailles. Berlin is now the Imperial capital of Germany.
1879 The Technical University is formed. Siemens and Halske demonstrate the first electric railway and electric lighting is introduced.
1888 Following the death of Wilhelm I and his successor Friedrich III, the third emperor in the space of 100 days dismisses Bismarck.
1902 Berlin's first underground line is opened between Zoo Station and Warschauer Brücke.
1914–18 World War I.

THE FIRST GERMAN REPUBLIC

1918 Kaiser Wilhelm abdicates in November. The ensuing disorder sees Philip Scheidemann proclaim Germany as a republic and Karl Liebknecht declare the nation as a socialist republic.
1919 The socialist Spartacus uprising is stopped as its leaders Karl Liebknecht and Rosa Luxemburg are murdered by government troops.
1920 Greater Berlin takes today's geographical form after territorial reform unites the city with a number of surrounding cities and towns.
1923 Hyperinflation hits its peak. A US dollar buys DM 42 billion. Three years later Hitler sends Goebbels to the city to "fight for Berlin".

THE THIRD REICH

1933 Hitler becomes Chancellor. Shortly after, the Reichstag is burnt down. A left-wing anarchist is blamed and Hitler uses this as an excuse to tighten his grip over the country.
1936 Nazi tyranny is suspended for two weeks as Berlin hosts the 11th Olympic Games.
1938 During *Kristallnacht* (9 November) the SA target Jewish shops, homes and businesses in a night of destruction.
1939 Outbreak of World War II.
1945 The Battle of Berlin. Hitler takes his own life in his bunker south of the Brandenburg Gate as Soviet troops close in. Germany surrenders. The de-Nazification of Berlin begins as the city is divided into four sectors.

THE FOUR-SECTOR CITY

1948–49 The Soviets cut off all transport into West Berlin during the Berlin Blockade. France, Britain and the US airlift supplies into the stranded city.
1949 Both the Federal Republic and the German

Democratic Republic (GDR) are formed.
1953 Soviet tanks hit the streets to quell the Workers' Uprising on 17 June.
1961 Railway links between the East and West are cut. The Berlin Wall is erected.
1963 US President John F. Kennedy gives his "Berliner" speech at Rathaus Schöneberg.
1971 Erich Honecker becomes GDR Head of State.
1972 The Berlin Agreement allows travel between East Berlin and the GDR.
1987 Berlin celebrates its 750th birthday.
1989 On 9 November, the Wall falls.
1990 On 3 October, Germany is officially reunified.
1999 The capital of Germany is officially moved from Bonn to Berlin.   ❑

PRECEDING PAGES: Unter den Linden in 1770.
LEFT: a 19th-century portrait of a member of the Prussian royal family.
RIGHT: Schinkel-designed statue on Schlossbrücke.

THE TOWN ON THE SPREE

Berlin outgrew the adjacent town of Cölln to become a beautiful and prosperous city poised on the edge of industrialisation

Present-day Berlin occupies an area once settled by Slavic tribes. After the unification of the Germanic tribes in the 10th century, Otto the Great extended his empire east of the Elbe as far as the Oder. It was only after a Slavic revolt, however, that a second military invasion enabled him to bring the region under permanent German rule. He named it the Brandenburg Marches after Brennabor on the Havel, the first Slavic town he had conquered.

By 1157 the Imperial Counts of the Ascanian dynasty received the Marches in fief. They took possession of the Fortress of Spandau, just a few miles west of present-day Berlin, and by the middle of the 13th century they controlled the entire area occupied by the present-day city of Berlin. Shortly after this, their power extended northwards as far as Pomerania, and in the east into lands beyond the Oder.

The first settlers

Berlin's 750-year history begins with two separate towns. Lying on adjacent islands in the Spree, the twin settlements of Berlin and Cölln were already closely linked by common economic interests when, at the start of the 14th century, they banded together under a joint municipal administration. The first settlers probably came to the islands during the last third of the 12th century. Cölln is mentioned in contemporary records for the first time in 1237, with Berlin appearing seven years later. Both received town charters before the end of the 13th century.

In those days the Havel-Spree region was an inhospitable, sparsely populated area. In places where the soil wasn't too sandy to cultivate, it was covered in dense forests, which were broken up by a network of lakes, watercourses and low-lying marshes. The inhabitants of the Slavic villages grazed cattle and scratched out a meagre living in their fields in the clearings. Only after the invention of the wheeled plough

---

LEFT: the Elector Joachim II of Brandenburg.
RIGHT: a statue of Albrecht the Bear who became margrave of the Northern March in 1134.

and iron ploughshare were they able to cultivate the clay soils, and the growth and prosperity of Berlin and Cölln increased considerably.

The Middle Ages

Throughout the entire Middle Ages, wood, linen, woollen cloth, and rye from the Marches

remained the principal trading commodities. Vassal noblemen and knights summoned by the Ascanians built a defensive network of castles across the land. To support these new strongholds, the knights founded new villages, recruiting peasants, craftsmen and merchants from the Lower Rhine, Flanders and the foothills of the Northern Harz, the original home of the Ascanians.

Unlike Spandau and Köpenick, the two other medieval towns lying within the area occupied by Germany's present capital, the twin cities of Berlin and Cölln owed their existence to trade. The Spree islands saddled the best place to ford the river for miles around. Not only did this situation divert carts through the cities, it also gave the burgeoning settlements control over river traffic. Soon the merchants and boatmen of Berlin monopolised the sup- ply of goods to the immediate hinterland, and controlled the Brandenburg Marches' long- distance trade.

With trade came wealth and increasing demands from merchants and the aristocracy. Arts and crafts flourished. Permanent housing gradually replaced the thatched-roofed wattle and daub houses; churches and monasteries sprung up. Magis-

> ### HERALDIC BEAR
>
> The consolidation of Hohenzollern power is marked when a chain and padlock is put around the neck of the city's heraldic bear.

in a feud with the Pope. Under the leadership of Berlin, the towns decided to act. They organised a local militia, yet reached no peace until 1411, when Burgrave Frederick of Nuremberg, a member of the Hohenzollern family, became governor and later Elector of the Marches.

The Hohenzollerns

The arrival of the Hohenzollerns in Brandenburg marked the end of the medieval power struggle among towns, knights and princes within the kingdom of Germania. During the

trates and noblemen acquired land, or entire villages, throughout the neighbourhood.

Compared with the well-established German trading centres on the Rhine and the Danube, Berlin's prosperity at the time must have seemed quite modest. During the Middle Ages the city played virtually no part in the cultural and economic life of Germany. Thus, the end of the Ascanian dynasty precipitated the collapse of power of other regional leaders, and consequently of law and order in the province.

The Marches, terrorised by highwaymen and bands of robbers, appealed in vain to the emperor. He, however, was beset by problems concerning his own crown and was caught up

reign of the second Hohenzollern elector a dispute arose in Berlin between the high-handed patrician town council and the burghers, who demanded the right to determine their own affairs. The common people called upon their ruler for assistance, but he took the opportunity to increase his own authority over the town and instated far-reaching decrees, which discounted the constitution of the community.

From this point onwards, the administrative council was subject to the will of the prince. He gave himself the right to approve the appointment of counsellors and seized the jurisdiction once more. His diktat prevented alliances with other towns and annulled the joint administration of the twin cities that had prevailed until this time. The citizens of Berlin rebelled to regain their lost civil rights, but the effort ended in failure.

The prince built a city fortress at Cölln, and half a century later, Berlin and Cölln became royal seats. Knights, officials, merchants and courtiers left the Hohenzollerns' Franconian possessions and took up residence on the Spree.

During the course of the Reformation, the city fortress was rebuilt in the Renaissance style; two castles in Grunewald and Köpenick

TOUGH TIMES

Famine and disease caused the population of Berlin-Cölln to dip to just 6,000 in 1648.

progress. There was no municipal refuse collection scheme and, in 1576, 4,000 citizens fell victim to the plague. The population was so afflicted that it didn't regain its old level of 12,000 until the beginning of the Thirty Years' War in 1618.

The Thirty Years' War

The three decades of war until 1648 marked a time of great privation for the city, although the actual battles were fought elsewhere. War contributions and general inflation swallowed up most of Berlin's wealth; a trade slump gob-

served as hunting lodges. A cappella, a royal choir, and a number of pictures by Lukas Cranach in the royal chapel were some of the first digressions into courtly culture. Amongst the bourgeoisie, too, culture and education were making great strides. New schools were being built, a printers' workshop and a pharmacy were established, and the first record of a theatrical performance dates to this period. In 1617 Berlin's first weekly newspaper made its debut.

Domestic sanitary conditions made slower

LEFT: Frederick William receives French refugees.
ABOVE: an engraving by Pieter von der Aa of Berlin-Cölln, 1729.

bled up much of what was left, and plundering Swedish and imperial troops took the rest.

Thousands of citizens lost their homes when one of the emperor's ministers, fearing an attack by Sweden, had the city suburbs burned to the ground. A magistrates' report dating from this period registers a rising suicide rate. Many Berliners were forced to emigrate.

Friedrich Wilhelm of Brandenburg, later known as the Great Elector, instigated an extensive rebuilding program for his capital, adding fortifications to protect it against attack. By the end of his reign in 1688, a transformation had taken place. Berlin had grown – it had a population of 20,000 – and become more beautiful. However, it remained a provincial backwater compared with Paris or even Vienna, which was seven times as big.

The Huguenots arrive

A series of shrewd ordinances by Friedrich Wilhelm, revived the ruined economy. A tax reform reactivated trade and business, and the construction of the canal linking the Oder with the Spree provided a waterway between Breslau and Hamburg.

The Great Elector's adroit policy of offering asylum to Jews and persecuted French Protestants also jolted economic and cultural development. He gave letters of protection and virtually unrestricted trading rights to 50 wealthy Jewish families who had been expelled from Austria. With their capital, experience and international contacts, they soon became a more or less indispensable part of the economic scene. Their influence protected them to some extent from envy and growing animosity on the part of their Christian competitors. Initially forbidden to build a synagogue, the Jews gradually acquired more privileges. But in the end, they became the financial victims of a special taxation system, and restrictive regulations passed during the 18th century forced all but the very richest Jews to flee the country.

Another influx of money and economic experience came to Berlin after the Edict of Nantes in 1685, when 5,000 French Huguenots fled to the city for refuge. Berlin profited from their skills as technicians and craftsmen, along with a touch of the more sophisticated lifestyle they brought with them from France. The Huguenots founded a number of new industries – silk weaving, and paper and glass manufacture – and introduced tobacco farming within the Marches.

Further groups of persecuted Protestants – from the Palatinate, Switzerland, Bohemia and the Salzburg region – were soon flocking to Berlin in considerable numbers. This cosmopolitan influence helped to establish the characteristic tolerance and open-mindedness for which Berliners were once famed.

The city's economic upsurge during the last third of the 17th century also had a favourable effect on culture and science. A daily newspaper already existed; a medical college supervised blossoming practitioners, and the alchemist Johann Kunckel discovered a procedure for the manufacture of ruby-coloured glass. The Academy of Arts opened in 1696, followed a few years later by the Academy of Sciences, whose first president was the philosopher Gottfried Wilhelm Leibniz.

Through cunning, force, marriage and inheritance the Hohenzollerns increased their possessions; and, with the acquisition of the Polish duchy of Prussia, their sway extended as far as the Russian frontier. In 1701 Friedrich I, the Great Elector's successor, demonstrated this new self-confidence by crowning himself King of Prussia. Berlin became a royal residence. The master builders Andreas Schlüter and Arnold Nering erected some fine examples of

baroque architecture. But the vast remodelling of the city palace, and the construction of the residences of Charlottenburg and Monbijou, as well as the Arsenal, the Academy and the two cathedrals on the Gendarmenmarkt drove the nation to the point of bankruptcy.

The soldier king

When Friedrich Wilhelm I ascended the throne in 1713, there was no room for further royal extravagance. "Army and Economy" were the twin overriding interests of the "Soldier King". He slashed four-fifths of the court maintenance budget. He planted the palace gardens at Charlottenburg with cabbages, and turned the pleasure garden into a drill ground. The king regarded art and science as unnecessary; his only exception was medicine. Thus, he ordained the foundation of the Charité, an innovation by virtue of its dual function as research institute and hospital. Furthermore, it was to the "father of militarism" that Prussia owed the introduction of compulsory education.

In order to be able to finance Friedrich Willhelm's well-trained army, the king also had to concentrate on the economic development of his country. At the beginning of his reign, Berlin suffered considerably under his universal conscription law. Over a period of two years

there was a mass exodus of 17,000 people – half of them skilled workers. Eventually, Friedrich Wilhelm excluded the city from the conscription regulations, and new manufacturing industries, mostly suppliers of military equipment, attracted recruits for the workforce. Under Friedrich II, who succeeded the "Soldier King" in 1740, courtly culture and pleasures flourished. An opera house was built and celebrations, music and plays returned to the city. The militarism remained, however. Friedrich's wars earned him the title "the Great" (he is

LEFT: Frederick the Great inspects the 1st Battalion.
ABOVE: the Berlin-Potsdam railway around 1850.

known as Frederick the Great), and increased the size of his kingdom considerably, making Prussia a major European power.

The Age of the Enlightenment

A policy of subvention attracted new industries; the city's population grew by a half over the next two decades. The restructuring of the city centre by Georg Knobelsdorff and Karl von Gontard had begun before the war with the building of the Opera House, the cathedral and the Roman Catholic cathedral of St Hedwig. It was now continued in the Gendarmenmarkt complex and reached its apogee with the remodelling of the Lindenallee to form a monumental avenue, today's Unter den Linden. Under Friedrich's successor, Friedrich Wilhelm III, the latter received its magnificent conclusion in the form of the classically inspired Brandenburg Gate, completed in 1795.

At this time, great thinkers like Gotthold Ephraim Lessing, Friedrich Nicolai and Moses Mendelssohn were making their contribution to the literary criticism of the Enlightenment and earning Berlin its reputation as the German intellectual capital. A century after the first Jew acquired full civil rights in Prussia, Jewish salons became the centres of "witty Berlin". The Romantic era began. Imitating the French, the nobility and the haute bourgeoisie cultivated a new kind of liberal democratic society.

French supremacy

In 1806, during the Napoleonic Wars, the Prussian army suffered defeat at the battles of Jena and Auerstädt. The French emperor and his troops marched victoriously through the Brandenburg Gate. Two years of occupation followed, giving way to many years of French supremacy. Meanwhile, intense feelings of patriotism were fermenting in the German capital. Friedrich Jahn, the father of physical education, trained the male youth of Berlin in preparation for the struggle against the oppressors; between 1813 and 1815 their fight for liberation was victorious. The French had to leave, but some of their ideas remained.

The sentiments of freedom expressed during the French Revolution found an echo in Prussia. The absolute rulers were forced to make concessions. But, as the forces of restoration started to regain ground, there came a time of increased repression, denunciations and police terror. In resignation, the bourgeoisie retreated into the safety of business and private pleasures. Berlin had been the seat of a university since 1810. A succession of important scholars, including Wilhelm von Humboldt, Johann Gottlieb Fichte, Friedrich Wilhelm Schelling and Georg Friedrich Hegel, ensured its growing reputation for academic excellence. A few decades later it was the largest seat of learning in the country, with over 2,000 students.

Industrialisation and poverty

Socially and economically, the long reign of Friedrich Wilhelm III (1797–1840) marked the

emancipation of the bourgeoisie and the beginning of industrialisation, accompanied by increasing impoverishment of the masses and the emergence of a working class. Whilst Carl Gotfried Langhans and Friedrich Schinkel were adorning the royal seat with neoclassical churches and palaces, the age of the tenement house had begun in the suburbs.

New industrial projects heightened the demand for underpaid workers. A few years before Friedrich Wilhelm III ascended the throne, the first steam engine was commissioned in the Royal Porcelain Factory in Dresden. Two decades later, the first steam-powered boat was sailing on the Spree.

Towards the end of the monarch's reign the first train connection opened between Berlin and Potsdam. Initially, the accession of Friedrich Wilhelm IV aroused great hopes. But social reforms linked to a new constitution did not occur. A loosening of censorship did little to alleviate the situation. The king drew up extravagant plans for the embellishment of his capital, and spent large sums of money persuading ageing cultural celebrities to come to Berlin, including poets, philosophers, and painters.

The Grimm brothers, exiled from Göttingen for their liberal politics, were offered asylum and academic positions. The composer Jacob Meyerbeer took over the direction of the Opera House. In 1844, Friedrich Wilhelm went so far as to open Germany's first zoo.

In the meantime, there was no respite from the growing misery of the impoverished masses. Half of Berlin's 400,000 inhabitants were members of the lower class. In 1847 the city was obliged to devote 40 percent of its annual budget to charity. The were several cases of unrest in Prussia, the most violent being the Silesian weavers' riots.

Revolution and reaction

When, in the spring of 1848, revolution broke out in Paris and Vienna, the middle and working classes of Berlin also took to the streets to demonstrate. The ensuing bloody battles claimed 200 victims, but the revolutionaries triumphed. The king was forced to pay his respects to the corpses as they lay in state on the Schlossplatz.

The dreams of a better future lasted for over six months. Improvements were discussed in democratic clubs and in scores of new newspapers in circulation (freedom of the press as well as freedom of assembly was guaranteed). But nationalists and democrats blocked each other with paralysing political disputes, and in 1848 General Wrangel occupied Berlin at the head of the royal troops. A further period of repression began. The constitution, when eventually approved, made only the smallest of concessions to the liberals, and cemented the autocratic position of the ruling dynasty. ❑

LEFT: overcrowded and insanitary living conditions in Prenzlauer Berg.
RIGHT: Wilhelm I holds a reception in the "White Hall" of the Berlin Palace in a painting by A. von Menzel.

FROM TOWN TO METROPOLIS

Berlin flourished during the late 19th century but triumph was to lead to disaster in the next century when political tensions in Europe erupted

During the second half of the 19th century, Berlin became the largest industrial city in Europe after Paris. As early as 1859, Karl Marx, who had studied on the Spree two decades previously, remarked: "People who saw Berlin 10 years ago would not recognise it today. In those days it was a sterile parade ground; now it is the bustling centre of German engineering." The king of steam locomotives, Borsig, led the industrial scene with a grandiose factory in the city. The Telegraphic Construction Company Siemens and Halske, which opened in 1847, pioneered new avenues in electrotechnology, and the invention of the dynamo made even further headway in the city's economic development.

At the same time, the workers' movement established itself as a counterbalance to this world of capitalist enterprise. Despite a 16-hour day, most workers were barely able to eke out an existence in their drab tenement houses. Socialist views found increasing numbers of supporters in the slums to the north and east of the city. In 1863 Ferdinand Lassalle founded the first social democratic workers' organisation, the General Association of German Workers. Berlin became the centre of the trade union movement and the bastion of the social democratic movement.

The Second German Empire

In the meantime, Prussia had increased its territorial possessions through wars with Denmark and Austria. North of the Main, it now ruled most of Germany between the French frontier to the west and the Russian to the east. With the dissolution of the German Alliance in 1866, Austria stepped out of its century-old political power struggle within Germany. Prussia had won the upper hand; the dream of Frederick the Great had come true. In the same year, Berlin became the capital of the Northern

German Alliance – the last step towards a unification of a "small" Germany that did not include Austria.

Basking in the wake of their successful war against France (1870–71), the German princes offered the imperial crown to the Prussian king five years later. The gesture wasn't one of pure

inclination, rather a bow to the gravitational forces of politics and economics, which required a unified nation state.

On 18 January 1871, the Second German Empire was proclaimed in the Hall of Mirrors at Versailles. King Wilhelm I of Prussia (1797–1888) was elected emperor of Germany. Otto von Bismarck (1815–98), the driving force behind the political union, became the first imperial chancellor. During his period of office (1871–90), Bismarck, the "Iron Chancellor", played an important role in shaping European politics from Berlin. Thus, the former residential city of the Prussian-Brandenburg monarchy became the capital of imperial Germany.

LEFT: lunch time at the Borsig factory (painting by Hans Baluschek, 1912).
RIGHT: Brandenburger Tor in the late 19th century.

The years of expansion

With its 826,000 inhabitants, the nation's new capital was by far the largest city in Germany. Nonetheless, compared with Paris – which was twice the size – or with cosmopolitan London, it retained a provincial air. But, after the foundation of the empire in 1871, Germany's economic and industrial expansion was no longer held back by small-state politics. Fuelled by French reparation funds, the country rapidly made up for lost time. Between 1871 and 1873 Germany experienced the boom years of the Gründerzeit, during which the German empire was caught up in the gargantuan economic and technical process of modernisation. The Industrial Revolution started later than elsewhere on the continent and therefore advanced extremely rapidly. National contracts and the repayment of war loans pumped large sums of money into industry. But many of the newly established joint-stock companies had no sound basis, or were even fraudulent. Crashes and financial scandals were especially commonplace in the booming building and land speculation markets.

A steady stream of new labour converged in Berlin from every corner of the empire. All these emigrants needed somewhere to live. Mass production tenement houses were built cheaply and quickly. In the rural communities on the edge of the city, land prices rose to 50 times their prewar levels; the farmers of Wilmersdorf, Schöneberg and Tempelhof were able to retire on their newly acquired wealth.

Land speculation continued to be a profitable business even after the stock market crash of 1873 and the following years of depression. Housing remained scarce although building continued apace. The industrial suburbs, the villages and the villa colonies grew ever closer to each other between the Havel and the Spree.

In 1920 the many urban and rural communities were finally joined together as a political and administrative unit. Greater Berlin had become a reality, with a population that almost reached 4 million.

The modern metropolis

This rapid transformation into the first modern metropolis in Germany reflected Berlin's economic prosperity. A new drainage system lowered the risk of infectious diseases; a covered market and a central slaughterhouse improved food supplies. Even traffic problems caused by the rapid expansion were solved with a circuit of railway and suburban trains, widened streets, and a network of horse-drawn trams.

In 1879 the Technical High School (now the Technical University) opened its doors, and the company of Siemens and Halske demonstrated the first electric railway. Only two years later, electric trains were running in the Lichterfelde public transport system. By this time, there were already electric street lamps and a telephone network with about 50 subscribers. At the turn of the century, horseless carriages and buses slowly began to supersede horse-drawn

BERLIN ON THE MAP

If you look at a map you will find Berlin to the east of the Elbe in the Brandenburg Marches, on about the same latitude as London and the same longitude as Naples. Before Germany was divided at the end of World War II, the capital also lay at the geographical centre of the German Empire, founded on 18 January 1871 by King Wilhelm I of Prussia. From a population of just 300,000 in 1850 the town's population grew to 1.9 million in 1900. During the post-war years Berlin served as a focal point in another respect: here the world superpowers, the Soviet Union and the United States, confronted each other more directly than anywhere else on earth.

vehicles. And in 1902, people could move even faster: the first over- and underground railway line was carrying passengers between the Warschauer Brücke and the Zoological Gardens in Berlin.

The Wilhelminian era

Kaiser Wilhelm I died of old age on 18 January 1888; so began what came to be known as the "year of the three emperors": His successor, Friedrich III, followed him to his grave only 99 days later. The next in line was Friedrich's ambitious and

THE IRON CHANCELLOR

Born in 1815, Otto von Bismarck, prime minister of Prussia 1862–90 and chancellor of the German Empire 1871–90, created a unified Germany using forceful diplomacy and war.

the economic and political centre. The city's rapid economic development and its equally rapid population growth produced a spirit of dynamism and modernity that characterised the next decade in spite of the Wilhelminians' conservatism. An influx of youthful, new ideas revived the literary scene, whose poets, radical thinkers and "cultural gypsies" dreamed of recreating the world through art.

The premières of Gerhard Hauptmann's naturalistic plays marked the beginning of a new

profoundly Prussian son, Wilhelm II. Whereas Wilhelm I had allowed Bismarck a fairly free hand in the formation of the new German empire, Wilhelm II saw a strong chancellor as an obstacle to his own aims. In March 1890, amidst much bitterness, Bismarck was forced to resign. The "pilot of German politics" left the ship of state, and the Wilhelminian era began.

It was a period which witnessed the completion of Germany's transition from an agricultural to a modern industrial state, with Berlin as

LEFT: the inauguration of the National Monument.
ABOVE: crowds on Potsdamer Platz at the wedding of Victoria Luise of Prussia in 1913.

chapter of German theatrical history. Berlin became a melting pot for all that was new and modern. The list of men and women of letters who lived and worked in the city after the 1890s reads like a litany of modern German literary history: from Heinrich Mann to Frank Wedekind and Rainer Maria Rilke, from Stefan George and Robert Musil to Expressionist poets such as Else Lasker-Schüler, Georg Heym and Gottfried Benn. Swedish dramatist August Strindberg spent a longish period in Berlin, as did the Norwegian artist Edvard Munch. An exhibition of Munch's paintings shortly before the turn of the century caused such a scandal that the Secessionist Group of artists formed in response. Their impressionist-realistic approach opposed the official school of painting patronised by state and court. A good 10 years later, with the arrival of Dresden's Die Brücke group – Ernst-Ludwig Kirchner, Erich Heckel, Max Pechstein, and so on – Berlin became the centre of Expressionist art, too.

The city flourishes

From the turn of the century, the imperial capital led the rest of the country in virtually every sphere. Berlin's press and its critics set the tone for the empire. The nation riveted its theatrical attention on the Deutsches Theater, under the

direction of Max Reinhardt. Hans Pfitzner brought his acclaim to the privately owned Theater des Westens, where he was the director. Richard Strauss set the pace in classical music as composer and conductor at the National Court Opera, and the Berlin Philharmonic grew in the nation's esteem, first under Hans von Bülow and then Arthur Nikisch.

A long list of names, including those of historian Theodor Mommsen, physicians Rudolf Virchow, Paul Ehrlich and Robert Koch and the physicists Max Planck and Albert Einstein, testifies to the significance of Wilhelminian Berlin as a centre of research and teaching in the humanities and, increasingly, in the natural

sciences. At the turn of the century, half-a-dozen future Nobel laureates lived in Berlin.

The road to war

During the early years of the 20th century political tensions in Europe intensified. International confidence dwindled as each country became drawn into the arms race. In 1914, the crisis climaxed. On 28 June crown prince Franz Ferdinand, the heir to the Austrian throne, was assassinated in Sarajevo. When Austria declared war on Serbia, Germany followed suit. Six weeks later, most of Europe was at war. In a burst of patriotism, German youth flocked to the front. The military leaders were predicting a six-month fight before victory was theirs.

Their estimates were utterly wrong. A sea blockade was erected around Germany, and soon the world was embroiled in war. Its consequences became increasingly evident in civilian life. Prices rose and a black market developed. In 1915 food was rationed and some items disappeared from the shops. During the winter of 1917–18, following a poor potato harvest, famine was rife. Starving crowds raided bakers' and butchers' shops in Berlin.

Meanwhile, under the leadership of Karl Liebknecht and Rosa Luxemburg, a group who opposed the war had broken away from the Social Democratic Party and was agitating for peace. The successful Russian revolution in 1917 aroused hopes that here, too, the old order could be overturned. Workers and sections of the bourgeoisie continued to press for a negotiated peace. In January 1918, 300,000 workers went out on strike. Military intervention put a brutal end to the rebellion.

As the war progressed, the Central Powers' bulwarks gradually collapsed. Despite Germany's victory on the Eastern Front, its military strength was exhausted. In November 1918, the navy mutinied in Wilhelmshaven and Kiel, and the rebellion rapidly spread to other places. A committee of workers and sailors called for a general strike in Berlin. After long hesitation, the Kaiser abdicated and fled to the Netherlands. On 9 November Social Democrat Philipp Scheidemann, standing at the window of the Reichstag, proclaimed the first German Republic. ❏

Left: Unter den Linden, 1913.
Right: reading out the mobilisation order on Unter den Linden, 31 July 1914.

FROM METROPOLIS TO BOMB SITE

At the beginning of the 1920s, Berlin was one of the most fashionable and vibrant capitals in Europe. Twenty-five years later, it lay in ruins

"The Kaiser went, but the generals stayed," was how novelist Theodor Plivier summed up Germany's problems in the period of turmoil following the abdication of Wilhelm II and the sudden ending of more than 500 years of rule by the Hohenzollern dynasty. November 1918 saw revolution in the air, with the country eager to see the toppling of the old order whom they blamed for defeat. Throughout the empire, workers and soldiers formed committees and the red flag fluttered above many town halls and barracks. A "People's Naval Division" of 3,000 mutinous sailors from Kiel arrived in Berlin, occupying the imperial palace and the royal stables and were supported by some locally garrisoned troops. The people, tired of war, marched through the streets shouting "Peace, freedom, bread!"

In the face of the popular revolution, the imperial chancellor, Prince Max of Baden, handed over the reins of government to Friedrich Ebert, the leader of the SPD. The Social Democrats had the majority of votes in parliament. The socialist workers' movement became the strongest element in what was otherwise a political vacuum. But divisions within the party meant that it was not prepared for this sudden rise to power. The socialists under Ebert and Philipp Scheidemann decided to go the way of parliamentary democracy, while a splinter group of independent socialists campaigned for a reform of the state along revolutionary principles. On the extreme left, the militant Spartacus League believed that government should be along the lines of that newly created in Russia by the October Revolution.

Scarcely had Scheidemann announced the birth of the German Republic before cheering crowds in front of the Reichstag building, than Karl Liebknecht, the leader of the Spartacists, proclaimed the Free Socialist Republic of Germany from a balcony of the palace. Thus, even on 9 November 1918, it was clear that the split in the German left was irreconcilable. It was this schism which, 14 years later, was to sound the death knell of the Weimar Republic.

Popular discontent

But to return to the beginning. When he fled into exile, the Kaiser left behind an empire in

chaos. In the industrial centres, demonstrations by starving workers blocked the streets. Wildcat strikes paralysed the economy. Some 2 million soldiers back from the front with the Western Army, including a lance-corporal by the name of Adolf Hitler, had little more to do than sit around the barracks in disillusionment.

Civil war was in the air. The provisional government in Berlin took draconian measures in order to re-establish its authority. For this it turned to troops from the old army, as some units had reformed as so-called volunteer corps following their demobilisation orders. During the winter of 1918, Berlin's historic city centre resembled a revolutionary army camp. Sailors

LEFT: mutineers in the November Revolution, 1918.
RIGHT: women demonstrate for the right to vote, 1912.

of the People's Naval Division and Red Workers' brigades patrolled the streets. At the end of December Gustav Noske, the minister of defence, had the palace forcibly cleared by government troops, with 67 fatalities. Bloody skirmishes finally escalated into an open power struggle when, on 5 January 1919, a mass demonstration protested against the dismissal of the revolutionary chief of police.

The Spartacus League, which had been rechristened the German Communist Party (KPD), called for a general strike. Armed Red Front fighters erected barricades by the Brandenburg Gate: the press district, near what later became

General strike versus military coup

Elections for the National Assembly were held that week with the Social Democrats gaining the most votes. The members of parliament retired from the restless capital to the small town of Weimar. There, on 11 August 1919, they approved the Weimar Constitution, which gave women the vote and established basic human rights, but was also full of flaws. Friedrich Ebert became Germany's new president, leading a broad coalition of left and centre left parties dominated by the SPD.

Meanwhile, faced with an ultimatum, the German negotiators acquiesced to the peace

Checkpoint Charlie, was transformed into a stronghold. It took some 3,000 government troops to drive the Spartacists out of their bases and crush the so-called "Spartacus Revolt".

Karl Liebknecht and Rosa Luxemburg, the two leaders of the November Revolution, went into hiding. On 15 January they were discovered in a flat in Wilmersdorf and brought to the Hotel Eden, the headquarters of the Infantry Division. After interrogation, they were assaulted by their guards during their transfer to the Moabit Criminal Court, and subsequently murdered in the Tiergarten park. Rosa Luxemburg's body was thrown into the Landwehr Canal; the killers were never brought to justice.

terms contained in the Treaty of Versailles. It is difficult to imagine a worse debt of guilt than that placed by the victorious allies on the new republic. The extremists of the right protested loudly against the "shameful decree"; monarchists and the military were reluctant to admit their own failure. With the words "unconquered on the battlefield" they spread the lie that in 1919 the front line forces only had to cede victory because of treachery from within their ranks. The "stab in the back" legend poisoned the political atmosphere, and provided fuel for the fires of right-wing and conservative anger.

The republic could not rely on public opinion, a fact demonstrated by the Kapp Putsch of

13 March 1920. Instigated by Baron Walter Von Lüttwitz, this latest coup attempt was led by one Wolfgang Kapp, a provincial director and arch-conservative official from East Prussia who was virtually unknown in Berlin. 6,000 soldiers of the Erhard Brigade marched on the city from their camp at Döberitz. Wearing swastikas on their sleeves and rallying behind the black, white and red battle standard, they forcibly occupied the government district and other strategic points, declaring the constitutional government to be null and void.

> ### BAUHAUS STARS
>
> Located in nearby Dessau, staff at the Bauhaus school included Paul Klee, Wassily Kandinsky, Ludwig Mies Van der Rohe, Walter Gropius (the school's founder), Oskar Schlemmer and Hannes Meyer.

With little resistance coming from the army, it was up to the people to act. Encouraged by the government (which had fled to Dresden) workers and unions staged a general strike which left Berlin once again in chaos. The city was without water, gas, electricity or telephone services. Post offices and banks remained closed. After only four days, the spectre of military dictatorship had vanished, along with Kapp himself.

The "Golden Twenties"

The "Golden Twenties" was characterised by Berlin in the years leading up to the great Wall Street Crash of 25 October 1929. But the start of the decade was anything but auspicious. The payment of war reparations led to a rapid currency devaluation, resulting in a huge rise in the cost of living. The US dollar, with a 1914 value of 4.20 Marks, was worth 7,500 Reichsmarks in 1922. One year later, when inflation had reached its peak, the exchange rate had rocketed to 4.2 billion. During the years of mass poverty, black marketers and speculators flourished. It was only the introduction of the Rentenmark in 1923 that brought about a period of economic stability.

The Berlin of the Weimar Republic was a city of stark contrasts. The former imperial capital blossomed into a metropolis on a par with London, Paris and New York. Its population grew between the wars from 3.8 million to 4.3 million. The immediate cause of this expansion was the controversial territorial reform of Octo-

ber 1920, which by a single act increased the city's area thirteenfold. Industry expanded into the outer districts. The citizens left the bleak tenements for the green belt communities on the periphery.

During this period, Berlin can lay claim to a number of exemplary achievements in the realm of local government politics. Thanks to the tireless endeavours of Ernst Reuter, the director of transport, the Berlin Public Transport Company (BVG) was founded on 1 January 1929. It was responsible for 92

tram routes, 30 bus routes and four underground railway lines. For a fixed price people could travel across the city in all directions. The Weimar years gave Berlin its trades fair centre and Tempelhof Airport – the "air crossroads of Europe". The suburban railway was electrified, and the city's countenance was enriched by the architecture of the Bauhaus movement.

A modern Babylon

Against a background of freedom and cosmopolitanism, tempered with political tension and social contrast, Berlin in the 1920s became the focal point of the arts scene for an entire continent. It was a latter-day Babylon to which

LEFT: troops join strikers during demonstrations, 1918.
RIGHT: the "Golden Twenties" – a show in the Admiralspalast at Friedrichstrasse station.

flocked men of letters, artists, architects, musicians, film makers and journalists from all over Europe. The new "West End" around the Kurfürstendamm became the centre of the city's nocturnal life, the meeting place of high society and bohemians alike. The streets were lined with cinemas, bars, dancehalls and artists' hangouts. As Günter Birkenfeld remarked, the Romanisches Café near the Gedächtniskirche was the rendezvous of "everyone from Reykjavik to Tahiti who could claim some sort of relationship, whether

INTELLECTUAL ELITE

Of the 19 German Nobel laureates of the Weimar years, 10 – including Max Planck and Albert Einstein – lived in Berlin.

character actors of sound films. In the theatrical world, Berlin experienced an unexpected Golden Age thanks to productions by Bertholt Brecht, Max Reinhardt, Erwin Piscator, Leopold Jessner and Jürgen Fehling. Max "The Wizard" Reinhardt staged the first Berlin productions of George Bernard Shaw's plays. In 1927, Piscator's political revue *Hurrah! We're Alive* had its première in the Theater am Nollendorfplatz. The theatrical life was at its most vibrant, with more than three dozen theatres in or around the city centre.

professional or amorous, with the Muses and the Graces".

The biggest film studios in Europe were built in Babelsberg, just outside the city limits, by Universum Film AG (UFA). World-famous films were produced here, from Robert Wiene's *The Cabinet of Dr Cagliari* and Friedrich Murnau's *Nosferatu* to Fritz Lang's *Metropolis*. Producers of world calibre – G.W. Pabst, Ernst Lubitsch and Erich Pommer – worked in Berlin. Billy Wilder was here as a reporter. Greta Garbo and Marlene Dietrich used the city as a stepping stone to Hollywood. Werner Krauss, Emil Jannings, Conrad Veidt and Peter Lorre (star of *M*) found fame as the first

The city was a magnet for artists from other countries. A large Russian artistic community developed, fleeing the excesses of the October revolution. Anna Pavlova danced here, Nabokov wrote here, Stanislavsky toured here. From England came the poet W.H. Auden and the author Christopher Isherwood. From the United States came the cubist artist Lionel Feininger, joining German names such as Otto Dix and George Grosz in making Berlin an international showcase for the Dada movement and avant-garde art.

Berlin also became an important centre of press and publishing, under such great names as Ullstein, Scherl and Mosse. Almost 150 daily and weekly newspapers reported political and cultural events from every conceivable angle adding to the intellectual maelstrom.

The rise of Hitler

Initially, there were few signs of Nazi activity in a city of such magnitude. Adolf Hitler's planned march on Berlin in November 1923 collapsed ignominiously, along with his putsch in the Bürgerbräukeller in Munich. In 1927, at a closed party meeting in the capital, he could claim 680 supporters. In 1928 he spoke for the first time in the Palace of Sports. As the newspapers reported, most of his audience consisted

ever controls the streets will rule the city. Whenever possible, he transferred his propaganda campaigns to the "red" working-class districts of Wedding, Kreuzberg and Neukölln. Brown-shirted raiding parties ambushed their political opponents and Nazi troops provoked bloody fights at party meetings.

During the elections for the town council in November 1929, Hitler's supporters gained only 13 out of a total of 225 seats. Meanwhile, however, Black Friday on the New York Stock Exchange had precipitated a worldwide recession and sparked off a new chain of worldwide events. The stage was being set.

of "curious observers who have come to see this strange man".

There seems little doubt that it was difficult for the Nazis to establish themselves in Berlin. For Hitler, this hectic, sharp-tongued metropolis was anathema. He set up his headquarters in Munich, but he was well aware that the road to power must lead through the capital. Josef Goebbels, his best agitator, was sent to Berlin in 1926 in Hitler's stead. Goebbels organised his "fight for Berlin" under the precept that who-

LEFT: the *Graf Zeppelin* hovers over Berlin, 1928. **ABOVE:** Nazi Minister of Propaganda, Josef Goebbels, 1931. **ABOVE RIGHT:** communist demonstrations, 1931.

The Weimar Republic ends

The social consequences of the lost war and subsequent inflation can be studied in the literature of the Weimar Republic. Dramatists such as Carl Sternheim and Ödön von Horváth described in their plays the moral eclipse of a broad spectrum of the middle classes and the petite bourgeoisie. A similar theme was treated by Erich Kästner in his novel *Fabian*, and above all by Alfred Döblin in *Berlin Alexanderplatz*.

George Grosz commented on the spirit of the times in his bitterly satirical drawings depicting the brutality of the ruling classes. Heinrich Zille ("Henry Paintbrush") portrayed the city's working classes in their tenement dwellings and back yards; Käthe Kollwitz wrote frank descriptions of the misery of the poor. The prevailing climate was one of hopelessness, which made the man in the street susceptible to both nationalist and anti-Semitic propaganda.

By the end of 1929, Germany's unemployed totalled 2.8 million. The following year, in the Reichstag elections, no fewer than 6.38 million voters placed their faith in Adolf Hitler, the man they saw as their saviour. In Berlin the Communist Party gained the majority of seats.

Early in 1932 the number of jobless had risen to 6 million, 600,000 of whom lived in the industrial capital, Berlin. In the Reichstag itself,

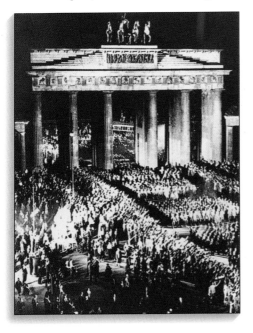

a radicalisation of right and left resulted in the parliamentary centre being unable to function. In the spring of that year, Paul Von Hindenburg's term as President expired. In his 80s and eager to retire, Hindenburg was nevertheless urged to stand for re-election by Chancellor Brüning, who saw him as the only alternative to Hitler. By this time violence on the streets and the strength of the SA meant many feared the outcome of Hitler obtaining power.

The road to dictatorship

After some hesitation Hitler stood against Hindenburg in a bitter campaign. Though he was defeated, and Hindenburg re-elected, the Nazi vote had almost doubled since 1930, and the weary president looked incapable of standing in the way for much longer. A succession of political blunders and double-dealings followed, beginning with the replacement of Brüning as chancellor. His successor, Franz von Papen, was a staunch monarchist whose policies were decimated both by the left and by the Nazis. Two Reichstag elections failed to break the political deadlock, until Papen was replaced by Kurt Schleicher. His efforts to appease the left resulted in a strong backlash from the right.

With the power of the industrialists seemingly moving behind Hitler, what little control Kurt Schleicher had was slipping from his grasp. Hitler had indicated he was willing to share power, and the tide in his favour seemed unstoppable. Schleicher resigned on 28 January 1933. Two days later Hindenburg received Hitler in audience and appointed him chancellor, with the task of forming a "Cabinet of National Concentration" with the German Nationalist Party.

Hitler did not seize power, but rather came to it by the back stairs, by political intrigue and double-dealing. In fact, making him chancellor was deemed to be the wisest move in keeping him under control. Von Papen, who had emerged as vice chancellor in the new cabinet, boasted to a friend that: "In two months we will have pushed Hitler so far into a corner that he'll be squeaking".

New elections for the Reichstag were planned for 5 March 1933. A week before, the parliamentary building on the Spree was engulfed in flames. Were the Nazis responsible for the fire or was it the work of van der Lubbe, a solitary anarchist? The question remains unanswered. Whatever the explanation, the burning of the Reichstag provided the National Socialists with an ideal excuse for embarking on a wave of brutal terrorism aimed at their left-wing opponents. The Communist Party was banned. Its leader, Ernst Thälmann, was arrested and sent to a concentration camp.

Although the Nazis had been waging a massive campaign of intimidation and already controlled virtually all media, especially radio, they failed to gain an absolute majority in the elections. They were able to achieve this result only by declaring the 81 Communist mandates to be null and void. The Enabling Act of 23 March 1933 enabled Hitler to change the constitution and decree laws without consulting parliament.

In March the KPD and the SPD were banned from the parliament and other parties disbanded. Hitler ruled alone.

The Third Reich

It became evident what this meant on 1 April 1933, when SA and SS troops marched through the streets of Berlin in support of a boycott of Jewish businesses. On 1 May there was a mass demonstration on the airfield at Tempelhof to mark National Labour Day. The next day, SA commandos stormed the trade union buildings.The Nazis set up concentration camps in the Columbiahaus in Tempelhof and in Oranienburg, outside Berlin.

During his first year in office, Hitler had 150,000 people arrested on political grounds and sent to the 100 concentration camps which had been built for the purpose.

Many opponents of the Nazi regime, including prominent artists and intellectuals, were forced to flee the country. As a result of this exodus of its German-Jewish cultural elite, Berlin lost its international appeal. More than 20,000 books by "Un-German" authors such as Heinrich Heine, Thomas Mann and Kurt Tucholsky, were burnt on the square in front of Berlin University. This act was to be the opening move in the process of bringing all public artistic and intellectual life into line with Nazi doctrine. Supervising the Gleichschaltung was the Minister of Public Enlightenment and Propaganda, Josef Goebbels. Those who believed that the police terror, the book burning and the first persecutions of Jews would prove to be short-lived excesses were taught the error of their ways by the Nuremberg Decrees of September 1935. Jews were now isolated from "Teutonic-blooded Aryans" and as members of a lesser race were deprived of their rights.

The following year, the youth of the world converged on a festive Berlin for the XI Olympic Summer Games. The Nazis hoped to impress the rest of the world with organisation and spectacle. During the Olympic summer of 1936 the city's nightlife was resurrected; even jazz was allowed. "No entry for Jews" signs and the anti-Semitic newspaper *Der Stürmer* disappeared for a few weeks. On 9 November

1938 Goebbels unleashed an orgy of anti-Semitic destruction after a young Jew from Hanover shot a German diplomat in Paris. During Kristallnacht (Crystal Night), SA and SS mobs laid waste to Jewish shops, flats and synagogues. In Berlin, the two main synagogues in Fasanenstrasse and Oranienburgerstrasse were set alight. Kurfürstendamm and Tauentzienstrasse were a sea of broken glass.

Plans dating from the 1930s show Hitler's scheme for making Berlin the capital of his "Thousand Year Empire". Entire districts were to be razed to the ground to make way for new party buildings. The focal point was to be a

boulevard, 7 km (4 miles) long, with a triumphal arch. At the end, occupying more or less the site of the present-day Platz der Republik, would stand a huge domed hall accommodating 180,000 people. Of all these grandiose schemes, Hitler's Inspector General of Works, Albert Speer, was to complete only one, the New Chancellery in Vossstrasse.

World War II

World War II would end the Führer's dream of "Germania", as he intended to name the capital of his new empire. This time, in contrast with the huge jubilant crowds who thronged the city streets of Europe in 1914, there was

LEFT: Nazi torchlight parade, 30 January 1933.
RIGHT: "Germans defend yourselves." SA men hold anti-Semitic placards in the streets of Berlin.

no cheering or celebration – not even in Berlin. "I can only say that the mood was one of extreme depression and gloom," wrote Neville Henderson, the British ambassador who handed over the British ultimatum at the German Foreign Ministry on 3 September 1939. A series of quick victories in Poland, Scandinavia and in the West restored the optimism of the populace as well as making any resistance to Hitler and his regime seem difficult if not hopeless.

As early as the summer of 1940, in the midst of the Battle of Britain, the Royal Air Force had started its night bombing raids on Berlin. In 1942 they began to bombard all major cities in

Germany. During the winter of 1943–44 it was the turn of the capital. A series of 16 devastating attacks followed. The Americans also participated in the closing phases of the Battle of Berlin. The air offensive escalated into a nonstop campaign; until mid-April 1945 scarcely a day went by without an air raid warning.

In January 1942, during the Wannsee Conference, the SS delegates had decided on what they termed as the "Final solution of the European Jewish question" – the annihilation of all continental Jews. In June 1933 some 130,000 Jews were living in Berlin. By 1942 there were 60,000, who were now systematically deported to extermination camps and murdered.

At the end of January 1945, Soviet troops reached the Oder near Küstrin. They set up a bridgehead on the west bank; their advance tanks were then only 70 km (44 miles) from the city boundary. That year, Berlin experienced a spring full of foreboding in the shadow of the Red Army. During January and February the capital suffered the worst air raids of the war. American bombers reduced almost the entire city centre to rubble. Theatres and concert halls had closed, victims of the "total war". Only a few cinemas remained open. The film they were showing was Veit Harlan's *Kolberg*. It was an oblique exhortation to hold out, portraying the defence of the fortress of Kolberg against Napoleon: now Berlin, too, was to be defended "to the last man and the last bullet".

The Battle of Berlin

On the morning of 16 April the window panes on the east side of the city shook. On the Oder front, almost 20,000 gunners began the main Soviet offensive with an artillery salvo. Ten days later, they closed the ring around Berlin. On 29 April the Russians launched a massive three-pronged attack on the inner defences of the "citadel". Their main targets behind the fortifications were the Führer's bunker and the Chancellery building. On 30 April Hitler committed suicide with Eva Braun, whom he had married the day before. One week later, Field Marshal Wilhelm Keitel, the head of German Supreme Command, arrived in Berlin. In the Russian headquarters, as the prisoner of the Allies, he signed the document of unconditional surrender on behalf of the German Reich.

During the course of the war, the Allied planes had dropped some 45,000 tonnes of bombs on Berlin. During the last offensive the Russian artillery had fired more than 1.1 million shells at the city. Berlin, which a megalomaniac dictator and his henchmen had planned to transform into the seat of power of a world empire, had been reduced to a pile of rubble. Harry Hopkins, the American presidential advisor, gazed down on the endless devastation as he flew over the Spree on 25 May 1945 on his way to Moscow. The capital of Germany had become, he said, "a second Carthage". ❑

LEFT: celebrations after victory in France, 1940.
RIGHT: May 1945 – troops of the Red Army fire their victorious salute atop the Reichstag.

THE RISE AND FALL OF THE WALL

The Berlin Blockade marked the start of Cold War tensions which were to climax in the construction of the infamous Berlin Wall

The Battle of Berlin raged for 12 days. In their fanatical attempts to avoid defeat the Nazis forced children and old people to defend the city with bazookas. Thousands were killed during the air raids and street fighting; others were hunted down by SS patrols, tried in mobile courts for desertion and executed and hanged from street lamps.

The balance sheet for Berlin during the Nazi dictatorship reveals 80,000 dead and 75 million cubic metres (98 million cubic yards) of rubble, one-seventh of the total for the entire country. The city centre was littered with corpses and burnt-out tanks. Of the capital's 4.3 million inhabitants, not more than 2.8 million – possibly as few as 2 million – remained. Most of them were women, children and old people who had managed to survive in the city's ruined buildings and cellars.

Experts seriously considered the possibility of rebuilding elsewhere from scratch. Of a total of 245,000 buildings 50,000 had been completely destroyed and 23,000 badly damaged. There was no electricity, no gas, and running water only in the outer districts. One-third of all underground railway tunnels were flooded; half the city's road bridges were unusable. Dysentery and other illnesses were rife – famine seemed inevitable.

Official food distribution satisfied no more than half the daily calorie requirements. Those determined to survive were forced to resort to barter, to make foraging trips to the countryside, or to buy goods on the black market. Practically every commodity became the subject of haggling.

The prime occupation of most Berliners came to be known as "organising". This involved the acquisition of food supplies, repair materials and equipment and other items in short supply. Winter was approaching fast. It was a fight for survival. The legendary

LEFT: the war reduced Berlin to 75 million cubic metres (98 million cubic yards) of rubble.
RIGHT: German soldiers are led to POW camps, 1945.

Trümmerfrauen, the women who cleared away the rubble, were the first to make an impression. They broke up stones – 125 per hour, 1,000 per day, for a weekly wage of 28 marks and a ration card – and created mountains of rubble like the Teufelsberg in Grunewald. During these early days, few Berliners exhibited

more than a passing interest in politics. They were powerless anyway.

The four-sector city

As far as the three western sectors of Berlin were concerned, the Red Army was a temporary caretaker of the city. This did not apply to the conquest of large tracts of central Germany by General Dwight D. Eisenhower's troops. During April 1945 they advanced as far as the Wismar–Magdeburg–Leipzig line, well beyond the predetermined boundary of the West–East zone. At the end of June the Anglo-American forces withdrew from Mecklenburg, Saxony and Thuringia, taking over their sectors in Berlin at the beginning of July. The French followed in August; Churchill had ceded them the districts of Wedding and Reinickendorf, originally part of the British sector. Three months after the surrender at Karlshorst, the former imperial capital had become the four-sector city of Berlin.

The London Protocol of 12 September 1944 was the basis for the exchange of troops between East and West. In this document the Big Three powers agreed on the division of Germany and the occupation status of Greater Berlin. By means of secured approach roads the Western Allies had thus moved on to a bomb site which lay more than 100 km (60

From this point onwards, Berlin was ruled jointly by the four victorious powers. The Allied Command consisted of the supreme commanders of the armies in question. Policy decisions depended upon unanimity. They were passed on to the politically neutral mayor, Dr Arthur Werner, who had been appointed to the city's first post-war municipal authority by Berlin's first Soviet commandant, General Bersarin, before the Western Allies even reached the city. The boundaries between the various sectors were of no significance to the populace. Food rationing was everywhere, and there was freedom of movement within the city.

miles) east of the Elbe, in the middle of the Soviet-occupied zone.

During the summer of 1945, America's Harry Truman, Russia's Joseph Stalin and Britain's Winston Churchill – succeeded during the negotiations by Britain's new premier, Clement Attlee – discussed the future of Germany within the framework of the Potsdam Conference. They agreed that the country should be completely demilitarised and de-Nazified, as well as deciding on reparations and the creation of a new administration along democratic principles. The unity of the country as a whole, with Berlin as the capital, was not questioned by the three superpowers in the Potsdam Agreement of 2 August 1945.

Berlin goes to the polls

The first, and what would prove to be the last, post-war town council elections for many years took place under Allied supervision on 10 October 1946. Out of the four parties which campaigned for power the German Socialist Party (SPD), gained the overall majority with barely 20 percent of the electorate voting for the Social Unity Party (SED), which was favoured by the Soviets. The elections were regarded as a reflection of the proportion of Berliners favouring the West and the East.

Regardless of the election results, the Soviets continued with the erection of a popular democratic society in their sector. A reappointment of public posts, which the Russians had filled before the elections with trustworthy German communists, did not take place.

In June 1947, the Soviet city commandant vetoed the election of the anti-communist Ernst Reuter (SPD) as the city's new mayor. At this juncture Louise Schröder, Reuter's courageous deputy, took on the job – thus becoming the first woman to head a Berlin town council.

LUFTBRÜCKE

Designed by Edward Ludwig, the Luftbrücke memorial at Tempelhof airport commemorates the 70 airmen and 8 ground crew who lost their lives in the Berlin Blockade.

The Berlin Blockade

The opposing interests of the victorious allies became increasingly clear. In February 1948, after the London Conference, the Western Allies agreed on a policy for the economic rehabilitation of Germany within their three zones. Moscow saw this move as a breach of the Four-Power Agreement and withdrew its cooperation from the Allied Control Council. Marshal Solokovski's departure on 20 March marked the end of the joint administration of Germany. The inclusion of the three western sectors in the West German currency reform provided an excuse for the Berlin Blockade.

On 15 June 1948 the Autobahn entering Berlin from West Berlin was declared "closed for repairs". Three days later, all road traffic was stopped crossing the sector boundaries and by 21 June no barge traffic was allowed to enter the city. On 24 June it was announced that due to "technical difficulties" no more rail traffic from West Germany would reach Berlin. It was confirmed the next day that no supplies would be crossing from the Russian sector into the Western parts of the city. Two-and-a-half million people were subjected to power cuts and severe rationing.

The American military governor, Lucius D. Clay, decided to react. Three air bridges connecting the city to West Germany were quickly set up; the first American transport plane, a Douglas Dakota bearing three tons of freight, landed at Tempelhof Airport on 26 June. During the following 11 months the Americans and British were to make thousands of flights to Berlin. By Easter 1949 an astonishing 7,485

tons of goods were being flown in daily – 1.8 million tons of essential supplies were delivered in total. For almost a year the local citizens lived without fresh fruit and vegetables, although trips to the surrounding countryside to gather food were possible for some people. Milk and eggs were available only in powdered form. Electricity was supplied for just a few hours daily.

In the autumn of 1949 the Russians offered the besieged West Berliners food ration cards in the Eastern sector. Only 100,000 accepted.

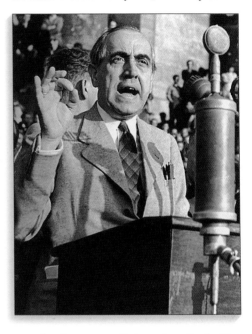

Following secret diplomatic talks in New York, the USSR lifted the blockade on 12 May 1949. Stalin had failed to achieve his aim of forcing the Allies to abandon Berlin. This marked a moment of victory for the city's population, but doubtless another stage along the road to partition.

The democratically elected town council had transferred its seat to West Berlin in September 1948; only the SED faction remained in the Eastern sector. The latter appointed a municipal council in accordance with the wishes of the Soviet authorities. As a counter-move the Western half of the city set up its own municipal council under the leadership of Ernst Reuter.

LEFT: US transport planes during the Berlin airlift.
RIGHT: Berlin's mayor, Ernst Reuter, addresses a demonstration for freedom in front of the Reichstag.

The formation of the GDR

On 23 May 1949, the split between Germany and Berlin was widened by the official birth of the Federal Republic of Germany with Bonn as its provisional capital – an arrangement originally intended as a temporary measure. A few months later, the German Democratic Republic (GDR) was formed in East Berlin. The law of the Federal Republic declared Berlin to be one of its constituent Länder with the Allied restriction that the city was not to be "governed by the Federal Government". The supreme command was to remain in the hands of the forces of occupation. The Soviet authorities

made no formal attempt to encroach upon the city's status, challenging it in practice only by their choice of Berlin (East) as the seat of government of the GDR.

Showcase of the Western world

Initially, the economic development of West Berlin was slow due to the political situation, the blockade, its isolated location and the correspondingly long haulage distances. In order to compensate for the city's geographical disadvantages, and above all to create a representative "showcase for Western democracy", enormous sums of money were invested by the United States and, increasingly,

by West Germany. As the political and economic links with the Federal Republic grew stronger, West Berlin became progressively more isolated from the eastern half of the city and the surrounding GDR.

In May 1952 the SED authorities cut the telephone lines; in January 1953 they severed the tram and bus routes within the city limits. West Berliners now required official permission to visit the surrounding GDR. The remaining passenger services (underground and suburban railway lines) within the city limits were not affected. Some 500,000 people continued to cross the sector boundaries every day in both directions. Since currency reform, well-stocked shops and stores were a major attraction in West Berlin. The building industry was booming, and factory chimneys were once more belching out smoke. In East Berlin, on the other hand, there was a shortage of practically everything – a situation exacerbated by the high level of war reparation due to the Soviet Union in the form of goods. There was universal discontent at the living conditions in the so-called Workers' and Peasants' State.

Rebellion in the east

Matters finally came to a head in the popular revolt of 17 June 1953. The catalyst was a decree by the SED government that the average work rate should be increased without a corresponding increase in wages. Next day workers building the Stalin-Allee downed tools and marched to the ministry offices in the Leipziger Strasse to demand that the decree be rescinded.

The rebellion quickly spread to other towns within East Germany. Workers took to the streets, demonstrating for higher wages, for the removal of the frontiers between the zones and for free elections. They stormed the SED offices in East Berlin, plundered official shops and lowered the red flag above the Brandenburg Gate. At 1pm the Soviet commandant declared a state of emergency. Police closed the border crossings to the Western sector. Russian T34 tanks rolled through the streets, crushing the revolt and in the process killing – according to official East German sources – 23 people. (Other sources believe the number to be in the region of 200.)

From this date until reunification in 1990, 17 June was marked in the Federal Republic and West Berlin as the "Day of German Unity".

Bolt-hole Berlin

Although the authorities used tanks to crush the protests within the Soviet sector of Berlin, they were unable to stop young, employable and in some cases highly qualified, East Berliners migrating to the other part of the city. During the 1950s the GDR was in danger of bleeding to death. It is estimated that 330,000 East Germans fled to the West in 1953.

The Soviet Union's leader, Nikita Khrushchev, came to the assistance of the GDR with his Berlin Offensive. In November 1958 he terminated the Four-Power Agreement. In an ultimatum he demanded a six-month withdrawal of the Western forces and the transformation of Berlin into a "free, de-militarised city". Otherwise he would negotiate with East Germany a separate non-aggression pact and would transfer Russian sovereignty over the Berlin air corridors to the SED government.

Talks held in Geneva by the Great Powers between May and September 1959 ended in stalemate. The crisis continued to deepen. By mid-1961 one in every nine GDR citizens had fled the country.

The Wall

The tension grew after Khrushchev and US President John F. Kennedy had parted as implacable opponents following their summit meeting in Vienna in mid-June 1961. America increased its defence budget by US$3.2 billion and large-scale air and land manoeuvres were reported in Carolina.

Khrushchev summoned Walter Ulbricht, the Secretary General of the SED, and other party chiefs of the Warsaw Pact countries to a secret conference in Moscow. He proposed that the sector boundary within the Berlin city limits should be turned into an East German frontier, in order to "guarantee constant surveillance and effective controls". On 13 August 1961, the border between the sectors was sealed off by the Communist People's Police who were assisted by what were known as "Working Class Combat Groups".

The next morning the barrier was complete. A few last-minute refugees dared to leap over the barbed wire, but most observers gazed in

LEFT: 17 June 1953 on Potsdamer Platz – Soviet tanks crush the uprising.
RIGHT: the Wall takes shape.

dismay at the new frontier, which severed every link between the two halves of the city. During the weeks which followed, closely guarded teams of building workers erected the "Anti-Fascist Protection Barrier", as the Wall was officially known. It was claimed that it afforded protection from possible attack. In reality, the sole purpose of the Wall's existence was to prevent the citizens of East Berlin from defecting.

Like a dissecting knife the Wall had cut the lively metropolis in half; in some places, like Bernauer Strasse on the border of Mitte and Wedding, it ran down the middle of the road or between houses. The suburban and under-

ground lines between the two sectors were cut off – even cemeteries were cut in two.

The ring around the city

Many East Berliners made desperate attempts to escape their situation behind the Wall. They dug tunnels, high-jacked boats, waded through the sewers, which were sealed off by underground gratings, drove heavy lorries at the Wall or dived into the Spree. The authorities eventually extended their "Ring around Berlin (West)" to form a border security system with alarms and obstacles, and fewer and fewer people were able to escape. The first-generation Wall was a hastily erected makeshift affair, but by the time the "fourth-generation" barrier went up in the city centre in 1976 it had grown to a height of 5 metres (15 ft). The Wall around West Berlin was about 165 km (103 miles) long. On the Eastern side, the area of No Man's Land, which was up to 50 metres (160 ft) wide in places, was demarcated by an electrically charged copper or barbed wire fence measuring 1.5 to 2 metres (5 to 6 ft) high.

The Wall proved a heavy burden for the crowded metropolis. With the dream of a united Germany at an end an awareness of the lack of security, the precarious nature of the city's access routes and its insular overcrowding

increased. The rag trade moved to Munich and Düsseldorf: the film studios became silent. Many firms transferred their headquarters to the Federal Republic. Experts and ambitious professionals packed their bags. Berlin seemed in danger of slipping into provincial obscurity in every sphere.

On the other side of the border, the authorities wanted the capital of East Germany to be a "spiritual and cultural centre" to provide the city's flashy Western counterpart with a socialist alternative as well as to be a worthy seat of the national government. In some cases, the SED leaders redesigned the historic city centre along lines in keeping with their socialist illusions of grandeur. Many of the nationally owned companies were either rebuilt or newly established. Ambitious town-planning programmes, such as the one at Alexanderplatz, were carried out at the expense of other parts of the country. Meanwhile, on the other side of the Wall, building projects like the Kulturforum were taking shape as part of capitalism's advertisement to the watching world. Neither of the idealistically opposing societies wanted to be outdone by the other.

Youth rebels

All over the world, 1967–68 was characterised by protest movements led by young people. This was the period of turbulent general meetings and sit-ins at the Free University and anti-Vietnam demonstrations and water cannons on the Kurfürstendamm. Student unrest brought Berlin into the public eye from a completely different angle. It became the capital of the anti-authoritarian movement which fought for the new freedoms and the new social order. Once again, Berlin had developed into a forum for new ideas.

Towards the end of the 1960s, a wind of political change was blowing. In Bonn, Willy Brandt's government introduced its new *Ostpolitik*, which involved recognition of East Germany. There was a relaxation of the tensions between the two superpowers and Washington and Moscow began talks on Berlin. In September 1971 the Quadrapartite Agreement was signed: although border posts for different categories of visitors were established, it introduced no new regulations and merely confirmed the status quo from 13 August 1961.

For West Berliners, however, the agreement assumed vital importance. There were improvements on the transit routes, along which the East German authorities now agreed to abandon their luggage and vehicle checks. It became possible to telephone from one half of the city to the other. Citizens of West Berlin were also permitted to visit East Berlin or the GDR for periods of up to 45 days. An exchange of permanent representatives led to the maintenance of normal relations between the two governments. The city seemed to be on the move again.   ❑

LEFT: the Kurfürstendamm in 1968 – demonstrations take place against the Vietnam war.
RIGHT: the left-wing 1968 student leader Rudi Dutschke speaks to fellow activists.

MODERN BERLIN

After the euphoria of reunification, a new metropolis has taken shape
and Berliners are seeking to establish it as a world city

"**R**ejoice, Berlin!" exalted the mayor of West Berlin, the day after the Wall fell. German citizens complied, piling into the city with champagne bottles. Many of them must have passed, without noticing, the small black letters near the Brandenburg Gate: "Thanks, Gorbi!" – an insistent reminder that the opening of the border didn't come completely out of the blue. Mikhail Gorbachev, the powerful leader of the Soviet Union, was responsible for introducing *glasnost* and *perestroika*, openness and restructuring – which led to a reawakening of national interests in the countries of the Eastern bloc, and to a new freedom of expression.

Hungary took the first step. During the summer of 1989 it opened its border with Austria. No one guessed how significant this removal of travel restrictions would prove to be. Thousands of East Germans spending their holiday in the "socialist brotherhood" took advantage of the opportunity to flee via Austria to West Germany. The West German embassies in Budapest and Prague were filled with refugees demanding the right to leave their home country. Despite Wall and border security, the flood of those voting with their feet rapidly reached unstoppable proportions.

In East Germany, work came to a halt as many holiday-makers failed to return home, fathers disappeared and parents abandoned their children. The economy was on the point of collapse. The protests of those who stayed grew louder – if they were to stay changes must take place at the highest level. The leaders of the SED, however, remained impervious to such demands. In towns throughout East Germany, demonstrators held silent protest marches every Monday. What started as a few thousand visionaries swelled every week. In October 1989, 70,000 people flooded through Leipzig. In Berlin, the restless energy first materialised as

a few minor street skirmishes. The SED party leadership refused to budge an inch. Indeed, it later emerged that the party chairman, Erich Honecker, even considered a "Chinese Solution" – a repetition of the bloody repression of the revolt which had taken place a few months previously on Beijing's Tiananmen Square. But

it was only a matter of time before the moribund regime would collapse.

Hundreds of thousands of East German citizens took up the cry "We are the people!" On 18 October the government made what was probably their first concession by dismissing their leader, Erich Honecker, who had held the reins of power since 1971. His successor, Egon Krenz, was Honecker's protégé, and he was slow to react to the people's mood.

The Wall falls

On 4 November, five days before the Wall finally fell, a crowd of almost 1 million East Germans gathered on the Alexanderplatz in

PRECEDING PAGES: German reunification celebrations outside the Reichstag on 3 October 1990.
LEFT: in party mood on the day the Wall came down.
RIGHT: popular protest takes to the streets.

East Berlin, and demanded the right to govern their own lives in freedom. The SED government was silent until the evening of 9 November when a radio announcement that the Berlin Wall was open took everybody, even the Russian guards at Checkpoint Charlie, by surprise.

There was now no stopping the course of events. On Christmas Day 1989 the Wall was opened at the Brandenburg Gate, the hackneyed symbol of German unity. Hundreds of television cameras had been waiting for weeks for just this moment. The New Year celebrations of 1989–90 at this historic place became a party of mammoth proportions, but not without tragic

received when, to mark the "historic hour", he cut short his visit to Poland and hurried to Berlin with his foreign minister and the honorary chairman of the SPD, Willy Brandt. Their attempt to sing the national anthem in front of the Schöneberg Town Hall failed to strike the right note. The citizens of Berlin had no time for demonstrations of nationalist fervour.

Invisible divisions

The idyll that replaced the Wall in the early stages was deceptive. "It will take longer to demolish the Wall in people's heads than contractors will need to deal with the visible Wall

results. The Quadriga was destroyed, a section of scaffolding collapsed under the weight of spectators and a number of people were injured. One man was found dead on the street in Unter den Linden. After their long closure, the underground stations were gradually opened again. The public transport system collapsed under the strain. The city, hopelessly overcrowded, was on the verge of grinding to a complete halt as thousands of East Germans from the surrounding area converged in the metropolis.

The department stores were jubilant at their unprecedented profits. Foreign heads of state and artists arrived in town. The West German chancellor, Helmut Kohl, was less rapturously

in the city", wrote the author Peter Schneider in his 1982 novel *The Wall Jumper*. There was no doubt that the people of Berlin could still be divided into East and West Berliners by their customs and social habits. Until currency union in July 1990, West Berliners exchanged their hard-currency D-Marks for the socialist "slot machine" money at a rate of 1 to 10, and threw it ostentatiously around on trips to East Berlin, in what was referred to as the "East Germans' Closing-Down Sale". East Berliners descended on West Berlin shops like vultures, snapping up anything they could afford. West Berliners mocked them. Envy and a ghetto mentality were widespread. Forty years of two different social and educational systems and 28 years of almost total separation were painfully obvious.

Reunited Berlin's struggle to regain its identity as a European metropolis rather than the "capital of an extended German Reich" was the struggle of its citizens, not of governments. After many years during which the citizens of Berlin had become accustomed to living in a divided city, the breaking down of the Wall on 9 November 1989 came as a surprise.

Building the new Berlin

The uncontrollable joy experienced during the first few weeks after the collapse of the Wall

projects, some of which are still at the planning stage, some already completed, but they are beginning to provide "Berlin-Mitte" with an identity. One of the most impressive is bound to be the new Lehrter Banhof – a railway station for the 21st century.

Since 1991, DM 30 billion per year has been invested in the modernisation of the city. The building boom anticipates the transfer of parliamentary offices and business headquarters as the metropolis slowly resumes its capital city status, taking 11,400 government jobs from Bonn. Although the "new Berlin" was only about half finished at the turn of the

soon gave way to sober pragmatism. In December 1990 the first elections for Greater Berlin took place and since then a joint city administration has been trying to come to grips with the many problems faced by the merger. Assimilating the two halves has not been an easy task, but a new city centre is taking shape.

Alexanderplatz and Zoo Station are now just main squares like lots of others in the city. The space between Friedrichstrasse, Unter den Linden and Leipziger Strasse has a host of building

LEFT: Brezhnev and Honecker kissing from the East Side Gallery.
ABOVE: Berliners unite on Glienicker Brücke, 1989.

millennium, more and more completed buildings are taking the place of the many busy construction sites.

Berlin in the 21st century

Berlin's project for the new millennium is the city itself, with a further DM 200 billion projected budget for modernisation. The theory is that, if the city can get rid of the most visible divisions between the former Eastern and Western sectors, the trickier mental and emotional boundaries will crumble too. To an outsider's eye, the progress looks promising.

Defying its numerous critics, the futuristic market centre erected in Potsdamer Platz continues to attract a wide selection of visitors. The swarms of illegal bars and apocalyptic clubs of the edgy 1990s are receding further and further in the former Eastern districts, replaced by the slim and chic interiors favoured by more a upwardly mobile clientele.

Every day, tourists queue up for hours to get a glimpse inside Norman Foster's completed Reichstag dome, its open glass structure symbolising a parliament that keeps no secrets from its people.

The word of the day is Weltstadt – world city. The streets are full of a writhing energy and Berliners are anxious finally to reap the luxuries

of a cosmopolitan metropolis that the city has so long been promised. Michelin-starred restaurants, unable to hold themselves back any longer, are serving baked pigeon with $200 bottles of wine on streets whose cobblestones have just been ripped away. But the business complexes projected to be the source of bustling wallet-heavy lunch crowds stand empty across the street, their facades mired by scaffolding and graffiti.

Their occupants have failed to materialise. Why should they? ask a chorus of voices wafting north from the Rhine. Powerful corporations such as Siemens, who fled when the city was still divided, are quite comfortable in their southern locations. Businesses, they argue, are not likely to relocate when their executives worry that their children would suffer in Berlin's struggling school district, where it is estimated that more than half the students can't speak German.

Surrounded by Brandenburg, Berlin is also an off-putting commute from every other European business hub. Without the companies established in the city, airlines are loath to schedule the same number of charter flights that they send, for example, to Frankfurt. There hasn't been a direct flight between the US and Berlin for many years. Lufthansa, the German national airline, announced that it would start running some flights between Berlin and Washington DC for embassy employees, but it declined to offer anything else unless it saw some capital coming into the city.

Problems to be solved

Airlines aren't the only ones waiting for capital – more than 250,000 Berliners are unemployed. It doesn't help matters that the majority of them grew up in the East, where the state assured them that they would never have to endure such a humiliation. Jaded and bored, they don't make any secret of their resentment. Immigrants, never a part of the East German economy, become an easy target, and the media pounces on stories of neo-Nazi violence in the Eastern developments. Working-class families also feel encroached upon by the young art students and media types who have settled into former Eastern neighbourhoods, pushing up rents and attracting property speculators.

As far as some "Easterners" are concerned, the city's development has provided an excuse to tear down the remains of their culture, and they point out that the bulldozers have shown no restraint when it comes to devouring icons of the former GDR.

But Berlin is a city with a knack for rebuilding itself, and this isn't the first time that Berliners have had to think hard about what they want to become. As the cranes start to disappear and the new embassy district start to establish itself, a question settles into the street like dust from a building site: "What next?" Anticipation drifts up after it: whatever happens now, it's going to be worth while waiting for. ❑

LEFT: waiting for a tram at Hackescher Markt.

Berlin Multikulti

Each year in summer, Berlin holds a "Carnival of Cultures", celebrating the contribution made to the city by its many non-German residents. Juxtapose this with the recent comments of a mainstream CDU politician that for him, "Leitkultur (dominant culture) means that there will never be mosques in Bavarian villages", and the difficulties inherent in the current immigration debate in Germany begin to become clear.

At the heart of the dilemma lies the deep-seated belief that culture equals national culture. Founded too late to get more than a few crumbs of the colonisation pie, the country has fortified itself with the ideal of a unified culture, bound together by a common language and a gently paternalistic system of government. Foreigners arriving in Germany are presented with a simple choice – either retain their culture with a view to returning home, or integrate completely. Multiculturalism is a bugbear, not a buzzword, sparking reactions ranging from polite indifference to racially motivated attacks.

All this is changing. Faced with declining birth rates which will reduce Germany's population to two-thirds of its current size by 2050, state and citizens are trying to come to terms with the inevitability of immigration. Despite providing sanctuary for more refugees than any other country in the European Union, Germany had until recently no policy enabling voluntary immigration. The most visible foreigners were the "guest workers", who for the most part are Turks, Italians, and Yugoslavs, bought into the country to reduce severe labour shortages. Recognising that a plurality of cultures can exist within a functioning society is a slow process, but one which is vital to Germany's continuing prosperity.

In this, Berlin is more fortunate than most of the rest of the country and many travellers rejoice at the immediately visible cultural diversity of the city. Berlin has traditionally welcomed cultural diversity. Located near the Germanic-Slavic linguistic border encouraged cross-cultural exchange when it was little more than a village. When the Huguenots were suffering persecution in France, Elector Frederick William invited them to settle in Berlin. Many were skilled traders and craftspeople who helped to build up the city's economy and

made important contributions to the arts and sciences. The Prussian Electors and later kings continued to recognise the benefits of a cultural mix, as can be seen in the jumble of architectural styles in Potsdam, where they built their summer residences. Berlin's vibrant Jewish community was also an integral part of the city until the rise to power of the Nazis. Jewish salons attracted prominent thinkers, scientists and artists who left their mark on Berlin society.

Today, Berlin has become even more diverse. The majority of foreigners living in the city still come from Turkey and Eastern Europe, but the mix has been broadened due to the return of diplomatic

life and the influence of a thriving art scene. One in seven Berliners is not German, and the proportion is growing. However, this is not the full story. While one-quarter to one-third of residents in the inner Western suburbs are foreigners, in the outer East the proportion drops to less than one in twenty. These monocultural enclaves have proven to be a fertile breeding ground for right-wing extremism, and a barrier to a greater acceptance of the benefits of a multicultural society.

As the immigration debates progress, this legacy of the division of Berlin needs to be addressed, in order to ensure the continued vibrancy of the city, and the sustainability of the cultural mix which is one of Berlin's primary attractions. ❑

RIGHT: Berlin's ethnic mix is one of its primary attractions.

THE BERLINERS

One in seven Berliners is not German by birth, and in this multi-ethnic city being a Berliner means different things to different people

A true Berliner is said to be someone whose family roots lie in East Prussia and Silesia. However, finding a Berliner of this descent is not an easy task. Long before the fall of the Berlin Wall in 1989, the city was a melting pot of nationalities. Today there are people from nearly 80 nationalities living in the city, according to the latest statistics.

For 40 years Berlin was a "capitalist island" in the centre of a Communist country and this made it special and very different from any other capital city. Because of its unique position as a showcase for capitalism in competition with the communist showcase East Berlin, and the heavy allied military presence, Berlin was given a special status students, people searching to for an "alternative" lifestyle and those who wanted to avoid military service found the perfect haven. Berlin offered an array of entertainment, intellectual stimulus and freedom to "live as you like". There was a sense that there was an urgent need to have a full and thriving city rather than an empty and "endangered" one. Political refugees were also offered asylum in West Berlin and this of course also contributed to the lively, colourful "multikulti" scene in the city.

A glance at the statistics shows that Berlin's population has been decreasing. Conservative estimates indicate that barely half of the city's 3.4 million inhabitants are natives of the city, while 130,000 who are registered as living here have been used to treating their residence as their second home. For safety's sake they used to have a suitcase ready to dash off to their other homes in the relative security of the Federal Republic of Germany.

The first settlers

The first settlers who made their homes in the Berlin area during the 13th and 14th centuries came from the region between the Harz mountains and the Thuringian forest, from the native

PRECEDING PAGE: relaxing in Gendarmenmarkt.
LEFT AND RIGHT: street entertainment.

district of the Ascanians around Bellenstedt and Bernburg, or from the Lower Rhine or Flanders. It seems highly probable that the name of Cölln on the Spree was derived from that of Cologne (Köln) on the Rhine. The seat of the electors of Brandenburg experienced a considerable influx of new residents towards the end

of the 16th century, when settlers from the Netherlands were encouraged to move to Berlin during a chronic labour shortage.

Then came the plague, carrying off 3,000 of the city's 12,000 inhabitants. The Thirty Years' War made further inroads. Berlin would still be just a small town in the Marches today if fresh blood had not flowed in from elsewhere.

During the 17th and 18th centuries the new arrivals were mostly refugees: Huguenots and Waldenses from France, Moravian Brethren from Bohemia, and 20,000 Salzburg Protestants from Austria. Swiss settlers and Jews swelled the ranks under Frederick the Great. During the empire and thereafter, country-dwellers – Poles,

Silesians, East Prussians and Pomeranians – were drawn by the city's expanding industry.

The "new residents" after World War II were refugees from Eastern Europe and *Gast-arbeiter* (guest workers) from Italy, Greece and a large number from Turkey. It is therefore impossible to generalise about origins of the citizens of Berlin. Goethe described Berliners as "that saucy race". Although set in northeast Germany, and enjoying no particular advantages of climate or topography, the city was a haven for immigrants. Most newcomers had endured injustice of some description and had been borne or driven along by forces beyond their control. Berlin offered them the chance of a new beginning, with all the attractions of the unknown.

Wall in the head

Perhaps Berlin is the most interesting place to get into a discussion regarding East-West relations. The expression *Mauer im Kopf* (literally Wall in the head) could not be more relevant than for Berliners who always had this physical wall around them. Many of them had experienced very directly the splitting-up of their families caused by the East Germans building in 1961 a "protective wall against the fascists".

Many Berliners no longer want to discuss the issue of reunification. There is a sense of resignation rather than enthusiasm for all that has changed since the fall of the Wall in 1989. With increased unemployment and growth in right-wing racist attacks, the city has suffered from the departure of the allies who perhaps had made the city more liberal.

Tough customers

Dieter Hildebrandt described the capital's inhabitants in *Deutschland, deine Berliner* (Germany, your Berliners). It gave people, he said, "the chance deal; the city was a pawnbroker's shop of possibilities for making a living. Here the future was cheap for the asking; there were prospects to be enjoyed without bothering to climb a tower; there was pleasure to be had – if you knew how to take advantage of it." In order to assert oneself effectively in a place like Berlin, one needed, according to Goethe, to be "a tough customer, and a bit coarse with it". In the years between the end of World War I, up until the Wall was built, West Berlin served as reception centre for a stream of immigrants from all over countries" arrived in droves. According to a local joke, the "reason they built the television tower at the Alexanderplatz so tall was so that the Saxons could see more clearly where there was an empty flat".

HARSH VIEWS

Poet Heinrich Heine believed that Berlin was not a city and wrote in 1822 "...it is simply a town where a lot of people are gathered together and many of them of lively temperament. The place itself is of no significance."

Berliner "Schnauze"

Although it is impossible to produce a character portrait of the "true Berliner", there are a number of traits which have always been cultivated by those who live here. First of all, there is the Berliner's traditional

LEFT: cycling past an East Side Gallery mural.
ABOVE: on the steps of the Deutsche Staatsoper (State Opera) building.

East Germany. In addition, with the assistance of the employment exchange, it recruited 370,000 new workers from the Federal Republic, the so-called *Wessis*. Roughly two-thirds of all *Wessis* eventually became permanent residents. They now consider themselves to be "true Berliners".

In the 1960s increasing numbers of Greeks, Italians, Yugoslavs and Turks began to move to the city. In East Berlin, workers from the surrounding GDR and "socialist foreign

tolerance of foreigners. It does not matter where anyone comes from.

Around half of the city's residents are elective Berliners – "trained Berliners" – and pejorative nicknames for newcomers are rare. Few of the city's most prominent political figures are native Berliners, and that includes its mayors. Anybody who makes his or her home here, and who learns to love the city, can become a Berliner.

To do so, however, they must come to terms with the local mentality. This reveals itself above all in a sharp tongue and a predilection for the city's unmistakable brand of humour. Berliners call a spade a spade. It disturbs them not at all whether, in doing so, they appear brash or put their foot in it. One Englishman in describing his short visit to Berlin suggested that it was important to be thick-skinned when dealing with Berliners.

He had arrived at 7am on a Sunday morning and wanted to find a safe place to rest before visiting some friends. Asking at a help desk, he was pointed towards the direction of the Bahnhof Mission, a place for the homeless.

This is a form of the *Berliner Schnauze* – a Berliner will always give an opinion on a subject – but it may not always be the most polite and well-researched one.

BERLIN'S ISLANDS

The islands of Berlin are little sanctuaries for dreamers, even if they do contain garden gnomes and vegetable plots. Some are uninhabited, being too small for anyone to set up home, or else they have been designated as conservation areas, but most of them are used by country recluses who have created their own little empires with a summerhouse and apple trees. The prettiest islands are on the Havel. Schwanenwerder – or Bonzenwerder (Bigshot Island) as it's sometimes called – is exclusive. The Pfaueninsel (Peacock Island), on the other hand, is a public park, a horticultural masterpiece with a small castle, built by the mistress of King Friedrich Wilhelm II.

Recreational activities

And then there is the Berliner's frequently quoted desire for amusement. During the 19th century it gave rise to the city's dancehall society, centred on such venues as Resi, Walterchen and der Seelentröster. On the outskirts of the city, popular pleasure establishments flourished: Neue Welt in the Hasenheide and Krolls in the Tiergarten. Here the local citizens amused themselves with all the popular cultural pursuits of music, dancing, theatre and art.

Also typical of Berliners is their love of nature – all the more surprising in this city of tenement houses and back yards where, apart from the Tiergarten, greenness is rare. A Berliner loves to grow flowers on the balcony, or at least a row of pot plants or herbs on the windowsill. A popular, long-standing tradition is the Sunday trip to the "country". Picnickers by the Havel will produce from their baskets meatballs, home-made potato salad and an adequate supply of Berliner Kindl. On Sundays each family seems to have its own particular place, and they sit there, cheek by jowl, in their seventh heaven, as if they were sitting on a palm-fringed beach instead of under a few sparse spruces and pines.

These weekly trips into the country invariably end up in the nearest pub. For this reason, a ring of tourist cafés mushroomed up around the former city wall, putting up signs saying: "Let the family make coffee here". Families would pay for the hot water and then unpack home-made cake. The landlord would make his profit out of the father who would inevitably treat himself to a beer, while his wife and children settled for their *Weisse mit Schuss* – local white beer with a dash of raspberry juice.

Consolation dogs

The Berliners' proverbial love of animals at times borders on the pathological. It is particularly evident in the large numbers of dogs which are kept in the city. Despite the overcrowding there are more dogs per capita here than in any other city in Germany: one for every 20 citizens. This statistic is linked to the age and social structure of Berlin's inhabitants. More than one-quarter of the city's population is over 60 years old, many of them living by themselves in council flats with their dogs as their only companions. Every year, a 16-tonne mountain of dog dirt is deposited on the city streets.

Native wit

Berliners are famous – and feared – for their quick-wittedness, for delighting in mockery and sarcastic repartee. They enjoy complaining about everyone and everything which may come between them and their desire for freedom – especially those in authority, who have always found it extremely difficult to extract from them a modicum of respect.

Frederick the Great, who wisely decided to release Berliners from military conscription, deliberately ignored the sarcastic jokes about him that circulated in the city. An informer wrote to him to denounce the treasonable remarks of a drunken citizen, but the emperor dismissed the matter, writing a message to be passed on to the informer: "Let him get drunk himself."

Adolf Glassbrenner described how Berliners used to grouse to let off steam in the newly established coffee houses of the post-Napoleonic era. "Only army officers eat cake for the sake of eating. All other Berliners eat cake in order to be able to read the newspaper. Most of them also go to the taverns for the same reason, because there are no other public places. Wine, however, makes them reveal their true nature, and criticism and humour soon give way to a mood of boundless enthusiasm. Before an hour has passed the newspapers have been swept from the tables and a conversation begins, becoming steadily more lively and delightful, as well as more animated, by the minute. The attraction of wit and freedom of expression know no bounds, and the champagne corks pop like the souls of Berliners who are released from convention and police repression…"

Claire Waldoff, alias Rosine von's Proj-ramm in the Linden cabaret *Who's Throwing Mud Around Here?*, ran into difficulties during the Third Reich. Berliners had no compunction about drawing parallels between *They Call Him Herrr-mann*, one of her songs written long before the Nazis came to power, and the prime minister of Prussia, Hermann Göring. The fact that many of the songs were filled with ambiguities and satirical jibes made such an assumption quite natural to Berliners, even though the song had nothing to do with Hitler's henchman, who was known in Berlin as "the bulging Teuton" because of his vast girth. The satire of the

pre-war Berlin shows was caught in Christopher Isherwood's play *I am a Camera*, which in 1972, along with his book *Goodbye to Berlin*, was loosely adapted to become the stage and screen musical *Cabaret*. Hitler, whose rise to fame had taken place in the beer cellars of Bavaria, found little popularity in Berlin – largely thanks to his lack of humour.

When bombs fell on their capital, the citizens of Berlin satirised the air raids with bitter irony: "Let's be practical and give Hitler a coffin", was their motto. Districts which were razed to the ground acquired new names: Charlottenburg became known as Klamottendorf ("Rag

Village"), Lichterfelde was known as Trichterfelde ("Craterfield"), and Steglitz was rechristened Steht nichts ("Nothing left").

The writer Kurt Tucholsky summed up the character of the Berliner thus: "There is much work done in this city – the people really slave away. (Even pleasure is hard work here; you roll up your sleeves before you get down to it, and you expect something in return.) The average Berliner is not industrious; he is permanently wound up. Unfortunately he seems to have forgotten the real reason for living. Even if he were in heaven – assuming he actually went to heaven in the first place – he would have an appointment at four o'clock." ❑

LEFT: dogs are very popular pets in Berlin.
RIGHT: waiting at Potsdamer Platz.

The Turkish Minority

Officially, about 435,000 foreigners currently live in Berlin. Approximately 150 different nationalities are represented, from Afghans to Vietnamese. There are large contingents of Poles (6.7 percent), (3 percent), Greeks (2.5 percent) and people from the Balkan states (about 13 percent). The Turks, however, constitute by far the largest group with about 127,000 residents (29.3 percent). Berlin has the largest Turkish population of any city outside Turkey.

The history of Berlin's Turkish community can

be traced to the construction of the Wall in 1961. Overnight the East German government barred over 50,000 East Germans from crossing to work in the West, thus depriving West Berlin of its source of cheap, skilled workers. To ease the severe labour shortage the Federal Republic "recruited" large numbers of *Gastarbeiter* (guest workers) from various countries – most came from Turkey.

Many of the first Turkish immigrant workers, whose time in Germany was originally intended to be temporary, found cheap accommodation in the working-class districts of Berlin and were soon joined by their wives and families. Nowadays the Turks represent a clearly defined ethnic minority group; they have developed a strong sense of com-

munity in every way, with their own tradesmen and wholesalers, restaurants, banks, clubs and even travel agents, who arrange regular flights to Ankara and Istanbul. There are Turkish doctors, Turkish secretarial agencies to help with the pitfalls of the German language, and Turkish driving schools to assist with the obstacle race of the German driving test. The Turks have their own daily newspapers, radio programmes, video libraries and cable television channel.

In the traditionally poor districts of Moabit, Wedding, Kreuzberg and Neukölln, Turkish immigrants, most of whom are Muslim, dominate the everyday street scene. The highest percentage of Turks can be found in Kreuzberg, and the district surrounding the Kottbusser Tor and Görlitzer Bahnhof. The underground line No. 1 is known locally as the Orient Express when it travels above ground from the Glassdreieck station onwards. The market along the Maybachufer on is an excellent example of this area of Kreuzberg, with frenetic haggling taking place over piles of brightly coloured fruits, clothing, fabrics and household goods.

Differences in language, culture and religion have have caused the city headaches in the past and were initially greeted with incomprehension on the part of many native Berliners. It is, however, true that the numerous Döner kebab stands have been accepted as a popular enrichment of the gastronomic scene, and many Berliners appreciate Turkish restaurants as a welcome change from local food. As an alternative to the anonymity of supermarkets they also like the personal service in the little corner shops – revived by the Turkish community. Nonetheless, for the majority of Berliners, their Turkish neighbours remain foreigners.

For a considerable number of Berliners prejudice has been further fuelled by the high unemployment rates over the past few years. Such people see the Turks as competitors for jobs and consequently as scapegoats for their financial difficulties, although they certainly would not want the immigrant worker's poorly paid manual job. The Turks' relatively high birth rate also aroused fears that the city would soon be dominated by the Turkish community, even though the population has decreased slightly in recent years. Racism and xenophobia are, of course, fuelled by members of the extreme right, resulting in chants of "Turks out" and sometimes even violence.

The Turks, on the other hand, who before their arrival had only a vague idea of the city which was to become their new home, felt increasingly insecure and discriminated against. The more difficult it became for them to establish contact with their new German neighbours, the more inclined they were to retreat into the reassuring familiarity of their traditional lifestyle, which provides clear guidelines for everyday life and behaviour.

Some 25 mosques have been built in Berlin, most of which are housed in former factory premises and are completely unobtrusive. Strictly segregated according to gender, children learn to recite sections of the Koran in Arabic and also receive value judgments from the imam, which are usually very difficult to reconcile with what they encounter in everyday life. This can cause family crises and conflicts within the Turkish community.

Torn between the relative freedom they experience at school, reinforced by materialistic consumer-oriented advertisements, and the strict religious and patriarchal structure found at home, second- and third-generation Turks divide their world in accordance with the principle "Germany in the morning, Turkey at night." Many parents would prefer to keep their daughters at home until they can be married off to an orthodox Turkish husband and marriages are often still "arranged" between families. Turkish parents tend to show little understanding for their children's desire to dress according to modern fashion rather than wearing the traditional headscarf or veil.

In recent years there have been a number of attempts to encourage understanding and interaction between the two cultures. In addition to joint Turkish-German playgroups and women's groups and the mixed district self-help associations, there are many common activities, particularly in the cultural sphere: German-Turkish theatre groups, music festivals and street parties.

The *Treffpunkt Berlin* was created as a coordinating body for integrated activities of all kinds. A publicity campaign under the rubric "Living together in Berlin" was started by the Berlin senator for immigration problems, with the aim of encouraging more tolerance. It is hoped that the readiness of members of the younger Turkish generation to orientate their lives according to their new environment will be encouraged by the gradual elimination of prejudice on both sides. Many of the Turks living in Berlin still cling to their cultural and religious traditions in order to maintain their sense of identity. Some strive to return to their native homeland one day with sufficient savings – and possibly with the senate's repatriation allowance – and make a fresh start.

Most younger Turks, on the other hand, set their sights on assimilation and integration, even when it is sometimes difficult for them to participate in the more casual lifestyle enjoyed by Germans of similar age. Yet, unofficially, they are essentially German, having been born, raised and educated in Germany. Many of them will also take advantage of the possibility of acquiring German nationality; more than half the Turks living in Berlin already meet the naturalisation requirements. Between the some older conservative Germans who traditionally

are averse to foreigners and the older Turkish generation who refuse to even learn the German language, it seems likely that several generations will have to pass before the integration process is complete. The conflicting feelings of expatriate Turkish community are summarised well in a poem by Aras Ören, a well-known Turkish writer who moved to Berlin in 1969:

In my case,
Whichever life they create for me,
I know it is a coat which does not fit.
But how will the next generation
Pass judgment on me?
If not on my reality,
Then on their own.

LEFT AND RIGHT: the Turkish community makes up nearly 30 percent of Berlin's population.

THE COUNTERCULTURE

Radical lifestyles, artistic expression and political views have flourished in Berlin.

But can they survive amid the bland consumerism of the reborn capital?

Berlin is not a quaint, European capital. Sightseeing is sometimes difficult here because there is no traditional city centre. Yet Berlin has recently surpassed much more stately cities like Munich as the most popular tourist destination in Germany. Who are these tourists and what do they want from this dusty metropolis? They aren't coming to see the Ku'-damm anymore: the word has spread that Berlin is full of a seething, revolutionary energy. From the student revolutions of the sixties to the Döner, a Turkish sandwich that beat out the *bratwurst* as Germany's favourite fast food, movements that have changed the entire country's temperament have started here.

Revolutionary background

During the era of the Wall, West Berlin attracted groups of people who found the prospect of a carefully planned existence in some federal provincial town too restrictive. "Normal" people, however, found little attraction in the idea of scaling the ladder of professional success in the permanently threatened island city. Correspondingly, individualists, survival experts and opponents of the system found opportunities within the hothouse atmosphere of the western half of Berlin even more enticing. Part of the political compensation for occupation in West Berlin was that Berliners didn't have to serve in the military. Young men escaping conscription fled to the island.

During the complacent time of the Economic Miracle such "deviants" had few chances of being accepted in the frontier town of the Western world. But during the 1960s a new generation accustomed to an affluent lifestyle had grown up in both the Federal Republic and West Berlin – a generation which longed for fresh ideals and which revolted against the black-and-white clichéd images of the Cold War.

As the horrors of the US involvement in the war in Vietnam surfaced, America's credibility

---

LEFT: sunbathing in the sculpture garden at Tacheles.
RIGHT: campaigning for gay rights in the 1990s.

as a "guardian of the peace" was destroyed. The simultaneous German student movement not only shook up the way universities saw themselves politically, it also blew away the fustiness hidden under academic gowns and with it the structure of private life as a whole, which non-conformist students found repressive. The

first communes and flat-sharing groups were formed. People became accustomed, slowly at first, to the existence of alternative lifestyles and to the unorthodox appearance of angry young people.

Skeletons were soon discovered not only in the cupboard of world politics, but on the domestic front as well. Some groups of protesters went underground and used violence in the fight against the capitalist system. Others, who wanted change without the use of violence, became involved in setting up citizens' initiatives in an attempt to end the destruction being wreaked on the environment and the quality of life in the name of social progress

Alternative projects

In the 1980s, alternative co-ops were full of Berlin's new breed of hippies. Playgroups and women's refuges, gay meeting places and women's centres were all part of the daily scene. Bar-keepers' and taxi-drivers' collectives, bicycle shops and craftsmen's associations were all part of the left-of-centre city infrastructure. The local magazine *Zitty*, which has since lost a bit of its alternative sheen, emerged as a guide to the left-wing scene. And the biggest alternative publishing project of all, originally serving only the Federal Republic and since reunification covering the entire

country, was the leftist daily newspaper *taz*, founded in 1979 in protest against the conservative press monopoly within the city. Finally, at the end of the 1970s, a new political force of the Alternative List (AL) was born, a green party which in 1989 stood for the Berlin Senate in alliance with the SPD. In 1990 it became the Association of Greens. The alternative lifestyle didn't bring peace to the social system and there were violent protests in 1980.

Housing shortage

In spite of a serious shortage of housing, unscrupulous landlords continued to permit some 20,000 cheap flats to remain empty. Entire blocks were like ghost towns. Once they were dilapidated, it was easy to obtain a demolition order and to make an exorbitant profit from the new building, especially with the assistance of public subsidies. By adopting this approach, many speculators destroyed and subsequently "restored" entire blocks. To fight against machinations of this kind, activist organisations occupied and renovated some 170 old buildings that had been standing empty. Most of them, unemployed young people, were not interested in spectacular protest: their concern was to create for themselves enough space to be able to determine their own lives.

Most Berliners adopted an understanding attitude towards the squatters. Although they were sometimes shocked at the unconventional and occasionally violent manner in which they defended the houses against the authorities, the local citizenry was aware of the social problems to which they were drawing attention.

The popular newspapers produced by the Springer publishing company and the senator for domestic affairs, Heinrich Lummer – notorious at the time as a conservative agitator – roused public opinion against the "anarchists", who were disturbing the peace of their smug fellow citizens. With a large contingent of police, Lummer had some of the houses cleared of their occupants.

On 22 September 1981 there was a bloody street battle, during the course of which an 18-year-old youth, Klaus-Jürgen Rattay, was knocked down and killed by a bus in the Potsdamer Strasse as he attempted to flee the police baton charge. The powerless rage of many of the demonstrators was unleashed in the shattering of shop windows.

The Conservative CDU-ruled senate maintained a hard-line approach, but the increased pressure of numerous supporters led to a change of heart. One-third of the occupations were legalised and the squatters were given the right of tenure. What was more, the CDU senator for social matters, Ulf Fink, released over the next few years a total of DM10 million from the senate's budget for self-help groups and self-administered businesses. The subsidy, which came to be known as the "Fink Bank", was not merely the result of sympathy for alternative lifestyles. Conservative politicians had recognised that these alternatives also served to correct the tense situation within the labour market. When the state itself was not able to offer more job vacancies, such measures at least provided support in the alternative sphere. Furthermore, environmental protection, the use of natural resources rather than a slavish adherence to technological progress, and a rejection of the throwaway society, can be regarded as conservative, rather than capitalist, objectives.

> ### 1980s KREUZBERG
>
> The Mehringhof was at the centre of the flourishing squat scene that developed in East Kreuzberg "SO 36" in the 1980s.

The subculture develops

Alternative organisations in the shape of the Grips children's and youth theatre, young writers and painters, musicians from punk to jazz, and subculture film makers like Lothar Lambert or Rosa von Praunheim jumped at the opportunity to subsidise their growing role in the community. Berlin became a centre for alternative large-scale industry.

The Mehringhof, a former factory containing almost 30 businesses and institutions ranging from Alternative Energy to the Network, the financing body for self-administered projects, was set up during the 1980s. Another popular gathering place was the UFA factory for culture, sport and handicrafts in the Victoriastrasse in Tempelhof. The varied activities ranged from ecological projects, dozens of courses and workshops on the active organisation of leisure time or self-fulfilment, to a wholemeal bakery which produced 2,500 loaves of bread per week. "No chiefs, one kitchen, one kitty and lots of beds" was the philosophy of some 70 alternative-minded Berliners, who lived and worked together in an extended family.

The Eastern scene

For the youth of the German Democratic Republic, East Berlin always represented a glittering, cosmopolitan ideal – even if the latter was relatively seldom visible under the stranglehold of the SED. The proximity of the "Showcase of the Western World", combined with the traditional tolerance found in a metropolis, permitted the creation of an alternative scene which stood comparison with the liveliness, if not the violence, of its counterpart across the Wall. It is clear that life on the eastern side of

the Wall was less spectacular than in the West, and that the censorship imposed by the omnipresent SED agents of repression prohibited adventurous undertakings, not to mention official recognition such as the "Fink Bank". Resistance was usually expressed in refusal or in the risky exposure of social and political misdeeds – a sort of alternative glasnost.

This was an approach that required considerable courage and imagination in the former GDR. Nonetheless, the young people of

East Berlin made for themselves their own "alternative" niches, such as on the Prenzlauer Berg, a district often compared with Kreuzberg in the West. Back in the 1980s there were alternative bars there – albeit not so loud as those in the West – and gay meeting places and flat-sharing schemes in occupied flats and houses.

Apart from the official cultural scene, independent groups formed; visitors from West Berlin watched their performances with enthusiasm. Eccentric fashions were created and shown in private. Artists made makeshift galleries in back yards and garages; fringe theatre provided countless opportunities to publicise matters usually veiled in silence. Only since the

LEFT: the bakery at the UFA factory still makes bread.
RIGHT: playing for the tourists on Unter den Linden.

removal of the Wall has it been clear just how extensive the alternative scene of East Berlin was. Freed of the restrictions of life uNdeR a socialist regime, a considerable number of projects took off within a few months. They were joined by their Western counterparts, who rushed into the cheap apartments in the East at the first opportunity. Entire housing complexes, hitherto abandoned to decay, were occupied and renovated in an improvised manner in order to experiment with new lifestyles.

However, the alternative scene in the East had other problems to solve. Here, it was not just a matter of the realisation of chosen

tion. The members of East Berlin's alternative scene are determined to pursue their aims in a non-violent manner. Their lack of experience in hard street fighting, and the years of repression – experienced every day and usually directed towards the individual – have given them a different resistance potential from their counterparts in the west.

Meantime, the various "scenes" are merging. Radical owner-occupiers are no longer fighting over properties in Kreuzberg; now it's Friedrichshain and Lichtenberg. Health food shops are everywhere in the city and alternative culture is infiltrating the establishment.

lifestyles, but a question of basic survival. The years of resistance to a system intolerant of non-conformists has led to the development of a political attitude different from that in the West. Before the 1989 October Revolution, the struggle against the potentates of the SED and their destructive approach to environmental and social questions was fought with great determination and personal energy.

Now priorities have changed: the scene must defend its beliefs vigorously against the bourgeois man in the street as he chases his personal, longed-for Economic Miracle and also against the radical right-wing youth who see a peaceful alternative lifestyle as pure provoca-

Modern revolutionaries

Today the initial segments of Germany's revolutionary population have come of age. The intermixing of former protesters among the mainstream has sparked friction on both sides.

The most visible manifestation of this trend is in the government. With three party members in the Federal Ministry, the Green Party has more official weight than ever before. Foreign Minister Joschka Fischer's experience, however, proves that this rise in stature doesn't necessarily mean that the revolution has won out. Times have changed since then, when Fischer trumpeted the Green Party's disgust with "normal" politics. In 1999, less than a year after Fischer became the prime minister, Germany joined the NATO campaign over Kosovo, in what was the first German combat since 1945. In a visible show of the disgust many of Fischer's pacifist party members left at this manifestation of "selling out" and Green Party members attacked him with paint bombs.

The former pride of the Green Party has also been lambasted with criticism from the other end of the spectrum. Conservatives think that Fischer's support of violent activism in the late 1970s and early 1980s went way beyond acceptable means of protest. In 2001, the leading news magazine *Der Spiegel* published photographs of Fischer beating up a policemen during a 1973 squatter riot. The report surfaced in the middle of a trail researching Fischer's role in a deadly guerrilla attack in 1975.

But it isn't only on the political front that a blurring of lines between radical and conservative elements of society has attracted criticism from everyone concerned. The Tacheles on Oranienburger Strasse, a former bastion against capitalist society, has recently worked out a deal with the huge developing firm that now owns the land it stands on. The real estate group wants to turn the Oranienburger Strasse into a consumer paradise, with the Tacheles as its crowning jewel. The artists who live there are paying the group a symbolic rent to stay in their squat. But many of their peers now look down their noses at the "sell out", leaving its exhibitions and events to the thousands of tourists who visit every year.

The government's move to the city in 1999 heralded further changes for the illegal club scene that had been flourishing in Berlin's abandoned buildings since the wall went down. Kunst and Technik, for example, was an illegal stronghold set up in a shack right on the Spree overlooking the Museum Island, just a few blocks away from the new Reichstag. In 2000, its building was razed to make room for some more "aesthetically pleasing" construction. Other spaces in the city's centre have been sold to developers and remodeled to house trendy clothing stores. Bars open up in Mitte

FISCHER'S SNEAKERS

When the Museum of German History opens again in 2002, you will be able to see the yellow sneakers Joschka Fischer wore when he was sworn into the parliament in 1983.

every other day, but each one looks much like the last. Some of the alternative living situations of the 1980s still flourish, and have become established fixtures of Berlin society. The Ufa Factory still bakes ecological bread and fixes bikes. Now they also offer tours as well. Some, like the Ex pub in the Mehringhof, have replaced their seething energy with a more nostalgic air.

Others have become more like parodies of themselves. The May Day riots, a yearly excuse for anarchists to stir up some

destructive impulses, are now frequented by "disaster tourists" and inarticulate activists. By the end of the evening, everyone throws a few cobblestones for posterity's sake, the police flaunt their riot gear, and then everyone goes home. But to say that Berlin's buzz of countercultural energy is being subdued by the tightening capitalist grip on the city would be going too far. Creative people are still flooding here from all over the world to live and work. In Berlin, many of them are finding the space and the inspiration to act on their ideas. To find the energy that keeps the new German capital always on the verge of a new revolution, all you have to do is step out on the street. ❑

LEFT: organic bread for sale.
RIGHT: creativity is thriving in the city.

MUSIC AND DRAMA

Top-class classical concerts, opera, musicals, "Off-Theatre" and
Berlin's status as "techno town" provide a vibrant mix

Berlin assumed its role as a national centre of music and drama somewhat later than other European capitals. As long as the town was nothing more than the residence of a provincial potentate in the backwoods of the Holy Roman Empire, the chances of it becoming a flourishing cultural centre were remote. To be a magnet for artists and the arts, Berlin first had to become the capital of a significant state. During the age of absolutism, this depended entirely on the personality of the ruling prince.

Musical drama

In 1740 there was a new king of Prussia who realised that the identity of state and subjects would be better and more permanently enhanced by cultural achievement than by rigid discipline and the regimentation of every aspect of life, which was what his father and predecessor, the miserly Soldier King Friedrich Wilhelm I, had prescribed. The artistically talented Friedrich II, known as Frederick the Great, lost no time in putting theory into practice. Frederick the Great, philosopher and musician, ruled for 46 years and, under his patronage, Berlin blossomed with cultural vitality.

Opera lovers of today still benefit from the legacy of the enlightened Hohenzollern despot. During the First Silesian War he had the Royal Opera House built on Unter den Linden. It was formally opened in 1742 with a performance of Karl Heinrich Graun's *Cesare e Cleopatra*.

The post-war division of the city deprived the west of the grand opera venue, and a new company, the Berlin German Opera Company, was founded. The ruins of the old Charlottenburg opera house formed the basis of a new opera house, designed by Fritz Bornemann. It opened in 1961 with Ferenc Fricsay as musical director of Carl Ebert's production of Mozart's *Don Giovanni*. Under the direction of

Gustav Rudolf Sellner and Götz Friedrich, the new company rose to international fame.

Musical drama received a boost in 1947 at the Komische Oper (Comic Opera House) where Walter Felsenstein began his much-admired campaign for the revival of realistic productions. His attention was devoted primar-

ily to the opéra comique, and to a lesser extent to classical operetta and the musical. Today the theatre offers reliable performances under the direction of Harry Kupfer.

Occupying the building near the Bahnhof Zoo, where the City Opera Company had occupied temporary quarters, is the Theater des Westens. Its production of *My Fair Lady* in 1961 marked a runaway victory for the American musical on the German stage. In recent years, the Theater des Westens has established a reputation for its musical and operetta productions, although it now has to compete with the Theater am Kurfürstendamm, which serves up plenty of farce-style musical comedy.

PRECEDING PAGES: *Flute Concert* by Adolf Menzel.
LEFT: an "Off-Theatre" performance.
RIGHT: a concert in Gendarmenmarkt.

Choirs and orchestras

For the citizens of Berlin, music and singing are a fundamental form of expression in spheres beyond that of opera. Numerous amateur choirs with fine reputations will sing you not only a litany, but also a variety of songs, cantatas and oratorios. These nightingales include the Philharmonic Chorus, the Choir of St Hedwig's Cathedral and the RIAS chamber chorus, as well as many small vocal groups and church choirs.

They are all following in the footsteps of the Academy of Singing, which first raised its melodic voice in 1791 and which, with its 1829 performance of the long-forgotten *St Matthew*

Orchester (DSO, formerly Berlin Radio Symphony Orchestra), which reached a first-class standing under Ferenc Fricsay and Lorin Maazel. In contrast to the relative conservatism of its more venerable rival, the DSO is well-known for its open-minded approach even to avant-garde music, an attitude sure to continue under new musical director Kent Nagano.

Not to be confused with the DSO is Berlin's second oldest orchestra, the Rundfunk Sinfonieorcheter Berlin (RSB), which plays to critical acclaim at the Philharmonie and the Konzerthaus. The same critical interest in innovation that made the Berlin of the legendary

Passion under the direction of the young Felix Mendelssohn-Bartholdy, inaugurated a revival of interest in the music of J.S. Bach which has lasted to this day.

The Berlin Philharmonic Orchestra, founded in 1882, played its way to international fame under Hans von Bülow, Arthur Nikisch and Wilhelm Furtwängler. By the 1970s, under the charismatic von Karajan, it could claim a reputation as one of the best orchestras in the world. The arrival in 2002 of Sir Simon Rattle as musical director is likely to alter the somewhat 19th-century repertoire to include some more contemporary material. Serious competition is present in the form of the Deutsches Symphonie

Golden Twenties the most exciting cultural centre in the world ensures that attitudes remain open to experiment.

Progressive unrest

If there is a hidden message to be heard, or sensed, in unfamiliar, revolutionary tones, a Berlin audience will be the most rewarding one imaginable. As far as music lovers of Berlin are concerned, half the fun lies simply in being present and being able to express an opinion. A festival première of a new work by Mauricio Kagel will receive the same attention as a fringe performance held in the Academy of Fine Arts or at the Bethanien Artists' Centre. Both these places have developed into settings where innovators can experiment with the frontiers of the arts, thus preventing any risk of stagnation. This is a characteristic of contemporary musical life in Berlin: as soon as an institution starts to rest comfortably on its laurels, someone else appears on the scene to challenge its reputation with something better, or at least more interesting. Often enough, they succeed.

Theatre

The drama scene in Berlin is just as varied. The decades during which the city was divided led to a parallel development, which

for comparable performances, and the Theater der Freien Volksbühne was built in the Schaperstrasse. The Free People's Theatre opened in 1963 but reunification resulted in a huge drop in attendance and it was closed.

The politically motivated subsidies given to support Berlin's theatres on both sides of the Wall now have no place in the unified city and many theatres are being forced to shut down due to lack of funds. A recent victim of cutbacks was the Metropol Theatre in Friedrichstrasse, which closed its doors in 1999.

Not so the Volksbühne on Rosa-Luxemburg-Platz which has regained its former name

has in some respects enriched its output. During the post-war years each sector of the city strove to demonstrate its cultural independence, or even superiority, as part of the general rivalry between the two systems. One example is the Volksbühne, the People's Theatre Organisation, which lay in the Eastern sector. It made theatrical history during the Wilhelminian Era (1890–1914) with its performances of censored plays by Gerhard Hauptmann, Strindberg and Ibsen. In postwar Berlin, the Western sector needed a stage

LEFT: Berlin has some of the world's finest orchestras.
ABOVE: the city has a long theatrical tradition.

thanks to the management of Frank Castorf, known as the "young Turk". Erwin Piscator, the creator of the "proletarian theatre" in the 1920s, was the first producer of this theatre in the heart of the old Scheunenviertel. In 1993, after years in the cultural wilderness, the Volksbühne under Castorf was voted theatre of the year by audiences.

Other highlights in the Berlin theatrical world which have resisted every threat of closure are the Maxim Gorki Theater and the most traditional of all the Berlin stages – the Deutsche Theater, which in the 1920s under Max Reinhardt grew to be one of the most significant in Germany. The names of the playwright Bertolt

Brecht (1898–1956) and the composer Kurt Weill (1901–50) are irrevocably linked to the city. The première of Brecht and Weill's *Threepenny Opera* in the Theater am Schiffbauerdamm (home of the Berliner Ensemble before it disbanded in 1999, although the theatre is still referred to by many by the name of its departed collective) in 1928 achieved worldwide fame.

After the war, Brecht returned from exile in the United States to East Berlin. His inspiration and authority, coupled with generous state subsidies, gave the Berliner Ensemble an international reputation, although this has suffered during the recent upheavals. Brecht's plays were beginning to get stale, and a new team is now trying to re-establish the theatre as a centre for experimental drama. Still a talking point in Berlin's drama circles is the Maxim Gorki Theater, where George Tabori's universal *Mein Kampf* received universal acclaim.

Musicals

The Grips Theater at the Hansaplatz has also achieved international fame. Youth drama performed here in some exemplary productions is imitated in many countries and languages. One musical, *Line 1*, can even claim to have become a hit. At its première in 1986, amazed

BERTOLT BRECHT AND MAX REINHARDT

After World War I a new battle erupted in Berlin for the cultural and political heart of the new Republic which raged until 1933. Accepted boundaries between art and politics were challenged, redrawn and blurred again. Young artists flocked to the city with a vision of producing art as politics. Bertolt Brecht, who arrived in 1920, threw himself into the vibrant theatrical scene and quickly caught the attention of the prominent director Max Reinhardt, an Austrian Jew. Reinhardt was incorporating elements of artistic Expressionism into theatre and had opened the experimental "Junges Deutschland" (Young Germany) theatre under the auspices of the prestigious Deutsches Theater. Expressionist drama painted an unashamedly stark vision of the world, and attempted to subvert any realism or naturalism in theatre. Drawing on Reinhardt's expressionism, but also on Marxism, Brecht developed his own theories, which encouraged audiences to think about the issues raised in a play, rather than the plot or characters. During the Nazi period Brecht went into exile; when he returned to East Berlin he set up the Berliner Ensemble. Both Brecht's Berliner Ensemble and Reinhardt's Deutsches Theater are open today, though their avant-garde tradition is more present in the Volksbühne than either of these now very established ensembles.

critics and audience witnessed a performance which could be considered to represent the birth of the Berlin – or even the German – musical. With *Line 1* (which refers to the then underground railway line between Bahnhof Zoo and the Schlesisches Tor, now between Krumme Lanke and Warschauer Strasse), the German musical emancipated itself from its American forerunners.

With typical Berlin wit it has come of age and become both cosmopolitan and exportable and recently travelled as far as India. In 1970, when it suddenly hit the headlines, the Schaubühne was on Hallesches Ufer in Kreuzberg –

Modern cabaret

East Berlin was the home of the city's first world-standard revue: in the Friedrichstadt-palast in Friedrichstrasse, artistes, ice dancers and jugglers continue to present classical variety theatre. Hoards of middle-aged German tourists pass through the doors every night for an evening of glitzy entertainment.

In the meantime, however, serious competition has emerged in the form of the Winter-garten in Potsdamer Strasse, with its amazing music hall acts although neither it nor the Friedrichstadtpalast can claim to host the true German *Kabarett* of the 1920s. Consisting

a location which, in those days, was far from the city's official temples of culture. When it opened with Brecht and Gorki's *The Mother*, with Therese Giehse in the main role, it set a high standard that continued with Ibsen's *Peer Gynt* and Gorki's *Summer Visitors*, produced by Peter Stein, and with its trend-setting Shakespeare cycles and classical plays.

In 1981 the Schaubühne acquired a new home near the Lehniner Platz, equipped with the latest technology, and fears for its imminent demise have not yet been confounded.

LEFT: glitzy entertainment at Friedrichstadtpalast.
ABOVE: Berlin has two jazz festivals a year.

more of original song and political satire than of jugglers and dancers, the brand of entertainment associated with Liza Minelli's cinematic appearance in the musical film *Cabaret* is now a rarity. If it's a more modern interpretation that you seek, then venues like Bar Jeder Vernunft and Chamäleon Varieté, which put on shows with everything from drag queens to quirky recitals, usually prove to be the most popular.

Fringe theatre

Berlin now has the opportunity to regain its former position of importance on the European cultural scene. Many of its numerous stages must be counted among the most celebrated in the German-speaking world and can stand comparison with the best anywhere. Unfortunately, lack of funding continues to be a real problem and it's not just the main theatrical institutions that are finding it tough. Fringe theatres have seen their already paltry subsidies dry up before their eyes and Off-Theater (as it is known) has been forced to battle to keep its head above water.

Only a small few of a once vast array of theatre companies still exist but the need for experimental and contemporary theatre will always ensure the existence of some sort of fringe scene even though some ventures find themselves

back on the pavement after only a few months. The work – indeed the very existence – of all these alternative stages and groups, which in the past gave birth to the celebrated Schaubühne, will ensure that the official, mainstream music and drama will not fossilise in complacency and repetitive routine.

Popular music

Berlin should by no means be remembered for just establishment art forms – several memorable records have been made here. In 1977, while trying to beat his drink and drug addictions, David Bowie moved to Berlin to escape Los Angeles and succeeded in making three

critically acclaimed albums with production guru Brian Eno, two of which were *Low* and *Heroes*. As well as making his own records, Bowie acted as producer for another Berlin arrival who was finding life in the fast lane a little too much – Iggy Pop. The albums *The Idiot* and *Lust for Life* virtually re-launched Pop's career and in so doing, although it appeared as a minuscule dot on the music map, the Berlin sound was produced.

Another contemporary, Lou Reed, made a record entitled *Berlin* without having been to the city, while U2 managed to reinvent themselves here in 1992 with the album *Achtung, Baby*. The unlikely origin of the name of their subsequent massive worldwide tour, "Zoo TV", was Bahnhof Zoologischer Garten.

Techno town

Berlin would, indeed, have a respectable musical CV if it were only into name-dropping but the city can, more importantly, claim to be one of the spiritual homes of a slightly different musical movement. The reunification of Germany coincided with the rise of the dance music culture. When techno (called *tekhno* by Berliners) burst onto the scene in the early 1990s it seemed to go hand in hand with the alternative post-Wall vibe as clubs like the infamous Tresor (which still supports its own record label) typified the hedonistic atmosphere of the time. As the techno-fuelled annual Love Parade gained an international reputation, Berlin became known as Techno Town.

In more recent years techno has had to make room for all the newer developing genres of music and the party scene has broadened to cater to Berlin's multicultural society.

Berlin has its fair share of major artists visiting on city tours and home-grown musical talent. Live music venues range from the huge open-air Waldbühne to small bars and cafés which have local bands playing every night. As it is always difficult to predict the changing face of the city's musical scene, the best way to determine what is groovy is to flick through listings magazines such as *Tip* and *Zitty* and go and see for yourself. ❑

LEFT: "Techno Town", as Berlin is known, still draws clubbers from around the world.
RIGHT: a performance of *Hamlet Machine* in the Deutsche Theater.

BERLIN CINEMA

*The German cinema had its heyday in the Babelsberg's UFA studios,
and today they still play a key role in the industry*

Shots can be heard in the Babelsberg studios again, film extras in full costume fight it out and lovers live happily ever after. What looks so genuine is part of the Babelsberg Studio Tour, a film theme park which includes a behind-the-scenes look at part of the working studios.

those involved was Kurt Maetzig, who under the Nazis was only allowed to work as cameraman in a small company which made cartoons – despite a higher degree and production experience – because his mother was of Jewish extraction. The "work team" formed the core of the DEFA (Deutsche Film AG), which received

In 1912, when German film-making was in its infancy, the film company Bioscop opened its first atelier in Babelsberg. A little later the German general staff attributed the disastrous course of World War I to poor propaganda. In order to avoid repetitions of the problem in future, the UFA (Universum Film AG) was set up under the auspices of the Deutsche Bank.

From 1921 the company transformed Babelsberg into its central film factory and continued to produce films until Soviet multiple rocket launchers rolled onto the site. The old management of UFA had its headquarters quietly moved across to West Berlin. A "film work team" took over what was left in the Eastern sector. One of

its official licence to make films from the Soviet authorities on 17 May 1946. Film production had already begun before the celebrations.

The news outside broadcast team and its leader, Kurt Maetzig, travelled around in a van with a wooden carburettor, and often arrived too late: Mrs Roosevelt's press conference was already over when they appeared. It is hardly surprising that the weekly news programme sometimes appeared only once a month.

On 4 May 1946 the clapboard fell in Babelsberg for the first post-war German feature film. *The Killers Amongst Us* is about war criminals who returned to their civilian jobs as if nothing had happened. The producer, Wolfgang

Staudte, was refused permission to film in the Western sector. DEFA thus gained a head start which was recognised in international circles.

A number of other highly regarded films followed and by June 1947 Babelsberg had 1,500 employees. By now the Cold War was heating up, and the newly created German Democratic Republic firmly controlled DEFA. The political film was succeeded by the party political feature, and critical realism gave way to social realism. Solutions and justice were no longer sought after; everyone knew what it was all about. Film makers like Maetzig still longed for the occasional "artistic experiment", but were forced to toe the political line. From 1955 Staudte worked in the West.

In East and West the film industry was faced with a crisis as a result of the arrival of mass television. In the GDR the problem was exacerbated by the monotony of dogma and the eternally positive heroes. This made no difference to the size of Babelsberg which now produced 40 to 80 films annually. An article published during the 1950s in the East German *Film Review* advised visitors to the studios, covering half a million square metres, that they would do well to take a "map and compass" with them. Meanwhile, following the construction of the Wall, the DEFA artists hoped that in the resulting "closed" society they would be permitted to speak and film more openly. "With you I would even go to see a DEFA film," remarked Manfred Krug in 1966 in *Spur der Steine (The Trace of the Stones)*. A week later the film had disappeared from the cinemas. A further dozen films suffered the same fate.

After November 1989, film production in Babelsberg was effectively brought to a stop. The market economy led to the decline of the whole complex and the staff feared for their jobs. The studio tours are the result of the workers' fight for survival.

The end of Germany's Hollywood loomed – that is, until a French firm, CGE, in cooperation with Bertelsmann, Germany's multimedia giant, acquired the land from the trust which was set up to administer the former GDR's assets. The two came up with grand plans for a "media city"; new film and TV studios were to be built, and radio and TV stations would move in. Managing director and film producer Volker Schlöndorff arranged some big film projects, which gave Babelsberg some the stimulus it needed. However, there is insufficient investment, and reconstruction work is still desperately needed.

The most important event in Berlin's cinematic calender is the annual Berlin Film Festival, known as the Berlinale. Founded in 1951 by the Western Allies, the event is Europe's third largest film festival, where film-makers compete for the coveted "Golden Bear" award. Although more of an industry gathering than the star-studded Cannes or Venice,

the Berlinale is an annual highlight for Berliners, and the city finds itself in the grip of film fever for a fortnight every February. A comprehensive programme of German and international films; fiction and documentary, feature-length and shorts, keeps the cinephiles happy, while every year the annual controversy rages over increased "Americanisation" and the prevalence of Hollywood productions over German films. Previously held in a dizzying variety of cinemas, East and West, the festival has in recent years found its home in the new Potsdamer Platz, and the world-class screening facilities to be found there. Check www.berlinale.de for details of each year's festival. ❏

LEFT: arriving at the opening of the Berlinale.
RIGHT: film set of an old Berlin street at Babelsberg.

MODERN ARCHITECTURE

Berlin's 20th-century buildings reflect the historic changes

wrought by decades of political turmoil and aesthetic innovation

Building in Berlin has frequently involved self-conscious statements, political and social as well as architectural. Never was this more true than during the 20th century. As one regime gave way to another, the physical fabric of the city suffered catastrophic damage and opposing ideologies eyeballed each other across the Berlin Wall. At the dawn of the new millennium, the reunited city is hard at work building new structures that reflect both its status as the country's capital and its hopes for the future.

Early Modernism

The industrial inner-city suburb of Moabit is the unlikely setting for a building which was a sensation in its time and is still the subject of pilgrimages by students of architectural history. The Turbine Hall, built in 1909 by Peter Behrens for the giant electrical firm AEG, was one of the pioneering buildings of architectural Modernism. Departing from a tradition which would apply some sort of historically relevant surface to the functional skeleton of workaday buildings such as factories, Behrens exposed the steel frame of his structure through a layer of glass. The classical weight and repose of its main facade was realised without resorting to the traditional language of columns, arches and neo-Renaissance ornamentation favoured in the Germany of the Kaiser.

The Turbine Hall stood alone as a harbinger of Modernism in the period before World War I. But the abdication of the Kaiser and the founding of the republic in 1918 ushered in a period of social concern and architectural experimentation. Preoccupied with the provision of public housing, the city council gave progressive architects a chance to prove their mettle. The English garden suburb provided a model for a number of residential developments, the archi-

tecture of which was forward looking rather than cosily domestic. The chief city planner, Martin Wagner, collaborated with Bruno Taut between 1925 and 1933 to build the famous Hufeisensiedlung (Horseshoe Block) in the southern suburb of Britz. The estate features functional houses and flats arranged in terraces with gardens and plenty of open spaces. Taut and Wagner were involved once again in the development of the estate at Onkel-Toms-Hütte among the pine and birches of Zehlendorf in the southwest of the city. The flat-roofed, straightforwardly designed houses and apartments here were grouped around a social and shopping centre (complete with a U-Bahn station), and given character by an inventive, varied colour scheme. Today, some 70 years later, such schemes remain a model of mass housing in an attractive environment.

Their equivalents in commercial architecture were structures such as the Berolinahaus and Alexanderhaus, completed in 1931 as part of

PRECEDING PAGES: the roof of the Sony Centre, designed by Helmut Jahn, Potsdamer Platz. **LEFT:** Quartier Schützenstrasse, Friedrichstrasse, by Aldo Rossi. **RIGHT:** a building on Friedrichstrasse.

Wagner's (for the most part unfulfilled) plans for a revitalisation of Alexanderplatz. Designed by the versatile Behrens, these eight-storey, sober, steel-framed edifices have shops at ground level, restaurants and exhibition spaces on the first floor, and offices above. The buildings had no problem fitting into the sombre townscape of Communist East Berlin.

Other architects, preferring to design buildings that expressed the dynamic spirit of the age in a more exciting way, shunned this kind of functionalism. The most extraordinary Expressionist building of the period, destroyed like so much else in the course of World War II,

originally intended to be an astrophysics laboratory and observatory, Erich Mendelsohn's Einstein Tower, located on a hilltop in Potsdam, is unique. Its fluid, organic shapes evoke the "mysteries of the unexplored universe".

In common with many modern architects, Mendelsohn fled Berlin after the Nazis were elected in 1933. With him went the designers associated with the Bauhaus, which had spent its final year in the city under the directorship of Ludwig Mies van der Rohe. Mies had designed a futuristic glass and steel skyscraper for a site on Friedrichstrasse as early as 1922, but unfortunately this never saw the light of day

was the Grosses Schauspielhaus by Hans Poelzig, which had a spectacular auditorium with great stalactite-like forms hanging from the ceiling. Expressionist architects gave new relevance to the traditional use of brick in eastern Germany, with their dynamic, angular forms evocative of the power of electricity or the excitement of jazz. A couple of the finest examples can be found at churches located in Wilmersdorf: the Kirche am Hohenzollernplatz by Fritz Höger, who was responsible for the world-famous Chile-Haus in Hamburg, and the Kreuzkirche, whose most striking feature is its pagoda-like porch. But the most singular structure of this type is to be found outside Berlin;

and the city had to wait until the 1970s to be endowed with a creation by this exemplary master of Modernism.

National Socialist monumentalism

After 1933 architecture entered a new phase, in the service of the megalomaniacal preoccupations of the National Socialist totalitarian state. Appointed general building inspector by Hitler, Albert Speer drew up plans for the future Berlin. As the capital of the Greater German Reich, the city would have a population of 10 million and be renamed "Germania". The grand avenue running west from the Brandenburg Gate was to form a right angle with an even grander thoroughfare, the North–South Axis, which would terminate in an impossibly vast People's Hall beneath the world's biggest dome. World War II brought these ambitions to a halt, although the lamp standards along the Strasse des 17 Juni are Speer's work, as is the quartet of pavilions around the Victory Monument. His gargantuan Reich Chancellery was gutted in the war, and its granite cladding subsequently used in the construction of the Soviet war memorials near the Reichstag and in Treptow Park.

The most significant structures from the National Socialist period still standing are Tem-

triumph that was the 1936 Olympic Games, it has remained in constant use, and is currently being refurbished to host the football World Cup in 2006. The city airport at Tempelhof is also still in use although, unlike the stadium, it no longer fulfils contemporary requirements. It consists of a series of severe, monumental buildings, such as a 100-metre- (330-ft-) long departure hall and a curving, 1,200-metre (400 ft), structure that leads to the hangars.

East versus West

As the Nazi nightmare came to a crashing end in May 1945, much of the city's physical fabric

pelhof Airport and the Olympic Stadium. The stadium was built for the Olympic Games of 1936, though work on the design began before the Nazi era. Built in the "stripped Classical" style of the time, its reinforced concrete hidden beneath the granite and limestone favoured by the Nazis, it can accommodate a total of 110,000 spectators. It is, however, an essentially functional structure, its gargantuan size mitigated by its submergence in its surroundings. Since successfully serving its purpose as a magnificent setting for the Nazi propaganda

lay in ruins; nearly half of Berlin's housing had been destroyed by the Allies, and few of its monuments had been spared. Reconstruction soon began; Hans Scharoun was appointed city planner in chief, but it soon became clear that the two halves of Berlin were destined to develop in different ways.

East Berlin obediently followed the model dictated by Moscow. The Soviet Embassy on Unter den Linden was rebuilt in 1950–53 in uncompromisingly neoclassical Stalinist style, at the same time as work began on the "First Street of Socialism" – the Stalin-Allee. This monumental, 90-metre- (300-ft-) wide boulevard, renamed Karl-Marx-Allee in 1961, runs

LEFT: the Bauhaus-Archiv designed by Walter Gropius.
ABOVE: Werner March's Olympic Stadium.

eastwards for 2 km (1 mile) from near Alexander Platz. It is flanked throughout by blocks of flats with shops and social centres on the lower floors. Here again the style is unmistakably Stalinist, though some of the detailing, such as the twin towers at Frankfurter Tor, was specifically designed to evoke the Prussian architecture of the past.

While East Berlin flaunted its architectural subservience to the Soviet Union, the other half of the city ostentatiously became the "Showcase of the West". Many of the architects forced to flee Nazism had successfully re-established themselves as teachers and practitioners, mostly free-standing structures, some of them 17 storeys high and grouped loosely around a central area with shops, church, cinema, library and kindergarten. One of the contributing architects was the great Le Corbusier, who had one of his *Unités d'habitation* built, though there was not enough room in the district for this 17-storey edifice, complete with 557 flats and "streets in the sky"; it was erected instead in the western suburbs near the Olympic Stadium.

West Berlin's greatest symbol

Although the Hansaviertel soon became an essential stop on city tours, the greatest new

particularly in the United States. Some now returned, bringing with them that triumphant version of Modernism known as the International Style, based on steel, concrete, glass and particular angles. The area around Zoo Station and the Kurfürstendamm was redeveloped in this manner, not always successfully.

The showpiece of the Western counterblast to the Stalin-Allee was the Hansaviertel. In 1953, the devastated Hansa district on the periphery of the Tiergarten was the subject of an international competition that resulted in the construction of some three dozen resolutely Modernist buildings. In contrast with the monolithic traditionalism of the east, these were symbol of West Berlin was the rebuilt Kaiser-Wilhelm-Gedächtniskirche. Centrally located at the end of the Kurfürstendamm, this somewhat bland neo-Romanesque church dating to 1895 had been almost completely destroyed by the Allies' bombs.

It might have been pulled down altogether, but its jagged, roofless tower was saved and, from 1959 to 1963 a new ensemble was built around it. This consisted of four free-standing buildings, a foyer, a small chapel, a belfry and an octagonal church. Its astounding combination of old and new enhanced the value of the ruined tower as a memorial, and instantly created an city landmark. The walls of the new buildings have a honeycomb-like structure; in the church, this contains a total of more than 22,000 stained-glass panels of a deep, heavenly blue shot through with flashes of brighter colours. The resultant atmosphere is one of calm contemplation, in contrast with the frenetic activity that surrounds it in this busy part of western Berlin.

Even more striking than the Gedächtniskirche was the Kongresshalle, the United States' contribution to the IBA (International Building Exhibition) of 1957. Located on the Spree's banks in the Tiergarten, this edifice – more of a sculpture than a building – was a radical

A new cultural district

One of city planner Scharoun's innovative proposals was the development of a new cultural district on land in the southeastern corner of the Tiergarten that had been cleared to make way for Speer's North–South Axis. The first significant building erected in the Kulturforum was Scharoun's own Philharmonie, a concert hall specifically designed for the Berlin Philharmonic Orchestra and completed in 1963.

The structure of the Philharmonie is as unusual as that of the Kongresshalle; the architect claimed that his tent-like shapes arose purely from considerations of function, in this

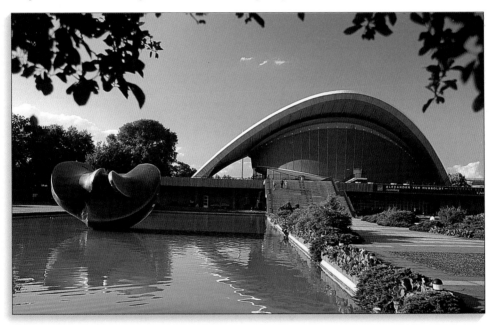

departure from the conventions of Modernism. Its extraordinary curving roof, which is supported at only two points, prompted witty Berliners to come up with the affectionate nickname the "pregnant oyster". The bold concept worked in structural terms, but water penetration caused the steel to rust, and in 1981 part of the roof collapsed. After reconstruction the building undertook a new, multicultural purpose and it was renamed Haus der Kulturen der Welt (House of the Cultures of the World).

LEFT: Kaiser-Wilhelm-Gedächtniskirche.
ABOVE: Haus der Kulturen der Welt, the "pregnant oyster" in Tiergarten.

case the placement of the orchestra platform in a central position, from which terraces of seating rise almost to the roof.

The building constitutes a quite remarkable contrast with its near neighbour, the Neue Nationalgalerie, the only Berlin work by the exiled Mies van der Rohe. Built in 1965–68, the New National Gallery expresses Mies's dictum that "less is more" to perfection.

Its 65-sq-metre (700-sq-ft) steel-coffered roof rests on a mere eight columns, thereby allowing light to flood freely through the glazed walls into the great foyer on its granite podium. Views out to the delightful little 19th-century St Matthäus Kirche (Church of St Matthew), with its patterned brickwork, serve only to emphasise the purity and restraint of this iconic Modernist work.

East Berlin has nothing that can compete with such genius; the Palast der Republik, the home of the Volkskammer, the parliament of the German Democratic Republic, features marble cladding and tinted windows, but is pedestrian by comparison. Constructed in 1976 on the site of the old royal town palace at a key angle in the processional way between the Brandenburger Tor and Alexanderplatz, it has none of the distinction necessary for such a significant location in the townscape. It

functioned well enough in its time, with public access to much of the interior, but since 1990 it has been closed due to the dangers posed by asbestos that was used in its construction.

Postmodernism

Postmodernism arrived in force in West Berlin with the International Building Exhibition of 1987, which aimed to reclaim the inner city as residential neighbourhoods. A whole range of projects scattered around the city demonstrated the extent to which architecture had progressed from the stylistic and functional considerations of Modernism to a more humane approach. The new attitude involved greater awareness of the

city's past and the complex context into which new buildings needed to fit. Some of the most sensitive residential schemes are to be found in the southern part of the Friedrichstadt; several architects worked together on the housing along the Lindenstrasse, an attractive, well-landscaped mixture of villas and apartment blocks well integrated with the older buildings around them. In marked contrast, the corner block at 45–47 Schloss Strasse in Charlottenburg is a striking individual design of great boldness that harks back to the Expressionism of the 1920s.

The architecture of unity

After 1990, the reunited city embarked on the colossal task of stitching itself back together and fitting itself out with buildings that would not only help fulfil its new role as capital, but express its identity, and the values of a nation at the heart of an expanding Europe.

The English architect Sir Norman Foster was responsible for creating the steel and glass cupola at the top of the Reichstag, which has helped that once forbidding neo-Renaissance mass of stone metamorphose into a superb new home for the country's parliament. In the bend of the Spree by the Reichstag, the genial plan for a whole new government quarter devised by Charlotte Frank and Axel Schultes is taking shape, its long ribbon of building leaping the river and the line of the Wall in a gesture charged with symbolism.

A commercial counterpart to the new government district is emerging at Potsdamer Platz, where teams of international architects have designed and knitted together a whole series of building complexes. Of these, one of the most spectacular is the Sony Centre, its focal point being a "covered arena cascading with light" by the German-born Helmut Jahn.

But the most extraordinary of the buildings that are playing a key role in defining the city's 21st-century personality is Daniel Liebeskind's Jewish Museum. The building's seemingly arbitrary and jagged forms and internal spaces are so charged with symbolism that many feel it should stand as sculpture in its own right rather than be filled with exhibits illustrating the long and often tragic history of the Jewish community in Germany. ❏

LEFT: Ludwig-Erhard-Haus housing the Berlin stock exchange was designed by Nicholas Grimshaw.

The S- and U-Bahns

Like Mussolini, Hitler was said to have "made the trains run on time" and Berlin's rail network was the pride of the country. But the Führer would have turned in his unknown grave if he'd seen what happened to it after the war.

In 1871, Berlin's first goods connection railway between the terminus stations Stettiner, Hamburger, Potsdamer and Anhalter and Görlitzer Station was experiencing difficulties due to narrow tracks and street traffic, so it was decided to construct the Ringbahn (ring railway) outside the then city limits. The complete circle finished in 1877. Soon a whole rail network was built, combining city, ring and suburban stretches. The main line through the middle of the city was Europe's first viaduct railway.

It wasn't until 1930 that the system took the name S-Bahn. Its finest hour came in 1936 during the Olympic Games when trains came every 90 seconds – a never-to-be-repeated performance.

The Battle of Berlin left much of the already depleted transport system in a terrible state. Drowned corpses were found in the underground sections of the north–south line and the U2 after the Nazis, close to capitulation, flooded the underground to halt the Soviet advance. The reconstruction process was not easy. The operation of the U-Bahn was given to the western BVG. East Berlin controlled the S-Bahn which, because it was run on electricity from the east, made it the cheapest public transport there.

From 1952, trams and buses no longer crossed the border between east and west, unlike the S- and U-Bahns. This was the time of the *Durchläufer* (through train) when rush hour trains travelling between two East Berlin stations would pass straight through West Berlin stations without stopping. The erection of the Wall in 1961 was to bring about the temporary demise of the S-Bahn in the West. The Stadtbahn line was interrupted at Bahnhof Friedrichstrasse, the terminus station for the east and west, and trains came to a halt at separate, partitioned platforms. The nearby Tränenpalast (Palace of Tears), the border clearance centre, witnessed numerous tearful farewells of people separated by the divided city.

Elsewhere, tracks travelling over the border were partially dismantled as west-bound lines were interrupted, breaking the circle of the Ringbahn.

RIGHT: the S-and U-bahn system is well integrated.

Gesundbrunnen became the last stop before GDR Berlin in the north, as did Sonnenallee in the south. On the north–south line, which operated as a western line, the stations at Potsdamer Platz, Unter den Linden, Oranienburger Str., Nordbahnhof and Bornholmer Str. were closed. The platforms of these so-called "ghost stations" were guarded by GDR soldiers, ordered to foil any escape attempts on the roofs of trains passing through. At Bornholmer Str., two tracks ran, and still run, side by side like repellent magnets on either side of the border.

A western call to boycott the S-Bahn was countered by a price increase for all Westerners boarding in the East. In 1984, the BVG took over the rail

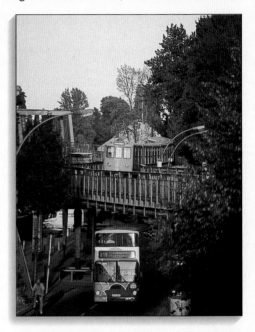

system and the western network began to expand gradually. Since the reunification of the city, a full transport network has been put into operation. The convergence of tracks at Gesundbrunnen, Schönhauser Allee and Bornholmer Strasse (Nordkreuz) will now serve as Berlin's northern rail crossroads and when the ambitious new Lehrter Bahnhof near the government quarter is completed it will be Berlin's first main central station.

The symbolic completion of the last stretch of track between Westhafen and Schönhauser Allee will give Berlin a complete Ringbahn or "Vollring" for the first time since 1961. Berliners hope the city's transport network, due to be completed in 2003, will once more be the envy of the world. ❑

PLACES

A detailed guide to the entire city, with principal sites clearly cross-referenced by number to the maps

Not content with its two centres during the Cold War, Berlin now finds itself with many centres of activity. The previous focal points of the Ku'damm (in the West) and Alexanderplatz (in the East) must now contend with Potsdamer Platz, the government quarter near the Brandenburg Gate, and Stadtmitte in order to be noticed. This should not come as such a surprise to a city which is the amalgamation of lots of little towns, and in part even village communities. Perhaps this explains Berlin's unique atmosphere.

The city is now divided into 12 districts instead of 23, but the changes are only administrative, and each of the original districts has its own distinctive features. This guide, therefore, will deal with the central districts before the Bezirk (district) reform.

The central districts are not divided into East and West but presented from the centre of the city outwards. Chapters on what to see in Mitte, and the area around Alexanderplatz, are followed by a chapter on the continuing redevelopment of Museum Island. Next is a chapter on Kurfürstendamm, which isn't a district but has its own chapter to reflect its importance in the divided city.

Following the Ku'damm is a chapter on Tiergarten, reflecting the district's prominence as the centre of the city's political and financial district. The book then moves on to chapters on historic Charlottenberg; Schöneberg, the focal point of Berlin's gay scene; Kreuzberg, the home of left-orientated politics and its much celebrated comrade in the East, bohemian Prenzlauer Berg.

Also featured in the chapter on Prenzlauer Berg is the more traditional working-class eastern district of Friedrichshain, which is now enjoying cult status, providing the right atmosphere not only for a number of night clubs but also for ambitious development projects.

Unfairly avoided by most visitors on a week-long holiday, the outer districts are grouped together in this book according to their area, either East or West. Although it is over a decade since the Wall fell, one can still notice each Bezirk's Cold War legacy. Whether it be the architecture (Karl-Marx-Allee and Marzahn being two examples of GDR design) or the people – the western districts still have the highest proportion of Turkish immigrants in Berlin – traces of the recent past remain extremely visible.

Finally, there is a chapter on Potsdam, capital of Brandenburg, with the fabulous palace of Sanssouci making it one of the most interesting cities in Germany. ❑

PRECEDING PAGES: the view from the dome of the Berliner Dom (Berlin Cathedral); the Gothic Marienkirche (St Mary's Church); the tubular sculpture *Berlin*, near the Europa-Center, symbolising the divided city (1987).
LEFT: Potsdamer Platz buildings.

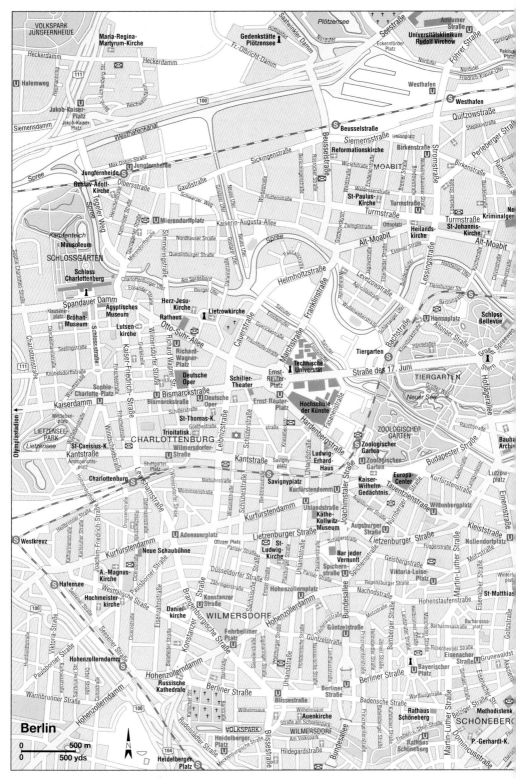

Berlin

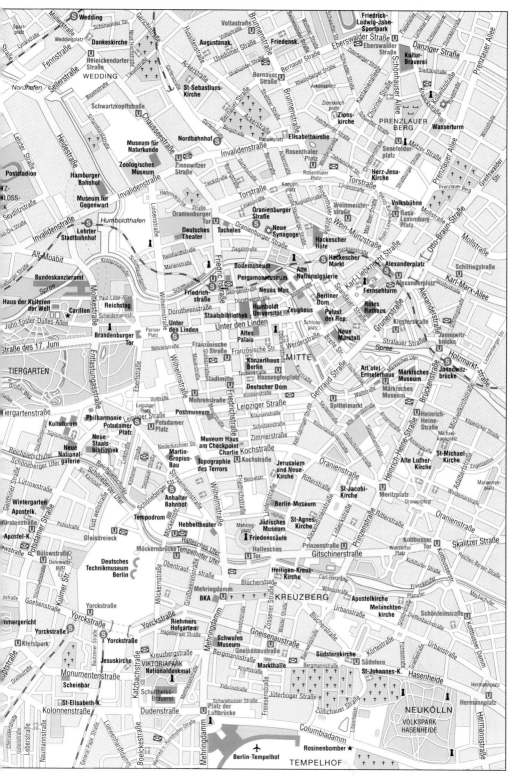

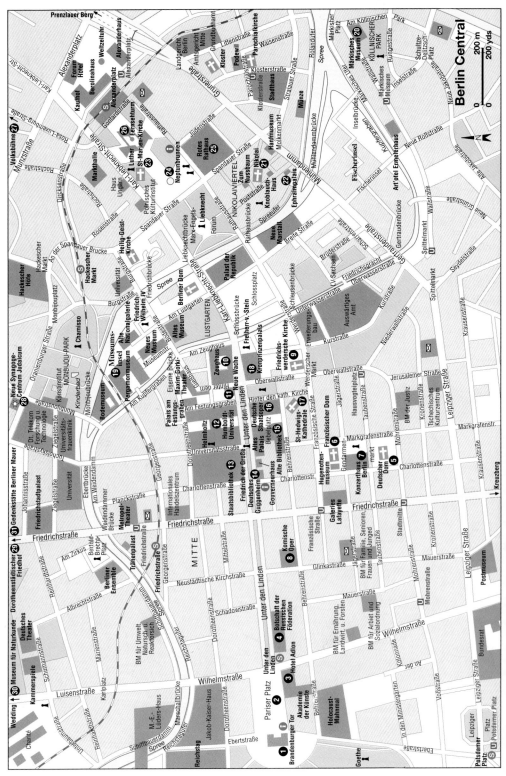

MITTE

Map on page 110

The Mitte district is at the centre of the city's historical, political and cultural life and reflects Berlin's past, present and future

Historically speaking, Mitte is the true heart of the city. Here, on the island in the Spree, the twin village trading settlements of Berlin and Cölln first grew up some 800 years ago. Here, too, was the centre of the residential cities of ruling electors, kings and emperors. Mitte was the power hub of the Nazi regime, and the seat of government of the German Democratic Republic. Here, the visitor comes face to face with Berlin's long history.

Mitte begins where East Germany once ended: at the **Brandenburger Tor ❶** (Brandenburg Gate). This symbol of Prussian glory and inter-German destiny must be the most-painted, most-photographed monument in the city. Built in 1788–91 as a triumphal focal point for the capital's magnificent boulevard, Unter den Linden, its history has often been an extraordinarily turbulent one.

The gate's famous *Quadriga*, the goddess of victory driving her four-horse chariot, has experienced a difficult fate as the representative of the "Triumph of Peace" – as the gate's architect, Langhans, described her. Captured by Napoleon in 1800 and returned to her original site eight years later, she was badly damaged in crossfire in 1945, then replaced in replica in 1958. The statue was destroyed once more, this time by over-enthusiastic revellers in 1989–90, during the first New Year celebrations following the opening of the Wall, but has been restored since.

PRECEDING PAGES AND BELOW: Brandenburger Tor, one of the city's most potent images.

Unter den Linden

Walking from the Brandenburg Tor along the avenue Unter den Linden gives an impression of the magnificence and splendour created by Frederick the Great when he had this symbol of Prussian supremacy constructed. A somewhat controversial statue of the great man on horseback was recently unveiled near the eastern end of the boulevard amid concerns that glorifying a, militaristic past such as Prussia's should not be on the agenda of a city trying to present itself favourably to a watching world. This may be easier said than done, considering that nearly every stone in the street in which Hilter used to parade his might bears witness to historical events, whether hidden behind a modern facade or carefully restored.

The first section, starting at the **Pariser Platz ❷** is nearly complete. Whether the square can be returned to its former, prewar glory, with its new hotels, banks, embassy buildings and the new **Akademie der Künste** (Academy of Arts) due to open in 2002, is for the people to decide. Until the USA can agree on the plans for the protection boundary around their proposed embassy next to the Brandenburger Tor where their prewar embassy stood, the full picture won't be seen. Some of the spirit of yesteryear has, however, already returned to the Pariser Platz. The

Kaiser Wilhelm II,
Greta Garbo,
Thomas Mann and
Charlie Chaplin all
stayed at the Hotel
Adlon (above)
during its heyday.

BELOW:
Gendarmenmarkt.

Hotel Adlon ❸, the former jewel in Berlin's luxury accommodation crown, has opened its doors again. After being consumed by flames in 1945, badly renovated in the 1960s and then torn down in 1984, the celebrities' favourite haunt has been rebuilt and refurbished for the millennium while still tipping its cap to a decadent past.

Further evidence of a less glorious past can be found in the former "political corner" of Berlin, surrounding the Pariser Platz. Hitler's architect, Albert Speer, was responsible for the construction in 1938 of the vast New Imperial Chancellery at the junction of what was then the Wilhelmstrasse and Vossstrasse. Beneath it lay the bunker that was to be the Führer's last refuge. Today, nothing can be seen of all this. Along with the existing apartments, the site will be, controversially, occupied in 2004 by the **Denkmal für die ermordeten Juden Europas** (Memorial for the Murdered Jews of Europe) – a gesture which has annoyed some of the less prominent set-upon minorities of the Nazi regime.

Continuing towards the city, you will pass the monumental building of the **Botschaft der Russichen Föderation ❹** (Embassy of the Russian Federation), constructed in the style of the Stalinist Era. Completed in 1953, it was the first building along this section of the avenue. The pulsating heart of the city once lay at the junction of Unter den Linden and Friedrichstrasse. However, the drab characteristic of social realism lent the scene an air of desolation in contrast with its former liveliness.

Since the Wall came down, the boulevard is gradually becoming a promenade once again, an avenue where people throng and push – more, at present, out of historical interest than in pursuit of pleasure. Here, too, the old elegance of Berlin is gradually re-emerging, as can be seen in the Grand Hotel Maritim.

Around Gendarmenmarkt

Turning right into Friedrichstrasse, one soon arrives in the new, glamorous heart of Berlin – Stadtmitte. The lavish and architecturally interesting **Galeries Lafayette** shopping centre is at the forefront of a move that was to bring back the glory days of Friedrichsstrasse. Unfortunately, the expensive shops, hotels, car showrooms and office spaces have yet to fire the imagination of the locals, even though wealthy tourists seem willing enough to inhale its costly perfume. On the corner of Friedrichstrasse and Behrenstrasse stands the Grand Hotel, the most prestigious hotel in East Berlin, opened in time for the city's 750-year celebrations in 1987. Its nostalgic decor and old-style pomp evoke memories of the luxurious lives of the haute bourgeoisie.

Map on page 110

The beautiful square of the **Gendarmenmarkt**, a few steps to the east along Mohrenstrasse, is dominated by the **Deutscher Dom** ❺ (Evangelical Lutheran Church, 1708) and the **Französischer Dom** ❻ (French Reformed Church, 1705). The **Hugenottenmuseum** (Huguenot Museum; open Tues–Sat noon–5pm, Sun 11am–5pm; entrance fee) is housed in the Französischer Dom. The museum documents the persecution of the Huguenots in France in the 17th century, and their contribution to the historical, intellectual and cultural development of Berlin. Today the cathedral's dome also houses a wine bar.

The Schauspielhaus, renamed **Konzerthaus Berlin** ❼ (open Mon–Sat noon–8pm, Sun noon–4pm; tel: 20 30 92 101), flanked by the two churches, is one of the finest buildings designed by that most Prussian of all architects, Karl Friedrich Schinkel. In his time the neoclassical masterpiece, built in 1871, was described as "tangible music". Since its reopening as a concert hall in 1984, it has remained true to the challenge contained in that description. The marble

BELOW: Galeries Lafayette interior, designed by Jean Nouvel.

The Friedrich Schiller monument by Reinhold Begas. The figures around its base represent History, Drama, Poetry and Philosophy.

BELOW: the ivy-clad exterior of the Staatsbibliothek (State Library).

pedestrian statue of Friedrich Schiller was returned to its original site here in 1986 as part of an exchange of cultural assets. The Nazis had banished the statue during the 1930s. Over at Behrenstr. 55 the **Komische Oper** 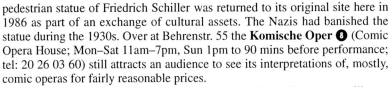 (Comic Opera House; Mon–Sat 11am–7pm, Sun 1pm to 90 mins before performance; tel: 20 26 03 60) still attracts an audience to see its interpretations of, mostly, comic operas for fairly reasonable prices.

Continuing along the Französische Strasse towards the Spree, you will next come to the Werderscher Markt. The impressive building on the far side was the former Führer-approved **Reichsbank**. One of the finest examples of Nazi architecture in the city, it was subsequently occupied by the Central Committee of the SED and, along with its newly constructed neighbour, now exists as the Foreign Office. The building over the street to the left is the **Friedrichs-Werdersche-Kirche** (Schinkel Museum; open daily 10am–6pm; entrance fee). Not only built to Schinkel's design, it now contains his museum documenting his life and work including some of his sculptures. If you take the Oberwallstrasse you will soon find yourself back on Unter den Linden, at the Lindenforum. "Here one magnificent building rubs shoulders with the next," enthused the poet Heinrich Heine.

The baroque splendour of the old **Zeughaus** (Arsenal), constructed in 1695, marked the first stage in the development of what was to become Berlin's show avenue. Today the Zeughaus is the site of the **Deutsches Historisches Museum** (German History Museum; open 10am–6pm, Thur 10am–10pm, closed Wed;), which has recently reopened after extensive renovation. The four allegorical female figures by the entrance represent Pyrotechnics, Arithmetic, Geometry and Mechanics. Particularly moving are the 22 masks of dying warriors by Andreas Schlüter contained in the inner courtyard.

A few steps further on is the Central Memorial of the German Federal Republic, housed in Schinkel's first neoclassical-style building, the former **Neue Wache** (New Guardhouse; open 10am–6pm daily). Built in 1818 and used by the Nazis as a memorial to Nazi heroes, by the communists as an anti-fascist memorial to the dead of two wars and, now, by the Federal Republic as a memorial to bad things in general, the statue inside, by the artist and pacifist Käthe Kollwitz, is quite fitting.

Humboldt-Universität

The students of the **Humboldt-Universität** (Humboldt University), next to the memorial, tread in the footsteps of many famous men. Their spiritual rector is Wilhelm von Humboldt, at whose suggestion the institute of learning was founded in 1809. The east and west wings encircling the courtyard of honour are extensions dating from the early years of this century. The **Staatsbibliothek** (State Library; open Mon 2–9pm, Tues–Fri 9am–9pm, Sat 9am–5pm; tours first Sat 10.30am each month) next door contains a collection of more than 7 million books.

Also part of the university buildings are the former Governor's House (Unter den Linden 11) and the **Altes Palais** (Unter den Linden 9; not open to the

public). The Governor's House originally stood in the Rathausstrasse, but had to make way for new buildings during the reconstruction of the city centre. In order to preserve the baroque facade it was transported and used to fill a gap left by a war ruin. Next door at No. 13–15, the tiny **Deutsches Guggenheim** ⓮ (open 11am–8pm daily, Thur 11am–10pm; free entrance Mon) hosts exhibitions by big names in the art world.

Around Bebelplatz

The Opernplatz opposite the university acquired a certain tragic notoriety at the beginning of the 1930s. On 10 May 1933, it was the scene of a huge bonfire, when more than 20,000 books, works abhorred by the National Socialists, were burned at the height of Nazi propaganda minister Josef Goebbels' "Campaign against the Un-German Spirit".

Today the square has been rechristened as **Bebelplatz** in memory of the workers' leader August Bebel. The building on the west side has a duplicate, which is part of the Hofburg in Vienna. The **Alte Bibliothek** ⓯ (Old Library; open Mon–Sat 10am–5pm, Sun 1–5pm) is affectionately known by Berlin residents as the "*Kommode*" (dressing table) because of its arched facade. Since its restoration in 1969 it has been used as a reading room.

The neoclassical jewel on the other side of the Bebelplatz is the **Deutsche Staatsoper** ⓰ (German State Opera House; open Mon–Sat 10am–8pm, Sun 2–8pm; tel: 20 35 45 55). Perhaps one of the unluckiest buildings on the street, this grand old building was damaged in a bombing raid in 1941, renovated for its bicentenary celebrations in 1943 and then totally flattened in 1945. Its reconstruction at the beginning of the 1950s followed, as precisely as possible,

BELOW: facade detail on the Neue Wache (New Guardhouse).

KARL FRIEDRICH SCHINKEL

Karl Friedrich Schinkel (1781–1841) was born in the small town of Neuruppin in Brandenburg. At the time Berlin, the capital of Prussia, was a second- or third-rate city by European standards. With the exception of the buildings surrounding the Bebelplatz, Unter den Linden, and the odd medieval remnant, there are few buildings or monuments in today's Berlin that were built before Schinkel's birth. In the 30 years to 1840 Schinkel designed over a dozen of the major constructions, including museums, churches, palaces and bridges, which would transform the architectural face of the city.

His work, and particularly his earlier designs such as the Neue Wache (1818), the Schauspielhaus (1819), and the Altes Museum (1925), is characterised by classicism, meaning it draws on architectural styles from ancient Greece and Rome. Schinkel's later work was influenced by a visit to England where he was impressed by the industrial styles that were already prevalent in that country by the 1820s. Elements of this style can be seen in the partial reconstruction of Schinkel's architectural school, the Bauakademie, and in the Friedrich Werdersche Kirche (1930), which now houses a collection of sculpture by Schinkel and members of his influential school.

the plans of the rococo architect Georg von Knobelsdorff. Friedrich II had the domed **St-Hedwigs-Kathedrale** ⓱ (St Hedwigs Cathedral; Mon–Fri 9am–9pm, Sat 9am–5pm), on the edge of the Bebelplatz, built for the 10,000 Catholics resident in Berlin during his reign. The former **Kronprinzenpalais** ⓲ (Crown Prince's Palace; Thur–Tues 10am–6pm) closes the square in on the eastern side. The palace was home to the royal family until the end of the monarchy. Schinkel was responsible for the design of the former Castle Bridge, now rechristened the **Schlossbrücke**, which crosses the Kupfergraben – one of the arms of the Spree – to **Museumsinsel** ⓳ (Museum Island, *see pages 127–130*). The Gallery of Goddesses, on the side of the bridge, depicting Nike and Pallas Athene and forming a cycle inspired by the anti-Napoleonic wars of independence, lead to Berliners calling the bridge Puppenbrücke (Puppet Bridge).

The Nikolaiviertel

At the south end of the Museumsinsel lies the **Fischerinsel**. Nothing indicates that the island was once the cradle of the twin founding settlements of Berlin and Cölln. After the war, plans for the reconstruction of the district, although technically feasible, were rejected in favour of total demolition and a policy of radical "rebuilding without nostalgia". In concrete terms, this meant that between 1967 and 1971 the entire area was razed to the ground before the construction of six 21-storey buildings.

While in the area, the visitor may be tempted to stop at the restaurant in the rococo palace **Ermelerhaus** on the Märkisches Ufer. From the nearby Gertraudenbrücke there is a fine view of the oldest railway bridge in the city, the Jungfernbrücke, constructed in 1798.

In the Köllnischer Park you'll find not only a monument to Zille but also the **Märkisches Museum** ⓴ (Museum of the March Brandenburg; open 10am–5pm, closed Mon; entrance fee except Wed), which houses the most extensive local history collection in Berlin and traces the history of the city from the earliest times until the present. The large tower was once part of the 17th-century fortifications. The city's furry mascots reside in the nearby bear pits, presumably not so honoured to be kept in such cramped conditions in what can only be described as an eerily quiet corner of Mitte.

The East Berlin authorities were particularly painstaking in their restoration of the **Nikolaiviertel** (Nicholas Quarter). With meticulous attention to detail they reconstructed many buildings which had originally stood elsewhere. The result was an island of history in the centre of East Berlin, a collage of antiquity which fulfils admirably the desire for a "showcase of the past". The houses clustered around the Nikolaikirche (Church of St Nicholas) were all restored, at least externally, with great attention to historical accuracy and loving insistence on period detail.

One of the most important structures is the arcade in front of the Law Courts, dating from the year 1270. The nearby "**Zum Letzten Instanz**", which backs onto a remaining piece of the Old City Wall in Waisenstrasse, is the latest incarnation of a restaurant

A statue outside the Märkisches Museum, which has collections relating to the history of Berlin and the Brandenburg region.

BELOW: the Gothic Marienkirche (St Mary's Church).

Map
on page
110

which has been on this spot since the 16th century. Napoleon, during his "tour" of Europe, Heinrich Zille and Mikael Gorbachev are all said to have enjoyed meals here.

The **Nikolaikirche** ㉑ (Church of St Nicholas; museum open Tues–Sun 10am–5.30pm; entrance fee), the oldest building in Berlin, is mentioned in records for the first time in 1264. It contains the sandstone *Spandauer Madonna* sculpture carved at the end of the 13th century. In the surrounding district the nooks and crannies of the cobbled streets invite visitors to browse in the little shops and stroll among craftsmen's workshops, bars and restaurants.

The Ephraimpalais to Rotes Rathaus

The **Ephraimpalais** ㉒ (Poststr. 16; open 10am–6pm; closed Mon) by the Mühlendammbrücke is one of 20 historic houses grouped around St Nicholas's. It was formerly considered to be the finest residence in the city and when completed in 1764 its magnificent rococo facade aroused considerable attention. Moved 12 metres (39 feet) from its original position for the 750th anniversary of Berlin, nowadays it houses changing exhibitions from the city's museums. Diagonally opposite, from the Molkenmarkt, the oldest market square in the city, the round domed tower of the former Rathaus (town hall) can be glimpsed.

The statues of the Marx-Engels-Forum are by Ludwig Engelhart.

On the eastern bank of the Spree, the **Marx-Engels-Forum** situated on the Karl-Liebknecht-Strasse is adorned with statues by East German sculptors. Rising up in the middle of the star-shaped square, dwarfing all the other exhibits, are twin bronze figures of the forerunners of socialism, Karl Marx and Friedrich Engels. With their fondness for nicknames, local Berliners were not slow to christen them "Vest and Jacket".

The Gothic **St Marienkirche** ㉓ (Church of St Mary; open Mon–Thur 10am–noon, weekend noon–5pm) is dwarfed by its modern surroundings in the shadow of the Fernsehturm (television tower). Visitors seeking refuge here from the roaring traffic of the Karl-Liebknecht-Strasse will find amongst the treasures in this 13th-century place of worship a 22-metre (70-ft) long late-Gothic fresco, *Totentanz* (*Dance of Death*, 1485), and a marble pulpit by Andreas Schlüter. Free organ recitals are held in the church on Saturday at 4.30pm.

BELOW: sculpture at Nikolaiviertel (Nicholas Quarter).

The **Neptunbrunnen** ㉔ (Fountain of Neptune) between Marienkirch and the Rotes Rathaus demonstrates the Berliners' predilection for Wilhelminian opulence. The bronze statue was completed by Reinhold Begas in 1891 as a gift from the citizens of Berlin to their emperor. The four figures of women splashing around the basin represent four rivers: the Rhine, the Elbe, the Oder and the Vistula.

The **Rotes Rathaus** ㉕ (Red Town Hall; open Mon–Fri 10am–6pm; closed for official functions) owes its name less to its political inclinations than to the red bricks from the Brandenburg Marches of which it was built. The fifth town hall in the history of Berlin, designed by Hermann Freidrich Waesemann and completed in 1869, is the city's main town hall. The frieze running around the outside of the building depicts scenes from the city's history. ❑

AROUND ALEXANDERPLATZ

The area around the former centre of East Berlin contains historic buildings, restored courtyards, stylish hang-outs and the heart of Berlin's Jewish district

Map on page 110

Visitors and locals can be seen rushing or strolling between the 39-storey Forum Hotel, the department store and the Teacher's House with its mural painting by Walter Womacka (which is also known as "Cummerbund"). They pass by the tacky **Weltzeituhr** (World Time Clock, 1969) and the nasty **Völkerfreundschaft** (Friendship of the Peoples Fountain), ironically named considering its former, unofficial, use as a pick-up point for ladies doing the night shift, all seeming just a little bit lost in the shadow of the overpowering architecture.

Two of the prewar buildings alongside the suburban train overpass, the **Berolinahaus** and the **Alexanderhaus**, are representative of the New Functionalism at the end of the 1920s. They blend unobtrusively with the characteristic socialist architectural style. The 365-metre (1,168-ft) high **Fernsehturm ㉖** (TV tower; open Nov–Mar, daily 9am–1pm, Oct–Apr daily 10am–midnight; entrance fee) with its unusual futuristic, triangular form at the base has become the former East Berlin's most familiar landmark. The revolving **Tele Café** (open daily 10–1am) takes about 30 minutes to do a circuit. Reconstruction of the square is due to start in 2004 but, at the time of writing, final plans had not been put in place, even though the architecture competition for its development had been won by Hans Kollhoff.

Reconstruction of a more avant-garde nature goes on at the **Volksbühne ㉗** (People's Theatre; tel: 247 6772) near Rosa-Luxemburg-Platz. Inside the impressive structure of the theatre renowned theatrical pieces are regularly reinterpreted by artists. The current director, Frank Castorf, sees no reason to change the format which regularly fills the auditorium.

LEFT: the Fernsehturm (TV Tower). **BELOW:** Hackesche Höfe.

Hackesche Höfe to Scheunen Viertel

Meanwhile at Hackescher Markt, one S-bahn station to the west of Alexanderplatz, things are a bit more conventional – a change of direction from its recent past. Only a stone's throw away from the Eastern capital's showpiece of Unter den Linden, the area was allowed to slip into a state of disrepair in the GDR, its buildings crumbling from neglect. The Fall of the Wall heralded an upturn in its fortunes as it became one of the beating hearts of the alternative post-Wende scene with bars, clubs and art workshops. Under the watchful eye of property developers, it was soon transformed into an ultra-chic cocktail and shopping spot.

The Hackesche Höfe, the renovated courtyard shopping complex on the corner of Rosenthaler Str. and Oranienburger Str., exemplifies how the new Berlin has a small habit of speculating on anything novel. A continuation of this theme is to be noticed in Sophienstrasse where a number of small, but renovated, art galleries sit alongside fashionable cafés in the heart of

the area named the **Scheunenviertel** (Barn District). Previously so far out of town that the hay barns were built there for safety reasons, the area was later a poor region, inhabited primarily by the Jewish proletariat. Having been completely wiped out during the Nazi era, the Jewish community here is starting to grow again. During its comprehensive renewal, the district has been reclaimed not just by bar owners, who have turned Oranienburger Strasse into a ready-made drinking destination, but by Jewish people too. Kosher restaurants, food shops and Jewish cultural centres are now established.

The splendid **Neue Synagoge** ㉘ (New Synagogue; open Sun–Thur 10am–6pm, Fri 10am–2pm; entrance fee) in Oranienburger Strasse, which was damaged by fire in the 1938 pogroms and suffered during the World War II bombing raids, is now topped by a gleaming golden cupola. It dominates this part of the city and forms the focal point for a reawakening of a Jewish and multi-cultural Berlin. However, the 24-hour presence of armed policemen outside the door is a blatant enough reminder that not everybody has opened their eyes yet.

The permanent exhibition inside in the **Centrum Judaicum** (Jewish Centre; opening as synagogue; entrance fee) tells the story of the original building and gives an account of how diverse Jewish life was in this part of Berlin. What remains of the world created by 160,000 Jewish citizens and wiped out by the events of history can also be studied in the occasional faded inscriptions, memorial plaques and buildings scattered across the city.

Friedrichstrasse

BELOW: the glitzy Friedrichstadtpalas.

There is no longer a faintly disreputable air hanging over **Friedrichstrasse**, for over 300 years a boundary as well as the city's north–south axis. During the long, hot nights of the "Golden Twenties" the street vibrated with wild vitality. Here the pulse of the metropolis beat more quickly than elsewhere and its citizens revelled in the high life in the velvet-and-kitsch atmosphere of the cafés, hotels and variety theatres. The citizens of East Berlin were consequently amazed when, in 1985, it was announced that along its entire 3-km (2-mile) length, the Friedrichstrasse was to be reconstructed in an attempt to recreate the "Berlin milieu of past decades". Today, Friedrichstrasse is the setting for a number of outstanding buildings, with new structures being built on the cramped spaces on the southern side of the train lines.

There's IHZ (International Trade Centre, on the junction of Dorotheenstrasse) and Bahnhof Friedrichstrasse, around which some new structures like the Friedrich-Carré building are taking shape; the Weidendammer Brücke, with an 1890s balustrade adorned once more by wrought-iron light fittings; the **Berliner Ensemble** (tel: 240 81 55) on the Schiffbauerdamm – Brecht's home theatre, with its international reputation; and – last but not least – the **Friedrichstadt-palast**, mockingly known as the "Stalactite Cave".

Famous names

For more than 40 years the producer Max Reinhardt was the dominant influence at the **Deutsches Theater** (tel: 28 44 12 22) and the nearby Studio Theatre in the

Schumannstrasse, where he was director between 1905 and 1933. Both establishments continue to support the tradition of critical drama as a mirror of contemporary issues. On the northern bank of the Spree around Schiffbauerdamm and Reinhardtstrasse, attempts to bring the theatre district up-market seem to have gone to plan. Nicely renovated flats and hotels have succeeded in bringing more gold cufflinks to the area but the endearingly obtrusive and immovable World War II over-ground flak bunker in Reinhardtstrasse must surely take the shine off it for some.

A real sign of the times came in 2001 when the post-Wende squat-come-art centre **Tacheles**, at the end of Oranienburger Str., renovated their dilapidated building. As one of the last bastions of resistance against the gentrification juggernaut, Berlin's 1990's stronghold of underground culture finally came into line with its surroundings. Like a boy who has had his hair combed to meet his father's boss, it still manages to keep some of its credibility in a city of entertainment where new concepts are now explained in business plans. For a symbolic rent of one mark per year, Tacheles will be listed as a historical building (in its past it was Friedrichstrasse Passage – one of the most important shopping arcades in Berlin) and made available for autonomous art events for the next few years. The surrounding project of some 40 buildings will be known as the Johannisviertel.

Not far away as the crow flies stands the **Charité**, the archetypal Berlin hospital. In 1710 Friedrich I had a plague hospital constructed on this site, purely as a precautionary measure, since he feared that the plague, which at the time was already devastating nearby Prenzlau, might also spread to Berlin itself. Once the danger of epidemic was over, the Great Royal Hospital was given over to the care of the indigent sick and rechristened the Charité (Mercy). The

Map on page 110

The three-day Berlin Welcome Card offers unlimited travel in Berlin and Potsdam.

BELOW: the Neue Synagoge.

Map on page 110

ivy-clad brick building was built as an extension in 1917; in 1982 the hospital was given a 15-storey tower and it now has beds for 7,000 patients. Testifying to the fame of the establishment are the names of distinguished medical men such as Ferdinand Sauerbruch, Rudolf Virchow and Robert Koch.

Buried in the nearby **Dorotheenstädtischer Friedhof ㉙** (Dorotheenstadt Cemetery; open daily) on the Chausseestrasse, are Bertolt Brecht and his wife Helene Weigel. The cemetery is overlooked by the flat where they last lived and which has, since, become their memorial museum: the **Brecht Haus** (open Tues, Wed, Fri 10–11.30am, Thur 5–6.30pm, Sat 9.30am–1.30pm). If you study the inscriptions on the graves you will notice a number of famous names. The philosophers Johann Gottlieb Fichte and Georg Wilhelm Friedrich Hegel lie here, as do the writers Arnold Zweig, Heinrich Mann and Johannes R. Becher and the artists Daniel Chodowiecki and John Heartfield, as well as many other famous personalities from German history and the more recent East German past.

Just off Chausseestr., known to some as "Silicone Allee" due to the number of internet start-ups in the area, the **Museum für Naturkunde ㉚** (Natural History Museum; Invalidenstr; open Tues–Sun 9.30am–5pm; entrance fee) is part of Humboldt University. One of the largest and best organised museums of its kind in the world, it contains a vast collection of fossils, skeletons and stuffed animals. Although much of the collection dates back to 1716, most of the exhibits can be traced back millions of years.

Reminders of the past

Up the hill to the north, passing the deserted no-man's-land on the left at Nordbahnhof, a less natural form of history is documented. Bernauer Strasse, the border between Mitte and the western district of Wedding *(see page 267)*, has witnessed many daring escape attempts to the West. Immediately after the building of the Wall, the second and third-floor windows of the flats on the Mitte side provided the escape routes to the western pavement below. When the GDR authorities emptied the houses and bricked up the windows, the escape attempts were forced underground. If you know of any tunnel dug under the Wall, it is most likely to be under Bernauer Strasse. The period of separation is remembered in a three-pronged memorial site ensemble.

The **Gedenkstätte Berliner Mauer ㉛** (Memorial of German Separation), a sectioned-off piece of the Wall complete with border defences and death strip, commemorates suffering under a communist regime and is the best place to see how the barrier worked. The neighbouring Kappelle der Versöhnung (Church of Reconciliation), built on the site of a church in no-man's-land destroyed during the 1980s, is a memorial to all those who died trying to cross the divide.

The **Dokumentationszentrum zur Geschichte der Berliner Mauer** (Berlin Wall Documentation Centre; Bernauer Str. 111; open Wed–Sun 10am–5pm) across the street provides information on the history of the Wall. Unfortunately, nothing remains of the houses on the Mitte side – they were destroyed by the GDR authorities to prevent any further exodus of people across the border. ❑

BELOW: Bertolt Brecht occupies a pedestal in the front of his theatre.
RIGHT: detail of the Neptunbrunnen (Neptune Fountain).

The Jewish Revival

Jewish communities had high and low periods in Berlin long before World War II. They were persecuted as harbingers of the black plague in the 14th and 15th centuries. In the 18th century they were granted commercial privileges that made many of them fantastically wealthy.

The Jewish salons in the late 18th and early 19th centuries drew all of Europe's attention to Prussian emancipation. The "Prussian Edict" on 8 March 1812 granted Jews equal rights as Christians. When Berlin became the capital of the first German Reich in 1871, Jews were in the perfect position to reap the benefits of a rapidly growing economy and play a leading role in Berlin's cultural heyday.

In 1880, these Jewish bourgeois families were joined by East European Jews fleeing persecution. The influx of immigrants sparked anti-Semitism all over the city. It was the beginning of the end. Nevertheless, a healthy Jewish culture flourished in the Scheunen-

viertel, a district only a few minutes' walk away from the Alexanderplatz. The tiny Auguststrasse in the heart of the district was a colourful Jewish street, awash with cultural vitality. Jews built up their community here, and lived peaceably with their German neighbours. Even today, you can still see traces of Hebrew script on the walls of the houses, showing through paint. In a doctrinal sense, it was more Jewish here than anywhere else in the city – much to the displeasure of Berlin's Jewish middle-class establishment, who saw the new arrivals as poor cousins who would ruin the family name.

By the time the Nazi party rose to power in 1933, Berlin had the biggest, most influential Jewish community in Europe: 180,000 Jews lived here. None of them would have believed that Jewish culture in the city would be eliminated 12 years later. Their disbelief explains why so few Jews managed to resist Nazi persecution, and why so few of them fled. And yet it was in this city that the Nazi policy of genocide was conceived. In the Wannsee-Villa, a house in the south of the city, which in January 1992 was designated an official memorial, the decision to eliminate the Jews of Germany was made.

On 8 May 1945, the day of German capitulation, 7,000 Jews were living in Berlin: 1,300 had hidden through the war, 1,500 had returned after they were released from concentration camps, and 4,200 had survived the war in Berlin as "privileged" Jews. Many of them trickled out of the city before a new Jewish community was founded in 1945–46. They were replaced by the 200,000 or so who fled to Berlin from Eastern Europe: "displaced persons" who were ironically flooding to Germany for asylum.

The experience of Nazi rule prevented many Jews from returning to Germany. Those who stayed felt they had a duty to rebuild a community where the Nazis meant to destroy every strain of Jewish life.

In Berlin today there are just two independent Jewish groups. In London, by comparison, there are 31. The next generation of Jews, who have not experienced *shoa*, the pain of the holocaust, is searching for its own identity and could well revive the rich traditions of Judaism. As well as the synagogue in Fasanenstrasse, the Neue Synagoge in the

Oranienburger Strasse has now been restored to its original splendour. Work on the building was completed in 1995 and now houses the Centraun Judaicum, a small museum, that tells the history of the building and the Jewish people of the city. On 9 November 1992, the 54th anniversary of *Kristallnacht,* when the Nazis systematically attacked Jews and their property, the foundation stone was laid in Kreuzberg's Lindenstrasse for a Jewish Museum.

Not only in the Scheunenviertel, but in all parts of the city, the Jewish community is re-establishing its culture. In Auguststrasse, which for many years has endured an impoverished existence, there is a kosher grocery store, Jewish library and a school. In Tucholsky Strasse, the Jewish Beth-Café sells kosher food alongside Israeli and German newspapers. The Oren, in Oranienburger Strasse is a popular Jewish restaurant for all Berliners. But in a very visible reminder that Germany hasn't managed to get rid of anti-Semitism, a security guard or police officer still keeps watch outside every Jewish institution.

On a political front, Germany has made a concerted effort to nurture relations with Israel since 1952 and it is now important political ally. The relationship annoys many American Jews, who often make a clean equation between Germany and the Holocaust. Internally, new rifts have entered Berlin's Jewish community that have more to do with reunification than with recovering from the Holocaust.

Tens of thousands of Jews have come to Berlin from the former Soviet Union. They were partly attracted by a German government policy that allowed Jews to enter the country with the same status as war refugees, and partly by Germany's economic stability. Russian Jews have found a society in Berlin that accepts their Jewishness much more than their former communist homeland, where they were unable to practise their religion. But that doesn't mean reintegration has been easy. Many educated, middle-aged Russians have had to come to terms with the realisation that lingual and cultural barriers will probably prevent them from ever practising their profes-

sions in Germany. German families who have been part of the Jewish community for the three generations since the war feel that the influx of Russian immigrants means their own needs don't get met as they should.

Contract disputes between the city's one liberal Rabbi, Walter Rothschild, and the community's official leaders have revealed deep-seated conflicts between liberal and orthodox branches, which also irritates the tensions that are already there between Russian and German Jews. These spats are necessarily tempered by the nature of the historical beast Berlin Jews are trying to tame.

At the same time, the way issues in the community are evolving resembles the internal difficulties that almost any public organisation deals with. Community leaders often express frustration that the press fixates on the Jewish community's internal conflict simply because the Holocaust's legacy makes a good story. Perhaps this is a sign that, one day, Berlin's Jewish community will once again be just one of many vital threads in Berlin's cultural mixture. ❑

LEFT: the Grosse Hamburger Strasse Memorial.
RIGHT: the Neue Synagoge.

MUSEUM ISLAND

Map on page 128

Museum Island is very much work-in-progress and it will be years before all the renovations and improvements – including a promenade linking the museums – come to fruition

Designated a World Heritage Site by UNESCO in 2000, **Museumsinsel** (Museum Island) in the heart of Mitte, a self-contained complex featuring five world-class museums and a number of other notable attractions, is the jewel in the crown of Berlin's historical sites. Having weathered a turbulent century, from the destruction wreaked by the Third Reich and World War II to the divisions of the cold war era, the various collections housed on the island have in recent years been experiencing their own reunification process. An ambitious programme of renovation, rebuilding and expansion, first approved in 1976, is due for completion in 2010.

Visitors can approach the Museumsinsel from a number of directions: over the two bridges that link the island to the eastern bank of the Spree (Hackescher Markt), by tram to the Kupfergraben side, or even by boat to one of the many jetties around the island. Approaching the island from the Unter den Linden side is perhaps most impressive; crossing the Kupfergraben via **Schlossbrücke ❶** (Palace Bridge) you're walking on one of architect and artist Karl Friedrich Schinkel's treasures, built from 1821 to 1824. The eight clusters of statues lining the bridge depict stages in the training of a Greek warrior, which must have been cold for the poor chap judging by his lack of attire.

LEFT: the interior of Berliner Dom (Berlin Cathedral).
BELOW: the monumental colonnade of the Altes Museum (Old Museum).

Around the museums

Looking to the right as you cross the Schlossbrücke, the view is dominated by the 180-metre (590-ft) long tinted glass façade of the **Palast der Republik ❷** (Palace of the Republic), seat of the GDR parliament until 1990. Built in a hurry and opened in 1976, the 'Palace' occupies what was once the site of the Berliner Schloss, a genuine royal palace that had stood for 500 years. Damaged in World War II, but still structurally sound, it was demolished in 1950 by the GDR government, deaf to pleas from stunned Berliners.

The brutal building that serves as its replacement is not high in the popularity stakes, and has lain empty since 1990. Fierce debate rages over the future of the shabby edifice – one idea is to rebuild the original palace in a modern style. An open-air exhibition at the Schlossplatz, the open ground before the Palast, gives details of this proposal, including a detailed pictorial history of the structure alongside architectural drawings and projected costs of rebuilding. Also on view is an archeological excavation of part of the cellars of the original palace.

Berliner Dom ❸ (Berlin Cathedral; open Mon–Sat 9am–8pm, Sun 12am–8pm; entrance fee), an imposing structure towering over the Lustgarten on the west side, was constructed as the court church of the Hollenzollern dynasty in 1905. Also damaged during

World War II, it is perhaps surprising that such twin symbol of the monarchy and the church escaped the swings of the GDR wrecking ball. Perhaps they were afraid of it – the exterior seems designed to inspire nervous awe rather than aesthetic delight in most observers.

A highlight is the huge copper dome crowning the roof; from inside the eye is drawn upward to the ornate detail of the ceiling decoration. The cathedral, used by members of the city's Lutheran community, is open to visitors if you want to go up to the dome's viewing gallery. On a sunny day, sit on the steps for free and enjoy the pleasant sight of Berliners and tourists alike frolicking in the Lustgarten. Access to the museum in the crypt, which features the ornate sarcophagi of members of the cathedral's founding family, is also available.

With the value-for-money three-day Museum Pass (above) you can visit the collections of Berlin's state museums without paying additional entrance fees.

RIGHT: the view of the Lustgarten and the Altes Museum from the Berliner Dom (Berlin Cathedral).

Lustgarten

Turning left from the Schlossbrücke leads you through the **Lustgarten ❹**, former kitchen garden of the king's palace, which dates from the 16th century. Remodelled as a military parade ground by Friedrich Wilhelm I (the "Soldier King"), remodelled again as a pleasure garden by Schinkel, it was paved over by the Nazis in the 1930s for a parade ground. Finally restored in 1997 as a recreational space complementing the Altes Museum and Berliner Dom, both look parentally over its lawns.

Standing in the Lustgarten just before the steps of the Altes Museum is a giant (7 metres/23 ft in diameter, 75 tons in weight) granite bowl, presented to the Altes Museum by master stonemason and businessman Christian Cantian. Originally intended to be displayed in the rotunda of the museum, the sheer size of the bowl made this impossible.

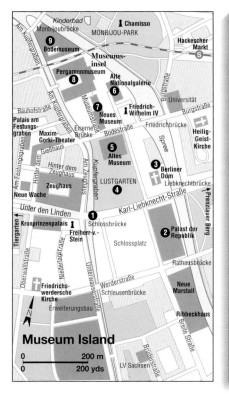

Old and new

Skirting around the great bowl and clambering up the steep steps we come to the entrance of the **Altes Museum** ❺ (open Tues–Thur and Sun 10am–6pm, Fri and Sat 10am–6pm; entrance fee). Berlin's first museum and Kaiser Friedrich Wilhelm III's answer to public demands to make available the treasures of the royal court, the museum was built to a design by Schinkel in 1830. Exhibited on the main floor is part of the collection of classical antiquities, mainly Greek works of art. This floor will also house an exhibition of Etruscan art upon completion of major restoration work, due to begin in 2005. On the upper floors can be seen special exhibitions and some of the artistic highlights from the Alte Nationalgalerie, which is also in the throes of restoration.

Directly behind the Altes Museum is the **Alte Nationalgalerie** ❻ (Old National Gallery; open Tues–Sun 9am–5pm; entrance fee), designed as a roman temple of the Corinthian order and featuring an impressive double staircase leading to the entrance. It was built as a showcase for the art of the fledgling German Empire in 1876. The sandstone exterior and interior has been splendidly restored. The museum houses German art treasures from the 19th century, as well as works by Monet, Manet, Renoir and Cézanne.

Of the five on the island, the **Neues Museum** ❼ (New Museum) beside the Alte Nationalgalerie is the one most obviously in need of restoration. Built in 1859 and badly damaged in World War II, with many treasures destroyed by fire, the Neues Museum is scheduled to reopen in 2005, when it will house the Pre- and Early History collections, the Egyptian collection and the Papyrus collection. The latter collections include some of the oldest treasures from the royal cupboards, including 1,500 objects donated by Mohammed Ali (no, not the

Map on page 128

Sculpture of Hebe *by Canova in the Alte Nationalgalerie.*

BELOW: sculpture of the Greek figures of Castor and Pollux on the top of the Altes Museum.

Map
on page
128

*For more information
on Museum Island
call the SMPK
(Staatliche Museen
zu Berlin Preussischer
Kulturbesitz)
information line on
(030) 20 90 55 66, or
check out their web
site at www.smb.spk-
berlin.de, available
in German and
English.*

BELOW: the main
entrance to the
Pergamonmuseum.
RIGHT: enjoying the
Lustgarten (Berliner
Dom behind).

boxer) to a Prussian delegation visiting Egypt between 1842 and 1845, and finds from excavations in Amama (1911–14). Exhibits in the Papyrus collection range from examples of classic Egyptian literature and illustrated books of the dead to manuscripts from Christian and Arabic times.

The Pergamonmuseum and Bodemuseum

We come at last to the mighty **Pergamonmuseum ❽** (open Tues–Sun 10am–6pm, Thur 10am–10pm; entrance fee), its twin wings embracing an open entrance courtyard reached via a bridge over the Kupfergraben. Last of the five museums to be constructed, the Pergamon is perhaps the most impressive. It has three major collections: the Collection of Classical Antiquities, the Museum of Near Eastern Antiquities, and the Museum of Islamic Art. The museum, built in 1930, is named after its most famous exhibit; the Pergamon Altar, taken in 1878 from the ruins of the ancient Hellenic city of Pergamon, situated on the west coast of present-day Turkey. The great marble altar, decorated with a partially reconstructed frieze depicting a mythic battle between the Olympic gods and a band of rowdy giants, formed only part of a great city complex – reconstructions at the base of the altar give an idea of the scale of the original.

Other highlights include the Market Gate of Miletus, a reconstruction of the entrance to the market square of the Roman town of Miletus in Asia Minor, dating from around AD 120; the world-famous Ishtar Gate and Processional Way from Babylon in the time of Nebuchadnezzer II; and the entrance to the Caliph's palace in Mshatta (an ancient city in Jordan), which forms the centre-piece of the Islamic collection. Aside from these genuinely stunning recon-structions (all the more stunning when you consider the size of the cities they were excavated from), the museum is stuffed with Greek, Roman, Babylonian and Islamic sculpture, art and architecture, and it's advisable to allow at least half a day to see everything properly. Personal CD players, available free on entry, give audio guides to the exhibits in a variety of languages.

Next up along the Kupfergraben on the northern tip of the Spree Insel, and unfortunately also closed for renovation until 2005, is the **Bodemuseum ❾**. Built in 1904 and originally called the Kaiser-Friedrich Museum, it was renamed the Bodemuseum in hon-our of Wilhelm Bode, general director of the Royal Prussian Museum from 1905. It will eventually dis-play the Münzkabinett (coin collection), one of the largest and most comprehensive collections of its kind in the world with around 500,000 objects. Coins in the collection range from some of the first coinage of the 7th century BC in Asia Minor to the coins and medals of the 20th century, including 102,000 Greek coins and about 50,000 from ancient Rome. The col-lection also contains paper money, historical seals, minting equipment and examples of different forms of money used by primitive peoples. Examples are cur-rently on display in the Pergamonmuseum.

The Bodemuseum will also be home to the Museum of Late Antique and Byzantine Art, with works orig-inating from Rome, Constantinople, Asia Minor, the Near East, Greece, Russia and the Balkans. ❏

KURFÜRSTENDAMM

Once the showcase of the Western world and one of the finest boulevards in Germany, Kurfürstendamm today is a great place to window-shop and people-watch

Map on page 134

"**W**ithout the Ku'damm, no Berlin," runs the birthday chorus sung by the Schöneberg Boys' Choir to mark the centenary of their "glorious boulevard" in 1986. The Kurfürstendamm was, is and will remain the focal point of the western part of Berlin. It's difficult to imagine the present city without it. Opinion is divided on the question of the exact birthday of the Ku'damm. The street existed as "Knüppeldamm" as far back as 1542. In the beginning it was a rough bridleway for Joachim II to his Grunewald hunting lodge. For centuries, the renowned boulevard was a track across the fields, through sand and marsh. But in 1871, Chancellor Bismarck set his eyes upon the Champs-Elysées in Paris, a thoroughfare through the Bois de Boulogne which had been drawn up by the ingenious master builder Le Nôtre "with a single chalk line through a wasteland".

The Iron Chancellor became obsessed with plans for a similar mighty avenue for the capital of the newly formed German Empire to enable "the Berlin population to circulate with ease in the open air" and to facilitate "the equestrian training of the upper classes". Construction on the country road proceeded slowly but by May 1886 steam-driven trams began running between Grunewald and the zoo. This event marked the real beginning of the Kurfürstendamm.

But, as with many things on the Ku'damm, the trams did not last long. If you wander through a hundred years of history on the Ku'damm today you have to look very closely to detect traces of its brilliant past. You shouldn't expect to find the golden good old days – the bad times are far too evident. In spite of this, the Kurfürstendamm is as lively as ever, as fun-loving, fast-living and full of contradictions as it was at the beginning of the last century.

Zoologischer Garten

The visitor's first impression of the area will probably be from the Hardenbergplatz, in front of Bahnhof Zoologischer Garten – known by many as Zoo Station. Hard to believe in what was, and still is, the busiest area in West Berlin, the signs pointing to the **Zoologischer Garten ❶** (open daily; entrance fee) are not a joke.

At the suggestion of naturalist Alexander von Humboldt, zoologist Martin Lichtenstein and landscape gardener Peter Lenné, construction of a menagerie began in the grounds of the Royal Pheasant Houses in 1844. The animal houses in the growing zoo, which was helped by donations from the nearby Imperial Colonial Army, were disguised as pagodas, temples and mosques. Completed in 1891, the Elefantentor (Elephant Gate) on the Budapester Strasse provided a magnificent entrance to the exotic animal world.

LEFT: sitting at a Ku'damm café.
BELOW: entrance to the Zoologischer Garten.

Destroyed during the war, it was reconstructed in 1984. An aquarium (open daily 9am–6pm; entrance fee) was added in 1913 under the aegis of the zoo's "father", Alfred Brehm. Today, housing some 4,000 species, it is one of the largest in the world. In November 1943 the work of an entire century was almost completely destroyed by a 15-minute air raid. When the smoke cleared, only 91 of the thousands of animals were still alive.

TIP

Berlin Tourism and Marketing has an office in the Europa-Center. Office hours are Mon–Sat 8am–8pm; tel: 25 00 25.

Around the Breitscheidplatz

With the exception of the protests against the threatened demolition of the ruins of the Gedächtniskirche, Kurfürstendamm escaped political demonstrations until the mid-1960s when student leader Rudi Dutschke (of the Association of Socialist German Students) repeatedly interrupted services to discuss the Vietnam war with church-going Christians. After the war the ruins were left standing where the church had always stood: in the thick of the traffic surging around Breitscheidplatz (named after the Social Democrat politician Rudolf Breitscheid, who was murdered in 1944 in Buchenwald concentration camp). The bare skeleton of the church was a thorn in the sides of the senate's architectural bureaucrats. It didn't fit in with their concept of an "auto-friendly city".

The *Tagesspiegel* newspaper carried out a survey in 1957, in which 90 per cent of the city's population voted to keep the "hollow tooth". Eventually in 1961 the ruins were integrated into the **Kaiser-Wilhelm Gedächtniskirche ❷** (Kaiser Wilhelm Memorial Church; open daily 9am–7.30pm), designed by Professor Egon Eiermann. A plaque was erected in the ruined tower, outlining its significance as a memorial: "The tower of the old church serves as a reminder of the judgement that God passed upon our people during the years of the war."

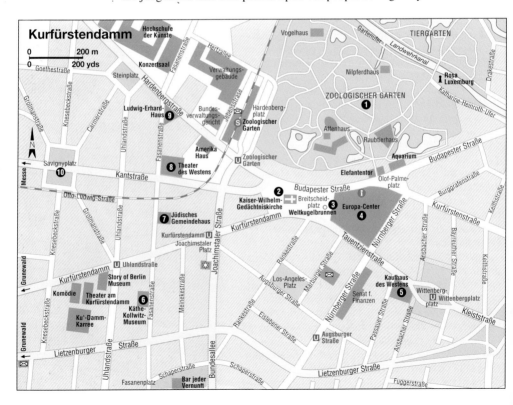

Map on page 134

Excellent gold-inlaid mosaics on the ceiling of the nave celebrating military campaigns from the Crusades on give a good idea of the original church. The rest of this area is usually taken over by kids doing flips and wheelies on their skateboards, roller blades and bikes.

The square is alive until late at night. People sit on benches, steps and the granite seats around the **Weltkugelbrunnen ❸** (Fountain of the Globe). The *"Wasserklops"* (Water Meatball) as it is popularly known, is a massive angular sphere of rust-coloured granite, which was built in 1983. Here they listen to the buskers or have their portraits drawn by one of the street artists. Or they read the fliers distributed by political groups and cults of every imaginable persuasion. Others linger over the market stalls.

A wrestling tent and a few wooden snack stands were all that stood on the present site of the **Europa-Center ❹** in the 1950s. It sprang up from the ground in 1965, prompting unprecedented debate and no shortage of deprecatory remarks. There are some 100 shops, restaurants, bars and cafés here, as well as a multitude of other "entertainment" venues. Berlin's biggest sauna is here, not forgetting the observation platform 106 metres/353 ft up, where there's a row of telescopes and a panoramic view. This was also the site of the neo-romantic apartment house, home of the legendary Romanische Café, until it was destroyed in 1943. Just as bohemian Berlin congregated at the Café des Westens, nicknamed "Café Grössenwahn" (Megalomania) in the years before World War II, so the Romanische flourished during the Weimar period.

When the Nazis expelled the Jewish intelligentsia from Kurfürstendamm, they also destroyed its spirit of liberalism. Ten years later British bombers reduced the zoo district to rubble and ashes in a single November night. The remainder was accomplished in the mania for demolition and modernisation in the 1950s and 1960s, which was on a scale barely imaginable even today. Thus the boulevard that exists today is a hotchpotch of modern glass architecture and historical stucco, lacking any coherent line.

Wittenbergplatz

So exactly where does the Kurfürstendamm begin? The answer is at No. 11 on the north side of the avenue directly behind Breitscheidplatz. There's no point looking for the first 10 houses. In 1925 the first part of Kurfürstendamm, where the Hotel Interconti-nental stands now, was renamed Budapester Strasse. Few people know that the Ku'damm once began on the outskirts of Tiergarten, on the Corneliusbrücke over the Landwehr canal. Others maintain that the street starts at **Wittenbergplatz**, where it goes under the guise of Tauentzienstrasse, but this isn't true. The boundary may be unclear, but there is a difference: on "Tauentzien", an out-and-out commercial street, there are no street cafés.

In their place, on the corner of Wittenbergplatz, is the **Kaufhaus des Westens ❺** (KaDeWe). The famous cathedral to consumerism is the largest department store in Berlin, with 24,000 sq. metres (28,704 sq. yards) of sales floor. The delicatessen floor (Fein-schmecker-Etage) on the sixth floor is worth a visit. In

"We watched the café and its terrace blow away, disappear with its spirit cargo, dissolve into nothing, as though it had never existed..." wrote Wolfgang Koeppen, a poet, describing the end of the Romanische Café in a bombing raid.

BELOW: the *Flow of Time Clock* by Bernard Gitton at the Europa-Center.

the central reservation in Tauentzienstrasse you'll see a strangely bent steel structure. Commissioned for the city's 750th anniversary in 1987, the *Berlin* sculpture – two halves of intertwined steel tubes that never touch – represents the then divided city.

The Ku'damm no longer shares the elegance of the KaDeWe. It's a great shame, claim those who have watched more and more stylish small businesses being driven out by escalating rents. Who cares, say others, who see the Ku'damm as a commercial centre where only the financially fit survive. In the 1970s it came under increasing fire from its critics. People talked of a "pizza, pop and porno promenade", of the "kebab mentality" and "meatball palaces". Kurfürstendamm had become the "nation's rubbish tip", complained others.

Nevertheless, responsible local politicians realised that the acclaimed "showcase of the Western world" was losing élan through ill-conceived urban development. Neon lights and peep shows were taking over.

New facades

To halt the decline, a city commission was set up by the City Business Association, a group of concerned business people, with representatives from the three relevant administrative bodies of Charlottenburg, Wilmersdorf and Schöneberg. Responsible for ensuring that development on Kurfürstendamm was in accordance with "the interests of the boulevard", the commission wanted to discourage amusement arcades, peepshows and snack bars in the "heart of the city" in a spirit of "liberalism, pluralism and multi-functionalism".

Stroll along the Ku'damm and the commission's efforts will be evident all around you. Between Breitscheidplatz and Joachimsthaler Strasse, on some of Berlin's most expensive building land, the last gap has now been filled between Marmorhaus and Café Kranzler. On the Kranzler corner itself a new complex of glass-fronted buildings, containing shops and offices, has shot up.

Opposite on the Ku'damm Eck (Corner), an attempt has been made to recreate the atmosphere of the 1920s intersection with the construction of an enormous building including a department store, a hotel and a gallery. The neighbouring Wertheim department store has replaced its horrible concrete facade with a tasteful, decorative glass frontage. Kiosks and advertising columns have been dolled up to give them an old-fashioned appearance, and stucco facades have been carefully restored in an effort to brighten up the rather tired-looking face of the Ku'damm. The thin line between elitism and modern mass tourism appears to have been reasonably well negotiated. The critics are steadily being silenced.

Things to do

There's a lot to see and do in the area, beginning with the old-established première cinemas, mostly concentrated between the Gedächtniskirche and Uhlandstrasse, and stretching as far as the Schaubühne am Lehniner Platz, the holy of holies of modern German theatre. The Maison de France on the junction with Uhlandstrasse runs lectures, films and language

BELOW: the
Berlin sculpture.

courses promoting the culture of Germany's western neighbour. Those interested in the turbulent history of the city should spend a few hours in the **Story of Berlin Museum** (Kurfürstendamm 207–208; open daily 10am–6pm; entrance fee). Tracing Berlin's history from the start, the exhibition is complemented by commentary in English on wireless headsets.

Kurfürstendamm 213 is the site of Café Möhring, a favourite location to drink coffee on a sunny day. Nearby, in the King's Teagarden (No. 217), there's a choice of 170 kinds of tea, which you can drink to the civilised accompaniment of classical music. The American poet Thomas Wolfe described the Kurfürstendamm as "Europe's biggest coffee house". Everywhere you turn, there's another ambient corner. Café Kranzler (Nos. 18–19), now reduced to one floor, just about preserves the feel of the good old days, while the Kaffeehaus Leysieffer (No. 218) is the haunt of the young trendies or "*Schickimickis*".

Off Ku'damm

Anyone who has been along the Ku'damm will be familiar with Berlin's cosmopolitan face, but not with the city itself, not by a long way. A detour into the side streets off Ku'damm gives a wider picture.

In **Fasanenstrasse**, which in recent years has become the art and gallery mile, you can catch a glimpse of life on the other side of the tracks. The street's crowning glory was the opening in 1986 of **Villa Grisebach** (No. 25). Having avoided demolition to make way for a proposed multistorey car park, the house is now used for exhibitions and auctions. The **Käthe Kollwitz Museum ⑥** (open Wed–Mon 11am–6pm; entrance fee) moved in immediately next door. On display there is a comprehensive collection of drawings, sculptures and graphics

Map on page 134

The Villa Grisebach organises two fine art auctions a year; during the rest of the time it houses the highly regarded Galerie Pels-Leusden.

BELOW: the showcase of the Western world in the 1950s.

Map on page 134

Käthe Kollwitz (1867–1945), one of Germany's best-known artists, is famous for her portrayal of the working classes.

BELOW: Theater des Westens.

by the artist. Kollwitz lived in the working-class district of Prenzlauer Berg and her work reflects the tragic living conditions of the poor of her neighbourhood and has a strong social and political content.

In the Wintergarten at the **Literaturhaus Berlin** (No. 23), Berlin's literary scene has found a focal point which includes a basement bookshop and a beautifully restored café-restaurant with a garden.

Along to Kantstrasse

On the northern side of Fasanenstrasse, diagonally opposite Hotel Kempinski, is the **Jüdisches Gemeindehaus** ❼ (Jewish Community Centre). A synagogue that once stood on this street was burnt by the SA gangs during *Kristallnacht* on 9 November 1938. Only a portal remains, but it sits comfortably with the simple new building, dating from 1959. The large hall on the top floor is used as a prayer room on Jewish holidays. The building also houses the Jewish College, which conducts courses in Hebrew, a library and a kosher restaurant.

The theatre on the corner of Kantstrasse, with Latin inscriptions along the gables, has had a chequered past. As a private venue for comedy and operetta, it went bankrupt several times. From 1950 to 1961, as the **Theater des Westens** ❽ (tel: 319 030; tickets: 0180-599 8999), it was the home of the Berlin City Opera, under Michael Bohnen, Heinz Tietjen and Carl Ebert. In 1987 the première of *Cabaret* starring Horst Buchholz Ende heralded a new era for the theatre as a stage for musicals. The lavishly renovated building dates from 1896, during Kaiser Wilhelm's time. At the top end of Fasanen Str. is the **Ludwig-Erhard Haus** ❾. This high-tech structure designed by British architect Nicholas Grimshaw houses the Chamber of Commerce (IHK) and the **Börse** (Berlin Stock Exchange).

Among the city's landmarks are the old-fashioned clock and the glass concourse of Bahnhof Zoologischer Garten (Zoo Station), for decades a blot on the whole district. In conjunction with the East German State Railways, the station underwent a 40-million mark overhaul for the jubilee celebrations in 1987. Since then, however, it has once again become a meeting place for shady characters, and visitors are advised to pay particular attention to their wallets.

Savignyplatz

To the west, Kantstrasse opens into **Savignyplatz** ❿. The numerous booksellers and trendy bars are reminiscent of St Germain. And, as in its Parisian counterpart, apartments in this corner of the city are much sought after. In contrast to Kurfürstendamm, the side streets here are fairly quiet. But a stroll through Bleibtreu, Knesebeck, Mommsen and Giesebrecht streets reveals plenty that's lacking in the main boulevard: delightful little boutiques, side by side with various junk and secondhand shops.

The neighbourhood makes a pleasant contrast to the honky-tonk atmosphere to be found around Lietzenburger Strasse, where between Uhlandstrasse and Knesebeckstrasse, clip joints, strip shows and brothels abound. Here in Sperlingsgasse you'll find an assortment of watering holes which claim to be "old Berlin", but Berliners are rarely found here. ❑

Rebuilding Berlin

On 20 June 1991 the Bundestag voted to move the seat of government of a united Germany to Berlin. The parliament officially moved from Bonn in September 1999, but the complete transfer will take more time owing to remaining construction work. In spite of this, what looked like just one big populated building site is slowly taking shape into something that resembles a city.

Although Berlin's infrastructure is good, the constant state of transition has meant that road links around the main construction areas have suffered. The congestion around Unter den Linden and Pariser Platz has eased but there are still tailbacks at Potsdamer Platz. In the initial stages of the project many of the problems experienced by the city planners were due to a lack of space created by the Wall which for many years prevented outward expansion. Where possible, government ministries have been housed in existing buildings. The Foreign Ministry, for example, has its offices in the centre at Werderscher Markt, in the former Nazi Reichsbank subsequently occupied by the Central Committee of the SED. The Finance Ministry has settled into what was Göring's Air Ministry building on Niederskircher Strasse.

The process of turning Potsdamer Platz, the old border between East and West, into the new commercial centre is almost complete. Before World War II, Potsdamer Platz was the busiest road junction in Europe. During the Cold War it was an empty strip of land beside the Wall and after the fall of the Wall it was left as wasteland. In 1995 it became the biggest inner-city building site in Europe.

The major part of the revitalised Potsdamer Platz was opened in 1998. The project is now in its final stages and the red Info Box on Leipziger Platz, which informed the public of progress, has been dismantled to make way for the further development of the complex. All eyes have now turned to the massive Lehrter Bahnhof (station) project just north of the nearly completed government quarter. Intended to be one of Europe's main high-speed rail crossroads, the transport intersection will also be incorporated into Berlin's underground and city railway system. Tunnelling for the extension of the U5 underground line to serve the government quarter is underway, but its completion is threatened by lack of finance. This will be accompanied by a road tunnel which will also connect with Potsdamer Platz.

Although Berlin has already attracted big money from the likes of Benz, Axel-Springer and Siemens, welcomed the arrival of the many media offices, and built seven large shopping complexes around the city, there is still an urgent need to attract more investment to the city. In contrast, there is a fear that if construction continues along the same lines, small businesses will be exposed to astronomical rents. With no small businesses, Berlin would stand to lose its unique character. As it stands, however, many of the new office complexes, like those in Stadtmitte, are standing empty without tenants. Berlin is still waiting to find out if anyone actually wants to live and work in the purpose-built city that has been created. ❑

RIGHT: the construction work continues.

TIERGARTEN

Map on page 142

Tiergarten is one of Berlin's most attractive areas. Situated at the centre of the city's new political and financial districts, it also contains the cultural centre of the Kulturforum

As long ago as 1764, the Scottish writer James Boswell enthused about the "magnificent park on the edge of the town, with carriageways and bridlepaths". And, he noted, there was also provision for those "desiring to exercise themselves". Even today, the mention of **Tiergarten ❶** immediately conjures up images of sauntering through Berlin's "green lung". Grosser Tiergarten, 3 km (2 miles) long and 2 km (1 mile) wide, stretches on both sides of the Strasse des 17. Juni, between Tiergarten S-Bahn station and the Brandenburg Gate. On sunny weekends, the playgrounds and lawns teem with umpteen holiday-makers, and Turkish families preparing their lunch or with their barbecues – much to the dismay of the city gardeners.

The 212 hectares (525 acres) of the park are the heart of the administrative district of the same name. Within its cramped 13 sq. km (5 sq. miles) both the glory and the decline of the former imperial capital are reflected in starkly contrasting scenes. The Grosser Tiergarten is a quiet haven in the centre of the district, with its mute stone witnesses to the nation's former greatness – the Reichstag, the Brandenburger Tor and the Siegessäule. To the south lies the once gentrified Tiergartenviertel, to the north the industrial, working-class neighbourhood of Moabit, an island surrounded by canals, where the majority of the 93,000 inhabitants live in late 19th-century tenements. Most of the district became part of Berlin in 1861.

LEFT: visitors at Potsdamer Platz looking up at the architecture.
BELOW: sculpture at Potsdamer Platz.

Potsdamer Platz

Hard to miss on the southeastern edge of the park is Berlin's largest commercial building project since the fall of the Wall – **Potsdamer Platz ❷**. At one point one of Europe's busiest intersections, the area was flattened in Allied bombing raids during the war and left to decay as wasteland in the following years owing to its close proximity to the Wall.

The potential of the site proved too good to pass up and, before anyone knew it, plans for the new US$4.8 million project were put into action. Logical from a sentimental point of view, the project proved to be a real test logistically with scuba divers and the excavation of millions of tons of earth being only part of the equation. The result: a heavily backed and highly stacked commercial venture which sees office towers from the likes of corporate giants Daimler-Benz and Sony stand alongside hotels, shopping centres and cinemas in what appears to be an attempt to produce a ready made city centre. Although top of most tourists' lists, the area hasn't been too enthusiastically received by the locals who don't really know what to make of it all despite being constantly reminded by the tourist board.

As a mark of Potsdamer Platz's importance to the

city, the hub of the annual Berlinale Film Festival was moved from the Zoo Palast near the Ku'damm to the Berlinale Palast on Marlene Dietrich Platz. One of the few remaining reminders of Wilhelmine on Potsdamer Platz is the old **Kaisersaal Café** from the Esplanade Hotel which was moved 75 metres (246 feet) from its original spot so as not get under the feet of one of the new arrivals. It was around this area, in the buildings of an old school alongside the hotel on Bellevue Strasse, that the Nazi People's Court used to sit.

In 1991 the architects Hilmer & Sattle won a competition to develop Potsdamer Platz site into "a metropolitan centre with round-the-clock vitality".

The Kulturforum

By heading off westwards along the reinvented Potsdamer Strasse one leaves Potsdamer Platz, and its conceptualisation of the future, and arrives at the **Kulturforum**, which is starting to show its age. To the right, as you enter the complex, is the **Philharmonie ❸** (Herbert-von-Karajan Str; tel: 2548 8232). Home of the world-famous Berlin Philharmonic Orchestra *(see page 147)*, its hall (which was completed in 1963 to the designs of Hans Scharoun) and its adjoining little brother, the Kammermusiksaal (Chamber Music Hall), which arrived in 1987, are said to provide near-perfect acoustics.

Next door at the **Musikinstrumenten-museum ❹** (Musical Instrument Museum, Tiergarten Str. 1; open 9am–5pm Tues–Sun; guided tour 11am Sun; entrance fee except Sunday) an unbelievable range of wind and percussion instruments are to be found which trace their evolution from the 16th to the 20th centuries. A star exhibit is a working Wurlitzer organ from the era of silent films.

Across Potsdamer Strasse stands another of Scharoun's babies – the **Neue Staatsbibliothek ❺** (New State Library; open daily 9am–9pm, Sat 9am–3pm). First opened in 1978, the contemporary structure is unfortunately dwarfed by Pots-

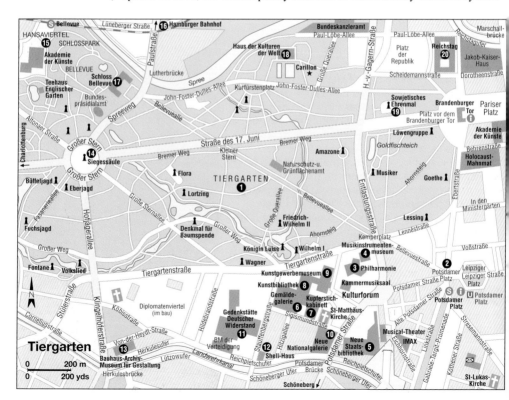

damer Platz, which is built directly behind. Across the open space of Matthäikirch-platz, the main body of the Kulturforum blends into its low-profile surroundings.

The **Gemäldegalerie** ❻ (Picture Gallery, Matthäikirchplatz 8; open Tues, Wed, Fri 10am–6pm, Thur 10am–10pm, weekend 11am–6pm; entrance fee) contains some of the most important works of western art and includes brush strokes from everyone who was anyone from the 13th to the 18th centuries. Known especially for its collection of more than 20 Rembrandts, the gallery also exhibits works by Giotto, Botticelli, Raphael, Breughel and Rubens, among many others. Important paintings in this collection include *Dutch Proverbs* by Pieter Breugel in Room 7, Rembrandt's *Portrait of Henrickje Stoffel* contained in Room X, *The Glass of Wine* by Jan Vermeer in Room 18 and Caravaggio's *Cupid Victorious* in Room XIV.

As part of the same complex, the **Kupferstichkabinett** ❼ (Museum of Prints and Drawings, open Tues–Fri 10am–6pm, weekend 11am–6pm; entrance fee) houses what is recognised as one of the world's greatest collections of graphic art. There are examples of work by every painter of significance, from Dürer to Brueghel and from Botticelli to Picasso. There is also an illustrated Bible. The holdings are displayed in rotating exhibitions.

The collection at the neighbouring **Kunstbibliothek** ❽ (Art Library, open Tues–Sun 9am–6pm; entrance fee) is dedicated to prints and exhibits that are more related to European applied art. It has approximately 350,000 volumes and is regarded as one of Germany's top institutions in that field. The last part of the complex to be completed was the red tiled **Kunstgewerbemuseum** ❾ (Museum of Applied Art; open Tues–Fri 10am–6pm, weekend 11am–6pm; entrance fee). Although the building was finished only in 1985, the museum is one of the oldest of its kind in Germany. Greatly depleted during World War II, it still stands as one of the best collections of European applied arts and crafts from the Middle Ages to the present day in the world.

The Neue Nationalgalerie

As one walks through Sigismundstrasse, the eye will be immediately drawn to a "temple of light and glass" on the left. The **Neue Nationalgalerie** ❿ (Potsdamer Strasse 50; open Tues, Wed, Fri 10am–6pm, Thur 10am–10pm, weekend 11am–6pm; entrance fee) contains late 19th-century and 20th-century paintings and sculptures from Germany, Europe and America up to the present day. The basis of the collection was a legacy of 262 contemporary works of art which the Swedish consul and banker Joachim Friedrich Wagener bequeathed to King Wilhelm I of Prussia.

The original home of the collection lay on Museumsinsel (Museum Island), but after being put into storage during the war a number of the paintings ended up in West Berlin. They were exhibited at various locations throughout the city until the present gallery was completed in 1968 in accordance with a design by the Bauhaus architect Ludwig Mies van der Rohe. Among the names to note are Kandinsky, Picasso and Klee, Bauhaus teachers Feininger and Schlemmer, German expressionists like Grosz and Dix, and American modernists Newman and Rothko.

The Kunstbibliothek has a huge poster collection. The library's full name is the National Library of the Foundation of Prussian Cultural Heritage.

BELOW: Holbein's *Portrait of the Merchant Georg Gisze* in the Gemäldegalerie.

At Stauffenbergstrasse 14, directly in the line of sight at the end of Sigismundstrasse, is the **Gedenkstätte Deutscher Widerstand ⓫** (Memorial to German Resistance; open Mon, Wed, Fri 9am–6pm, weekend 10am–6pm), a permanent exhibition in the former Wehrmacht headquarters. It was here in the courtyard of the former Bendler block that Colonel Claus von Stauffenberg and four of his co-conspirators were executed by firing squad on 20 July 1944, after the abortive attempt on Hitler's life. They are commemorated in a sculpture by Richard Scheibe – *Der gefesselte Jüngling* (Youth in Chains).

The Diplomatenviertel and beyond

The Bauhaus school in Berlin was shut down by the Nazis, who claimed the designs were un-German in 1933. Many of the leading lights in the movement remained in exile after the war.

BELOW:
the Reichstag.

In the years before and shortly after World War I, representatives of numerous foreign countries settled in Tiergartenviertel, with the result that the area north of the Landwehrkanal, to the north and west of the Kulturforum, became known as the Diplomatenviertel (Diplomatic Quarter). In recognition of the Axis federation with Hitler's Germany, Japan and Italy built prestigious mansions on Tiergartenstrasse. Left as wasteground for a long time, the area is slowly coming to life again. The Japanese embassy, destroyed in the bombing, has been faithfully restored and how houses the Japanese–German Centre.

The curvaceous structure at the corner of Reichspietschufer and Stauffenbergstrasse was never one of Hitler's favourites. Built between 1930 and 1932 to the design of Emil Fahrenkamp, the **Shell-Haus ⓬**, which is now used by the BEWAG electricity company, was one of the first steel-frame high-rise buildings of the time.

Further along the Landwehrkanal, the **Bauhaus Archiv-Museum für Gestaltung ⓭** (Klingelhöferstrasse 14; open Mon–Wed 11am–5pm; entrance

THE REICHSTAG

After its recent renovation the Reichstag is now one of Berlin's most popular tourist attractions. Built between 1884 and 1894 by Paul Wallot, its Italian high Renaissance style and ornate facades exemplified the Wilhelminian taste for pomp and prestige. The glass dome and the plenary session hall were destroyed in 1933 by fire, and after 1945 only a bombed-out shell remained with black holes for the windows. Considered one of the main prizes of the victorious Soviet troops, the building was eventually rebuilt by 1970.

In December 1990, the newly elected German government held its first meeting in the Reichstag after reunification. In 1995 the whole building was wrapped up by the artist Christo before another final renovation project took place from 1995 to 1999. The ensuing design competition for the renovation was won by the British architect, Sir Norman Foster. His new glass dome provides an opportunity not only to see the surrounding city but also into the parliament below. Mirrors and light abound in the rooftop – a symbolic gesture to the people that will take German politics into a new future where there is no secrecy.

The dome of the Reichstag is open 8am–midnight daily; the Assembly Hall Mon–Fri 9am–4pm, weekend 10am–4pm. Guided tours are held at noon daily.

fee), the world-famous school of architecture, crafts and fine arts, provided a forum for a number of progressive teachers and students who attempted to achieve a unity of art, technology and science during the 1920s. The museum exhibits teaching material and works by artists who graduated from the Bauhaus or taught there, among the best known being Gropius, Mies van der Rohe, Kandinsky, Klee, Breuer and Itten. The southwestern corner of Tiergarten park, too, has its places of interest. As well as enjoying a coffee at the huge, lakeside Café am Neuen See, a hunt for the two monuments, which commemorate the murders of the communist rebels Rosa Luxemburg and Karl Liebknecht by members of the Reichswehr in 1919, would easily pass half an hour.

The Berlin Pavilion at the Tiergarten S-Bahn station is a short walk away and features exhibitions on architectural history.

The Siegessäule

At the centre of Grosser Tiergarten stands the mighty 67-metre (223-ft) **Siegessäule** ⑭ (Victory Column). Friedrich Drake's golden "Viktoria" – also known as "Gold Elsie" – was erected in 1873 to commemorate Prussia's victory in the wars against Denmark (1864), Austria (1866) and France (1870–71). The last of the four patriotic bronze reliefs around the base of the column that were removed by the occupation forces in 1945 was brought back to Berlin from Paris by the French president, François Mitterrand, as a gift on the occasion of the city's 750th jubilee.

Opposite the Siegessäule is the monument of war hero Field Marshal Helmuth von Moltke.

The reliefs show events from the successful military campaigns. The Siegessäule originally stood in Königsplatz (now Platz der Republik) but was moved to Grosser Stern and increased in height in 1938 as part of the development of the east–west axis into a parade ground and boulevard for Hitler's new "Germania". The bronze Bismarck Memorial by court sculptor R. Begas (1901) and the monuments to Generals Roon and Moltke (1904) were moved at the same time to the northern side of the square. A footpath leads past statues of Lessing, Goethe, Wagner, Lortzing, Fontane and many others who were honoured during a veritable mania for monuments at the turn of the century.

BELOW: the Viktoria statue.

To the northeast lies a housing project that, for some, is best forgotten. The **Hansaviertel** ⑮, a modern family housing district, was conceived for the 1957 International Housing Exposition which brought together 54 international architects from 13 countries to design a living space for the rehabilitated Germany. Combining all the necessary elements of a modern residential area – a church, a school and so on – it will be remembered as an all too realistic representation of the contemporary architecture of the time.

Over the river lies Moabit. Although there is much of significance here, including the market halls on Beusselstrasse, the Westhafen (West Harbour) and the Kriminalgericht **Moabit** (criminal courts), it was pushed into the shadows when the Wall went up. Many Berliners associate Moabit with its prison, widely referred to as "the clink". The name encompasses the criminal courts and the detention centre on Turmstrasse, which is notorious in certain circles.

Map on page 142

BELOW: the Sowjetisches Ehrenmal (Soviet War Memorial).

Hamburger Bahnhof to the Sowjetisches Ehrenmal

Up next to the Mitte border, the Museum for Contemporary Art in **Hamburger Bahnhof ⑯** (50–51 Invalidenstr.; open Tues, Wed, Fri 10am–6pm, Thur 10am–10pm, weekend 11am–6pm; entrance fee), opened in November 1996, is dedicated to modern art. As well as including works from the Berlin State museums, it also exhibits pieces from the collection of private contemporary art collector Erich Marx and acts as a venue of numerous special exhibitions and events. If the art inside doesn't impress, the building, which was completed in 1947 and is the only surviving old terminal station in Berlin, will.

Schloss Bellevue ⑰, to the north of the Grosser Stern, was once a minor palace belonging to the Kaiser. These days it is the permanent home of the Bundespräsident (German Federal President, not the Chancellor) after the government's move from Bonn. The eco-friendly elliptical building to the side with solar panels on the roof is his offices and was built as the winner of a Europe wide competition. The Kongresshalle (Congress Hall, 1957) is known locally as the Pregnant Oyster. Its concrete cantilever roof was donated by the United States. After an accident in 1980 when the roof fell in, the buildings officially opened for the second time in 1987 with an exhibition entitled "The Sciences in Berlin". Today it is known as the **Haus der Kulturen der Welt ⑱** (House of World Cultures; John-Foster-Dulles Allee 10, open Tues–Sun 10am–9pm; tel: 397 8175) and puts on a broad range of world culture exhibitions and events ranging from musical gatherings to cinema screenings.

Just off Strasse des 17 Juni, and flanked by two of the first enemy tanks to roll into Berlin in 1945, the **Sowjetisches Ehrenmal ⑲** (Soviet War Memorial) was constructed using some of the red marble taken from Hitler's New Chancellery. Guarded, until reunification, by two Red Army soldiers, the monument is now approachable by visitors.

The Government district

Along the northern edge of the park at the Spreebogen complex ("Bogen" meaning "bend" in the river), the newly built **Band des Bundes** is the new government and parliament district. The outcome of a huge design competition, the complex, which spans the Spree twice and has buildings on both sides of the previous Wall boundary, symbolises the togetherness of the re-unified city. Attacting most media attention is the new **Bundeskanzleramt** (Chancellor's office) which cost DM 465 million to build. The ambitious Lehrter Bahnhof project, to be completed in 2004, will serve the government quarter and will give the city its first main central railway station while acting as a major European rail crossroads. Among the construction work is the extension of the U5 line which, it is planned, will connect the area with old city.

Now that the renovated **Reichstag ⑳** *(see panel, page 144)*, which along with the Swiss Embassy is all that remains of the former Alsenviertel empire centrepiece, has become the seat of the new German Bundestag (Federal Parliament), the area before its steps has been restored, as has the **Platz der Republik** which became the focal point of Germany's reunification celebrations on 3 October 1990. ❏

The Philharmonie

At the opening ceremony in 1963, the Philharmonie was praised as one of the great concert halls of the world, an architectural wonder with remarkably excellent acoustics. Echoing the avant-garde lines of the exterior is the interior, designed by Hans Scharoun, who moved the orchestra and its conductor to the centre of the auditorium and distributed the audience on nine levels around the pentagonal podium. Rising up like vineyard terraces, they enclose the platform on all sides so that the sound can soar unhindered to the furthest seats. The Kammermusiksaal (Chamber Music Hall) which was tacked on to the original building in 1987 follows the same acoustic principles.

The Philharmonie is home to the Berlin Philharmonic Orchestra, which is in some respects the official national orchestra. Its tent-shaped silhouette has given it the popular name of "Karajan's Circus" after the celebrated conductor Herbert von Karajan, who was appointed the musical director of the Philharmonie in 1964.

During his directorship, conflict between von Karajan and the equally self-confident orchestra was exacerbated by the maestro's frequent absences and autocratic behaviour, leading eventually to their final split a few months before von Karajan's death in 1989 at the age of 82. Von Karajan had been elected the orchestra's musical director for life, thereby inheriting the legacy of three former conductors from the days when the orchestra's headquarters were in the Bernburger Strasse near the Anhalter Bahnhof.

Here Hans von Bülow, Arthur Nikisch and Wilhelm Furtwängler wielded the baton until the concert hall was destroyed during an air raid on 30 January 1944. Only a week after the Berlin Philharmonic had made its début in the former roller-skating rink on 17 October 1882, the first series of subscription concerts had begun, an innovation at the time.

The formation of an independent symphony during the authoritarian Wilhelminian era must have seemed quite revolutionary. By 1882, the 54 musicians had all parted company from their employer and conductor, Benjamin Bilse, and decided to form their own orchestra, based on democratic principles. Enhanced by a modern payment structure, their democratic constitution continues to underline the *esprit de corps* of what *Le Figaro* called "the most famous orchestra in the world".

In 1982 the centenary of the orchestra was celebrated as the "anniversary of a musical republic". The conductor since 1990, Claudio Abbado, who has succeeded in integrating 20th-century music into the programme of classical and romantic works, is the first non-German in the job. He will be succeeded at the start of the 2002–03 season by the British conductor Sir Simon Rattle, who is set to alter the image of the orchestra once more. As principal conductor and musical director, he plans to reinvent the ensemble by introducing a new repertoire. Although the building in which they play may look slightly outdated compared to the modern backdrop of Potsdamer Platz, the orchestra certainly appears willing to go with the times. ❑

RIGHT: the Philharmonie; opened in 1963.

CHARLOTTENBURG

Map on page 152–53

Charlottenburg is one of Berlin's most interesting districts. In addition to the treasures contained in its palace and museums, it is surrounded by beautiful countryside

Those who have explored Kurfürstendamm and the surrounding area will already be familiar with one part of Charlottenburg. The entire district covers 30 sq. km (12 sq. miles) and occupies the whole northwest of the inner city. The district of Charlottenburg merged with Wilmersdorf for administrative purposes at the beginning of 2001, with a total population of 316,000 inhabitants. Charlottenburg alone has a population of 176,000, making it as large as the towns of Kassel or Mainz, and has many sights of interest, including the Funkturm (radio tower) and, further out, the Olympiastadion (Olympic Stadium). Above all, though, the former royal seat represents a little piece of old Prussia in western Berlin, and is a major tourist attraction.

The Zoologischer Garten area

At **Zoologischer Garten** (Zoo Station) cross the railway bridge and follow Hardenbergstrasse to Steinplatz, the heart of Charlottenburg's student quarter. En route, you pass the Bundesverwaltungsgericht (Supreme Administration Court) on the corner of Jebensstrasse. The area became the student quarter in the early part of the 20th century, when an increasing number of professors, artists and wealthy citizens began to move into Uhlandstrasse, Fasanenstrasse, Carmerstrasse and Knesebeckstrasse as part of the "move West". Today the area buzzes with bars, galleries and cafés, as well as a first-class selection of bookshops.

Three of Charlottenburg's main thoroughfares: Bismarckstrasse, Otto-Suhr-Allee and Strasse des 17. Juni meet at Ernst-Reuter-Platz, one of the city's busiest roundabouts and site of the **Technische Universität ❶**. With around 30,000 students, the Technische Universität is one of Berlin's largest universities. It originated as a mining school founded by Frederick the Great in 1770. Engineering and technical subjects are its strengths, but it offers over 50 courses, including social sciences and humanities. With 6,000 students from abroad, the university has the highest percentage of foreign students in the country. Former students of the university include the Berlin architect Schinkel and Ernst Ruska, who won the Nobel physics prize as the inventor of the first electron microscope.

About 4,500 of the students in Charlottenburg are enrolled at the prestigious **Hochschule der Künste** (HDK). This is Berlin's College of Arts and offers courses in the fine and performing arts, music, multimedia and architecture. The HDK organises numerous cultural events open to the public (check the local press for details). Günter Grass, Germany's famous contemporary writer and winner of the Nobel prize for literature, is among HDK's alumni.

PRECEDING PAGES: Schloss Charlottenburg. **LEFT:** the Porcelain Collection, Schloss Charlottenburg. **BELOW:** synagogue in Pestalozzistrasse.

To the Rathaus

The eastern boundary of the Technische Universität campus which abuts the square is marked by the Charlottenburg Brücke over the Landwehrkanal and the Charlottenburger Tor, featuring the bronze statues of King Friedrich I and his wife Sophie-Charlotte, who gave her name to the district. The wealthiest town in Prussia at the time, Charlottenburg erected the gateway on the border with Berlin in 1905 as a mark of its 200th anniversary and an expression of civic pride.

At the weekends an antique and flea market is held in front of **Ernst-Reuter Haus**, the home of the German Institute of Urban Studies and the Berlin branch of the German Association of Municipal Authorities. The lively stalls stretch along the Strasse des 17. Juni offering a great selection of souvenirs, bargains and locally produced arts and crafts. Connoisseurs of antique rococo porcelain from the time of Frederick the Great shouldn't miss the opportunity of a visit to what used to be the Royal Prussian and is now the **Staatliche Porzellanmanufaktur** (State Porcelain Factory; open daily; tel: 39 00 92 15) at Wegelystrasse 1 in front of Tiergarten S-Bahn station.

Bismarckstrasse leads to the western focus of Charlottenburg, Theodor-Heuss-Platz. Once the home of the British Army, it now hosts the Wühlmäuse cabaret and good local shops, with the Reichsstrasse offering a selection of speciality stores. On Bismarckstrasse, the **Schiller-Theater** ❷ (tel: 61 40 11 11) built in 1951 and **Deutsche Oper** ❸ (German Opera House; tel: 341 0249; ticket line: 343 8401) built in 1961, both offer prestigious cultural programmes.

Otto-Suhr-Allee was named after a mayor of West Berlin. It has a great beer hall, the Luisenbräu, which brews its own ales. The 88-metre (293-ft) clock tower of **Rathaus Charlottenburg** ❹ (Town Hall) is an unmistakable part of

BELOW: floating restaurant in Charlottenburg.

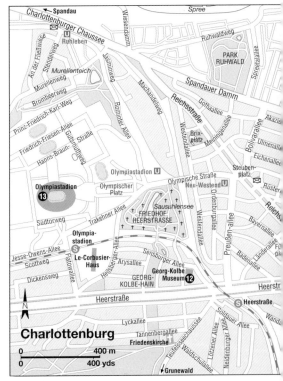

the local skyline. The rather subdued art nouveau construction was inaugurated on 20 May 1905 for the city's 200th jubilee. Alt-Lietzow street, behind the Rathaus, serves as a reminder of the district's origins as the village of Lützow or Lietzow. No. 28, the former **Villa Kogge** (open daily; entrance fee), built in 1864 and used today as a registry office, is worth a visit.

Many of Charlottenburg's famous families are buried in the Luisenfriedhof cemetery on Guerickestrasse, which dates back to 1815. In the traditional petty-bourgeois district or "Kiez" around Gierkeplatz, one of the last smallholders' homes can be found at Schuhstehrusstrasse 13. This is part of the local history museum and provides an insight into how Charlottenburg looked when it received the status of city from King Frederick I in 1705.

Schloss Charlottenburg

Schloss Charlottenburg ❺ (Palace of Charlottenburg; open Tues–Fri 9am–5pm, weekend 10am–5pm; entrance fee) was built by a succession of architects of the baroque and the rococo periods as a royal seat. In 1695 Sophie-Charlotte, countess and later queen of Prussia (1658–1705), had a summer residence built 8 km (5 miles) outside the gates of Berlin, designed by the master-builder Arnold Nering. During the 18th century this was extended into a royal residence, with an Ehrenhof (Memorial Courtyard) and French-style gardens.

Schloss Charlottenburg was the last remaining Hohenzollern residence to be left standing in Berlin after the City Palace on the Spree and the Monbijou Palace both fell victim to the destruction of war. Although it suffered considerable fire and bomb damage in World War II, careful restoration has returned it to its former Prussian glory. Its magnificent 550-metre (1,830-ft) frontage is

Map on page 152–53

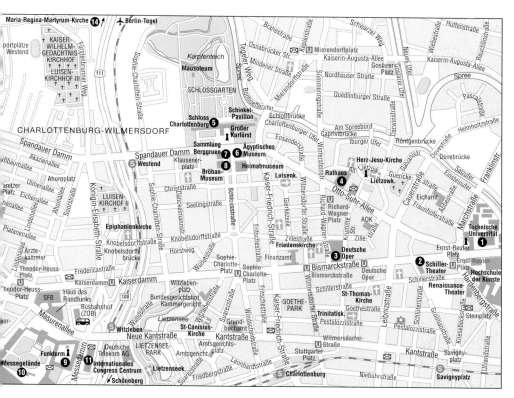

the result of almost a century of building and rebuilding. The **Belvedere**, in the Schlossgarten (palace gardens), houses a collection of Berlin porcelain; the Schinkel Pavilion, an unadorned building with a square ground plan, contains Biedermeier miniatures and vases. On the second floor of the Knobelsdorff Wing are works formerly in the possession of Frederick the Great, by court painters such as Watteau and Pesne.

Court architect Eosander von Göthe added the 143-metre (470-ft) **Orangerie** on the west side, and erected the distinctive dome on the central section, where the temperamental goddess Fortuna spins in the wind, 48 metres (160 ft) up. Under Friedrich II, court architect von Knobelsdorff added the Neuer Flügel (New Wing) to the east. The Theatre, designed by C.G. Langhans in 1790 and now the Museum für Vor- und Frühgeschichte, together with the Small Orangery, completes the palace precinct.

The **Museum für Vor- und Frühgeschichte** (Museum of Pre- and Early History, Langhans Building; open Tues–Fri 10am–6pm, weekend 11am–6pm; entrance fee) has some great Bronze Age exhibits and Trojan treasures. The collection used to be in the Monbijou Palace and included the legendary Priam Treasure, a spectacular collection of jewellery, discovered by Heinrich Schliemann in 1873. Unfortunately this treasure disappeared without trace during World War II.

The **Reiterdenkmal des Grossen Kurfürsten** (Equestrian Monument to the Great Elector, 1698) in the Ehrenhof occupies its current location because of a wartime blunder. The bronze statue, modelled by Andreas Schlüter, originally graced the Langebrücke (bridge) in front of the city castle on the Spree. During the war it was moved to Potsdam for safekeeping. As the baroque statue was

BELOW:
Reiterdenkmal des Grossen Kurfürsten (Equestrian Monument to the Great Elector).

being shipped back to Borsighafen on Tegel Lake en route to Berlin, the over-loaded barge sank under the weight. Several years later the statue was raised and restored and finally erected outside Charlottenburg Palace in 1965.

Restoring the historical rooms to their original state took decades of painstaking artistic work. They are now open to the public as a museum. The Goldene Galerie from the Frederican rococo period is on the upper storey of the **Knobelsdorff Wing**, where the collection of paintings and the library of Frederick the Great are displayed in his private rooms.

The **Schlosspark**, planned and laid out by Simon Godeau in 1697, was the first garden in Germany to be designed in the French style popular under Louis XIV. At the beginning of the 19th century Lenné gave the baroque park a face-lift along English lines. It is now one of Berlin's favourite spots for Sunday strolls, picnics and frisbee games.

The Neo-Classical mausoleum of Queen Luise, wife of Friedrich Wilhelm III, can also be found in the park. Designed by Karl Friedrich Schinkel, the mausoleum also houses the tombs of Kaiser Wilhelm I and his wife.

Court officials and the militia, lived opposite the palace, at the northern end of Schlossstrasse. The two officers' barracks of the Gardes du Corps (1859), designed by August Stüler, a pupil of Schinkel, now house the Ägyptisches Museum and the Berggruen Collection.

The bust of Nefertiti, the star exhibit at the Ägyptisches Museum.

Other Charlottenburg museums

The **Ägyptisches Museum ❻** (Egyptian Museum; Tues–Fri 10am–6pm, weekend 11am–6pm; entrance fee), in the Schlossstrasse 70, is housed in a barracks designed by the master builder Friedrich August Stüler. The collection contains items covering the period from approximately 5000 BC until AD 300. The most famous exhibit is the bust of Nefertiti, a limestone sculpture of the wife of Akhenaton, the Egyptian Pharaoh who reigned from 1375–58 BC. Some 48 cm (18 inches) tall, it was discovered in 1912 by the German archaeologist Ludwig Borchardt in the atelier of the master sculptor Tutmosis, as he was excavating for the lost royal city of Akhetaten on the banks of the Nile. The bust arrived in Berlin in the 1920s as part of an exchange.

Other celebrated exhibits include the Green Man, a bald head in green stone from about 300 BC, the ebony head of Queen Tiy and the remarkably well-preserved Kalabasha Gate. Ancient papyri, the oldest bearing a text over 3,000 years old, also recall the remarkable civilisations of the land of the Nile. Utensils, pottery, and chronometers bear witness to everyday life in Pharaonic Egypt.

Across the road, in Schlossstrasse 1, is the **Sammlung Berggruen ❼** (Berggruen Collection; Tues–Sun 10am–6pm; entrance fee). Opened in 1996, Heinz Berggruen's private collection is on loan to the city of Berlin for 10 years and contains around 100 paintings, sculptures and drawings by Picasso, Klee, Cézanne, Matisse, van Gogh, Braque, Laurens and Giacometti. The collection is noted for the high quality of its Picasso works which include paintings, sculptures and drawings. An excellent personal CD

BELOW:
the Ägyptisches Museum (Egyptian Museum).

guide to some of the best paintings in the collection is available at the cloakroom and included in the price of the price of the entrance fee.

Next door is the **Bröhan Museum** ❽ (Tues–Sun 10am–6pm; entrance fee), which houses a splendid collection of of art nouveau and art deco design by Berlin artists. A series of mock drawing rooms named after leading 1930s designers or furniture makers such as Hector Guimard, Louis Majorelle and Edgar Brandt are hung with outstanding contemporary paintings and equipped with gorgeous designer furniture and ornaments.

Along the road in Sophie-Charlotten-Strasse 17–18 are the workshops of the **National Plaster Casting Company** (open Mon–Fri 9am–4pm, Wed 9am–6pm, closed weekends). From a stock of 6,000 casts you can buy a plaster copy of the Nefertiti bust or of other exhibits in the national museums.

The Funkturm to the ICC

The western part of Charlottenburg is dominated by the **Funkturm** ❾ (Radio Tower; observation terrace open daily 10am–11pm; entrance fee), reminiscent of a mini Eiffel Tower. This Berlin landmark is 150 metres (500 ft) high including the aerial. The steel girder construction dates from the pioneering years of wireless, when Germany's first radio broadcast was made from the Voxhaus on 23 October 1923. Six years later it beamed out the world's first public television broadcast. Today the aerial is only used by the police and fire brigade. There's a lift to the observation platform 125 metres (416 ft) up.

The Broadcasting House on Masurenallee opposite is one of Europe's most modern broadcasting centres and has been planned so that all its studios face onto a central courtyard. Hans Poelzig designed the blue-black clinker building,

BELOW:
the triumphal march into the Olympiastadion, August 1936.

Map on page 152–53

which dates from 1931. The 14-storey block next door houses the SFB television studios, which are sometimes used for concerts. The 160,000 sq. metres (191,358 sq. yds) of the **Messegelände ⑩** (Exhibition Centre; tcl: 30380) with over 26 exhibition halls stretch out below the radio tower. Some 44 major exhibitions and trade fairs are held here every year.

A covered bridge leads from the exhibition centre on Hammarskjöldplatz over the motorway to **Internationales Congress Centrum ⑪** (International Congress Centre (ICC); tel: 30380), resembling an aluminium futuristic spaceship. Built between 1973 and 1979 for just under a billion marks, the construction is 320 metres (1,050 ft) long and 80 metres (260 ft) wide providing exhibition space of 800,000 sq. metres (960,000 sq. yds). An equally outsized surreal iron sculpture presides over the square outside – *Alexander the Great of Ectabene* by Romanian sculptor Jean Ipousteguy, popularly known as the "Klettermaxe".

Around the Olympiastadion

Heerstrasse and Reichsstrasse lead to the Olympiastadion. A worthwhile detour on the way is the **Georg-Kolbe Museum ⑫** (open Tues–Sun 10am–5pm; entrance fee) at Sensburger Allee 25, off Heerstrasse, the erstwhile home of the famous sculptor and illustrator (1877–1947). The house and the sculpture grove in the garden feature a substantial part of his work.

Olympischer Platz affords the first view of the Third Reich's sports grounds (Reichssportfeld). Commissioned by Hitler from Werner March for the Summer Olympics in 1936, this is one of the largest sports complexes in Europe. The **Olympiastadion ⑬** (open daily 8am–sunset; entrance fee), the main focus, is an enormous oval construction of whitewashed concrete, which holds as many as 90,000 spectators and is home to Berlin's premier league soccer team, Hertha BSC. The stadium has been undergoing reconstruction to host the World Cup in 2006. The area around the Olympiastadion is popular with rollerbladers and learner drivers, and the open-air pool is a popular summer retreat.

The neighbouring **Waldbühne** is a great summer venue for rock concerts. At the Rolling Stones' legendary appearance in September 1965, 21,000 fans wrecked the arena and it wasn't opened again for concerts for many years. Now it provides an atmospheric stage for the Berlin Philharmonic, classic film screenings and open-air opera performances.

Nature-lovers will enjoy the nearby **Grunewald**, Berlin's expansive forest, dotted with lakes and the odd restaurant. The view of Berlin from the **Teufelsberg** (Devil's Mountain) is one of the city's best and should be enjoyed before private developers go ahead with their plans to build a leisure complex atop the man-made hill.

At the northeastern tip of Charlottenburg there is a moving memorial on Hüttigpfad to victims of the Third Reich; 1,574 resistance fighters were executed here in what was once Plötzensee prison. Berlin's Catholics dedicated the **Maria-Regina-Martyrum-Kirche ⑭** (open daily) on nearby Heckerdamm to the memory of the "Martyrs for freedom of belief and conscience in 1933–45". ❏

Georg Kolbe is one of Germany's best-known sculptors. When he died he left 180 of his works to the city which are now displayed at the museum bearing his name.

BELOW: the Funkturm (Radio Tower).

SCHÖNEBERG

*Chic Schöneberg, home to Berlin's gay and lesbian community,
contains historic buildings, restored 19th-century apartments,
and trendy cafés, restaurants and bars*

Map
on page
162

One image of Schöneberg may be familiar to visitors: the former city hall with its square clock tower and the flag with a bear on it. Here prominent guests from around the world would enter their names in the city's golden book. On 26 June 1963, 400,000 Berliners gathered on the square outside to cheer US President Kennedy, when he broadcast those stirring words from the balcony: *"Ich bin ein Berliner!"* In honour of the murdered president, it is now known as John-F.-Kennedy-Platz. At midday every day the Freedom Bell rings from the tower of the town hall, which you can climb as far as the observation platform. A copy of the Liberty Bell in Philadelphia, this was a gift from the United States and is inscribed with the words: "May this world, with God's help, see a rebirth of freedom."

When the mayor of the then independent district laid the foundation stone of **Rathaus Schöneberg ❶** (tower open daily 10am–5pm) nobody could have guessed that, just four decades later, the imposing municipal building would become the political centre of the western half of the city, the official seat of the local mayor and the mayor of West Berlin. After the collapse of the Wall, it once more reverted to a borough council chamber, and the city administration moved into the Rotes Rathaus in Berlin-Mitte.

The population and architecture of the district is marked by distinct social divisions. You need only cast a glance at Friedenau and the "Rote Insel" (Red Island), the Bavarian Quarter and Potsdamer Strasse, to recognise the differences. Berlin's third smallest district in terms of area – 12 sq. km (5 sq. miles) – Schöneberg has proportionately few open spaces. To the aggravation of its 149,000 inhabitants, it also has the greatest area of roads. Schöneberg's prettiest park, Rudolf-Wilde-Park, begins immediately behind the Rathaus. On a bronze plinth stands the *Goldener Hirsch (Golden Stag)*, Schöneberg's heraldic mascot and a reminder of the original inhabitants of this once thickly forested area. At Kufsteiner Strasse, the park merges with the Wilmersdorfer Volkspark.

Historical Schöneberg

Dominicusstrasse leads from the town hall to the old centre of Schöneberg. The oldest building, the Frederican Dorfkirche, dating from 1766, stands on a rise beside the main street, Hauptstrasse. The main section of Hauptstrasse between Kaiser-Wilhelm-Platz and Dominicusstrasse still has a grassy promenade, a throwback to its village past. The first official mention of Schöneberg in writing appeared as long ago as 1264, when the Askanian Prince Otto III of Brandenburg donated to the Benedictine nuns of Spandau "five hides of land in 'Villa sconenberch'". After the

PRECEDING PAGES: statue in Schöneberg. **LEFT:** Rathaus Schöneberg detail. **BELOW:** magazine cover of US President John F Kennedy.

A bronze plaque on the entrance of Rathaus Schöneberg commemorates the visit by John F Kennedy on 26 June 1963. "Ich bin ein Berliner!" from his famous speech actually translates as "I am a doughnut!".

BELOW: Rudolf-Wilde-Park with the *Goldener Hirsch (Golden Stag)* statue in the background.

village was acquired by Elector Joachim I in 1506 and became a sovereign domain, it gradually increased in stature. It was strategically placed on the Berlin–Potsdam road, but this proved its undoing in the Seven Years' War: in 1760 Russian troops burnt the entire village to the ground.

One of the most important things to come out of the rebuilding was the surfacing of the carriageway to Potsdam. Standing on Prussia's first high road, Schöneberg was brought even closer to Berlin. Many travellers stopped off here, and inns, craftsmen and market gardens moved in to the area. In spite of the expansion, Schöneberg retained its quaint rural identity, and became a favourite place for day trips from Berlin – a tradition that survived well into the 20th century.

Between 1875 and 1898, the district's population grew from 7,500 to 75,000 people. Schöneberg was given a town charter and more and more new housing was erected to accommodate the expanding population. The area of Friedenau in the southwest corner was a typical example. Development began there in 1871 of a genteel country estate for wealthy government officials and retired gentlefolk. The war with France had just come to its conclusion with the signing of the Treaty of Frankfurt, hence the name Friedenau, which means peaceful meadow. With its tree-lined streets, leafy squares and stuccoed town houses with front gardens, Friedenau retains a definite peaceful quality to this day.

Its inhabitants weren't too happy when Schöneberg was integrated into Greater Berlin in 1920. They felt that Steglitz would have been an address with more class. Writers such as Max Frisch, Uwe Johnson and Günter Grass came to Friedenau in search of a quiet place to work. Federal Germany's first president, Theodor Heuss, lived here in Fregestrasse during the Weimar period.

Around **Friedrich-Wilhelm-Platz ❷**, where Friedenau and Wilmersdorf merge, the geometry of the original street plan is still discernible in the curved streets. On the corner of Schmargendorfer Strasse you can marvel at the Burg, or castle, a particularly stunning example of Friedenau villa architecture dating from around 1885. On Perelsplatz, in the north of the district, there is a notable art nouveau fountain, the Sintflut-Brunnen (Fountain of the Flood). Like Schöneberg, Friedenau was keen to demonstrate its independence by building a prestigious town hall. The Rathaus dominates Breslauer Platz, on the Hauptstrasse which continues south as Rheinstrasse.

The Insulaner

On Torgauer Strasse by Schöneberg S-Bahn station, an enormous gasometer serves as a symbol of Schöneberg's proletarian past. Railway bridges and sections of track crisscross the area west of the Schöneberg motorway intersection. On Priesterweg, out towards Tempelhof, Berliners tend small garden plots in allotment colonies with romantic names such as Spot of Happiness. The colonies are an ecological oasis, a miniature, waist-high jungle, which has grown up between the rusted railway lines.

Just to the south of the allotments (off Munsterdamm and Prellerweg) is the Insulaner, a park consisting of hills which were created from the ruins of the Bavarian Quarter after the war. With its swimming pool and toboggan run it provides an important recreational space for the Schönebergers.

On the summit of the Insulaner, with 75 metres (250 ft) by far the highest of the hills, glistens the dome of the **Wilhelm-Foerster-Sternwarte ❸** (open Tues, Thur–Sat 10am– 9pm, Sun 3–6pm; entrance fee), the largest public

 Map on page 162

There are over 350 taxi ranks in Berlin. Charges at night and during the weekend are higher than during the day.

BELOW: Rathaus Schöneberg, former seat of the West German senate.

observatory in the old Federal Republic and a regular meeting place for amateur astronomers. At the foot of the hill, the Zeiss Planetarium simulates the course of the stars under its 20-metre (67-ft) aluminium dome.

Exterior décor at the Wilhelm-Foerster-Sterwarte Planetarium, a regular meeting place for amateur astronomers.

Rote Insel (Red Island)

The "Rote Insel" (red island) is an "island" of high density tenement buildings and industrial areas between the former Anhalter rail-freight station and S-Bahn bridges on Yorckstrasse in the north, and S-Bahn tracks to the east, west and south, not to mention the Autobahn junction to the south. It can only be reached over various railway bridges or underpasses.

In the early part of the 20th century, this working-class district developed into a stronghold of the labour movement. If no longer rebellious, "Rote Insel" has kept its run-down appearance, contrasting with the affluent area just a bit further to the west of the S-Bahn tracks and Hauptstrasse. The tenements, workshops and corner bars together typify petty-bourgeois Berlin.

Incidentally, two Berliners from these parts later found fame and fortune in America. Marlene Dietrich and Hildegard Knef both started life in what is now Leberstrasse, then Sedanstrasse.

Around Kleist-Park

From the island it's only a few minutes' pleasant walk to **Kleist-Park ❹** (open summer 7am–8pm; winter 7am–4pm) on Potsdamer Strasse, a neighbourhood brimming over with history. From 1679 this area was used as a royal kitchen garden and courtyard. Later, Berlin's first botanical garden was founded here. The much-travelled poet and naturalist Adalbert von Chamisso, author of *Peter*

BELOW: fast food Berlin-style.

BERLIN CUISINE

Although not especially famed for its cuisine, Berlin has benefited greatly from its multicultural make-up. Originally influenced by the early Germanic and Slavonic settlers, the *Speisekarte* (menu) was further expanded, in the 17th century, by the French Huguenots who introduced, notably, vegetables. The traditional Berlin menu is not very accommodating for vegetarians – Berlin cooks have the habit of using *Speck* (bacon) in almost every dish, not considering it to be meat. In restaurants you will be able to find elaborate meals consisting of the staples pork, beef and chicken, and fish like herring or carp *(see Travel Tips for details)*. Most dishes come with vegetables, although they are not the main focus.

At the many street *Imbisses* (stand-up food stalls) you will see the locals eating *Bouletten* (Berlin's own hamburger, made of meat, breadcrumbs and herbs), *Kartoffelsalat* (potato salad) and *Currywurst* (spicy sausage served with tomato sauce and sprinkled with curry).

But many traditional fast foods have been usurped by "delicacies" from afar. The start of the 1970s heralded the introduction of what is now a symbol, nay icon, of Berlin life – the Turkish Döner kebab. The mix of bread, salad, meat and sauce has been taken to heart by the city's inhabitants.

Schlemihl, was custodian here from 1819 to 1839. In 1897 the botanical garden moved to Dahlem and the site was turned into a public park, which was named after the poet Heinrich von Kleist.

The elegant *Königskolonnaden* (King's Colonnades) at the park's main entrance were originally designed in 1870 by Carl von Gontard for the Königsbrücke at Alexanderplatz. The sandstone baroque columns have stood here only since 1910.

The **Kammergericht** (Courts of Justice) ❺, to the rear of the park, dates from 1913. The *Rossebändiger (Horse-Breakers)*, two bronze groups which stand in front of it, are particularly fine examples of 19th-century Prussian sculptural art. The sight of this north-German baroque building provokes an involuntary shudder. During the Nazi regime this was the seat of the infamous Volksgerichtshof (People's Court) for a time, where the officers of the 20 July conspiracy and other victims were sentenced to death in show trials. From 1945 until 1948, occupied Germany was governed from here by the Allied Control Council, composed of representatives from the US, UK, France and the Soviet Union. Today the building is used by the Berlin Constitutional Court.

The **Bayrischesviertel** (Bavarian Quarter) begins to the west of Martin-Luther-Strasse, a genteel residential district which before 1933 was known locally as "Jewish Switzerland". At that time many Jewish academics lived in the spacious apartments, the most famous being Professor Albert Einstein, whose home was at No. 5 Haberlandstrasse (now No. 8 Nördlinger Strasse) when he received the news that he had been awarded the Nobel Prize for his work in the field of quantum physics in 1921. The house was bombed during the war but the remaining original houses are a reminder of its former character.

Map on page 162

Rummage for bargains in Schöneberg's many antique and second-hand shops.

BELOW: Allied flags on the former Allied Control Council buildings.

Map on page 162

Nollendorfplatz

Schöneberg meets the city at Wittenbergplatz, location of one of the city's first and grandest U-Bahn stations (built in 1913) on its first line (Linie 1). Treasures of another kind are waiting to be unearthed in Schöneberg's antiques district. The big names, with prices to match, are on Keithstrasse. Eisenacherstrasse and Motzstrasse are also treasure houses for collectors on the look-out for Meissen porcelain, Russian ikons, old militaria and other rare items. There is also an awful lot of rubbish masquerading as art.

The ambience of **Nollendorfplatz** ⑥ is dominated by neon-lit cafés, bars and restaurants and the Metropol, Berlin's biggest disco, housed in an art-deco theatre building. This area, stretching down towards Winterfeldtplatz and Goltzstrasse, and even beyond, has acquired the reputation of Berlin's gay quarter and is one of the crucial parts of Berlin's social scene. Not only did the number of bars and cafés, gay and straight, increase dramatically during the 1990s, but also the resident population of gay men (and fewer lesbians) with significant disposable incomes. Rainbow flags in windows of shops and apartments are part of the scenery, and a street festival is held annually on Motzstrasse (Strassenfest) in the early summer. On Goltzstrasse you find antique shops and boutiques with all sorts of crazy clothing, new and second-hand and esoteric shops. This street epitomises the affluent, lefty-liberal part of Schöneberg.

On "Potse"

In between the two parts of the district runs Potsdamer Strasse, a section of the former Reichsstrasse 1 from Königsberg to Aachen. Dominating the street at the corner of Pallasstrasse is the so-called Sozialpalast ("Social Palace") an unprepossessing 1970s apartment block, built on the site of the former **Sportpalast** (Sports Palace) where Goebbels proclaimed "total war" after the fiasco at Stalingrad. It's a dreary prefabricated concrete slum, representing something of a social trouble spot. At one end it rests on an old bunker, and on the other side it is propped up by an underground garage.

While the Wall was standing, the "Potse" – as locals affectionately refer to their Potsdamer Strasse – became a cul-de-sac and a problem area. Prostitution and drug-trafficking have since been forced into the side streets, and brothel owners have turned their cheap hotels into more lucrative hostels for asylum seekers. One of the highest proportions of foreigners live in Schöneberg and their shopping and social activity is centred along this main street and the eastern part of the district. Thus the local immigrant community grew up in a district where banks alternated with amusement arcades, and supermarkets with sex shops, pawnbrokers and Turkish traders. The area has been cleaned up and now has more respectable forms of evening entertainment to choose from.

One of Berlin's biggest Turkish markets is held on Crellestrasse on Wednesdays and Saturdays – a lively and bustling place where you can purchase vast amounts of fruit and vegetables for little money. As a sign of the times, the Turkish traders have started to label their wares in Russian, too. ❏

BELOW:
the Metropol club.

Gay Berlin

The self-styled "gay capital of Europe", Berlin occupies a prominent place in gay and lesbian history. Seventy-two years before the 1969 Stonewall riots in New York, Magnus Hirschfeld founded the world's first organisation dedicated to ending the legal and social intolerance of homosexuals in Charlottenburg, This was followed in 1919 with the Institute of Sexual Science, another first, which made significant contributions to establishing sexuality research as a scientific discipline. Berlin's liberal atmosphere in the years following World War I encouraged a flourishing gay and lesbian scene, centred around Nollendorfplatz in Schöneberg and catering for a wide social cross-section.

Marlene Dietrich was born in Schöneberg and was part of the lively scene there, as was Christopher Isherwood, who lived in Nollendorfstrasse from 1929 to 1933. Isherwood's "Berlin Stories" *Mr Norris Changes Trains* (1935) and *Goodbye to Berlin* (1939) give modern readers a glimpse into the heady lifestyle of the era, and were the basis for the hit musical and film *Cabaret*.

Gay and lesbian life in Berlin darkened with Hitler's rise to power. The Nazi party doctrine of racial purity was also directed against "social degenerates", including homosexuals. Tens of thousands of gays and lesbians were rounded up and deported to concentration camps, where they were forced to wear a pink triangle. The appalling conditions, including forced labour, starvation rations and medical experimentation, meant that very few survived to bear witness after the war. A memorial plaque was erected at Nollendorfplatz station in 1989, part of the ongoing battle for recognition and compensation of the forgotten victims of National Socialism.

Recovery after the collapse of the Nazi state and the subsequent division of Berlin was slow. The continuing existence in the West of the notorious Paragraph 175a, under which homosexuality was a criminal offence, meant that a return to the glory days of the 1920s was impossible. Nevertheless, the gay and lesbian scene gradually began to grow on both sides of the wall. In the East, cut off from its traditional haunts, a small and mostly underground scene developed in Prenzlauer Berg. In the West, liberal Kreuzberg provided the atmosphere necessary for the re-establishment of a once-vibrant community.

Today, homosexuality has long since been decriminalised in Germany and Berlin draws many gay Germans and tourists alike. Public displays of affection between same-sex couples rarely raise an eyebrow, and there is an abundance of gay and mixed venues throughout the inner suburbs. The nightlife is legendary, with everything from cheesy German pop to hardcore sex on offer most nights until the early hours.

The Lesbian Film Festival and the Verzaubert Queer Film Festival attract large audiences, as does the three-day gay and lesbian street party. The highlight of the year is the Christopher Street Day parade, when over 400,000 people make their way from the Ku'damm to the Victory Column in a celebration of the richness and diversity of Berlin's gay and lesbian community. ❑

RIGHT: celebrating at a gay parade

KREUZBERG

At the heart of the new Berlin, Kreuzberg is slowly being gentrified while losing little of its radical and multicultural character

Ever since the city was divided, Kreuzberg has become something of a legend that extends far beyond the borders of Berlin. A small district in the West that was surrounded by the East on three sides, Kreuzberg progressed from a no-man's-land in the early 1960s into a hotbed of immigrant communities, political activism and alternative lifestyles in the 1970s and 1980s.

As the "least German" of all districts and the scene of numerous violent clashes between young political demonstrators and police, Kreuzberg's reputation became notorious throughout Germany. Many considered the district the dubious refuge of draft dodgers, squatters, anarchists and Turkish immigrants. Others, however, saw it as a haven for struggling artists and students, an open and tolerant environment in which people from a variety of cultures and persuasions live together in relative peace. Although these distinctions have lost their edge since the fall of the Wall, Kreuzberg still remains both the most famous and most infamous district of Berlin.

For a quick introduction to the unique character of Kreuzberg, take the subway (Line 1) from Zoologischer Garten and head east towards Schlesisches Tor. Labelled the "Istanbul Express" by locals, the train travels above ground after the Gleisdreieck station and the following six stops provide an excellent tour through the heart of Kreuzberg. Outside you can observe how the well-kept buildings of west Kreuzberg give way to the run-down housing projects surrounding Kottbusser Tor and beyond.

More interesting, however, is to observe the exotic assortment of passengers on the train. It is not uncommon to see Muslim women veiled from head to toe sitting next to leather-clad punks with mangy mohawk haircuts and dogs.

Kreuzberg is as unique as its residents and its innumerable bars, cafés and hang-outs harbour an infinite number of eccentrics. Utopian revolutionaries dreaming of an autonomous Kreuzberg, of separating their "Kiez" from the rest of Berlin; starving artists hoping for their big break; self-sufficient hippies growing grain and herbs on balconies and outhouse roofs; underground radicals diligently preparing for the May Day riots and Turkish immigrants propagating a breath of Turkey – here in Kreuzberg life pulsates in colours seen nowhere else in Berlin.

Early history

Unofficially, Kreuzberg is divided into two separate districts which coexist in a kind of love–hate relationship. The first is known by its postcode, "61", the other by its prewar code, "SO 36", or southeast 36. Anyone living in 61, possibly in one of the renovated town houses in the middle-class area around

PRECEDING PAGES: the Jüdisches Museum. **LEFT:** Checkpoint Charlie. **BELOW:** the Kreuzberg, with its artificial waterfall.

Mehringdamm, is usually regarded as a yuppie by those from SO 36. By contrast, someone from "Kotti", the working-class area around Kottbusser Tor, is immediately suspected of being a troublemaker or anarchist.

Such an unusual blend of people living together in one district, like so much dry tinder just waiting to be sparked off, can be traced back to the founding of Kreuzberg. As with all other districts in modern Berlin, Kreuzberg was first established through the great administrative reforms of 1920. The historic districts of Friedrichstadt, Luisenstadt and Tempelhof Vorstadt were combined into one single administrative district at the southern edge of the city centre. The new district was named after the most prominent feature of the area – the 66-metre (217-ft) high Kreuzberg, or cross mountain, in the south.

In the 1920s Kreuzberg was largely a residential district. In the northeast, Luisenstadt saw its population explode during the Industrial Revolution as millions of immigrants from the east poured into Berlin in search of work. The city was thoroughly unprepared for such an influx of people and although vast numbers of tenement blocks were built, Luisenstadt, present-day SO 36, turned into a working-class slum of deplorable conditions. Tempelhof Vorstadt in the south, on the other hand, was the upmarket, bourgeois counterpart whose residents were predominantly white-collar workers and government employees.

The exquisite Riehmers Hofgarten and the well-preserved residential buildings surrounding Chamissoplatz provide a clear example of the area's middle-class roots. Friedrichstadt, the third historical district of Kreuzberg formerly located in inner-city Berlin, was very different in character from its suburban neighbours to the south and east. It was home to a host of important government buildings during the reign of Kaiser Wilhelm II, including the presidential

A cabaret artiste summed up the underlying rivalry between Kreuzberg's two halves thus: "The guy from 61 drives a Mercedes; the guy from 36 breaks off the star emblem."

BELOW: Heilig Kreuz Kirche, Kreuzberg.

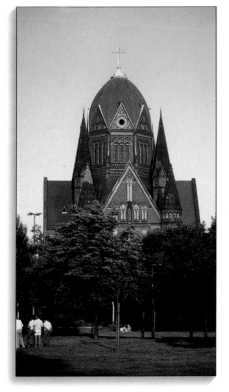

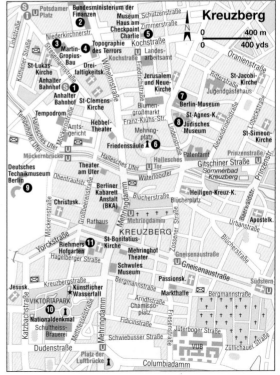

palace, the chancellery and the foreign office. Nearby Kochstrasse was Berlin's equivalent to London's Fleet Street with its high concentration of press and media businesses and Friedrichstrasse was wildly popular for its cinemas, dance halls, and shopping areas. The origin of Kreuzberg was essentially both proletariat and bourgeois in composition. Throw in a busy government, business, and entertainment district and you can see that Kreuzberg was a unique blend of diverging social and demographic elements from the beginning.

Although the world wars and the Wall irrevocably changed the face of Kreuzberg, its long tradition of cultural and social diversity is readily revealed to the observant traveller. A good starting point to explore this tradition is the Askanischer Platz, which can be reached with the No. 129 bus or by taking the S-Bahn (S 1 or 2) to the Anhalter Station.

Around the Anhalter Bahnhof

On the eastern edge of the Askanischer Platz stands the brick ruin of the **Anhalter Bahnhof ❶**, all that remains of one of the largest train stations in Europe and a once proud symbol of the wealth and power of industrial Berlin. Damaged during World War II and demolished shortly thereafter, its crumbling entrance used to welcome people from Frankfurt-am-Main, Basel, Leipzig, Munich and Dresden; now it frames a desolate wasteland.

Before World War II, the surrounding area was a bustling thoroughfare due to the Anhalter and nearby Potsdamer train stations. Film and insurance companies had their offices here, luxurious hotels like the Excelsior and the Stuttgarter Hof catered to wealthy guests, and cafés, restaurants and clubs were busy late into the night. A short distance to the north lay the main government quarter of the Third Reich, which was home to Hitler's Chancellory, Goebbel's Ministry of Propoganda and many other important ministries and agencies. Nazi Berlin's most feared address was also here; Prinz-Albrecht-Strasse 8, the official headquarters of the Gestapo (the secret state police). Housed in the former Prince Albrecht Palace, it was from here that Himmler, Heydrich, and their henchman planned, implemented and administered widespread terror and mass murder from 1934 to 1945.

Like so much of Berlin, the buildings in this area were badly damaged during the last two years of the war. After Germany surrendered, the once-feared address of the Gestapo headquarters turned into one of the many stretches of neglected ruins during the immediate postwar years. Ironically, this locus of Nazi power marked the border between the Soviet and American sectors; hence the Berlin Wall ran the length of the Prinz-Albrecht-Strasse after 1961. It was later renamed Niederkirchnerstrasse by the East Berlin government. On the other side, the West Berlin government blew up the damaged remains of all Nazi buildings in 1949, including the notorious Prince Albrecht Palace.

Heading north from Askanischer Platz, walk up Stresemannstrasse and then along the Niederkirchnerstrasse. Here you can witness something of a rarity in modern-day Berlin – the crumbling remnants of

Map on page 172

Anhalter Bahnhof, designed by Franz Schwechten, was built in 1870. The area that the station once stood on now houses the tents of the Tempodrom, a music venue.

BELOW: the ruins of Anhalter Bahnhof.

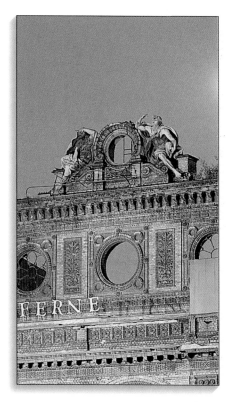

the Wall. The street is an eerie reminder of Berlin's past. And not just because of the Wall. The enormous building across the street is actually the former Aviation Ministry of the Third Reich, which, after the war, was attractive real estate for the East German government because of it large size and intact state.

Despite the obvious Nazi architecture, the building became the home to a dozen ministries of the GDR until 1990. In the early 1990s, the building served as the headquarters of the Treuhand, the special government agency charged with liquidating East Germany's state-owned economy. It is now the **Bundesministerium der Finanzen ❷** (Ministry of Finance). On the other side of the street, behind the Wall, are the Martin-Gropius-Bau and the Topography of Terror.

Martin-Gropius-Bau and the Topographie des Terrors

The **Martin-Gropius-Bau ❸** (open Tues–Sun 10am–8pm; entrance fee) is a magnificently restored museum that is home to a permanent collection entitled "Art in Berlin" and temporary exhibitions on art, photography and architecture. Designed by Martin Gropius in 1877, the Gropius-Bau was home to the Museum of Applied Art until its destruction in the war. The building was restored and renovated in 1981 and hosted the main historical exhibition marking Berlin's 750th anniversary in 1987. In preparation for the anniversary, an excavation of the adjoining area revealed ruins long thought destroyed – the foundation walls and cellars of the Gestapo headquarters.

Only a few steps from the Gropius-Bau's entrance, the unearthed ruins of the Nazi past could not be ignored and were soon incorporated into an open-air exhibition entitled the **Topographie des Terrors ❹** (Niederkichnerstrasse 8; open 10am–8pm daily; entrance fee). Walking among apparently nondescript

BELOW: the Martin-Gropius-Bau.

ruins, visitors are greeted by a sign announcing: "You are standing on the grounds of the former torture chambers of the Gestapo." Designed to preserve and explain the site and its history before and during the Nazi regime, the exhibition reveals in chilling detail the authority once exercised from the desks upstairs and the fate of the prisoners in the cells below. The exhibition, far from being complete, has many supporters and its fair share of detractors as well. Mounds of dirt still cover a large part of the ruins and, unfortunately, the main documentation is not yet available in English. In some ways, the unfinished status of the Topography of Terror is an interesting reflection on how Germany is coming to terms with the problems of its past.

From here it's a 10-minute walk down Wilhelmstrasse, along Kochstrasse and up Friedrichstrasse to the site of Checkpoint Charlie, one of the most famous names associated with Berlin during the Cold War.

Map on page 172

Soviet-style souvenirs from the days of Berlin's Soviet sector are still on sale today.

Friedrichstrasse and beyond

Checkpoint Charlie was an allied military post marking the border between East and West Berlin until 1990. As the official gateway to the Soviet Sector, it was the scene of numerous border incidents, most notably a heated standoff between Soviet and American tanks for a few tense days in 1961. With its dramatic "YOU ARE NOW LEAVING THE AMERICAN SECTOR" sign, Checkpoint Charlie conjured up images of spies and border guards and became synonymous with the mystery and intrigue of the Cold War. Nothing remains of the actual military installation today, although a small guardhouse was rebuilt in the middle of street. For more information on the general history of the Wall, visit the nearby **Museum Haus am Checkpoint**

BELOW:
Friedrichstrasse and Checkpoint Charlie.

Charlie ❺ (open daily 11am–6pm; entrance fee) at Friedrichstrasse 44. One of the most interesting aspects of the museum is its documentation of the elaborate escape plans made by East Germans to get over the Wall.

Continuing down Friedrichstrasse, the architectural transgressions of the past are impossible to ignore. In the 1960s, unimaginative concrete blocks were erected in the East and West alike, although **Mehringplatz** ❻ is a pleasant exception, a modern complex which is worth seeing for its unusual structure. Originally, this was a large circular plaza built in the 1730s on the inside of the **Hallesches Tor**, one of the major gateways in the old fortifications protecting Berlin. Granted, not much is left from that time, but the old gateway now serves as a U-Bahn station of the same name and the overall structure of the historic Mehringplatz, formerly Belle-Alliance-Platz, remains. From a distance the buildings today look like one massive group of uninspiring tower blocks, but when you enter the estate, laid out in the round, you find yourself in a pedestrian zone dotted with open spaces and shopping arcades. The pedestrian zone is surrounded by rings of houses of various heights, beginning with three-storey buildings in the inner circle and leading out to 17-storey blocks on the outside. In the middle of the ring towers a monument to peace.

To the east of Mehringplatz runs Lindenstrasse, where you can see an interesting juxtaposition of the old Berlin Museum and the new Jewish Museum.

Kreuzberg's museums

BELOW:
the Berlin Museum.

The **Berlin Museum** ❼ is an exquisite Baroque building dating back to 1734. It originally housed an exhibition detailing the history and development of the city through paintings, prints and crafts. It served as West Berlin's answer to the

Märkisches Museum in the East, which housed a similar exhibition. When the city was reunified, the Märkisches Museum took over as the main exhibition on Berlin's history, making the Berlin Museum superfluous. It is currently closed awaiting the opening of a major extension that will hold the Jüdisches Museum.

Map on page 172

The **Jüdisches Museum** ❽ (Jewish Museum; open Tues–Sun 10am–8pm; daily tours; entrance fee) stands in striking contrast to the Baroque architecture of its immediate neighbour. Designed by Daniel Libeskind, an American architect of Jewish origin, the large metallic structure was built in the form of a distressed Star of David with an open space in the centre, creating a void into which one can look, but cannot enter. The museum hosts a permanent exhibition on the long history of Berlin's Jewish citizens.

Another museum in the area worth seeing is the **Deutsches Technikmuseum Berlin** ❾ (German Technology Museum of Berlin; open Tues–Fri 9am–5:30pm, weekend 10am–6pm; entrance fee). Located just south of the Anhalter station at Trebbiner Str. 9, the museum is impossible to miss due to the huge twin-propellered plane suspended high above the entrance. A veritable playground of technology, visitors here can play with antiquated machinery and computers, and stroll through a superb collection of old planes, steam engines, and automobiles. For a nice change of pace from exploring museums and ruins, head south to the beautiful parks and well-preserved residential areas of Kreuzberg 61.

The Deutsches Technikmuseum is great fun for children, who will enjoy the interactive displays.

Around Viktoriapark

Take the No. 119 bus or the U-Bahn to Mehringdamm station and walk south towards **Viktoriapark** ❿ (or the Kreuzberg as it's popularly known. Situated on the slopes of a hill, the park is one of city's prettiest and claims to be

BELOW: Karneval der Kulturen (Carnival of Cultures).

PARADE CULTURE

There's nothing the Berliner likes more than an excuse to party, and if they can swathe the proceedings in some sort of gesture-based parade, all the better. The Karneval der Kulturen (Carnival of Cultures), which takes place in Kreuzberg on Whit weekend in June, celebrates the cultural diversity of the city. The Christopher Street Day Parade in June is a chance for Berlin's gay and lesbian community to commemorate the Stonewall riots of 1969 and celebrate free sexuality. But for size, it doesn't match the Love Parade. Since 1989, attendance at the world's biggest dance music street party, which converges on the Grosser Stern in Tiergarten, has soared to 2 million people. Because it is registered as a demonstration the parade wasn't, until recently, obliged to clean up after itself, leaving that mess to the council. Aside from litter, the environmental damage done to the park is a worry – leading to the fear that the parade's days are numbered. For some, the event is already past its best – the excessive commercialisation in recent years has prompted a rival parade on the same day. In August as many as 50,000 citizens make their way from Alexanderplatz to Unter den Linden as part of the Hanf (Hemp) Parade demonstrating for the legalisation of the stigmatised plant and its numerous eco-friendly advantages.

Germany's northernmost vineyard. Atop the hill sits the Cross, a monument from which the hill and the entire district get its name. It was built by the architect and sculptor Karl Friedrich Schinkel to commemorate the 1813–15 war of liberation. The 20-metre (66-ft) Gothic column topped with a massive iron cross was erected in 1878 on a stone base 8 metres (27 ft) high.

Surprisingly, the park also has a waterfall which roars down the hill towards Grossbeerenstrasse. It is an imitation of the Zackelfall in the Sudeten mountains, and in summer a favourite place for dogs and small children to splash around. Climbing to the top of hill rewards you with a spectacular view of the surrounding area. Looking to the north and east, you can behold the entire expanse of Kreuzberg. There's scarcely a patch of green to be seen, except a few swathes which a closer glance reveals to be cemeteries. People live very close together in Kreuzberg: in 1910, more than 420,000 people were crammed together in an area of 11 sq. km (4 sq. miles). Today, Kreuzberg is still the most densely populated district in Berlin, with about 150,000 inhabitants per hectare.

But there are perfectly pleasant places to live in Kreuzberg, particularly around Viktoriapark. Perhaps the best example of upscale housing in this district is **Riehmers Hofgarten ⓫**, a historic estate which is protected by a preservation order and is only a stone's throw away from the waterfall. The bourgeois residential complex, named after its founder Wilhelm Riehmer, dates back to 1871. The gateways on the Yorckstrasse, Grossbeerenstrasse and Hagelberger Strasse lead into a large estate consisting of 24 buildings surrounding an expansive central courtyard. There is plenty of evidence of the care taken by the architects in planning the estate. The apartments and the spacious courtyard were built so that the various nooks and crannies effectively mask the noise of the traffic that roars along Yorckstrasse at all hours of the day and night.

Viktoriapark is a favourite venue for New Year's Eve celebrations when the hill fills with people enjoying fireworks and music.

BELOW:
U-Bahn Line 1, immortalised in a musical.

Riehmers Hofgarten is worth seeing, if only for the painstakingly restored stucco facades modelled on those of the Renaissance architect Palladio. Little wonder that upmarket cafés, cinemas and a club have moved into the neighbourhood. The **Berliner Kinomuseum** (Cinema Museum; Grossbeerenstrasse 57; open daily), however, is a fleapit which shows black-and-white films from the early days of cinema and does not seem to fit into the up-market ensemble.

To the Südstern

Nearby Chamissoplatz is also an impressive residential area. The square was left largely unscathed during the war and escaped the demolition mania of the reconstruction period which followed. Its petty-bourgeois character has barely changed since it was built in the second half of the 19th century. It is even home to one of Berlin's few remaining Wilhelmine pissoirs. The rectangular square is surrounded by four- and five-storey buildings distinguished by facades of varying colour, simple stucco ornamentation and harmoniously balanced windows and balconies. The square is definitely worth a visit, as are the restaurants, flea-markets and antique shops found in the adjacent Bergmannstrasse.

Keep walking down Bergmann-strasse and, passing

a large 18th- and 19th- century cemetery, you end up at the Südstern (South Star). Seven main roads meet here to form a star, in the middle of which stands the former Garnisonskirche (Garrison Church), which has not been used as a place of worship for many years. Further to the northeast, heading towards Kottbusser Tor, it is clear where bourgeois Kreuzberg 61 changes into proletarian SO 36.

Map on page 172

East Kreuzberg SO 36

Renovated old houses, new houses and completely derelict houses stand side by side. The working-class milieu of SO 36 has changed considerably since the "Strategy for Kreuzberg" was unveiled in the 1970s by the city government. The IBA international building exhibition played a major part in this strategy, introducing the concept of "informed development" to save the district from deteriorating into a complete slum. The concept involved reconstructing or renovating old buildings and initiating new projects designed to blend in harmoniously with their older surroundings.

Although many areas such as the Mariannenplatz were effectively restored, whether this concept was a total success is debatable. Simply take a walk around Kottbusser Tor and form your own opinion.

A visit to the Tükenmarkt gives a good insight into the life of Berlin's Turkish community.

In this neighbourhood the exotic Kreuzberg blend is evident: trendy cafés, punk bars, and kebab stands line the streets in a completely random manner. The neighbourhood is also known as Germany's "Little Istanbul" because of large number of Turks residing here. Invited by the West German government to offset serious labour shortages after the war, thousands of Turks immigrated in the 1950s and 1960s as *Gastarbeiter* (guest workers). Most of them settled in Kreuzberg because of the cheap housing and soon afterwards were joined by their families. Over the years a lively Turkish community has developed right in the heart of Kreuzberg.

BELOW: a trendy café in Kreuzberg.

This community can be experienced in its undiluted form at the Türkenmarkt (Turkish Market), held every Tuesday and Friday on the Maybachufer. A bazaar atmosphere reigns until well into the afternoon and the riverside pavements are busy with women in veils and men with beards. Prices are haggled over, fruit and vegetables tested for their quality, and oriental delicacies and household goods from around the world are offered for sale. The smell of kebabs hangs in the air, mingling with the aroma of oriental spices, which are slowly but surely finding their way into German cuisine. And the Germans living in the area have grown to accept their Turkish neighbours. It is now taken for granted that long-established Kreuzbergers buy their vegetables from Turkish market stalls and that the Turkish döner kebab has replaced the traditional *currywurst* as Berlin's favourite snack.

Kreuzberg surpasses all other districts in Berlin in terms of social and cultural diversity. This should be evident after exploring the historical areas around Friedrichstrasse, the upscale residences of Kreuzberg 61 and the multicultural makeup of SO 36. Although officially fused with the district of Friedrichshain in January 2001, it is hoped that the tolerant atmosphere and racial harmony characteristic of Kreuzberg will continue to flourish for a long time to come. ❑

PRENZLAUER BERG

The working-class district of Prenzlauer Berg has a bohemian reputation while its neighbour Friedrichshain is home to Berlin's clubbing mile

Map on page 184

What Kreuzberg was to West Germany in the 1980s, the "Prenzelberg" was to the GDR. A refuge for misfits unable to conform back home in the provinces; a playground for drop-outs wanting to try alternative ways of living; a meeting place for punks, gays, opposition groups, alternative lifestylers and artists from near and far; in short, a centre for the subculture of the whole country.

In Prenzlauer Berg it was possible to live largely beyond the control of the state and the norms of socialist society. The state housing department lacked an overall picture of the run-down workers' district, and it was possible to squat in empty apartments or simply to occupy them and thus circumvent the usual waiting list. Experts estimate that between 20 and 30 percent of the Prenzelberg population obtained their flats in this way. Musicians, painters, theatre groups and political groups found space here, too, in order to work on their projects.

Private galleries and bars sprang up. The Prenzelberg scene, more a jumble of different subcultures than one distinctive social entity, flourished on the edge of legality – closely watched by the state, sometimes treated like a child, but by and large tolerated.

The Berlin scene continues to influence the shape of the district. After the Berlin Wall came down, a lot of West German squatters came here to take advantage of the chaotic housing situation, but the present gentrification process is slowly taking over, forcing most to find pastures new. The only remaining question is whether the new administrative centre, which goes under the name of Pankow, will be able to supply the district with enough money to reinforce its support groups and local initiatives. Long-term residents are beginning to notice that the character of Prenzlauer Berg has changed recently. In reunited Berlin, the "wild child" of the city's districts counts as a prime city centre location. It is proving very easy for investors with plenty of capital to oust the incumbent and less well off population – students, artists, the unemployed and the elderly – from their homes.

PRECEDING PAGES: mural at the East Side Gallery. **LEFT:** cow sculpture on the side of a café wall. **BELOW:** sunny street café.

Historical rapprochement

Prenzlauer Berg is within walking distance of the city centre. Head northeast from Alexanderplatz and you're in the thick of its historical past. Beyond Torstrasse, the southern boundary of the district, there is a marked incline – the old Windmühlenberg (Windmill Hill). This once lay beyond the city gates. At that time it was fields and meadows, and few people lived here. The district's main traffic routes – Schönhauser Allee, Prenzlauer Allee and Greifswalder Strasse – were country roads, leading out from the city to the

northeast. Along them are several old cemeteries, including (on Schönhauser Allee) what was the most fashionable Jewish cemetery in Berlin, where the painter Max Liebermann is buried.

Vines were cultivated in Prenzlauer Berg right up until the middle of the 19th century. But the quality of its wine was more cause for jest than praise. The 19th-century satirist Adolf Glassbrenner described it as "three-man wine". "If a man wants to enjoy this grape juice, he needs two others to hold him."

Housing in Prenzlauer Berg

After 1861, a whole town of tenements was blasted out of the ground on the outlying hill. By 1920, when the administrative district of Prenzlauer Berg came into being, 312,000 people were living here. There are very few individual attractions, but the district as a whole is of cultural and historical interest. Prenzlauer Berg was largely spared during the air raids, and the few new buildings and redevelopment projects since 1945 haven't altered its essential face.

Around 90 percent of the houses are five storeys high, set close together on absolutely straight streets. Gateways lead into a labyrinth of alleys, passageways and narrow dark courtyards. Behind the showy stucco facades, poverty escalated. Damp, dingy apartments, overcrowded rooms, inadequate sanitation, horrendously high rents – these were the social conditions which were to lead the painter Heinrich Zille to comment caustically that you can kill a man just as well with a flat as you can with an axe.

Today, the old houses are starting to look as good from the outside as they do inside. Fragments of stuccowork clinging to crumbling plaster and balconies in imminent danger of collapsing are less frequent sights. The once elegant facades are returning to their former glory, the bullet holes nearly all filled in. The faded inscriptions like " Herrings and potatoes", revealing the specialities sold by the former owners, are slowly disappearing, being covered by the signs of a variety of new businesses. Although not many tower blocks have been built, Pren-

BELOW: Karl-Marx-Allee with the Fernsehturm (TV tower) in the background.

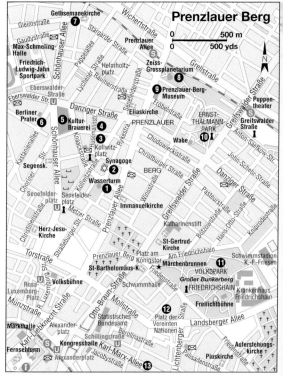

zlauer Berg has the highest population density of all the former eastern districts. People have furnished the remaining non-renovated buildings as well as they can and made them habitable. But standards of housing are still quite low and a few apartments still have no indoor toilet or bath.

Map on page 184

Around Kollwitzstrasse and Kollwitzplatz

The emblem of Prenzlauer Berg, part of its coat of arms, is the **Wasserturm** ❶ (water tower) on Windmühlenberg (Knaackstrasse), which was built in 1875. Over the years, the narrow tower next door has been used by various political parties as a flagpole. The last flag to flutter there, as on so many houses, was the black and red squatters' standard. This is one of the city's oldest waterworks, erected in 1855–56 by an English firm at their own expense. Beneath are the old brick vaults, which are all that remains of the then open reservoir. Today they are used for performances and temporary exhibitions and the roof space of the water tower is residential.

If the iron gates at the foot of the hill happen to be open, take a peek into the sinister place beyond. In 1933 the National Socialists set up a torture chamber here, to which communists were brought from the workers' district. A memorial stone commemorates its victims. Opposite the water tower, behind Rykestrasse 53, is the red-brick **Synagoge** ❷, built in simple classical style in 1904. It was badly damaged by the Nazis in 1938, but because of the adjoining houses they didn't set fire to it, and between 1976 and 1978 it was restored as Germany's first post-war synagogue.

To the rear lie **Kollwitzstrasse** and **Kollwitzplatz** ❸. The artist and sculptor Käthe Kollwitz and her husband Karl, a doctor who looked after the poor, lived

BELOW: keeping cool outside a Prenzlauer Berg bar.

in the house on the corner of Knaackstrasse (formerly Weissenburger Strasse 25). In the grounds of the bombed out building, a statue, based on one of Kollwitz's drawings, the *Schützende Mutter (Guardian Mother)*, commemorates the artist. Käthe Kollwitz herself sits facing it, larger than life in bronze, and the children playing in Kollwitzplatz regularly leap onto her lap and climb up around her neck.

With the opening of several very popular bars and fringe theatres in the 1990s the area around Kollwitzplatz has become the centre of an exciting local scene, with a lively atmosphere. Recognition of the area came in 2001 when Bill Clinton, on a presidential tour of Europe, was seen dining in the Gugelhof restaurant with German Chancellor Gerhard Schröder and Foreign Minister Joschka Fischer.

For the purist, however, the post-Wende scene of underground bars and clubs has virtually all been raised to street level. No longer the place where truly original projects are likely to be germinated, Prenzelberg is at risk of becoming the one-dimensional landscape its original dwellers were opposed to. The choice of bars, restaurants and art outlets now goes on without end. Those discontented with the arrival of the mainstream bandwagon are heading eastwards to Friedrichshain but the new set of upwardly mobile, multicultural parents has found the right atmosphere in which to bring up their young children.

Husemannstrasse

"Honnywood" is what the locals call **Husemannstrasse ❹**, which leads off to the north from Kollwitzplatz. The shopping street was originally built around 1890, then rebuilt, in 19th-century style, in 1987 to commemorate the 750th

BELOW:
eating al fresco
on Kollwitzplatz.

anniversary of the city. Ornamental plasterwork, window frames, doorways, shop signs and signposts were painstakingly copied, with the result that the street now resembles a film set. More often than not you'll come across a film crew, shooting location shots for television or the cinema.

If you follow the Knaackstrasse to its end at the corner of the Danziger Strasse you will come across the huge complex of the old Schultheiss-Brauerei (Schultheiss Brewery), which covers an area of 7,500 sq. metres (8,970 sq. yds). Here you will find the **Kultur-Brauerei ❺** (Culture Brewery; Knaackstrasse 97, tel: 441 9269) a multicultural centre with exhibition halls, theatres, pubs and a club. Franz Schwechten, Wilhelm II's favourite architect, started to construct the exterior buildings of the brewery complex in 1891. A 1990s Prenzlauerberg-style refit has put the shine back into the brickwork but, for some, has removed a bit of the atmosphere.

Schönhauser Allee and Helmholtzplatz

This loud, lively shopping street with lots of cafés is best reached by U-Bahn (Eberswalder Strasse station). The "Boulevard of the North" can't yet compare with similar shopping centres in the western districts. The junction of Danziger Strasse and Kastanienallee is one of the city's busiest for traffic. The **Berliner Prater ❻** (check press for details) is also located here, an old-established assembly hall and function rooms which today is used as a venue for a variety of cultural and musical events. It's pleasant to stroll under the monorail, even in the rain. Ever since it was built in 1911–13, the locals have called it "the municipal umbrella". West of the railway the redevelopment zone begins around Arnimplatz, the socialist counterpart of Kreuzberg's "informed reconstruction".

There now exists a more relaxed atmosphere around **Gethsemanekirche ❼** (Gethsemane Church), under cover of which the East German opposition came together and which became a symbol of the 1989 revolution. On 7 October 1989 the church opened its doors to give sanctuary to protesters being attacked by the Stasi and the police on the 40th anniversary of the founding of the GDR. Many things have changed around the nearby **Helmholtzplatz** since the frenetic years of squatting and hell raising in the early 1990s. Known to its profligates as LSD, after its Strassen Lychener, Schliemann and Duncker, it was a hive of subversive activity and helped Prenzlauer Berg on its way to being the most fashionable Bezirk in town. Remnants of the more radical edge of the epoch can still be found in Café Schliemann in Schliemann-strasse, restlessly coming to terms with the mass gentrification around them.

At the end of Stargarder Strasse glistens the silver dome of the **Zeiss-Grossplanetarium ❽** (planetarium; Prenzlauer Allee 80; tel: 4218 4512; open Mon–Fri 10am–noon, Wed, Sat 1.30–9pm, Thur–Fri 6–10pm, Sun 1.30–6pm; entrance fee), where you can embark on a journey through the solar system or be talked through the skies over Berlin.

South of the planetarium is the local history museum. At the main entrance to the **Prenzlauer-Berg-Museum ❾** (Prenzlauer Allee 227–228; open

Map on page 184

The dome of Zeiss-Grossplanetarium houses the most up-to-date telescope in Berlin.

BELOW: the Gothic towers of Oberbaum Brücke.

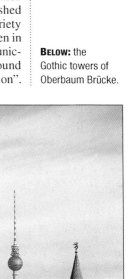

Tues–Wed 10am–5pm, Thur 10am–7pm, Sun 1–5pm) a relief commemorates the head of the city planning department Hermann Blankenstein, under whose leadership the public building was erected between 1886 and 1889.

On the site of a former gasworks stands **Ernst-Thälmannpark** , a vast open space with an arts centre, playgrounds, a swimming pool and accommodation for 4,000 people. The massive Thälmann monument on Greifswalderstrasse was unveiled in 1986 to mark the centenary of the leader of the labour movement. Lengthy debate surrounded the Thälmann project, which was envisaged as giving the district a prestigious new centre. These days, the area looks quite dated and, as it is removed from the bustling hub between Schönhauser Allee and Prenzlauer Allee, it tends to be forgotten. Jump onto tram No. 20 and, after a few minutes, you'll be in Friedrichshain.

Friedrichshain

With a population of 100,000 and covering just 10 sq. km (4 sq. miles), this is Berlin's smallest district. Traditionally working class, the area is more authentic East Berlin than its neighbour, Prenzlauer Berg. Anyone taking a walk in Friedrichshain in the first half of the 18th century would have looked out over waving cornfields and fertile meadows. Here, beyond the city gates, was a rural haven. At the beginning of the 18th century, when Prussia's first king, Friedrich I, decided to develop Berlin as his royal seat, the city boundaries were extended to the east.

BELOW: remembering past times.

A new suburb was formed which stretched from today's Frankfurter Tor, along Palisadenstrasse, over Platz der Vereinten Nationen and up to the Königstor, although at that time the district did not yet have a name. Craftsmen

Map on page 184

and workers began to settle here. But the industrial boom was just getting under way, and with it the rush to build tenements. Friedrichshain soon developed its own brand of poverty. It became a town of tenement blocks full of cramped apartments and without proper sanitation. The small workshops became manufacturing companies and later large industrial concerns. The new factories required a lot of labour, "human resources", for badly paid 16-hour shifts on dingy factory floors. The Berlin–Frankfurt/Oder steam railway was built specifically to guarantee supplies of manpower and raw materials, with an extra station near today's Ostbahnhof. The population expanded rapidly. By the beginning of the war Friedrichshain had the largest population in Berlin.

The suburban population was already plagued by poverty and disease even before industrialisation brought misery on a grand scale. In 1840, during the period before the March Revolution, when wealthy citizens were beginning to doubt the legitimacy of absolute rule, Berlin's city fathers decided to create a recreational park in the east of the city. In the west there was already the spacious, feudal Tiergarten, mainly frequented by the elite of the royal city, but this was far away from the poor inhabitants in eastern Berlin. Gustav Meyer, who later became the court gardener at Sanssouci Palace, laid out the **Volkspark Friedrichshain ⓫** (open daily) to plans by the landscape designer Lenné.

Volkspark Friedrichshain

The "Poor People's Park" was called Friedrichshain to commemorate the centenary of Frederick the Great's succession to the throne. In 1868 it was reduced in size to permit the building of the city's first hospital, initiated by Rudolph Virchow because of the high incidence of sickness among the poor. But what is

BELOW: Volkspark Friedrichshain.

MAY DAY

May Day in Berlin is much more than an occasion for labour unions to demonstrate workers' solidarity and for politically minded citizens to protest against global oppression and tyranny. It is also an occasion for revolution among Berlin's left-wing radicals, an annual one-day uprising marked by violence, property damage, and heated clashes with the police. May Day begins with peaceful demonstrations and traditionally ends with riots well into the night. The riots originated during the 1980s in Kreuzberg. May Day then was extremely violent with rioters rampaging through the streets and destroying anything smacking of capitalism.

Although the riots today are nowhere near as violent, due in part to the 7,500 police armed with riot gear and water cannons, street battles still occur. The radical left from all over Europe coalesces in either Kreuzberg or Prenzlauer Berg and are joined by an army of riot "tourists", who want to see and participate in this yearly spectacle. For this reason, May Day will invariably end in the occasional riot, despite government measures to curb violence or ban the demonstrations outright. The legend of the May Day riots, although in diluted form, remains alive.

most unusual about the park is the proliferation of memorials. The *Märchenbrunnen* (Fairytale Fountain) in the western corner dates from 1913 and is a token to the children of east Berlin under threat from typhoid and rickets. The neo-baroque fountain, decorated with characters from Grimm Brothers' tales, was built to a design by city architect Ludwig Hoffman.

The park is also home to the Gedenkstätte für die Deutschen Interbrigadisten, a monument to those German members of the International Brigades who fought against the fascists in the Spanish Civil War, one for the dead of the 1848 March Revolution and one for the Red Sailors' Revolution at Kiel in 1918. Engraved on the sailors' plaque is a line from the memorial address given here by Lenin in 1919: "Lay firm the foundations of working-class rule, unite against the opposition." Stirring stuff indeed, but it is unlikely that these powerful inscriptions cross the minds of the crowds who flock here with their families and frisbees at the weekend.

Dominating these monuments are two artificial hills – Grosser Bunkerberg and Kleiner Bunkerberg – which were created when well over one million cubic yards of rubble from bombed-out Berlin was dumped over a couple of war-time bunkers. Between them is a small shaded lake, alongside which are giant outdoor chess boards.

Stalinist streets

The bare expanse of what was formally Leninplatz has been renamed **Platz der Vereinten Nationen** ⓬ (United Nations Square). In the middle of the square, a 19-metre (60-ft) statue of the Soviet hero once watched solemnly over his comrades, but after vehement protests from both East and West, the statue

BELOW: water sculpture near Karl-Marx-Allee.

was dismantled. The city's great east–west axis, **Karl-Marx-Allee** is astonishing not only for its colossal proportions but also as a monument to the socialists' early programme of reconstruction.

By the time the war was over, what was then Frankfurter Allee had been reduced to nothing more than a great expanse of ruins. In the early 1950s the SED (German Unity Party) leadership decided to build here Berlin's "first socialist street", which would not only offer comfortable living conditions for the working population but would also "take into account today's traffic conditions".

The boulevard is 80 metres (260 ft) wide, a whole 20 metres (65 ft) wider than the mighty Prussian Unter den Linden. The young state pointed proudly to the fact that the first phase of building was completed in record time. No mention was made of the fact that the construction workers had protested against the raising of building targets, a protest which culminated in the storming of the Brandenburg Gate on 17 June 1953. Everything appears over-proportioned here: the shopping arcades, the gateways, the wide pavements and above all the boulevard itself, where the traffic thunders along its marked lanes and the air is thick with fumes. So bad are the fumes that the cheap plastic tiles, used to replace the original ceramic cladding that often fell off the buildings, became terribly discoloured. Since the whole street was bought by a western bank, renovation work is well underway and examples of such tiles are few and far between.

Regeneration

Little by little, Friedrichshain is coming alongside its former eastern neighbour Prenzlauer Berg. Having already received refugees from the gentrification process up the hill, it is now receiving a lick of the old brush itself. **Simon-Dach-Strasse**, the Friedrichshain version of Oranienburger Strasse, buzzes of an evening with the sound of fun-seekers, some of whom may be on their way to Berlin's "Clubbing Mile". Along the river from Ostbahnhof to beyond the Oberbaum Brücke there are several trendy clubs, although the immediate vicinity is depressingly industrial.

This haven of hedonism along the **Mühlenstrasse** is ideally complimented by the longest remaining stretch of the Wall, the **East Side Gallery**. Decorated by predominantly political works of art, it is supposed to convey the attitudes towards the fall of the Wall at the time. If nothing else, it is the longest outdoor gallery in the world. Exposed to the elements for too long, it now looks like everyone and everything else along Mühlenstrasse – a little bit the worse for wear. This will not be the case for long.

Things are happening in the East. Plans for the rejuvenation of the stretch of land on the river behind the Wall, with unobtrusive buildings and parkland are set. More buildings are to be added to **Oberbaum City**, an ambitious commercial and service centre project at Oberbaum Brücke. The Rummelsburger Bay waterside development at the old town of Stralau, to be known as **Watercity Stralau**, is to receive 5,900 dwellings, 425,000 sq. metres (508,296 sq yds) of office space and a further list of amenities by 2015. Berlin is growing upwards and eastwards. ❑

> Map on page 184

The East Side Gallery is the longest remaining section of the Wall (1,300 metres/4,265 ft). It runs along Mühlenstrasse between Hauptbahnhof and Oberbaum Brücke.

BELOW:
local club DJ.

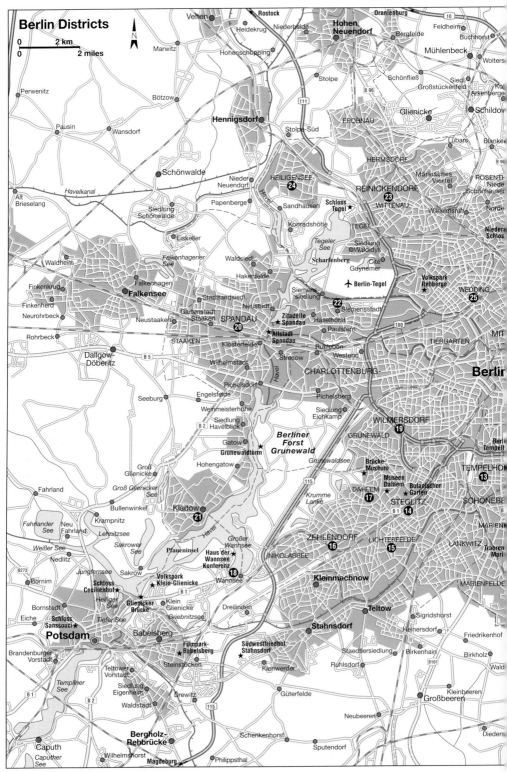

Berlin Districts

0   2 km
0   2 miles

N

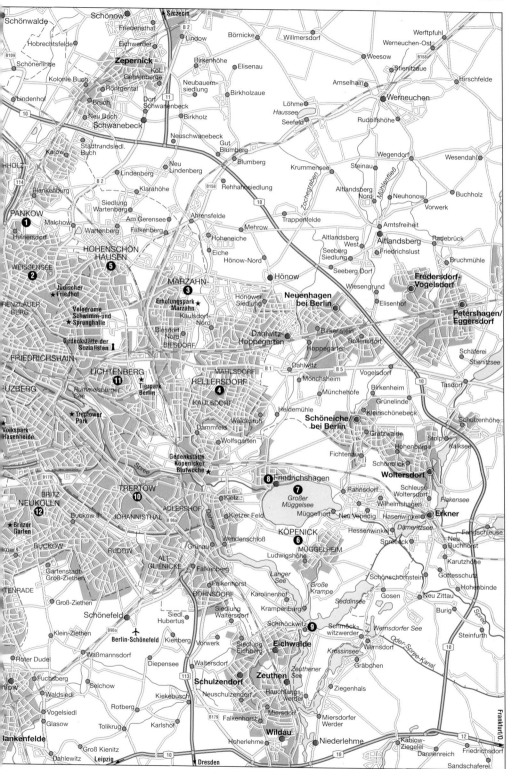

THE OUTER DISTRICTS

Berlin's outer districts provide an opportunity to explore the city's waterways, open spaces and different ways of life

Berlin's individual districts are much older than the city itself. In its present form, the metropolis has existed only since 1 October 1920. This move provided the basis for the city's rise to a metropolis of international stature. Six communities formed the heart of the original city: Mitte, Tiergarten, Wedding, Prenzlauer Berg, Friedrichshain and Hallesches Tor (Kreuzberg).

After unification, Charlottenburg, Köpenick, Lichtenberg, Neukölln, Schöneberg, Spandau and Wilmersdorf, all independent towns until then, retained their names and their imposing town halls. Other rural communities and estates were united to form a further seven administrative districts, each one bearing the name of the most populous village lying within its boundaries: these were Pankow, Reinickendorf, Steglitz, Tempelhof, Treptow, Weissensee and Zehlendorf.

On 1 January 2001 the district boundaries were changed again. In a move to cut administrative costs, the previous 23 districts were reduced to 12. Only the densely populated Neukölln, way-out Spandau and the huge Reinickendorf avoided being merged with neighbouring districts. The reorganisation, which was supported by some and opposed by others, has thrown up one or two strange partnerships as well as fused some supposedly like minds. Fancy Schöneberg must share its funds with industrial Tempelhof whereas the former western working-class Kreuzberg finds itself joined with its ex-eastern comrade Friedrichshain.

The government districts of Mitte and Tiergarten are sensibly united, but they find themselves being gooseberried by "red" Wedding. Official sources are keen to emphasise the boundary changes but it is unlikely, at least for the first few years after reform, that the residents will have an affinity for their new partners.

Unfairly avoided by most tourists on a week-long holiday, the outer districts are grouped together in this book according to their area, either East or West. Although it is more than a decade since the Wall fell, one can still notice each Bezirk's Cold War legacy. Whether it be the architecture (Karl-Marx-Allee and Marzahn being two examples of GDR design) or the people – the western districts still have the highest proportions of Turkish immigrants in Berlin – traces of the recent past are still extremely visible.

Finally, there is a chapter on Potsdam, capital of Brandenburg, with the fabulous Schloss Sanssouci making it one of the most interesting cities in Germany. ❏

PRECEDING PAGES: preparing to take to the water.
LEFT: the peaceful schlossgarten at Lübbenau.

NORTHEAST DISTRICTS

This chapter details Pankow's best sites, the Jewish cemetery in Weissensee, and the districts of Marzahn, Hellersdorf and Hohenschönhausen

Map on page 194–95

Upper-class **Pankow** ❶ with around 124,400 inhabitants is Berlin's northernmost district, and has always been a bit grander than its proletarian neighbours, the districts of Wedding and Prenzlauer Berg. Its villa district in Niederschönhausen began to take shape between about 1880 and 1900, as rich Berliners moved out beyond the boundaries of the city.

Nowadays, former SED bigwigs still live in this pleasant neighbourhood, as do the diplomatic representatives of many countries. For reasons of wealth and prestige, therefore, the villas in Pankow were noticeably better maintained than in some other parts of the city but the paint is beginning to peel once more. Town houses are more frequent here than tenements. Among the suburbs on the district's outskirts, with their typical wooden houses, there is still the occasional flash of village character. Fields and allotments characterise the area.

Pankow takes its name from the river Panke which rises at Bernau and winds its way largely underground through Wedding and joins the Spree at Schiffbauerdamm in Berlin Mitte. Formerly a farming village, probably a Slavic settlement, it is officially mentioned for the first time in 1230. At that time there were only a few huts on the village green, which was later renamed Breite Strasse. Around 1800, Pankow had only 286 inhabitants. In 1920, it was incorporated into Greater Berlin.

A walk through Pankow

A short stroll up Berliner Strasse from S & U Bahnhof Pankow, **Breite Strasse** used to be known as Johannes-R.-Becher-Strasse, after the 1920s Expressionist poet who was later the GDR's first Minister for Culture. The **Alte Pfarrkirche** (old parish church) which stands on the village green island in the middle of the street is invariably called the Church of the Four Evangelists and is the oldest building in the district. The eastern part was built in the 14th century from grey stone and the red tower on the west side was added at the turn of the 19th century, which accounts for its rather uneven appearance.

Further along the street, the red-brick **Rathaus Pankow** (town hall), which was built in 1903 in art nouveau style, has increased in significance now that Prenzlauer Berg and Weissensee are both in the administrative district of Pankow.

You can find out more about the history of Pankow in the **Stadtbezirkschronik** (District Museum, open daily; entrance fee) at Heynstrasse 8, near Wollankstrasse. Housed here is Max Skladanowsky's revolutionary invention, the first cinema film. Not as hot on the marketing front as the Lumière brothers, Skladanowsky organised the first Berlin film show in the Winter Gardens in Pankow in 1895. While you

LEFT:
Pankow market.
BELOW:
getting married at
Rathaus Pankow.

are in the area, take a look inside the Hartmann bakery at Wollankstrasse 130, which has a shop counter dating from the turn of the 20th century. Closed since 1964 and reopened in 2000, it sells Christmas decorations and the owners have plans to turn it into a museum of childhood.

Not far away is **Pankow Bürgerpark**, popular with day visitors from Berlin. Through the high gateway, ornamented with figures like an Italian triumphal arch, you find the most romantic surroundings: well-kept gardens, flower beds, fountains, statues of animals, and outdoor cafés, ideal for relaxed coffee-drinking and people-watching. The park radiates a peace regrettably disturbed by aircraft landing at Tegel airport. The Bürgerpark merges with the **Städtischer Friedhof Pankow** (cemetery) and Waldfriedhof park, and eventually runs on to the **Schönholzer Heide** (heath) where there is a cemetery for Soviet soldiers. The heath can be reached from the Bürgerpark via the quiet Bahnhofstrasse between the S-Bahn platforms and the cemetery, where the Wall used to be.

Famous inhabitants

If you pass through the quiet, tree-lined Heinrich-Mann-Platz, you will see Leonhard-Frank-Strasse 11, the once home of Ernst Busch. Busch was one of the many writers and artists who volunteered to fight against the fascists in the Spanish Civil War, but was latterly known as a political songwriter.

A short walk away, at Homeyerstrasse 13, you can find the former apartment of writer Arnold Zweig. In the 1920s many other artists and writers such as Heinz Knobloch, Hans Fallada, Willy Bredel and Arno Holz lived around **Majakowskiring**. After the war, it was home to many GDR-approved people of

BELOW: Schloss Niederschönhausen.

note – the style of the houses point to their privileged position in society. Carl Ossietzky, a winner of the Nobel Peace Prize and publisher of the magazine *Weltbühne*, also lived in Pankow at around this time, in what is now designated Ossietzkystrasse 24-6. Ossietzky was arrested by the Nazis in 1938 and tortured to death. His grave is in Niederschönhausen cemetery on Buchholzer Strasse, alongside that of his wife Maud, who refounded *Weltbühne* in East Berlin in 1946.

Map on page 194–95

Pankow's Schloss Niederschönhausen was the venue for the signing of the treaty to reunify Germany in 1990.

Schloss Niederschönhausen

Pankow's reputation, however, was founded on its castle, **Schloss Niederschönhausen**. The castle is reached from Pankow S and U-Bahn station by tram No. 52 in the direction of Blankenfelde. It was built in 1664 as a country house for Countess Dohna of the house of Holland-Brederode. It was subsequently altered a number of times, until barely anything of the old building remained. At the end of the 18th century, Queen Elisabeth Christine, the unloved wife of Frederick the Great lived in the castle. Between 1945 and 1989 it was used by the East German government to accommodate important guests.

The palace itself is not accessible but the **Schlosspark** (castle grounds), which is open to the public daily during March–Oct, was laid out as a French-style rococo pleasure garden in 1764. In the mid-19th century it was restyled into an English landscape park, with sweeping lawns. The Panke river flows through the park, crossed by several small bridges. On the other side of the street Am Schlosspark is the local landmark, Pankow open-air swimming pool, which was opened in 1960.

Historic buildings

The old village smithy which stood on Dietzgenstrasse in Niederschönhausen was built in 1757 and was Pankpow's oldest building but for safety reasons it had to be pulled down. The **Holländerhaus** (Dutch House), a two-storey patrician house on the junction of Dietzgenstrasse and Platanenstrasse, dates from the same period. At the end of Dietzgenstrasse is the Pankow tram depot, dating from early this century. Berlin's first horse-drawn tram travelled to and from the Rathaus to Gesundbrunnen S-Bahn station in around 1895.

The village churches in Buch and Blankenfelde are 13th-century granite constructions, extended in the 19th century, as is the church at Buchholz, known as Französische (French) Buchholz after a group of Huguenots established themselves there in 1688. Between Rosenthal and Blankenfelde there is a **Botanischer Garten** (botanical garden; open daily; entrance fee). Completed in the mid-1990s, it has a tropical greenhouse and a palm house.

BELOW: Rudolf Dörrier chronicled Pankow's history.

Weissensee

On the northeastern edge of the city is the district of **Weissensee ❷**, hemmed in by Pankow to the west, Prenzlauer Berg to the south, Marzahn to the east and Lichtenberg to the southeast. Visitors without cars should take the S-Bahn to Greifswalder Str. and then board one of the numerous tram trains that travel out from the city centre every five minutes heading for the Berliner Allee. A lot of routes go via Antonplatz, straight to the small-town dream-world of Weissensee. The low rows of houses which line the main roads are relieved now and then by modern looking four- or five-storey buildings. In spite of the many colourful window displays in the shops, some still adjusting to a market economy, and the bright signs luring customers to restaurants and little cafés, the facades arouse little interest. Weissensee was viewed as a suburb by the old city fathers, and had no significance either as a showcase or as a prestige district.

The history of Weissensee

The little Brandenburg village is mentioned for the first time in 1313. In the late-Middle Ages three manors emerged from the settlement. In 1745, von Nüssler, the head of the area, united these manors under his control. After its sale in 1872 the estate of Weissensee came into the possession of the powerful merchant Adolf Schön, who speculated with the land during the industrial boom, in order to build tenements. In 1872 the settlement of Neu Weissensee was founded to the southwest of the old village. This became an independent district in 1880 and was united with Weissensee in 1905. The extended district was chiefly populated by the working classes.

The amalgamation of the villages of Weissensee, Hohenschönhausen, Malchow, Wartenberg and Falkenberg followed in 1920. Currently the district covers an area of over 30 sq. km (11.3 sq. miles) and is home to 74,948 people. Weissensee offers plenty of contrasts: factories and commercial concerns, workshops, nurseries, small farms, quiet leafy residential streets, allotment

BELOW: proud garden owner in Weissensee.

gardens, picturesque parks, lakes and ponds. The most important stretch of water is the **Weisser See**, originally the Grossen See, which covers 10 hectares (25 acres) to the west of the Berliner Allee.

Map on page 194–95

A walk through Weissensee

At first sight the lake takes you by surprise: a floating classical fountain in the midst of fields, poplars and robinias, and a very popular recreation area. The park was founded in 1859, together with a country house which in 1874 was to become the venue for the famous Sternecker fireworks displays.

On the eastern side of the lake there is an open-air swimming pool with a man-made sandy beach beside it. Boats for hire, rose gardens, an open-air stage, an animal zoo designed for children, a large playground, a paddling pool and a sunbathing area: everything that visitors, especially with families, might need in order to unwind.

Nearby at Berliner Allee 185 is the **Brecht-Haus Weissensee** (tel: 926 80 44) where Bertolt Brecht and his wife Helene Weigel lived before they moved to Mitte. These days it is used as a gallery and for various cultural gatherings.

Where Falkenbergerstrasse joins the Berliner Allee lies the original site of the village meadow of Weissensee. Here stands the largely medieval church, which was extended to its present size in 1863 and 1899. The architect Bruno Taut left his legacy in Buschallee when he designed this row of houses, around 1 km long, which were built between 1926 and 1930 and stretch almost to Hohenschön-hausen. On the other side of the lake, at Parkstrasse 82, is **Rathaus Weissensee** (town hall). Immediately outside the front door is another picturesque pond in a parkland setting. The district council buildings were built by Mettmann in

BELOW: Brecht-Haus Weissensee.

At the entrance to Jüdischer Friedhof Weissensee are plaques commemorating Jews who died during the Holocaust.

BELOW:
walking through Jüdischer Friedhof Weissensee.

1929 as a school and are a classic example of the architectural style known as New Objectivity. In Pistoriusstrasse is the **Kreuz-pfuhl**, a park with a pond, surrounded by four-storey red brick buildings with ornamental gables, curved balconies, decorative brickwork and large leafy courtyards. The estate, built between 1908 and 1910 as part of a communal "forum" but never finished, was set out by architect Karl James Bühring. Structurally interesting, it is a valuable document of social history and a pleasant contrast to the usual city tenements.

North of the Weisser See, off Rennbahnstrasse, in the Radrennbahn Weissensee, was an open-air cycle racing track which could seat 9,000 spectators. The area around the racecourse became a home for bike enthusiasts, and also a venue for various rock extravaganzas (the SED drafted in ZZ Top and James Brown to play here) and other entertainment. After the discovery of harmful substances in the ground in the mid-1990s, the stadium was shut down for renovation. It opened again in 2001 and has mainly become a venue for football and athletics meetings.

Weissensee's Jewish cemetery

In the past, the Berlin authorities moved the city's cemeteries out to Weissenhof. One of the most important from a cultural and historical perspective is the **Jüdischer Friedhof Weissensee** (Jewish Cemetery; Herbert-Baum-Strasse; open Mon–Thur and Sun 8am–5pm, Fri 8am–3pm; men must cover their heads before entering the cemetery grounds).

Berlin's Jewish community, which by 1880 had reached over 65,000, bought the 40-hectare (100-acre) plot because they were running out of space in the old cemetery on what is now Schönhauser Allee. At that time it would

have been far away from the city gates. The architect Hugo von Licht was responsible for the design of the yellow brick entrance, which still survives in more or less its original state. The famous names on the family graves give an indication of the Jewish contribution to the economic, scientific, spiritual and artistic might of Berlin.

Among those buried here are: Hermann Cohen (d. 1918, philosopher); Eugen Goldstein (d. 1930, physicist); Lesser Ury (d. 1931, artist, impressionist and member of the Berlin secession); Rudolf Mosse (d. 1920, newspaper advertiser and publisher of the *Berliner Tageblatt*); Samuel Fischer (d. 1934, publisher and founder of S. Fischer Verlag); Lina Morgenstern (d. 1909, women's rights campaigner and a socially committed writer who founded the first Women Workers' Educational Society and was on the committee of the German Peace Group); and last but not least the founders of the two large and well-known Berlin department stores, Adolph Jandorff (d. 1931, KaDeWe) and Hermann Tietz (d. 1907, father of the Her-Tie group). Near the main entrance is the grave of the Jewish resistance fighter Herbert Baum (d. 1943).

Another Jewish cemetery can be found to the east on Wittlicher Strasse just east of the Weisser See. This belongs to the Orthodox Jewish community Adass Jisroel, and was closed by the East Berlin authorities in the mid-1970s. It subsequently fell into disrepair and has only recently been restored.

While Weissensee itself is an industrial and residential area, Falkenberg, Malchow and Wartenberg are more rural. A large part of East Berlin's farming land is centred here, and is used mainly for vegetables.

The Berliner Allee leads north to **Malchow**. The former landmark of the town, the imposing tower of the 13th-century church, was blown up in the last days of the war. Only a few segments of wall betray the existence of the sacred building. The late Romantic 13th-century church in nearby Wartenberg met a similar fate: it was destroyed in an air raid in 1945. Even less remains of the church in Falkenberg. The mother of Alexander and Wilhelm von Humboldt had the tower constructed in 1795 and a family vault built for herself and her two husbands on their death.

Marzahn

The district of **Marzahn ❸** was founded in 1979 and 138,600 people live here, housed in 60,000 apartments. The neighbouring districts of Hohenschönhausen and Hellersdorf were founded between 1985 and 1986. Today, 109,800 and 127,700 people (respectively) live in the area: some were here before the new districts were founded, but three-quarters of them have moved here since 1979. In particular, young families with children have settled here.

This satellite town in East Berlin was the heartland of an ambitious housing programme devised by the East German government and designed to eliminate the housing shortage in the GDR by 1990. Building workers from all over East Germany were assembled to turn the project into reality. There was no time for town planning, nor was there the scope or materials for anything other than rows of high-rise blocks. Boxlike houses, known as "six-floorers", "10-floorers"

Map on page 194–95

BELOW: housing estate in Marzahn district.

and 30-storey "beacons" were pieced together like a jigsaw on the drawing board into entire housing estates, together with the usual shopping centres and hospitals, crèches and schools.

There's a good overall view of the new estates from the vantage point of three "rubble mountains" which stand on the border between Marzahn and Hellersdorf: Ahrendsfelder Berg in the north, Hellersdorfer Berg alongside the Berlin Garden Show grounds, and the hill alongside Wuhletal S-Bahn station. The flat, scarred landscape is broken only by the concrete mountains of high-rise towers.

During its first few years, Marzahn was denounced as "the largest concrete desert in Europe", a political project that had completely failed to take into account the human needs of the residents. People moved into the flats before the roads were tarmacked. There was no street lighting, no playgrounds, no trees, no grass, not even any shops. In spite of this, it proved a popular choice for many because of the modern amenities available inside the flats.

Today, however, few people would leave the PDS stronghold of Marzahn. (In the 1999 parliamentary elections, over 44 percent of people living in Marzahn voted for the successor to the SED.) Local facilities have been sorted out, and the people are proud of their district, for it is they who have made it habitable. Trees and flower beds were planted, cables laid for street lighting, and inner courtyards and entrance halls painted. In addition, there was a wide range of cultural activities on offer in the Kulturhaus (community arts centre) and the youth clubs, which also attracted members from other areas.

If you want to discover Marzahn it is best to do it on foot. The best points to start a walk are from Springpfuhl or Marzahn S-Bahn stations. Here you'll find

Mahlsdorf, 5 km (3 miles) from Marzahn, is home to Gründerzeitmuseum (guided tours Wed and Sun 10am–6pm; entrance fee) which houses a collection of artefacts and furniture from the Gründerzeit showing the expansion of Berlin in the late 19th century.

BELOW: Marzahn high-rise developments.

Helene-Weigel-Platz and the Marzahner Promenade, the two shopping and recreation centres of the new district with a variety of shops and department stores, galleries and cafés. Just north of here is **Alt-Marzahn**, the Old Town.

Map on page 194–95

A walk through Marzahn

Hemmed in by the high-rise blocks, Marzahn's old town, is a wonderful little village built around a village green which was mentioned for the first time in the 14th century. Excavations have also uncovered traces of early history, remains of pre-Christian settlements and an 8,000-year-old stag mask. The village was painstakingly restored in tandem with the construction of the new estates.

On the old village street stands August Stüler's lovely brick church, and some 60 houses and courtyards from the mid-19th century, among them the village inn, Marzahner Krug, and the **Friseurmuseum** (hairdressing museum; open Tues–Thur 10am–6pm, Sun 1–5pm; entrance fee).

A few minutes' walk from Alt-Marzahn, on the Blumberger Damm, is a side entrance to the showgrounds of the **Berliner Gartenschau** (Garden Show; open daily). For a minimal entry charge you can visit the show gardens (now called Erholungspark Marzahn), special displays and water fountains. For children, there are playgrounds and a children's zoo, where they can stroke the patient goats. The showground is easily accessible on foot from the new S-Bahn and U-Bahn station at Wuhletal.

Standing on the station platforms it is possible to view the fertile ground and varied vegetation, running alongside the new housing estates at Hellersdorf, 1 km (half-a-mile) wide. From the Wuhlgarten, a thickly wooded park, peer the ruined church tower and neo-Romanesque dome of a castle-like building. This

BELOW: public transport is good in the outer districts.

Map on page 194–95

is part of the Central Clinic for Psychiatry and Neurology. Patients live in neat brick villas set among high trees, and the public are free to wander where they like in the beautiful grounds.

Hellersdorf and Hohenschönhausen

Alternatively, the visitor can take the opposite direction from Wuhletal station and go towards Kaulsdorf and Mahlsdorf. Both places belong to the new district of **Hellersdorf** ❹. As in neighbouring Biesdorf, which also comes under Marzahn, courtyards and villas, houses and gardens from the turn of the century are typical. The village is on the main road to Frankfurt and has views across cornfields to the countryside.

An attraction of particular interest is the **Schloss Biesdorf**, a small castle in the centre of the historical village which was built in 1868 in late classical style. It was owned until 1927 by the industrialist Werner von Siemens, who experimented with wireless telegraphy from the castle tower. The castle now houses Marzahn's arts centre.

North of Kaulsdorf and Mahlsdorf is the Hellersdorf Development Zone. Often compared with Marzahn a few years back, it is actually better than its awful reputation.

The contrast between rural communities and satellite towns common to all three new districts, is less obvious in **Hohenschönhausen** ❺, because of its proximity to the city centre. The names of its four neighbourhoods – Falkenberg, Hohenschönhausen, Malchow and Wartenberg – come from the original Middle Age villages. Sports enthusiasts should go to the **Berlin Sportforum** (associated with Weissensee but actually in Hohenschönhausen), which covers an area of 45 hectares (110 acres). The sports hall, together with the swimming centre and the ice stadium, are occasionally used for major sporting events, tel: 91 17 00 for details.

If you want to be shocked, visit the **Gedenkstätte Berlin-Hohenschönhausen** (Genslerstr. 66; open Mon–Fri 9am6pm, Sat 9am–4pm; guided tours are available by appointment tel 98 24 219; Mon–Thur 11am, Fri–Sat 11am and 1pm). Another memorial site to Berlin's murky past, it started its life as "Spezial-lager Nr. 3", a pre-trial confinement camp. It later became a prison, first for the Soviets and then for the Stasi until 1989 and was notorious for the torture that was carried out behind its cold walls.

Excursions

If you have the time, take a trip to the Malchower See, which lies between the new estates at Wartenberg and the old village of Malchow. On the way, you will see the prettiest corner of the whole district, the area around **Orankesee** and **Obersee** which contains some lakes set in lovely countryside and a villa district.

Further on you will come upon a jumble of well-tended allotments, cemeteries, blocks of flats, 19th-century tenements, factories and shopping streets – surrounded by greenery. In the nature reserve around **Fauler See** you can listen to the chorus of more than 100 species of birds. ❑

BELOW: the countryside is never far away.
RIGHT: Jüdischer Friedhof Weissensee (the Jewish cemetery in Weissensee).

SOUTHEAST DISTRICTS

*This chapter takes visitors through a relaxed tour of Köpenick,
Berlin's lake district, Trepow, Lichtenberg and on to
the chilling museum of the Stasi headquarters*

Map
on page
194–95

East Berlin's largest district is familiar to the rest of the world only for the
pranks of the cobbler Wilhelm Voigt, the "Captain of Köpenick". However,
Köpenick ❻ has more to offer than this tragi-comedy from the days of the
German Empire. Now merged with Treptow, it is Berlin's greenest district with
woods and lakes covering three-quarters of the once-independent district in the
southeast of the metropolis, between the river Dahme and the Spree. There is
also plenty to see here: the historic old town, the castle island, the regatta course
at Grünau, the open-air pools by the lakes and the Müggelberge hills with their
numerous inns. In addition, some large businesses, such as the VEB Oberspree
cable factory (known as AEG before the war), boatyards and clothing manufac-
turers have moved in on the edge of the district.

Köpenick's old town

Köpenick was officially mentioned for the first time in 1209. Archaeological
excavations, however, have ascertained that a stronghold stood here as early as
the year 800. The town of Köpenick apparently did not receive its charter until
around 1300, but no record remains of this event.

In the middle of the old town centre, where the river Dahme joins the Spree,
is the brick Rathaus and its red tower. In 1904, barely
two years after its completion, the town hall became
famous the world over when the unemployed cobbler
Voigt marched on it in a borrowed captain's uniform,
with an escort of soldiers whom he had picked up off
the streets. Voigt had the mayor arrested and took control of the town coffers, in order to obtain a pass. He
was soon caught but the story swept around the world
as a striking example of the Prussian propensity to
follow without question anyone in uniform. The
emperor himself is said to have laughed over the trick.
Carl Zuckmayer's farce based on the event, *Der
Hauptmann von Köpenick (The Captain of Köpenick)*,
was premiered in Berlin in 1931.

Immediately next to the **Rathaus** (town hall),
alongside Luisenhain, the tourist steamers of the
Weisse Flotte (White Fleet; Lange Brücke; tel: 0331-
275 92 10) dock several times daily, although only
from May to September. In good weather, it's always
worth taking a ride through the sprawling countryside in the direction of Müggelsee, Woltersdorf or
Schmöckwitz – coffee and cakes are included in your
ticket. Meanwhile, confirmed land-lubbers may like to
take a look around the Protestant church next to the
neo-Gothic Rathaus, which dates from 1841, and the
Heimat Museum (local museum; open daily except
Fri and Sun; entrance fee) in the Rathaus, which documents the story of the Captain of Käpewick.

PRECEDING PAGES:
Schloss Köpenick.
LEFT: Schloss
Friedrichsfelde.
BELOW:
Rathaus Köpenick.

From the Rathaus, cross the busy Müggelheimer Strasse to reach the old **Köpenicker Kiez**, the grey single-storey, badly neglected, dwellings which line a cobbled street date in part from the 17th and 18th century. The houses back onto the Frauentog, a bay that separates the Schlossinsel from the mainland, where Köpenick's fishermen formerly cast their nets. The Kiez – the word comes from the Slavonic Chyza, meaning "hut" – was built in 1260. The baths on the Dahme River behind were closed down after the purity of the water was found to be questionable.

Schloss Köpenick

A narrow wooden bridge leads over to the **Schlossinsel** (Castle Island), the site of the Wendenschloss, which was built on stilts around AD 825. A few remains of the castle have been uncovered, but sadly they are no longer on display. Around 1100, the castle was run by the legendary Count Jaczo de Copanic. Count Jaczo won hegemony in Brandenburg by defeating the Christian army of the Askanian Albrecht the Bear. In 1157 Albrecht succeeded in ousting Jaczo from Köpenick. After the battle in Gross-Glienicke, he is alleged to have swum the Havel on his horse. He hung his shield and hunting horn on an oak on Schildhorn peninsula – in what is now the Grunewald – and was converted to Christianity, as he had sworn he would if he was fortunate enough to survive.

The Wendenschloss was pulled down in the mid-16th century. Today, the only reminders of the lost castle are the signposts pointing "Zum Wenden-schloss" ("To Wendenschloss"). These signs direct you to the villa neighbour-hood of the same name and to a freshwater swimming pool, by the side of which you can obtain refreshments. In 1558, Elector Joachim II built a splendid

BELOW:
Friedrichshagen waterworks, erected in 1893 in English country-house Gothic-style.

moated castle on the same spot, but this didn't last for long either. The present baroque pile was built for the Grand Elector Friedrich Wilhelm by architect Rutger von Langerfeld between 1677 and 1682. There's a particularly fine view of the warm yellow facade from the water. In 1806 the French laid waste to Köpenick during their campaign towards Moscow, and occupied the castle. From 1830 to 1848, after the war of liberation against Napoleon, it served the Prussians as a prison for young rebels, and was later used as a teaching college and a student hostel.

Map on page 194–95

The castle was first restored after World War II. Today, three floors of the extravagant rococo interior house the **Kunstgewerbemuseum Standort Köpenick** (Museum of Arts and Crafts; the museum is closed until 2004 for renovation). The museum's collection includes wood-carved antique furniture, which includes a wonderful Biedermeier desk with inlaid panels and countless secret drawers, tiled stoves, porcelain, glass, silverware and Empress Griselda's famous jewellery from the 11th century.

Before restoration, regular weekend chamber concerts were held in the restored chapel throughout July and August, and, on the stage outside, evening serenades were performed under the open skies.

Close to the S-Bahn station on the Spree, opposite the island with the tree nursery, is the **Platz des 23. April** which commemorates the anniversary of Köpenick's "liberation" by the Soviet army, while a stone column 6 metres (20 ft) high recalls the *Köpenicker Blutwoche* (Köpenick Bloody Week) in June 1933, when 90 people, mostly communists and social democrats, were murdered by Hitler's SA. The monument depicts a symbolically clenched, raised fist. Behind are reliefs from everyday life in the Democratic Republic.

BELOW:
Schloss Köpenick.

In the northwest of Köpenick, on the border with Lichtenberg, is the Volkspark Wuhlheide, an idyllic area of woodland where you will find the **Freizeit- und Erholungszentrum Wuhlheide** (FEZ; tel: 5307 1146; open Tues–Sun 10am–6pm, Sat from 1pm; entrance fee), a children's recreational centre. Attractions here include a small lake, a mini-tourist village and a disco to enable Berlin's kids to let off steam. The very young will love the Pioniereisenbahn, a narrow-gauge railway that runs 7-km (5-mile) circuits of the grounds.

The **Gendenkstätte Köpenicker Blutwoche** (Memorial to the Köpenick Blood Week; Puchanstrasse 12; open daily Tues, Thur and Sat). This memorial museum documents the terror tactics by which the SA eliminated their political opponents in Köpenick during the Spring of 1933. These opponents included members of the KPD (Communist party), SPD (Social Democratic Party), Jewish citizens and Union members. The SA killed, wounded, tortured and imprisoned over 300 members of the then predominantly middle-class, professional community. The prisoners were tried and held in the court building, that had, like several other establishments in Köpenick and indeed all over Berlin, been annexed by the SA to be used to implement their National Socialist ends.

The complex still stands, having been used in the 1960s and 1970s as a wardrobe depot for the East German television industry. It was dedicated to the memory of "Anti-Fascist Opposition in Köpenick" in the 1980s, and in 1993 opened in its present form under the care of the local department for sport and culture. The exhibition is informative and well presented (although all in German), and provides a demonstration of how formerly misused buildings can, when preserved, serve as the best form of memorial.

BELOW: watersports on the Müggelsee.

Müggelsee and environs

Three kilometres (nearly 2 miles) southeast of Köpenick lies Berlin's largest lake, **Müggelsee ❼**, covering an area of 7 sq. metres (8 sq. yds). It is also the city's main supply of drinking water. For years it has been threatened by an acute pollution problem, and motorboats were banned in 1989. Along the shore, several not particularly cheap restaurants, such as the Müggelseeperle and the Rübezahl, invite day-trippers to partake of their hearty fare. By the freshwater swimming pool on the west beach, the Spree River flows out of the lake.

Located midway between the town of Köpenick and the Müggelsee, **Friedrichshagen ❽** was founded in 1753 by Friedrich II as a spinners' village. At this time the whole of Köpenick was experiencing a boom as a centre of the textile industry, particularly of silk spinning. The avenue of 200-year-old Chinese mulberry trees on Bölschestrasse, now in a sorry state, is all that remains as a reminder of these affluent days. Before the turn of the century, many artists and anarchists moved in to the little village, which at that time couldn't be reached by road.

Among them was Gustav Landauer, who published the magazine *Der Sozialist* and is said to have answered the telephone with the words: "This is the revolution – who's that?", but this could be apocryphal. Gerhard Hauptmann also lived here for a time.

The community, known as the Friedrichshagener Dichterkreis (Poets' Circle), flourished for a while, but after 1900 it slowly broke up. Nowadays, Friedrichshagen is country-cottage territory, as too is Rahnsdorf which lies between the eastern side of Müggelsee and the Müggelspree. From Rahnsdorf S-Bahn station you can take an immaculate, almost 100-year-old tram to Woltersdorf, a rather sleepy place on the banks of the Flakensee.

Map on page 194–95

South of the Müggelsee, in the middle of the vast **Berliner Stadtwald** (Berlin city forest), loom the Müggelberge hills, another favourite with day-trippers from Berlin. When it snows in winter you can even sledge here. The hills rise to 110 metres (360 ft) above the mirror of the lake. In Brandenburg terms, that's almost Alpine. On a clear day there's a wonderful view from the Müggelturm (tower) all the way from the radio tower at Königswusterhausen to the Rüdersdorf cement works. Unfortunately, Köpenick's woodland and its recreational facilities are having their tranquillity rapidly destroyed; the area is now the preserve of the whole population of Berlin, and people flock here on the weekend in huge numbers.

Langer See, Seddinsee, Zeuthener See

The three lakes of Langer, Seddinsee and Zeuthener converge on the old fishing village of **Schmöckwitz ❾**, southeast of Köpenick town which has been settled since prehistoric times. Seddinsee to the east is linked to Müggelsee by the Gosener Kanal; Langer See to the west flows into the Dahme, with the result that it is possible to make a relaxing circular trip by boat, starting from Köpenick. In June each year the Grünau international rowing regatta takes place on Langer See. You can hire rowing boats in the summer to cross the lake.

BELOW: riverside restaurant.

Treptow

The sculpture of two wrestlers, known as Molecule Man, is by Jonathan Borofsky. The sculpture measures 30 metres (98 ft) above water, it is situated at a former meeting point of East and West and represents human relationships.

BELOW: a system of canals connects Berlin's waterways with the industrial quarter of Treptow – here, the Kabelwerk Oberspree (KWO) cable factory.

In the district of **Treptow** , economic prosperity and leisure are interwoven with the more sorry aspects of the city of Berlin. Spacious parks on the banks of the Spree, heavily built-up industry along the Landwehr canal and, as a historical reminder, the Sowjetisches Ehrenmal (Soviet memorial). The district's symbol today is the Allianz building and the stainless steel wrestlers rising out of the Spree, an impressive first glimpse of Berlin as you cross the Ironbridge at Ostkreuz arriving by train from the south east.

In 1261, Margrave Otto III donated the heath to the town of Cölln and in 1435 it was extended to become the 1,200-hectare (3,000-acre) Cölln Heath, by the purchase of lands belonging to the Tempelhof order. In 1568 the fishing community of "Trepkow" is officially mentioned for the first time. It first appears as "Treptow" in 1740. The Spree's supplies of fish, naturally good lines of communication, the man-made waterways of the Landwehr, Spree and Teltow canals, as well as the forest, provided a variety of commercial opportunities.

At the beginning of the last century and in the years of industrialisation, they contributed to Treptow's economic growth. The timber, chemical and metal industries continue to dominate the economic face and the infrastructure of the district. Industrial development along the Landwehr Kanal, the Wiener and the Schlesische Brücke began as early as 1750, with the construction of the Lohmühlen (tanneries). After 1871, a number of industrial enterprises were established here. The Elektro-Apparat-Werke site north of Treptower Park S-Bahn, which was later extended to become an electrical appliance factory for AEG, was one of East Berlin's largest firms, employing 10,000 people. Treptow's popularity with Berliners and tourists alike is based on its spacious parks.

Treptow's parks

Treptower Park (open Wed–Sun 2–6.30pm; guided tours Thur 8pm, weekends 3pm) which covers 230 hectares (570 acres), stretches northwards from Bulgarische Strasse on either side of the plantane-lined Puschkinallee. Plänterwald lies between Neue Krugallee and the Spree. Whereas in the past, summer holiday-makers and those in search of recreation would be driven in their horse-drawn carriages out beyond the city gates to Treptow, now the S-Bahn (Treptower Park station) is the simplest way to reach the green lung on the banks of the Spree and the Berlin stop of the Weisse Flotte (White Fleet).

To the left of the S-Bahn station are the jetties, from where passenger "steamers" chug up and down the Spree. These run during the summer, offering tours of the eastern waterways. You can walk upriver along the airy, wide promenades to the Rosengarten (Rose Garden). The lawns, copper beeches, chestnuts and plantanes, along with the immaculate gardens, provide landscape designers and sculptors with an inspirational backdrop for the regular summer and autumn exhibitions of flowers and sculpture. People stroll, amble, jog and skateboard through the grounds. In spite of its neat, "cultivated" air, this green corner provides space for a wide variety of plants and trees, to the joy of conservationists and ornithologists. Further down the bank, past the restaurants, is the Abteiinsel, a small island linked to the bank by a swing bridge. Among its attractions are an open-air theatre and a large bathing beach, as well as boats for hire.

Pisa is not the only place with a leaning tower. If you look out over the Spree from the Rosengarten, you'll see on the opposite bank behind the trees, the tower of the 15th-century **Alt-Stralau** (Old Stralau) village church. It was displaced in an air raid in 1945 and has tilted ever since. Further along the river

Map on page 194–95

Weisse Flotte is a Potsdam-based boat cruise company. Tel: 0331-275 9210 for details.

BELOW: Treptow's Sowjetisches Ehrenmal (Soviet Memorial).

Statue of a kneeling soldier at the Sowjetisches Ehrenmal (Soviet Memorial).

bank is the Zenner Restaurant, a popular place to drive out to for a meal. In 1602 the local authority bought a fishing hut on this spot, and the occupants ran a bar here. In 1702 a brewery was added, and then a century later Carl Ferdinand Langhans built the Neue Gasthaus an der Spree in place of the Spreebudike. The inn, which was regarded as very elegant at the time, opened its doors on 11 June 1822. It was later given the name Zenner after one of its landlords.

Past Bulgarische Strasse you come to the old Kaiserbad and the terraces of the Spree. There's a lovely view from here over Stralau, Abtei and the little islands in the Spree. From here it's not far to the 12-hectare (30-acre) **Spree-Park** (open daily March–Oct; entrance fee), stretching to the north of the Plänterwald. In the past this was where the Berliners' Rummel, or annual fair, was held. Nowadays, bumper cars, colourful carousels and other rides spin non-stop from spring to autumn. The landmark of the Spree-park is a 45-metre (150-ft) giant ferris wheel, with 40 cars. Over a million visitors flock here every year. Further south is an open-air stage and various sports pitches.

The Sowjetisches Ehrenmal (Soviet Memorial)

In the part of Treptower Park away from the Spree, to the right of Puschkinallee, is the imposing **Sowjetisches Ehrenmal** (Soviet Memorial), constructed between 1946 and 1949. This is the major monument in Berlin to the 5,000 Red Army soldiers who fell in the Battle for Berlin in 1945.

The monument has a scale all of its own, as if harmonising with the distant architecture of the fatherland. At the southern end, carved from a 50-tonne granite block, is the kneeling figure of Mother Russia; she has no inscription, her silence is immense. Southwards, along a corridor of silver birches, are two walls of red granite, parted in the middle; representing Soviet flags lowered in mourning and they are said to resemble wings or cliffs. Through the flags the viewer glimpses the Hill of Honour, and the figure of the soldier, child under one arm, swastika underfoot, rising above the tree line.

A series of white tombs, each carrying a relief and inscription of Stalin's words, border the expanse leading up to the mausoleum. Having climbed the narrow steps, the viewer can look back over the monument, under the protective shadow, as it were, of the Red Army soldier. Today's visitor still gains a sense of the ideological power the monument must have conveyed through the architectural grandeur alone. Three wreaths are maintained here by the embassies of Russia, Belarus and Kazakhstan.

Further north, past the picturesque Karpfenteich (Carp Pond) ringed with beautiful ancient trees, you come to **Archenhold-Sternwarte** observatory (open Mon–Thur 2–5.30pm, Fri–Sun 2–7.30pm; demonstrations Wed 6pm, weekend 3pm; entrance fee). The observatory, which opened in 1896, owes its existence not to its trades fair but rather to the financial generosity of the people of Berlin, and to the enthusiasm of its founder, the astronomer Friedrich Simon Archenhold. The 21-metre (68-ft) long, 130-tonne giant outdoor telescope is claimed to be the longest refracting telescope in the world. In 1959 it was

Map on page 194–95

expanded to include a Zeiss planetarium, which can project the movement of around 5,000 stars on its heavenly dome which measures 6 metres (20 ft) in diameter. In addition, the observatory also possesses a reflector telescope and a code-refractor. Since 1970 it has also housed a research department for history and astronomy. Near the observatory is the Hain der Kosmonauten with busts of Yuri Gagarin and the GDR's own cosmonaut, Sigmund Jähn.

Lichtenberg

Lichtenberg , now merged with Hohenschönhausen, is an industrial and working-class district, one of the most densely populated in the east. Lichtenberg was almost completely destroyed during the war and the area was rebuilt as a residential district during the expansionist period in the 1970s. Housing here today is still predominantly public, nearly all of it high-rise. The blocks have modernised sanitation and amenities, along with colourful new cladding. The architectural contrast between East and West Berlin is nowhere more clear than in Lichtenberg. While West Berlin was compelled to build inwards, there were no outer limits in the East; the architects' brief was build big, build fast, and build outwards.

Although the architecture creates a degree of space unthinkable in Western cities, the effect is to remove public life from the streets. In its place are the newly opened shopping centres (Ring Centre Frankfurter Allee, Forum Centre Landsburger Allee) which the East Berliners have taken to in a big way – most will say they approve of Sunday opening hours, with none of the disdain shown by those for whom consumer goods have always been a fact of life. Outside the centres, the area is silent, apart from the constant traffic, which flows through Lichtenburg on its way elsewhere. You either don't mind this architecture or you hate it, but a walk down Frankfurter Allee and its environs is essential to an understanding of the dichotomies that have formed Berlin and continue to shape the lifestyles of its diverse inhabitants.

BELOW: Karlshorst racecourse.

A walk around Lichtenberg

There is a place in Lichtenberg which local historians credit as being the "cradle of the district". This is Loeperplatz, on what is now Möllendorffstrasse, where there's an early **Gothic church** (1250) on the former village green. The church is well preserved and the square around it well cared for. But in the rush hour the green is little more than a forlorn island in a sea of traffic. The village is officially mentioned for the first time in 1288, but it did not receive a town charter until 1907.

The imposing brick **Rathaus** (town hall) was built a few years before, also on Möllendorffstrasse.

In 1920 Lichtenberg became part of Berlin. The marsh land, fields, and coniferous and deciduous forests had long since given way to tenements and smoking chimneys. Only Friedrichsfelde and Karlshorst retained their village character. Since the beginning of this century, the district of Lichtenberg has been home to working-class people, many of them very poor. The closest you'll probably get to the atmosphere of those long ago years is the area around Tuchollaplatz (between Rummelsburg and Nöldnerplatz S-Bahn stations), which was spared in the war. The painter and artist Heinrich Zille lived here for almost 20 years. Many of his drawings are rooted in this neighbourhood, in the plight of the poor, the grimy streets and the grey, treeless world where children would play. In recent years part of this area has been given a make-over.

Friedrichsfelde

Founded in 1955, the **Tierpark Friedrichsfelde** (Tierpark Zoo; Am Tierpark 125; open daily 9am–5pm; entrance fee) now keeps over 900 species in an area twice the size of the Zoologischer Garten, making it one of the largest zoos in Europe. It is beloved by Berliners young and old, who can wander along the winding paths through the estate and be amazed at the animals appearing at every turn. Peacocks roam the woodlands, animal calls ring out over the meadows, and bronze sculptures line the paths. (The bronze used for the sculpture of the lions was recycled from a bust of Stalin formerly on Karl-Marx-Allee, molten down during de-Stalinisation).

The racecourse at Karlshot holds races every Sat at 2pm and Tues at 6pm. Tel: 50 01 70 for details.

The big cats, fast asleep or furiously pacing their enclosures; the elephants, playing to the adoring crowds at bath time; the giraffes, as shy as schoolgirls; all are well represented and in good condition. More rare for a city zoo are the bison and buffalo, and the sea cow, next-of-kin to the elephant. Bird lovers will be delighted: Tierpark keeps a large variety of exotic birds, as well as eagles, vultures and owls. There is a "stroking area" where children can get to know the goats and sheep. There is so much to see that a full day is barely enough; parents with children may want to hire a baby wagon for the day.

BELOW:
statue at Schloss Friedrichsfelde.

Also of interest is the **Schloss Friedrichsfelde** (open Tues–Sun 10am–6pm; entrance fee) at the north entrance, built in the late 17th century in the style of a Dutch country house. The last owners of the castle and park were the lords of Tresckow. One member of this family was among the officers who made the failed assassination attempt on Hitler on 20 July 1944 and who were later sentenced to death. The castle was restored in the 1960s and the early 1970s. The rooms are now used as a wallpaper museum, and chamber concerts are sometimes held in the evenings.

Karlshorst

Not far from the zoo, in Karlshorst, the racecourse was built. Bets were being taken here back in the days of the German empire. Diagonally opposite the entrance to the racecourse you can see a large, rather dilapidated wooden building. This is Rennbahn Station where the emperor always used to alight whenever he came to the race meetings. The notice of surrender was signed in the villa at the end of Rheinsteinstrasse on 9 May 1945. The house used to function as a commemorative museum administered jointly by Russians and Germans. In 1995, on the fiftieth anniversary of the surrender, a new exhibition which downgraded the former emphasis on Soviet army history was displayed in what is now the **Museum Berlin Karlshorst** (open Tues–Sun 10am–6pm).

Gedenkstätte der Sozialisten (Socialist's Memorial)

The **Gedenkstätte der Sozialisten**, (Socialist's Memorial; open daily) is in the Zentral Fiedhof Friedrichsfelde, East Berlin's main cemetery, a short walk from Lichtenberg S- and U- Bahn station. Rosa Luxemburg and Karl Liebknecht were buried here in January 1919, having been murdered by officers of the Reichswehr. Several years later, the German Communist Party had a memorial built on this spot. The simple structure, created by architect Mies van der Rohe, consists of a circular wall around a 4-metre (17-ft) high porphyritic stone, bearing the inscription *Die Toten mahnen uns (The Dead Remind Us)*. The monument was ceremonially unveiled in 1926.

The Nazis destroyed the memorial but it was rebuilt after the war. Numerous tablets were added to commemorate murdered anti-fascists and victims of the Spanish Civil War. Over the years, the Socialists' Memorial became the burial ground of the party elite. Wilhelm Pieck, Otto Grotewohl, Walter Ulbricht, Ernst Thalmann and Franz Mehring are all buried here.

These figures play an iconic role in the contemporary left wing movement in Berlin, and the PDS, the leadership party in Prenzlauer Berg, maintain a wreath at the memorial. Every January a 50,000 strong procession goes through the city in commemoration of the murder of "Karl and Rosa", and their memory, or legend, provides a unifying banner for a party two-thirds of whose support is over 60 years old.

Map on page 194–95

Stasi headquarters

Not far from the Magdalenenstrasse U-Bahn station is the **Forschungs- und Gedenkstätte Normannenstrasse** (ASTAK; Research and Memorial Foundation Normannenstrasse; tel: 030-553 68 54; open Mon–Fri 11am–6pm, weekend 2–6pm; entrance fee; guided tours in English can be arranged within a week's notice), part of the former residency of the despised ministry for State Security for the GDR and its secret service, the Stasi.

Presided over by the shadowy figure of Erich Mielke and established in the mid-1950s the Stasi continued to pursue and persecute "class enemies from outside and within" until the the collapse of the SED in 1989. During "the peaceful revolution" the site became a focal point for demonstrations against the regime, and was eventually stormed, revealing a hive of offices and archival material of vertiginous proportions. Control was given over to a citizens' committee, which decided that the site should serve as a permanent memorial to the victims of the Stasi, and the main building Haus 1 (House 1) was opened in 1990 as a museum, library and research centre.

The interior has been immaculately preserved, from the marbled foyer, conference room, lounge and cafeteria to the offices of the former high ranking ministers, including that of Mielke himself. Walking through these rooms is an unnerving experience: a *mise en scène* of socialist chic, with the characteristic wall-to-wall wood panelling, but lacking the bodies for whom this comfort was the reward of a paranoid relation to the society outside its walls (it is estimated

BELOW:
Eric Mielke's desk at the Forschungs- und Gedenkstätte Normannenstrasse.

Map on page 194–95

that 95 percent of the overall budget of the Stasi was spent on spying on its own people). Other floors have permanent exhibitions with photos, facsimilies, texts and memorabilia covering aspects of the permanent struggle the ministry faced in controlling the will of the people it claimed to represent. While the exhibition at Museum Haus Checkpoint Charlie documents the daring of escapes attempted and achieved, the focus here is on the regime's untiring effort to wear down the people's resistance, whose heroism was in the equally determined refusal to allow it to do so.

In 1991 former citizens of the GDR were given the right to apply to see their Stasi files, although to this day few have succeeded in doing so.

The Swimming Hall and Velodrom

The **Schwimm- und Sprunghalle** (Swimming and Diving Hall, Europasportpark, S-bahn Landsberger Allee; opening times subject to change; entrance fee; tours available) complex was designed as one of a pair of facilities to head Berlin's bid for the Olympics in 2000, alongside the **Velodrom** next door. The projects were given the go-ahead by the then-minister for buildings, Wolfgang Nagel, and retain their Olympian stature, minus the express shuttle to the venue. Nagel's decision was brave and flew in the face of heavy opposition: the cost of the complex totalled 550 million marks and it shows: these buildings are in a class of their own.

BELOW AND RIGHT:
the Schwimm- und Sprunghalle at Europasportpark.

The architect commissioned for the project, Dominique Perrault, responded to the monumentality of the Olympia Stadium by almost "burying" the complex. Some 800 thousand cubic meters (285 thousand cubic metres) of earth was removed to this end. So unimposing is the resulting structure that you zoom past it on the S-bahn and, save a flash of turquoise at the bottom of your vision, barely register the existence of the complex. The two buildings protrude only a metre above ground level, and from above the swimming hall and velodrome form a rectangle and circle respectively. In the 1950s and 1960s the site was occupied by the Werner Seelenbinder Halle – a venue for sporting, entertainment and party-political events, before these moved to the Palast der Republik. The buildings were then used as a slaughterhouse and meat market, and were out of bounds until 1991, holding apart the three districts the site intersects Friedrichshain, Prenzlauer Berg and Lichtenberg.

The new development provides the missing link between the three. The interior space created by the sparse design and clean, artificial light is impressive. So are the swimming facilities: two 50-metre pools and a state-of-the-art diving platform. There is also a sauna/fitness area and therapy pool. The competition pool is available only for swimming clubs, leaving the second pool for the "serious amateurs" (those seeking wave machines and water slides try the Sport and Erlebnis Zentrum down the road).

It goes without saying that the running costs for the complex cannot be met by the entrance tariffs alone, and it is to the credit of the Berliner Bader Betrieb that the 5-mark entrance fee (3 marks for concessions) is not higher. ❏

SOUTH AND SOUTHWEST

This chapter follows a route through Neukölln, Tempelhof and Steglitz to the museum complex of Dahlem and then on to the beautiful countryside of Wannsee and Grunewald

Map on page 194–95

Neukölln , in the southeast of the city, is part of that ring of concrete suburbs that encircled the German capital in the 1870s, when Berlin grew at an astonishing rate. Hundreds of thousands of people, especially from the eastern provinces, were lured to the new metropolis during the industrial boom years. Property speculators hurriedly erected the notorious tenements that were to prompt the graphic artist Heinrich Zille's comment that you can "kill a man as well with an apartment as with an axe".

Nowadays most tourist routes tend to bypass this traditional working-class district, although there is more historical interest here than in Kreuzberg – for example, the Britzer Dorfmühle (windmill) in Buga-Park, Berlin's first Muslim cemetery on Columbiadamm and "Bohemian Rixdorf", which journalist Egon Erwin Kisch once considered worth writing about. Unlike Kreuzberg, whose boundaries follow the line of Südstern, Hermannplatz and Kottbusser Damm, the visitor has no high expectations of Neukölln, and it is therefore free to weave its unsophisticated charm without prejudice. When you alight from the U-Bahn or the bus at Hermannplatz, the "gateway to Neukölln", expect to encounter a genuine piece of Berlin.

PRECEDING PAGES: racing at Mariendorf. **LEFT:** watching planes during the Berlin airlift. **BELOW:** the *Dancing Couple* sculpture on Hermannplatz.

Hermannplatz and around

Hermannplatz was restored for Berlin's 750th anniversary celebrations. In the centre glitters the *Tanzendes Paar (Dancing Couple)*, a bronze by the Berlin sculptor Joachim Schmettau, who was also responsible for the popular *Wasserklops* (in the inner city centre). The sculpture is ringed by old Berlin apartment buildings and offices with renovated facades. Hermannplatz is an ideal starting point for exploring Neukölln for the first time.

The district's three most important roads and shopping streets start here: Sonnenallee (which became famous for the film *Sonnenallee*), Karl-Marx-Strasse and Hermannstrasse. Two of the locals' favourite recreational places – Neue Welt and the Hasenheide – are close by. In the past, the Neue Welt was a venue for dances, beer festivals and political gatherings. Since being restored, it has become a shopping centre and roller-skating park.

Adjacent to the Neue Welt is the **Volkspark Hasenheide**, a public park with ancient trees, meadows and open-air cinema. In this old hare reserve – hence the name, which means "hare heath" – Friedrich Ludwig Jahn established the first German gymnasium in 1811. The Jahn Monument recalls the father of national gymnastics, and gym clubs from all around the world have added their own inscriptions and commemorative plaques to the plinth.

The history of Neukölln

Even from a distance **Rathaus Neukölln** (town hall) and its 65-metre (213-ft) high tower dominate Karl-Marx-Strasse, the district's main boulevard. Neukölln U-Bahn station brings you to the historic heart of what became the town of Neukölln. The town, which was originally called Richardsdorp, then Rixdorf, was first officially mentioned in 1360. Richardsdorp stood on the road from Cölln to Köpenick and consisted of farmhouses clustered around an elongated village square. The 15th-century Bohemian-Lutheran church, **Bethlehems-Kirche**, still survives from those times, along with Berlin's oldest village smithy. Kutschen Schöne, a carriage business founded in 1894, has also survived. Twelve of its 153 carriages are white wedding coaches, hired to take couples to the church or registrar's office.

Some 400 Protestant refugees from Bohemia, almost all from the same village, set up a new home in Rixdorf in 1737. Thus Richardstrasse and the area around Kirchgasse became the Böhmisches Dorf (Bohemian Village). With its own assembly room and squat farmhouses, run by the starkly simple Herrnhuter brotherhood, it stood on its own as an "almost misplaced idyll" (Egon Erwin Kisch), a mere stone's throw from the hurly-burly of Neukölln.

To distinguish their settlement from old Richardsdorp, it was called Böhmisch-Rixdorf. The two were merged in 1874, and in 1899 Rixdorf received its town charter. In 1912, the town authorities decided to revive the name of Berlin's old sister town and renamed the district Neukölln.

In the reforms of 1920, Neukölln was united with the villages of Britz, Buckow and Rudow to the south, to become Berlin's 14th administrative district. All three places retain their rural character to this day. The Federal Garden

BELOW: concert in Körnerpark.

Show (Buga), held in the south of Neukölln in 1985, presented the town with its own beautiful recreation area, the **Britzer Garten** in the grounds of Schloss Britz (Alt-Britz 73; open daily). The 100-hectare (250-acre) terrain, with forest and meadows, streams, flower beds, and a large man-made lake attracts regular visitors from all over the city.

Map on page 194–95

The Hufeisensiedlung (Horseshoe Block)

In the past the oppressive living conditions in the proletarian quarter of Neukölln turned the place into a powder keg. Between 1925 and 1931 a massive estate with 2,500 flats was built in the grounds of the Britz estate. Part of it, the **Hufeisensiedlung** (Horseshoe Block) designed by architects Martin Wagner and Bruno Taut, is a perfect illustration of the way in which progressive engineering techniques can be used to realise the concept of social housing. These revolutionary Weimar apartments are still regarded as exemplary throughout the world – in stark contrast to the **Gropiusstadt**, Neukölln's second major experiment in town planning.

The foundation stone for this satellite town was laid in 1962. The founder of the Bauhaus school of architecture, Walter Gropius, designed the ground plans for the modern complex, which today houses over 60,000 people. One of Gropius' own tower blocks dominates the skyline. Thirty-one storeys high, this is the highest residential block in Berlin and is surrounded by buildings that vary in height from one to 16 storeys, forming a semicircle open towards the south. Even at the planning stage, the architects had an eye on the location of playgrounds and open spaces. Of central importance in this respect is the sickle-shaped flash of green which encloses four U-Bahn stations. In spite of these

Schloss Britz (Alt-Britz; tours Wed 2–6pm) next door to the Horseshoe Block has a small museum and is a venue for concerts and exhibitions. The Britzer Garten is open daily.

BELOW: Hotel Estrel in Neukölln.

seemingly well-intentioned facilities, living conditions in Gropiusstadt are pretty disastrous. Drug-dealing, racism and right-wing extremism are the morbid consequences of a hostile living environment. It is far from coincidental that this was the stronghold of the reps, the extreme right-wing republicans, during the 1989 elections.

Around the "Kiez"

The Neuköllin Opera puts on a mixed bag of unconventional performances from classical pieces to experimental and children's shows.

Meanwhile, the Neuköllners can be satisfied, indeed proud, of the cultural range on offer in their part of the city. The **Neukölln Opera** (Karl-Marx-Str. 131–133; tel: 688 907-0; box office: 688 90777), an independent musical theatre group, has long established a reputation outside the district. The days are long gone when Neukölln artists had to draw attention to themselves with the battle cry: "There's life in the desert." Today they've found an ideal exhibition space in the Galerie im Körnerpark, where their work is shown to best advantage.

Lying in the heart of Neukölln, between Hermannstrasse and Karl-Marx-Strasse, the **Körnerpark** is a horticultural gem, with sweeping flights of steps, water fountains and ornamental flower beds. Visitors don't expect to find such a refuge here, for Neukölln is not only densely populated but also has a lot of industry, including a film processing plant, a cement works, the Berlin Kindl brewery and the Trumpf chocolate factory. In Neukölln, tradition rubs shoulders with today, city bustle contrasts with the quiet village atmosphere and it's possible to experience "Berlin Kiez" (local Berlin) still largely unchanged.

Tempelhof

BELOW:
the Luftbrücke Denkmal (Airlift Memorial) at Tempelhof Airport.

The name **Tempelhof** ⓭ is automatically associated with the airport, which has brought worldwide fame to this part of the city. The birth of commercial flights, the rapid increase in air traffic after the blockade, right through to the age of the jet engine, all has been witnessed at close hand by the people of Tempelhof. The town of Tempelhof is very much older. It was founded in the 13th century by the Knights Templar, as too were the southwest districts of Mariendorf, Marienfelde and Lichtenrade.

Like Tempelhof, all three were once simple Brandenburg farming communities. Friedrich Wilhelm I turned the fields and meadows north of Tempelhof into an exercise and parade ground for his troops in 1722. As Tempelhofer Feld, it became a recognised showground for numerous military events outside the gates of Berlin.

The first world airport

Other aeronautical spectacles were offered after 1883 when the new airship troops of the imperial army were installed on Tempelhofer Feld. In 1909 Orville Wright, one of the famous American flying brothers, rattled across the airfield on a bold test flight. The era of mechanised flight had just begun.

On 23 October 1923, Berlin Airport was officially opened in the eastern part of the former parade ground. To start with, there was very little to see beyond the signpost, a few aircraft hangars and a customs shed. Planes took off and landed on open grass runways. It was not until at least five years later that the huts and sheds gave way to a respectable terminal with a hotel, restaurants and concrete air-field. From 1936 to 1939 this terminal became the centre of the present mas-sive complex at the Platz der Luftbrücke. The war interrupted its completion and not until the 1950s was Tempelhof Central Airport finally opened to civil-ian traffic. When the large commercial airlines rerouted their flights to Tegel in 1975, Tempelhof became quieter.

Map on page 194–95

Tempelhof and the Airlift

Before 1989, some of the administrative offices and maintenance sheds were leased out to local businesses and the Americans used the airport terminal on Platz der Luftbrücke as an airbase. Further east at Gate 5, as a reminder of the blockade, the Americans have preserved a four-engine DC-54, one of the "raisin bombers" that delivered food parcels in 1948. Now over 45 years old, the vet-eran of the airlift stands alongside the fence. The **Luftbrücke Denkmal** (Air-lift Memorial) on the airport forecourt is also dedicated to the airlift.

The concrete sculpture by Eduard Ludwig represents the arch of a bridge, while the prongs at the top symbolise the three air corridors to the west, which kept West Berlin alive with food supplies during that period. Listed in bronze on the base of the memorial are the names of 70 Allied pilots, as well as four German assistants who gave their lives in the airlift. Barely was the memorial inaugurated in 1951, before the locals had given it an appropriate nickname: with grim humour the work of art was christened "the hunger claw", in mem-ory of the meagre rations that were available during the blockade.

On Alt-Tempelhof street, to the right and left of Tempelhofer Damm, you'll

The Berlin Blockade (1948–49) started when the Soviet authorities blocked all the roads leading to West Berlin. During the next 11 months US and British pilots made 541 flights to Berlin to supply food (see page 47).

BELOW: Tempelhof Ullsteinhaus.

find the old town centre with its village green and the last remaining farmhouses. Opposite the Rathaus (town hall), built in the 1930s, the half-timbered tower of a 13th-century fortified church peeks out from a little park. It was rebuilt in 1956 after having been badly damaged in the war.

The old school on the village green in Alt-Mariendorf houses the **Heimatmuseum und Archiv Tempelhof** (Templehof Local Museum and Archives; open daily; entrance fee), displaying furniture, folk art and old documents. In the former estate of Alt-Lichtenrade, weeping willows ring the village pond. The surroundings, complete with traditional village inn and old fire station, are idyllic. The granite village church at Alt-Marienfelde, in late Romanesque style, dates from 1220 and is the oldest building on Berlin soil.

Races are held at the Trabrennbahn Mariendorf on Sun at 1.30pm and Wed 6.30pm, when entrance to the racecourse is free.

About 800 horses are stabled in Tempelhof – no longer on farms, but in the stalls of the **Trabrennbahn Mariendorf** (Mariendorf racecourse; tel: 740 1212). The racecourse was opened in 1913 and has always been popular. With its new grandstand, it is one of southern Berlin's major attractions. The five-storey building is well equipped with restaurants and bars. Gambling fever is rife on here Wednesdays and Sundays.

Industry in Tempelhof

Tempelhof plays a vital role in the economy of the capital as one of the largest industrial districts in Berlin. The building of the Teltowkanal at the beginning of the century fostered industrialisation in the south. Tempelhof's industrial area also follows the canal in part. From Stubenrauchbrücke (bridge) on Tempelhofer Damm, you can look out over the cranes and warehouses of Tempelhof harbour. Tempelhof's most striking piece of industrial architectural design

BELOW: a performer at Ufa-Fabrik.

is the expressionist facade of the Druckhaus Tempelhof (printworks) at Ullsteinstrasse U-Bahn station. The plant was built in 1925–26 by Eugen Schmohl and was Berlin's first reinforced concrete tower block. Under the name Ullsteinhaus the complex on Mariendorfer Damm housed the editorial staff, printworks and administrative offices of the Ullstein Brothers' enormous newspaper and magazine publishing company. Since the final closure of the main printing works, the publishing house, which is itself a listed building, has been leased out to smaller businesses.

Map on page 194–95

The Ufa-Fabrik

"Three things have come into the world from Tempelhof: films, planes and the Knights Templar," proclaimed the district authorities proudly on the occasion of their 750th anniversary celebrations. Tempelhof was the largest production centre of the Ufa film company after the "film city" of Babelsberg. Countless cinema classics were made at the studios at Oberlandstrasse 26.

The first silent movie studio was operating here as early as 1909. In April 1945 Herta Feiler and Heinz Rühmann, the superstars of German cinema, went in front of the cameras for *Sag die Wahrheit (Tell the Truth)*. In the 1950s, however, Berlin's film industry enjoyed its last commercial success.

In Viktoriastrasse, not far from the printworks, dreams of a "great Germany" were filmed for propaganda purposes during the Third Reich. In 1976 the print laboratory occupying the former Ufa site was declared bankrupt, and the old production halls fell into disuse.

In June 1979 a crowd of activists occupied the run-down dream factory. Under the slogan "The second wind of Ufa" they transformed the empty complex into a self-governing multifunctional centre, catering for everyday needs. Since then, the new **Ufa-Fabrik** (Viktoriastr. 10–18; tel: 75 50 30) has become a lively splash of colour in a district otherwise notorious as a "cultural desert" with its circus, Tempelhof's only cinema (Ufer-Palast), bar, cabaret stage and the café Olé.

Ufa Fabrik (tel: 75 50 30) has open-air theatre performances between June and September: check the local press for details.

BELOW: village church in Alt-Marienfelde.

Steglitz

"Life is peaceful here in Steglitz, the children look healthy, the beggars don't press you too hard," wrote Franz Kafka to a friend in 1923. Apart from the bustle of shoppers on Schlossstrasse, it is still very peaceful in **Steglitz ⓮**. Today, the district has a population of 189,000, but it has retained its traditional bourgeois atmosphere. New housing and industrial estates may have appeared, but the quiet alleys about which Kafka enthused in his letters, can still be visited.

People come to this highly respectable neighbourhood to marvel at the marvellous orchids in the Botanischer Garten, to enjoy some highbrow entertainment in the Schloss Park Theater, or sometimes, to receive treatment at the university clinic.

Above all, though, Steglitz is famous for its **Schlossstrasse**. There are five streets of that name in Berlin, but usually the name is used in reference to the main shopping street in Steglitz, which starts at the U-Bahn station on Walther-Schreiber-Platz. This

street, known at its peak as "little Ku'damm", runs all the way from Steglitz Forum, a five-storey "multicentre", to the Rathaus (town hall). While the Titania-Palast remained open, people also flocked to Schlossstrasse in the evenings to enjoy all sorts of artistic events: cinema, concerts, ballet, operetta and variety. In the 1960s, Marlene Dietrich was among the stars to perform here. Since the 1970s, however, its glittering past as a palace of culture can no longer be detected from the outside and the building is under a preservation order as an example of 1920s architecture.

Since 1976 Schlossstrasse has gained one landmark. On the corner of Schildhornstrasse, immediately beside the motorway flyover, is the **Turmrestaurant Steglitz**. A lift takes you up to the three restaurant levels, where diners can enjoy a magnificent view.

At the bottom end of Schlossstrasse you'll find **Rathaus Steglitz**, built in 1896–97 in Brandenburg brick Gothic. In the cellars, which no longer exist, the founders of the Wandervogel met in 1901. This New Romantic youth movement began in Steglitz and caught the imagination of hundreds of thousands of young people before it was disbanded by the National Socialists.

Diagonally opposite, on the corner of Albrechtstrasse, Berlin's highest office block towers over the town. Like so many other concrete blocks, the 130-metre (425-ft) **Steglitzer Kreisel** is a product of the frantic building boom in the late 1960s when tax concessions attracted a lot of capital into the city. But in the 1970s the tower block was seen primarily as a scandalous indictment of the policy of "write-offs" and was put up for auction. After a new investor had been found and the Kreisel completed, a hotel moved in here, together with the office of the mayor of Steglitz and several of his administrative departments.

BELOW: the Turmrestaurant, Steglitz.

Wrangel Schlösschen (Wrangel Castle)

The old farming village of Steglitz was conveniently situated on the road to Potsdam. In 1375 it was officially mentioned for the first time as the seat of a Lord von Torgow zu Zossen. In 1920, when it was the largest village in Prussia with 84,000 inhabitants, it became part of the 12th administrative district of Greater Berlin, along with the rural communities of Lichterfelde, Südende and Lankwitz. On the corner of Wrangelstrasse an old Prussian manor house has been preserved from the days of the lord of Steglitz manor, Karl Friedrich von Beyme. The building now houses the **Schlosspark Theater** (tel: 793 1515; open Mon–Sat 1–7pm, Sun 5–7pm).

Built in 1804, it was named **Wrangel Schlösschen** (Wrangel Castle; tel: 7904 3924) after its most popular resident. Field Marshall Count von Wrangel was known locally as "Papa Wrangel". In 1921 the actor Paul Henckels opened a theatre, which was later converted to a cinema, next door to the manor house. Badly damaged in the air raids, it was opened again in November 1945, before all the rebuilding work had been completed, as the first functioning theatre in the American Sector, under the directorship of Boleslaw Barlog. The repertoire included *Hokuspokus* by Curt Goetz, bringing to the stage an up-and-coming young star, whom Barlog had discovered for this production: Hildegard Knef. The Schlosspark Theater, which has a small auditorium seating only 478, attracts large enthusiastic audiences every night with its reputation for staging first-class plays, mostly light works and comedies, by leading playwrights.

Berlin's often deplorable weather may not come from Steglitz, but it is forecast there hour by hour. Since 1983 the Meteorological Institute of the Free University has been based in the old **Wasserturm am Fichteberg** (water tower),

Map on page 194–95

BELOW:
the Botanischer Garten in Steglitz.

remodelled for its new function at a cost of millions. The technological heart of the water tower lies on the 6th floor. Printers spew out an unceasing stream of numbers; a screen relays the radar picture from the weather fronts within a 200-km (125-mile) radius; 40 metres (133 ft) up, on the roof of the tower, an aerial receives data from weather satellites. The tower also has its own studio for telephone weather reports. Four to five million calls are logged annually.

In Klingsorstrasse, near the Teltowkanal, the **Klinikum Steglitz der Freien Universität** was erected between 1961 and 1969, with the support of the Benjamin Franklin Foundation of America. The 1,400-bed clinic is Europe's most modern centre in the field of medical research and teaching.

Botanischer Garten

The Freigelände in the Botanischer Garten features an extensive geographical section, where flora from the Pyrenees, the Alps, the Carpathians, the Balkans and the Himalayas are on show.

BELOW: water plants in the Botanischer Garten.

Another natural scientific institution which is a favourite with day-trippers is the **Botanischer Garten** (Botanical Gardens; open daily; entrance fee). The Steglitz entrance lies at the bottom end of Schlossstrasse, which joins the widened Fernstrasse Unter den Eichen south of Hermann-Ehlers-Platz. An avenue leads to the 16 filigree greenhouses on a hill, which look out over the 51-hectare (126-acre) site.

The most eye-catching is the large **Tropenhaus** (Tropical House; open daily), a palace of glass, 25 metres (83 ft) high. Altogether there are around 18,000 different types of trees and plants in the gardens. In the **Freigelände** (open-air gardens) you can wander along winding, marked trails, all beautifully laid out, through the flora of the earth's temperate zones. To the north, the garden borders on Königin-Luise-Platz in Dahlem. At the entrance is the **Botanisches Museum** (open daily 10am–5pm; entrance fee) – the only museum of its kind in Germany – with a specialist library of over 60,000 volumes.

On what is now Finckensteinallee, Wilhelm Carsten, who was known as the "Napoleon of land speculators" endowed the Prussian military with a tract of land, on which the **Hauptkadettenanstalt** (Main Cadet School) was built in 1878.

In 1934 the SS was stationed here. In the cellar of the Lichterfelde college, death squads killed around 40 Berlin SA-leaders who were involved in Röhm's alleged putsch on 30 June 1934.

Litchterfelde

In **Lichterfelde** ⓰ in 1881, the inventor Werner von Siemens made a name for himself with the so-called "Electric". On 16 May, on a test ground that stretched from the cadet school to Lichterfelde-Ost station, he started up the first electric tram for public passenger service: a converted horse-drawn tram with an electric motor installed under the floor. Lichterfelde is also the cradle of German aeronautics. Otto Lilienthal who, it is claimed, was the "first flying man" lived on Boothstrasse. In 1894 he built a 15-metre (50-ft) hill near his house from where he tested his flying machines and glided through the air for over 90 metres (100 yds). Today a staircase leads to the top of this grassy mound where a stone globe, surrounded by a circular observatory pavilion, open to the sky, symbolises mankind's conquest of the air.

Zehlendorf

Zehlendorf ⑯, Steglitz's neighbour to the west, enjoys the reputation of being Berlin's most exclusive district. Statistics show that the people of Zehlendorf live in the biggest apartments and enjoy the best medical care and have the highest level of education in all Berlin. Here you'll find the most attractive parks in western Berlin: Volkspark Klein Glienicker in the south, the Havel River, Grunewald Forest and a chain of lakes from Nikolassee down to Grunewaldsee.

One place at the southern tip of the district became internationally famous over the years: the **Glienicker Brücke** (bridge) across the middle of which ran the former border with the GDR. From here in February 1986, pictures were relayed around the world, as hundreds of journalists waited for days in the freezing cold for the arrival of Anatoly Scharansky. After years of imprisonment, the Jewish lawyer from the Soviet Union was finally allowed to emigrate to the West in exchange for Soviet spies. The Glienicker Brücke had been used before as a gateway to freedom for top agents from East and West. In 1962 the U2 pilot Francis Gary Powers, who had been shot down over the USSR, was exchanged for the Soviet master spy Ivanovitch Abel.

The history of Zehlendorf

More than 200 years ago this crossing point already held special significance for Zehlendorf. Prussia's first traffic-carrying paved road, the Potsdamer Strasse, crossed the Havel River here over a wooden bridge. Sleepy Zehlendorf came to life. A travelling speed of up to 10 km (6 miles) an hour was possible on the "Steinbahn". The coach journey from Berlin to Potsdam took just three hours,

Map on page 194–95

Enjoying the sunshine at a restaurant in Zehlendorf.

BELOW: the Tropenhaus (Tropical House), in the Botanischer Garten.

and Zehlendorf lay directly between the two. Barely 50 years after the road was completed, the wind of technological change blew once more through the venerable village, which was officially mentioned for the first time in 1241.

The Berlin–Potsdam Railway was built, and in 1838 the first train stopped in Zehlendorf. Villa enclaves grew up beside the railway in the second half of the 19th century, changing Zehlendorf and the surrounding villages into urban suburbs of Berlin. In the centre of present-day Zehlendorf, life is anything but sleepy. At the crossroads of Potsdamer Strasse, Teltower Damm and Clayallee is the district's city area, where you will find assorted shops, the town hall, finance offices and other institutions. Only the small baroque village church to the west of the crossroads remains from the olden days, somewhat protected from the traffic by an old stone wall.

On Potsdamer Chaussee, which leaves the city area and goes westwards towards Wannsee and Potsdam along the route of the old Reichsstrasse, you will find the **Waldfriedhof Zehlendorf** (Zehlendorf Cemetery). Here are the graves of mayor Ernst Reuter (d. 1953), theatre director Erwin Piscator (d. 1966) and other well-known theatrical people and writers. On Clauertstrasse in Düppel, a former manor on the city boundary towards Kleinmachnow, is the **Museumsdorf Düppel** (open Apr–Oct Tues–Thur 3–6pm, Sun 10am–5pm; entrance fee), a reconstruction of an old Prussian village community from around 1200. It is run by volunteers, who demonstrate medieval handicraft skills on Sundays in the various workshops. In the western side of the forest, bordering the Havel River, stands the Grunewald Turm (Grunewald Tower) which was built at the end of the 19th century as a memorial to Kaiser Wilhelm I. From the tower the visitor can enjoy beautiful views across the lakes.

BELOW:
East and West
exchange agents
on Glienicker
Brücke (bridge).

The Dahlem museum complex

This section of Zehlendorf, where it crosses into Wilmersdorf at Roseneck, is known as **Dahlem** ⓐ. Once a country estate, Dahlem is now a centre of scientific research, as well as a treasure-trove of artworks.

Map
on page
194–95

Near Dahlem-Dorf U-Bahn station are the museums of the **Stiftung Preussis-cher Kulturbesitz** (Foundation for Prussian Cultural Possessions). This museum complex, known as the Dahlem museum complex, was built to fill the cultural institutional gap caused by the city's division after World War II. The collections in this complex are some of the most comprehensive in Europe. The four museums housed here are: the Ethnologisches Museum (Museum of Ethnology); Museum für Ostasiastische Kunst (Museum of East Asian Art); Museum für Indische Kunst (Museum of Indian Art) and Museum Europäischer Kulturen (Museum of European Cultures). It is worth planning the visit well because it can be a rather overwhelming experience trying to fit all four museums into one day.

The **Ethnologisches Museum** (Museum of Ethnology; Lansstrasse 8; tel: 830 14 38; open Tues–Fri 10am-6pm, weekend 11am–6pm; entrance fee) holds around 500,000 objects from all over the world, a large collection of sound recordings, documentary films and photos. It is ranked as being one of the largest and best of its kind in the world. Included in the building are the following collections: Africa, American archaeology, American ethnology, Europe, the Islamic Orient, Eastern and northern Asia, south and southeast Asia, the South Seas and Australia.

There is also a collection on the ethnology of music, a children's museum and a museum for the Blind. The permanent South Seas exhibition presents cultures from Oceania and Australia. A great variety of vessels can be seen in the "Boat

BELOW: Glienicker Brücke today.

Hall". If you are travelling with a family, you can also enjoy the chance of walking onto the twin-hulled boat from Tonga. The creativity of the West Africa people is demonstrated in the masks and ceremonial figures, musical instruments and everyday objects from the turn of the century.

The site for the **Museum für Ostasiastische Kunst** (Museum of East Asian Art; open Tues–Fri 10am-6pm; weekend 11am–6pm; entrance fee) has been completely renovated and the collections cover the periods from the Stone Age to the present day. Art objects from China, Japan and Korea are exhibited in individual galleries. In the centre of the museum is a room dedicated to Buddhist art common to all three cultures. A small porcelain goblet, which used to part of the Electors of Brandenburg's art collection and dates back to the early 17th century, is of particular cultural and historical importance. There is also a throne, which is a masterpiece of lacquer work. It consists of jacaranda wood with an inlay of mother-of-pearl in a lacquer and gold base.

The **Museum für Indische Kunst** (Museum of Indian Art; opening hours as above; entrance fee) contains works of fine and applied art from India, Southeast Asia and Central Asia dating from the second century BC to the present day. The museum's "Turfan" collection from Central Asia is internationally famous and of particular beauty are the wall paintings, fabric paintings and the clay and wooden figures. Palm leaf, paper and birch manuscripts, paper in different languages demonstrates India's written tradition. The main attraction here, however, is the domed cave temple, which has been reconstructed in the original size.

BELOW: exhibits from the Dahlem museum complex.

In June 1999, the Museum für Volkskunde (Museum of Folklore) and the European holdings in the Museum für Völkerkunde (Museum of Ethnology)

were united to form one collection, the **Museum Europäischer Kulturen** (Museum of European Cultures; Im Winkel 6/8; opening hours as above; entrance fee). This museum is divided up into two sections covering an area of 1,700 sq. metres (2,033 sq. yds).

In the first part, there is a section which displays the increasing importance of pictures in people's daily lives. Until the 15th century, the majority of pictures were displayed purely in churches. With the introduction of photography, the outside world started to become a visual pleasure in ordinary homes – from church views to market places. Painted furniture, magic lanterns, camera obscura, film and digital images are part of the exhibits on display in this section of the museum.

The second area of exhibits contains 19th century pictures of life in that period with visuals showing the diverse use of pictures in European religions and also how people's perception changed due to these pictures.

Not far from the museum complex, at Bussardsteig 9, is a low building at the edge of the Grunewald called the **Brücke-Museum** (Bussardsteig 9, tel: 831 2029; open Mon–Wed 11am–5pm; entrance fee). This was planned in 1964 on the initiative of the 80-year-old painter Karl Schmidt-Rottluff a surviving member of the Die Brücke (The Bridge) group of artists who were very influential between 1905 and 1913.

Paintings of the Die Brücke group, including works by leading lights Karl Schmidt-Rottluff, Ernst Ludwig Kirchner and Erich Heckel, can be seen displayed in each of the Brücke's four rooms but the museum also displays works by other contemporary artists in a variety of mediums. The pleasant gardens surrounding the museum contain metal sculptures.

The functionalist building housing the Brücke-Museum was built by Werner Düttmann in 1966–67.

BELOW: exhibit in the Museum Europäischer Kulturen.

MUSEUMS IN DAHLEM

Berlin's world-famous museums shared the fate of the divided city. When in 1953 art treasures were returned to Berlin from their wartime homes in bunkers and mines, those stored in central Germany went to east Berlin, while those from western Germany ended up in west Berlin, where the Dahlem museum was expanded as a consequence. For decades the divided city developed two parallel collections. Both halves claimed to be the rightful trustees of Prussian heritage. East Berlin expanded the historic Museum Island, while west Berlin countered with the Foundation for Prussian Cultural Possessions based at Dahlem.

For a long time the Dahlem museum was the most important museum in the western part of the city, but after reunification of the east and west many of its most important collections were rehoused. The Gemäldegalerie (Picture Gallery), for example, has been moved to the Kulturforum in the Tiergarten. Today former differences of opinion concerning the city's cultural legacy have become superfluous and the unification of all the capital's museums under The State Museums of Berlin (SMPK) should be completed by 2010. Regardless of their geographical location, Berlin's museum collections are certainly worth a visit.

The Freie Universität

During term-time, tens of thousands of students flock to Dahlem every day. This is the main site of the **Freie Universität** (FU). The university was founded in 1948–49 under difficult conditions. Political pressures at the well-established Humboldt University in the eastern part of the city had become intolerable to some of its students and lecturers. Prompted by these individuals and with the help of the American military governor Lucius D. Clay, the first educational programme began in Dahlem in December 1948.

When the Freie Universität opened its doors in 1948 there were 1,500 students compared with more than 53,000 today.

Before World War I, several scientific research institutes of the Kaiser-Wilhelm Association had already been established in Dahlem. Here were based the laboratories of famous academics such as Max Planck, Albert Einstein and other Nobel Prize winners. In 1938 at Thielallee 93, the old Chemical Institute, the atomic age was ushered into the world when Otto Hahn and his colleague Fritz Strassmann succeeded in splitting the first uranium atom. Despite vociferous opposition from anti-nuclear campaigners, a test reactor continues to operate in the **Hahn-Meitner-Institut** on Glienicker Strasse in Wannsee.

Towards the end of the 1960s, the FU went through a turbulent phase when the "non-parliamentary opposition" (APO) and the protest movement against the American war in Vietnam were formed here under the leadership of the Socialist German Students (SDS). Today, the university is Berlin's largest higher education institute, with about 53,000 students.

Dahlem-Dorf

BELOW:
Dahlem-Dorf.

One memento of the former rural idyll of Dahlem has been preserved in the old section called **Dahlem-Dorf**. The history of this village probably goes back more than 750 years. The simple manor house, with Renaissance traces, opposite the thatched entrance to the U-Bahn station dates from 1679 and is now used partly by the university and partly by the "Friends of Dahlem Desmesne", who are committed to preserving Dahlem's rural heritage.

In the first years of National Socialism, the presbytery of Dahlem parish was used as a base for the "Confessional Church", under Pastor Martin Niemöller, who strongly opposed the pro-Nazi stance of the German Evangelical Church. Niemöller, who spoke out courageously against the Nazi regime in his sermons, was thrown into a concentration camp by the Nazis in 1937. The presbytery is now known as **Martin-Niemöller-Haus** and contains a centre for peace studies.

Not far from here, on the shores of **Grunewaldsee** (Grunewald Lake), stands a small hunting lodge, built around the mid-16th century in Renaissance style for the Elector Joachim II. **Jagdschloss Grunewald** (open May–Oct 10am–5pm, closed Mon; Nov–Apr weekends only 10am–4pm; entrance fee; info line tel: 0331-969 4202) is now a museum, containing a collection of hunting weapons and equipment as well as paintings by German, Dutch and Flemish masters from the Hohenzollern collection. The architect is thought to be Caspar Theiss, who was also responsible for building mansions in Berlin. Its current appearance can be attributed to the Baroque work carried out by Johann Arnold Nering and Martin Grünberg (1669–1709) who were commissioned to re-do the exterior, which still remains today.

Map
on page
194–95

Wannsee

In the last 30 years of the 19th century, Berlin acquired a highly modern local transport system, the Schnell (fast) or S-Bahn. The construction of the **Wannsee-bahn** terminus was largely responsible for Zehlendorf's rapid development, once again, as an exclusive place to live.

The line from Zehlendorf station to **Wannsee** ⑱ passes through some of the prettiest residential districts in the western part of Berlin. The stations have been designed to blend in with their surroundings. Outstanding sights on the route include **Mexikoplatz** station, a perfect example of art nouveau, and **Nikolassee** in the centre of the villa district of the same name, which has been wonderfully preserved in the architectural style of a neo-Gothic castle.

From Nikolassee station, a footpath leads to the city's main freshwater swimming pool, **Strandbad Wannsee**, the largest outdoor pool in Europe. There has been a freshwater pool here since the turn of the century, although until 1907 swimming in Berlin's lakes and rivers was officially banned.

Between 1927 and 1930, a huge public bath was built to designs by the head of the Berlin city planning department, Martin Wagner, and architect Richard Ermisch. Their aim was to provide recreational facilities for those Berliners "who live in dark, airless tenements and can't afford the luxury of a trip to a spa". Today, Wannsee pool is crowded on hot summer days with Berliners sunbathing along the sandy shore or yatching and windsurfing on the lake.

The log cabin at Nikolskoe, now a popular café, was built in 1819 on the orders of Frederick William III for his daughter Charlotte.

BELOW:
boats at Wannsee.

Greek curiosities in the grounds of Schloss Glienicke.

BELOW: Volkspark Klein-Glienicke.

Around Wannsee

At Sandwerder 5 near Wannsee S-Bahn station is a magnificent villa, no longer used as a family home. Carl Zuckmayer had the opportunity to work in the "Schloss am Wannsee" (Castle on the Wannsee) during the summer of 1925. For over 20 years now this has been the home of the **Literarische Colloquium Berlin** – a studio, meeting place and hostel for writers' conferences and authors from all over the world. The concept was initiated by the writer and professor of literature Walter Höllerer. He founded the Literary Colloquium in 1964 to demonstrate that literature "occupies the area of tension between science, politics and everyday life". The group's work gives particular emphasis to adapting printed material for broadcast media, such as radio, film and television.

Devotees of the poet Heinrich von Kleist regularly make the pilgrimage to the **Grabstätte von Heinrich von Kleist** (the grave of Heinrich von Kleist) on Kleiner Wannsee. In the grounds of Bismarckstrasse 3, you can visit the exact spot on the lakeside where the writer, born in 1777, committed suicide with his married lover Henriette Vogel on 21 November 1811. The reddish stone on Kleist's grave bears a line of verse from his play *Der Prinz von Homburg*: "Now, O Immortality, you are wholly mine".

Königstrasse is the main route through the district of Wannsee, a favourite stamping-ground for day-trippers and watersports enthusiasts. Here and in the neighbouring streets, the Rathaus and low-built houses recall Wannsee's rural past. The Mutter Fourage gallery has taken over an old farmhouse in Schäferstrasse, with a nursery and pottery, while yacht clubs, sanatoria and private villas line the banks of the **Grossen Wannsee**.

Despite being slightly off the beaten track, the **Haus der Wannsee-Konferenz** (House of the Wannsee Conference; Am Grossen Wannsee 56–58; open Mon–Fri 10am–6pm, weekends 2–6pm) certainly merits a visit on account of the unique place it holds in 20th-century history.

Built in 1914–15 by the industrialist Ernst Marlier and situated in charming surroundings by the side of the lake Wannsee, the villa formed the setting for the infamous Wannsee Conference of January 1942 when, in the space of roughly 90 minutes, the Nazis finalised their plan to deport and brutally exterminate all the Jews of Europe in the "Final Solution". Reinhard Heydrich, chief of the Reich's main security office, headed the conference of 14 high-ranking civil servants and SS officers which, with ruthless efficiency, agreed the set-up and logistics for the implementation of this monstrous undertaking.

After the war the villa was occupied in turn by Soviet navy personnel and American officers before being converted into a community college in 1947. From 1952 to 1988 it served as a holiday home for children from the Neukölln district. In 1992, 50 years after the Wannsee Conference, the efforts of historian Joseph Wulf led to the villa finally being recognised as a Holocaust Memorial Centre and historical site. The permanent exhibition which the villa contains encompasses information on the conference, the events which led to it, and documentation on the segregation, persecution and genocide of the Jews.

Castles and gardens

In the south of Zehlendorf, on the banks of the Havel, lies one of the loveliest areas of parkland to be found in Berlin. **Volkspark Klein-Glienicke** (open daily 7am–8pm) was reserved for the sole use of royal guests when Prince Karl, a brother of Fredrich Wilhelm III (1797–1840), lived in the former manor house. The prince employed K.F. Schinkel, the country's first master architect, to rebuild the house and had a leading landscape designer to lay out the beautiful estate. Over on Königstrasse is **Schloss Glienicke** (open May–Oct, weekends 10am–5pm; entrance fee), with a gentleman's residence and coachhouses.

The two round, temple-like buildings on the street are the "Large and Small Curiosities": observation turrets which Prince Karl had built so that he could watch the traffic moving past on the main thoroughfare. In the era of horse-drawn carriages 150 years ago, this may have been a more exciting pastime than it is today. Set in a park on the opposite side of Königstrasse is the former royal hunting lodge, rebuilt for Prince Karl in French baroque style by Ferdinand von Arnim. Jagdschloss Glienicke is used as a conference centre. In the woods south of the avenue, opposite the road to Nikolskoe, you'll find another unusual piece of architecture: the **Loggia Alexandra**. This semicircular building on Böttcherberg was built in 1869 as a scenic look-out for the owners of Klein-Glienicke castle.

Directly opposite Am Böttcherberg road, **Nikolskoer Weg** branches off. A winding road brings you to your destination: an idyllic inn on the hill over-looking the Havel, built in the style of a Russian log cabin. Beside it is an ornate church complete with onion dome. King Friedrich Wilhelm III had the **Blockhaus Nikolskoe** built in six weeks as a gift for his daughter Charlotte, wife

Map
on page
194–95

BELOW: the
beach at Wannsee.

No cars are allowed on Pfaueninsel: take the ferry from Nikolsloer Weg (the fare includes admission to the island). Banned items and activities include smoking, swimming, cycling, dogs, radios and CD/cassette players.

BELOW: a horse-drawn carriage at Pfaueninsel.

of the later Czar Nikolaus I. At that time, relations between Prussia and Russia were dictated by family connections. Just behind the Nikolskoe is the charming church of St Peter and Paul which was designed by August Stüler and whose onion domes continue the Russian theme of the Nikolskoe. It is a favourite for weddings and the Christmas service is also popular, when Nikolskoe looks even prettier under a covering of snow.

Pfaueninsel (Peacock Island)

At the end of Nikolskoer Weg is the **Pfaueninsel** (Peacock Island) from where there's a wonderful view over the Havel. One of the most romantic spots in Berlin, this is a favourite lovers' haunt. Friedrich Wilhelm III, the unmilitaristic successor to Frederick the Great, bought the island in 1793 as a refuge for himself and his beloved, and ordered the construction of a steward's house and dairy farm. The summer palace that looks like a ruined castle was intended for his mistress, "Minchen Encke", who became Countess Liechtenau.

"Superb little place for a summer house, ruined knight's castle springs to mind, will have them build something Gothic straightaway," the pleasure-loving monarch noted in very basic German. Between 1793 and 1797 work continued on the half-timbered building. From a distance the oak panels give the impression of white stone. On the third floor, gaping window frames give the appearance of romantic ruins. The illusion was continued throughout the entire castle, right through to the round turret room. Today the castle houses a small museum (open April and Sept, Tues–Sun 10am–5pm; Oct, Tues–Sun 10am–4pm; entrance fee). In 1822 the island was converted into an English-style landscape park by Peter Joseph Lenné. Peacocks were brought over from the

manor of Sakrow on the opposite bank of the Havel. In time, the birds and their offspring took over the whole island and gave it the name by which it is still known today.

Wilmersdorf

From the air, **Wilmersdorf** ⓲ looks like a topographical cross sitting between the city and Grunewald. The district stretches from the Bundesallee right to the very heart of western Berlin and then westwards to the banks of the Havel. Of its 34 sq. km (13 sq. miles), almost half consists of pine forest. The combination of the city on one side and trees on the other is what gives Wilmersdorf its attraction. This district is by and large middle-class and includes an above average proportion of well-educated professional and well-to-do widows.

For most of its over 700-year history, Wilmersdorf was a simple farming community. At its historical heart on Wilhelmsaue the inscription on a granite slab pouts out that "farmsteads surrounded by fields gave Alt-Wilmersdorf its identity in the olden times". A farmhouse on the old village green is the last surviving monument to that rural era. The Shoeler-Schösschen was built in 1754.

The Bundesallee leads from the Zoo quarter south to the Bundesplatz. As a former royal boulevard it was among the grandest addresses in western Berlin. What was left standing of the avenue after the air raids was sacrificed to an eight-lane through road during the route planning which is sometimes called the "second destruction of Berlin".

Of architectural interest is the former **Jaochimstalsches Gymnasium** (high school), a neoclassical brick building with a 150-metre (50-ft) arcade dating from 1880 and inspired by Schinkel. Hidden behind the ancient trees at

Map on page 194–95

BELOW: the Summer Palace on Pfaueninsel.

Map on page 194–95

Statue of Chancellor Otto von Bismark in the Grunewaldturn.

BELOW: the Russian church on Hohenzollerndamm in Wilmersdorf.
RIGHT: Pfaueninsel (Peacock Island).

Schaperstrasse 24 is the venue is **Bar jeder Vernunft** (tel: 883 1582; daily shows 8.30pm; late night shows Fri and Sat 11.30pm), a permanent marquee in the car park of a former Theater der Freien Volksbühne. This cabaret theatre, with interiors resembling a "mirror-tent" from the 1920s, brings together local celebrities on stage as well as offering unknowns the chance to display their talent.

Wilmersdorf prides itself on being a haven of religious tolerance. This arose from the emigration wave in the 1920s when thousands of Russians came to Wilmersdorf. A Russian Orthodox church was built for them. There is also a Swedish church, an Islamic mosque and three synagogues. The Jewish population at that time was nearly 30,000. West of the city motorway, Wilmersdorf merges with the suburban idyll of Schmargendorf, where at Berkaer Platz you can admire the Rathaus (built in 1902) which is an especially fanciful example of Brandenburg Gothic. Because it is now a registrar's office, its romantic turrets and towers are immortalised in countless wedding albums.

Grunewald

At Roseneck, Schmargendorf borders on the Grunewald area, where you'll find Berlin's most expensive residential area. At the end of 1981, the **Wissenschaftskolleg zu Berlin** (Berlin School of Sciences), modelled on America's Princeton University, opened its doors at Wallotstrasse 19. Top international scientists of all fields pursue their research here as "fellows", free from the usual obligations of university life. Berlin's upper classes meet in the Rotweiss tennis club on Hundekehlesee, where Steffi Graf is a member. Its reputation as Berlin's most feudal tennis club dates back to the early days of the villa community at Grunewald. Conceived in 1890 as the crowning glory of the extended Kurfürstendamm, Grunewald was an ideal choice of home for affluent citizens keen to avoid paying city taxes. Until it became part of Greater Berlin in 1920, the town came under the financial control of Teltow, whose taxes were more lenient.

On a hill on Havelchaussee stands the 55-metre (183-ft) **Grunewaldturm** (Grunewald tower; Havelchaussee 61; open daily; entrance fee), a favourite with day-trippers from the city. The neo-Gothic building was commissioned by Teltow in 1857 in memory of Emperor Wilhelm I, and designed by Franz Schwechten, who was also responsible for the Gedächtniskirche in Charlottenburg. At the base of the tower is a pleasant restaurant.

The superstructure of a radar station on **Teufelsberg** shimmers in the distance like the holy dome of Sacré-Coeur or some Russian cathedral. The highest point in western Berlin at 115 metres (383 ft), Teufelsberg was piled up after the war from 25 million cubic metres of rubble. From the summit American and British personnel listened through the ether to what was going on in the former Eastern Bloc.

During the winter a lower plateau on Teuffelsseechaussee provides an imitation Alpine setting for Berlin's amateur sports enthusiasts. Climbers and hanggliders practise on the slopes of the "rubble mountain", which offers a wonderful panorama. There is a small lake, the Teufelsee, at the bottom of the hill. ❏

NORTHWEST DISTRICTS

*This chapter details the historic town of Spandau and
its surroundings, places of interest in Tegel and
the changing face of Wedding*

Map
on page
194–95

I n the centre of **Spandau ⑳** there was, and probably still is, a slogan spray-
painted on a railway bridge: "It has always been something special to be a
Spandauer!" There is some truth in the saying, which has also become the district administration's motto. Spandauers – the inhabitants of the formerly independent town on the Havel – have always been conscious of their origins,
especially with regard to their relationship to Berlin. "I have 11 districts and one
republic – Spandau," Mayor Reuter once joked about the distinctive local patriotism of the Spandauer smallholders.

They fought passionately against absorption into Greater Berlin in 1920.
Town councillor Emil Müller anticipated the approaching storm before World
War I, when a splendid town hall was built in Spandau costing almost 3½ mil-
lion gold marks. "May the Emperor's hand protect us from Greater Berlin and
administrative union," he stormed in 1911 during the ceremonial laying of the
foundation stone. The emperor departed and Greater Berlin came into being.
Spandau became the focal point of the administrative district of the same name.
Its 86 sq. km (33 sq. miles) make up almost one-sixth of the total area of the old
West Berlin and it is the second largest Berlin district.

Spandau is the only part of Greater Berlin on the west bank of the Havel,
and shares a 32-km (20-mile) boundary with Nauen in
the former East German district of Potsdam. Of the
historic sights in Berlin, the Zitadelle Spandau with its
Juliusturm (tower) ranks at the top of the list. After the
war, Spandau's name drew worldwide attention
because of its prison for war criminals and the high-
ranking Nazis imprisoned there. The German Overseas Development Agency (DED) has its headquarters
in Kladow, which includes a school that prepares 250
aid workers a year for work in the Third World.

Economically and commercially, Spandau plays a
major role in the life of Berlin. The largest industrial
district in the old Western sector, its chief claim to
fame is that it is the home of Siemens, the Reuter
power station and BMW's sleek motorbikes.

Spandau, along with Köpenick, is one of the oldest
parts of Berlin. Thanks to its suburban location on the
Havel's west bank, it has preserved much of its
original rural frontier character. The Old Town was
threatened with demolition in the 1960s, but it now
has protected status.

Its grid of narrow streets and the Nikolaikirche are
two reminders of Spandau's original autonomy. It is
proud to be five years older than Berlin and was first
officially mentioned in 1232 when a royal letter
awarded the Civitas Spandowe market and customs
privileges. Some people believe that Spandau's union
with Berlin was only properly finalised with the

PRECEDING PAGES:
Zenerbrücke at
Tegel.
LEFT: painting of
Nikolaikirche.
BELOW: Zitadelle
Spandau,
Juliusturm (tower).

There are plenty of places to eat and drink in Spandau; many are concentrated around the Kolk.

BELOW:
Zitadelle Spandau.

advent of the underground. Since 1 October 1984, the extended line 7 has been transporting people between the city and the heart of Spandau in 25 minutes.

As if to make up to her older sister for the loss of her independence, the Berlin Board of Works took great care with the decoration of the last three U-Bahn stations. In the terminus by the **Rathaus Spandau** (town hall), "Spandau at the gates of Berlin" (as it advertises itself) welcomes visitors with all the trappings of the post-modern age: ornate black marble columns, gleaming brass and old-fashioned light fittings.

Zitadelle Spandau (Spandau Citadel)

Spandau's importance as a trade and fortress town rested on its choice waterside location. The copper-plate engraver Magnus Merian captured this in 1652 in one of the earliest drawings of the city. Directly outside the Old Town, on what is now Lindenufer, two navigable rivers meet. The Havel flows from Mecklenburg in the northeast and joins with the Spree on its course to the Elbe. Furthermore, in the Middle Ages the trade route from Magdeburg to Poland also passed through the town. Such a strategically important spot therefore had to be well guarded. The Brandenburg nobility was quick to recognise this. Documents reveal that Spandau has had a fortress since 1197. In 1557, Elector Joachim II ordered it to be extended into an "impregnable modern stronghold".

The master builder Chiaramella de Gandino designed an imposing moated castle in high-Renaissance style with four angular bastions. The resulting **Zitadelle Spandau** (Spandau Citadel; open Tues–Fri 9am–5pm, weekend 10am–5pm; entrance fee), is considered to be a masterpiece of "modern Italian fortress construction". No other European fortress of its like has been so well

Map on page 194–95

preserved. As the mighty brick walls come into view through the trees beyond the Zitadellenbrücke (Citadel Bridge), they glimmer with a reddish hue. The oldest part of the citadel is the 12-metre (40-ft) wide **Juliusturm** (tower), which dates back to the time of the medieval Spandau castle, the residence of the Brandenburg princes and nobility. A wooden spiral staircase leads 30 metres (100 ft) to an observation platform, from where you can enjoy a marvellous panoramic view over the diverse Spandau countryside.

The heavily fortified citadel was intended to guard the river-crossing on the road to Berlin. When the Prussian court, including the queen, her sisters-in-law and heir to the throne, fled to Spandau in the Seven Years' War they took with them the royal finances, silverware and secret documents.

The castle also served as the Prussian state prison, where the rulers had officials and political hot-heads locked up. These included "Turnvater Jahn" (the father of modern gymnastics) and 1,495 revolutionaries from the Berlin uprising of March 1848. After the 1870–71 war, the 2.3-metre (8-ft) thick walls of the Juliusturm protected the state war coffers that were filled with French reparation payments: 120 million marks in gold mint packed in 1,200 crates. In 1919, the gold was returned to the new victor as reparation for war damages.

The citadel, which from the air looks like a huge star, was used by the military until 1945. As long ago as 1817 it housed a secret rocket laboratory. More recently the German army experimented with highly toxic substances in the military defence installation. At the end of World War I, these were either buried or sunk into wells. Now life is peaceful in the citadel.

In the Kommandantenhaus (Commander's House) on the right just after the railway bridge, the **Stadtgeschichtliches Museum Spandau** (Spandau museum,

LEFT: reflection of the Juliusturm and Zitadelle.

Am Juliusturm 35; open Tues-Sun 10am–6pm; entrance fee) mounts exhibitions such as a series on "Spandau and the History of Europe". Concerts, art exhibitions and poetry readings are held in the former Palais (Knights' Hall). In the evenings, visitors can enjoy a medieval banquet to a minstrel serenade in the atmospheric setting of the crypt. It is also favourite hibernating place with bats, 10,000 of whom spend the winter here.

Spandau Altstadt (old town)

The citadel lies on an island outside the town centre. The bridge Am Juliusturm crosses to the right bank of the Havel and the **Altstadt** (Old Town). The oldest part of Spandau, the Kolk, stretches to the north, just downstream from the bridge. Time seems to stand still as you stroll along the cobblestones past quaint 18th- and 19th-century dwellings. The names of the three streets recall the old settlements that once stood here. The first, Behnitz, already belonged to Spandau in the 13th century.

The **Kolk** used to be directly linked with the citadel. The house at Behnitz 3 formerly belonged to the military. In the evenings, the castle guards used to make merry in the three village inns. The fishing village Damm lay on the edge of the Kolk and, to this day, the allotments still possess royal fishing rights.

At the Kolk, or to be more precise, at the intersection of Möllentordamm and the Behnitz, there is a small "balcony", from where you can observe the **Schleuse Spandau** (Spandau lock) in operation. Paddle boats, motorboats, yachts, tugs and barges, and even the tourist steamer *Moby Dick*, must pass through this needle's eye linking the upper and lower reaches of the Havel. The lock is soon to be enlarged by a second chamber to allow European traffic to

BELOW: portal detail from Nikolaikirche in the Altstadt.

reach the industrial zone on the upper Havel. At present more than 35,000 boats use the north–south route every year. Berlin has a weekend flotilla of about 75,000 yachts and motorboats and about 100 watersports clubs have sprouted on Spandau's shores. At the Weinmeisterhorn, downstream from the Frey-Brücke, is the start of a 2,000-metre (2,200-yd) regatta course. In the peak season for weekend sailors the lock is in operation up to 17 hours a day.

The medieval Altsadt which sprawls on the other side of the bridge was built to an oval ground plan in the first half of the 15th century. In the middle rises the church of St Nikolai, one of the oldest Gothic town churches in the Brandenburg March. Rochus, Count of Lynar, who completed the construction of the citadel in 1594, donated the Renaissance altar. A bronze statue outside the main entrance commemorates Elector Joachim II's conversion to Protestantism is 1539. The daily life of Spandau has been preserved around Reformation-splatz. The Middle Ages are in fact just under the street paving. During excavation work for a new building, the foundation walls of a 13th-century Dominican abbey were discovered. The ruins are carefully preserved in an "archaeological basement", and can easily be viewed from the outside through the large glass panes.

Until the beginning of this century, Spandau led the life of an enclosed fortress town. As early as the 14th century, it had already surrounded itself with a defensive wall, some scenic remains of which are still to be seen in Kinkelstrasse. Spandau grew into a military town and the arsenal of Prussia. The first factories were erected for military purposes: in the 18th century the Prussian army set up a carbine factory. Ammunition factories, artillery works and a cannon foundry followed in the 19th century. Products from these are displayed

Map on page 194–95

BELOW: Schleuse Spandau (lock).

COFFEE CULTURE

One of the first things on a Berliner's mind after work is a "Molle" (a glass of beer). Usually frequented by men, the "Kneipe" (German pub) is a typical piece of German culture – Berliners drink around 140 litres (296 pints) of Bier (beer) every year. So important is it that all German Bier must adhere to the Reinheitsgebot (purity regulation), which ensures that water, hops and malt are the only ingredients to pass your lips. The new breed of Berliner doesn't frequent the Kneipe so much, preferring to drink a beer or have coffee in a café-bar.

Today, café-bars and coffee shops are all over town. Most of them offer breakfast till late in the afternoon (adapting to the lifestyle of the Berlin youth) and the relaxed licensing hours mean that some establishments stay open till the last person drops. Berlin received its first café in 1791, when an Italian introduced the concept to the Lustgarten. In the following years, coffee drinking became so popular that, in order to stop money leaving the country, Friedrich the Great prohibited it in Prussia. The last word in coffee shop etiquette should be left to the ones who know best. A hallowed institution, "Kaffee und Kuchen" (coffee and cake) should be taken in the same way as the English take afternoon tea in the late afternoon.

today in the inner courtyard of the citadel. It was only after disarmament in 1903 that Spandau began to grow beyond its old limits and the **Neustadt** (New Town) grew up along the roads leading to the north.

The Allied war prison

Rudolf Hess (1894–1987) was appointed Hilter's deputy in 1932. He was in charge of Nazi party organisations until his flight to England in 1941 where he was held as a prisoner of war until 1945 when he was tried as a war criminal at Nuremberg and imprisoned.

Until 1987 Spandau's former **Allierte Kriegsverbrechergefängnis** (Allied War Criminal Prison) on Wilhelmstrasse 21–24 was surrounded by high walls and warning signs in a multitude of languages. It was erected in 1878–81 to accommodate up to 600 prisoners. In 1947, the four victorious powers agreed to intern seven of the main defendants in the Nuremburg war crimes trials here, including Rudolf Hess, Hitler's former deputy, who was sentenced to life imprisonment. After 1966 he was the only remaining inmate of the prison. Guarded by French, British, American and Russian troops on a monthly rota, he led an eerie hermit's existence. A pardon would have been possible only by a unanimous decision on the part of the four Allied powers. However, although Hess was over 90 and half-blind, the Soviets blocked his release for 40 years. So the old man's last days were divided between the prison and the British military hospital. On the first day of every month there was a ceremonial Changing of the Guard, a sorry spectacle to which Hess himself finally put an end by his suicide on 17 August 1987. The building has since been torn down and replaced by shops.

Towns around Spandau

BELOW: half-timbered house in Spandau Altstadt.

A trip to **Gatow** and **Kladow** ㉑ reveals the delicate charm of the area around the Havel. The BVG ferry line operates a regular passenger service from Wannsee. Both villages in Spandau's deep south were incorporated into the

district in 1920. They still lead an independent existence, centred on their historic churches, although more and more villas and bungalows are forcing their way between the last few remaining farmhouses.

About 40 percent of Spandau is either water or greenery. The district has 69 working farms, cultivating a total of 650 hectares (1,605 acres). Billowing wheat fields are not an unusual sight around Kladow in summer, and in Gatow you might get a farmer to sell you milk from his cows or some fresh free-range eggs. In the former sewage fields around Gatow, rare ferns and different species of birds have reappeared.

The **Gatower Heide** (heath), a 350-hectare (865-acre) nature reserve, is a beautiful place to enjoy long walks. Out towards the north, just beyond Hakenfelde, is the expansive **Spandauer Forst** (forest), which includes several small moor nature reserves, lakes and streams. The largest reserve is Teufelsbruch, which provides a habitat for rare animals, birds and plants including wild boar. Another old small town, Hakenfelde is also interesting for the Evangelisches (Prostant) Johannesstift, an ensemble of hospital, therapy centres, school, church, conference and seminar venues, dating from 1910.

Any description of Spandau would be incomplete without mentioning its industrial counterpart to the east, **Siemensstadt** ㉒. In 1899, the rapidly expanding electrical firm of Siemens and Halske opened a cable and dynamo factory on the Nonnendammallee. Land along the Spree then cost seven pfennigs per square yard, but the workers had to contend with a long walk to the factory or with commuting by steamer. By 1906, the factory at the gates of Charlottenburg employed 10,000 people. It was absorbed by Spandau and officially christened "Siemens Town". In the 1920s it developed into a model of a green-field factory

Map
on page
194–95

BELOW: old house in a rural village.

town, with its own housing areas, which now spread from Siemensdamm to Jungfernheide. The skyline of the "electropolis" is dominated by Hans Hertlein's functional cubic brick architecture. Its most distinctive feature is the **Siemensturm** (tower) at the Werner-Werk für Messwerktechnik (Werner Instrument plant), which is over 70 metres (233 ft) high. About 60,000 people worked in Siemensstadt in the 1930s. Today, the number has fallen to 20,000 employees. Siemens has now moved its headquarters to Munich but remains Berlin's top employer in the electrical industry.

Reinickendorf

About 4 million passengers pass through the hexagonal customs hall at Tegel Airport every year. Few are aware that they have landed in **Reinickendorf ㉓**, which, with Pankow, form the northernmost of Berlin's districts.

Tegel was already making its mark on the history of aviation at the beginning of the century. In 1909 Count Zeppelin's airship Z3 landed on what was at that time a rifle practice and exercise ground. In 1931, on the disused military land, 19-year-old Wernher von Braun launched the first liquid-fuel rocket, the predecessor not only of the V2 which was used to bomb London, but also the American space rocket. This makes Tegel one of the birthplaces of world space travel. The first runway for planes was constructed in 1948–49 during the Berlin Blockade. The 2,400 metres (8,000 ft) was completed in just three months and was at that time the longest in Europe. From then on the four-engine "raisin bombers" droned daily over north Berlin. On 14 April 1949, 362 American airlift planes landed in the space of 24 hours. Tegel has been in use as a civilian airport since 1960 and after the main airport at Tempelhof could no longer cope

BELOW:
Zenerbrücke, Tegel.

with the mounting number of passengers, it was expanded to become one of the most modern airports in the world in 1974. Arriving at Tegel from the air, woods and lakes stretch out beneath you. As in Spandau, they make up a large part of the district. Not for nothing is Reinickendorf known as the "green north": almost one-quarter of it is woodland. But its profile includes fields and meadows and former villages such as Lübars, where some farming is still carried out. Then there are villa communities such as Frohnau and Hermsdorf and, as a contrast, the tower blocks of the Märkisches Viertel, probably Germany's most famous housing estate from the 1960s.

The city's second largest district, covering an area of 90 sq. km (34 sq. miles), Reinickendorf is not only a favourite recreation spot. In the industrial area north of the airport, the old-established Borsig works have been going for 90 years. The Berlin inventor and engineer August Borsig had chased the English competition from the market by the mid-19th century with his steam engines. The Borsig-Werktor at the works entrance on Berliner Strasse – an arch embellished with Gothic turrets and battlements – bears witness to the company's importance at the turn of the century. In the year 2000 the Borsigturm (tower) was modernised and turned into attractive offices for new up-coming enterprises in the branches of communication, internet, multimedia and consulting.

The old village of Tegel, the centre of which lies just a few hundred metres to the north, lost its rural character with the advent of industrialisation. It is now the only place in Berlin where the shopping centre is accessible by steamer. The street Alt-Tegel, which has been a pedestrian zone since 1976, links the shopping centre with the jetties on Tegeler See and the **Greenwichpromenade**. The promenade around the 4-metre (13-ft) deep Havelbucht (Havel Bay) is the

Map on page 194–95

The chapel at the Russian cemetery at Wittestrasse 37.

BELOW:
Tegel Centre.

starting point for some attractive shore walks. But the lake's scenic appearance is deceptive. Even in the early 1970s, biologists were raising the alarm when increasing phosphate levels threatened to pollute the lake. A phosphate elimination plant, which is cleverly shaped like a steamer, went into operation in 1985, in an attempt to improve the quality of the water.

Schloss Tegel

The gem of Tegeler Forst (forest) is **Schloss Tegel** (guided tours Mon 10am and 11am and 3pm and 4pm; entrance fee). Built by the Grand Electors as a hunting lodge, the building has been in the possession of the von Humboldt family since 1766 and was redesigned by K.F. Schinkel in 1820. The building is open to visitors in the summer months but the parks are open all year round.

Across the lake on the Reiherwerder peninsula, you may catch the facade of a castle-like building shimmering through the trees. Ernst Borsig, the nephew of the locomotive king and owner of the Tegel works, had this palatial residence built in 1911 – **Villa Borsig**. Not far from the Villa Borsig on the junction of Karolinenstrasse and Heiligenseestrasse, two public houses vie for the title of Berlin's oldest inn. The Alte Fritz was still called the "Neuer Krug" when the young Crown Prince Friedrich allegedly changed his horses and drank beer here in the old posting-house on the road to Rheinsberg.

Other famous guests of the house were the Humboldt brothers and Goethe, who stopped here in 1778 during his only journey to Berlin. It is said that the innkeeper told him ghost stories, which he later used in Faust: "The devil's pack, it pays no heed to rules, we are so clever, and yet in Tegel there are ghouls." Directly opposite the Alter Fritz is the Alte Waldschenke, which only became popular with day-trippers from Berlin during the 20th century. Until then it was a workhouse. It is hard to give the simple, half-timbered building an exact date, but it is said to have been erected between 1760 and 1770.

Reinickendorf's heritage as part of the Brandenburg March is reflected in its country manor houses. In the genteel villa suburb Frohnau, on Edelhofdamm, is one slightly different house – the **Buddhistisches Haus** (Buddhist House). Set in a park on a hillside, featuring pagodas, it was built in 1924 for the doctor and homeopath Dr Paul Dahlke. He had converted to Buddhism on a journey to Sri Lanka and after his death was buried in the temple gardens. The centre, the oldest Buddhist centre in Europe, belongs to the German Dhammaduta Society in Sri Lanka and is organised by two monks from Sri Lanka. The house is open all day – the temple for meditation, a library for reading and study, and the grounds for reflection.

Reinickendorf, or more accurately the area of Wittenau, is also famous for an institution known disparagingly and sometimes discriminatorily as "Bonnie's Ranch". The nickname originated among drug users and refers to the **Karl-Bonhoeffer-Nervenklinik** on Oranienburger Chaussee, Berlin's largest psychiatric hospital, which is also involved in treating heroin addicts – of which Berlin has its share. The clinic was founded in 1880 under the name

Schloss Tegel houses the Humboldt Museum. The extensive park was probably laid out by the celebrated Prussian landscape gardener Peter Joseph Lenné. The park contains the Humboldt family tomb, designed by Schinkel and constructed in 1830.

BELOW:
Schloss Tegel.

Map on page 194–95

Irrenanstalt Dalldorf (Lunatic Asylum). The farming folk of Dalldorf found it distasteful to be so closely associated with such an institution. So in 1905, approval having been cleared at the highest levels, the town was renamed Wittenau, after its leader Peter Witte. The hospital remained and achieved a reputation in specialist circles for its early attempts to provide its pitiful inmates with therapy as well as sanctuary. During the Third Reich, the clinic's history was less distinguished. Behind these walls, crimes of euthanasia were committed by unscrupulous Nazi doctors and wardens.

Märkisches Viertel

A few kilometres away, a 16-storey block towers into the sky, notorious throughout the entire federal republic as an architectural disaster. The **Märkisches Viertel** is a prime example of the dehumanising, purely technocratic building styles of the 1960s. The tallest, ugliest building stands on Wilhelmsruher Damm immediately behind the Postbrücke. The residents' name for it speaks for itself – "Langer Jammer" (long lament). The satellite town with space for 50,000 people in 17,000 apartments was built between 1963 and 1974 to rehouse those displaced in the inner-city "redevelopment zone" in "light, air and sun", designed by about 20 architects. Progress came in the shape of concrete. Now the authorities are trying to soften the bleak architecture by painting it and making various other improvements. Germany's first adventure playground was built here on the initiative of local parents and children, who found recreational facilities inadequate. At Senftenberger Ring 25 there's also a children's playhouse, the first heated house to be built in Europe in the so-called "earthern construction style" – the work of architect Engelbert Kremser.

BELOW: the Buddhistisches Haus, Tegel.

HANNA HÖCH

Hanna Höch was born in 1889 and studied graphics in Berlin where she became involved in the Berlin Dada movement through her lover Raul Hausmann. After World War I Germany experienced rapid industrialisation and the growth of consumerism. This resulted in the rapid growth of mass media and a social shake-up that included the redefinition of the role of women in society. Within this changing environment a group of Berlin-based artists called the Dada Painters questioned the political situation and its social implications amid the disillusionment after the war and the shift away from imperialism to capitalism. Through their art they aimed to challenge bourgeois values and reflect the hopes and fears of the new society.

Within this framework Hanna Höch created a remarkable group of photomontages. Taking photographs from magazines such as *Biz*, for whom she worked, she juxtaposed images of modern German women with images of their pre-war counterparts. In doing so she challenged cultural representation of women, raising questions of women's sexuality as well as their gender role in the new society.

In 1938 she married Kurt Matthies and in 1945 exhibited in Berlin and in the Museum of Modern Art in New York. She died in Berlin in 1978.

Taking to the Water

Berlin is a city built on water. It has six rivers, 50 large lakes and more than 100 smaller lakes and ponds, two major canals within the city boundary (as well as those which link the biggest rivers, the Havel and the Spree, with the Oder and the Elbe), about 35 islands, 31 summer bathing beaches (most of which are beautiful sandy lakeside spots) and 1,662 bridges.

The city started out as a tiny fishing village on an island and waterways have played a big part in Berlin's growth and prosperity. As an inland port Berlin once belonged to the influential Hanseatic League which controlled international shipping routes. The canals which flowed into the Oder and then the Baltic or into the Elbe and then the North Sea, and subsequently the Atlantic, were the vital arteries of a wealthy bourgeoisie. This trade along the internal waterways has seen something of a revival recently, although it doesn't have much economic significance.

Today the main function for the city's lakes and rivers is recreational. Both the major beaches in the city, say Berliners, measure up to any Mediterranean resort. Well, almost. The seething mass – of families unpacking their picnic hampers, of young bikini-clad women on parade along the promenade and of macho men displaying their tanned muscles on the beach – does convey something of the feel of St Tropez.

The view over the bay does not focus on a solitary white ship on the distant horizon, but on a sea of white sails and chugging motorboats. There are over 35,000 sport and sailing boats in Berlin and on some days it seems as though it ought to be possible to cross the Wannsee using the densely packed boats as giant stepping stones.

If you haven't got access to a boat, then find out when the Ausflugsdampfer (pleasure steamers) sail. A steamer trip is just as much a part of Berlin life as beer and meatballs. Make the trip at night if you get the chance. Then it's a "moonlight cruise", so loud and boozy that the moonlight usually becomes a minor detail. It is also possible to take a three or four hour boat trip along the Spree river and the Lanwehrkanal which take in some of Berlin's major sights. Longer trips also travel along the Spree and Havel rivers.

The islands of Berlin are little sanctuaries for dreamers, even if they do contain garden gnomes and vegetable plots. Some are too small for habitation or else they have been designated as conservation areas, but most of them are used by country recluses who have created their own little empires with a summerhouses and apple trees. The prettiest islands are on the Havel. Schwanenwerder – or Bonzenwerder (Bigshot Island) as it's sometimes called – is exclusive. The Pfaueninsel (Peacock Island, *see page 248*), on the other hand, is a public park, a horticultural masterpiece with a small castle, which King Friedrich Wilhelm II's mistress had built.

In Treptow there is a small island called Liebesinsel or Love Island. It's uninhabited and there is no ferry service, but when did such minor inconveniences deter true lovers? ❏

LEFT: taking a ferry trip.

Lübars and Heiligensee

A popular rural spot for day-trippers from the city is the village of **Lübars**, whose fields reach right up to the high-rise blocks. Some farming still goes on here, about 140 hectares (350 acres) of corn is grown every year. In the west of Reinickendorf, wedged between Tegelwald and the Havel, are the villa suburbs of Konradshöhe and Tegelort. This is also where you'll find Berlin's only car ferry, which runs from Tegelort across the Havel to the Aalemannufer at Spandau, operating a regular service.

Map on page 194–95

Right in the north is the sleepy fishing village of **Heiligensee ㉔**, one of 30 settlements to have grown up around Berlin in the Middle Ages. The courtyard on the village green on Alt-Heiligensee street betrays traces of the original village character.

The artist Hanna Höch (1890–1978, *see tint box on page 265*), probably the most famous inhabitant of Heiligensee, is buried in the cemetery beside the 16th-century church. Höch is credited with inventing collage. In the 1920s she was the only female member of the "Berlin Dada" school of artists. Denounced as "degenerate" by the Nazis in 1939, she moved to a house at An der Wildbahn 33 where she harboured several irreplaceable works by her fellow artists of the Dada school until the end of the war.

The signpost for Heiligensee. Artist Hanna Höch is buried in Heiligensee's church cemetery.

Wedding

"Red Wedding, welcome your comrades, hold your clenched fists high. Keep your ranks unwavering, for our day draws nigh…"

Erich Weinert's proletarian battle song from the late 1920s was once typical of the **Wedding's ㉕** reputation. It was already a stronghold of the socialist labour movement at the time of Germany's industrial expansion in the late 19th century. On 9 November 1918 workers at the AEG and Schwartzkopff plants marched on the government quarter with their revolutionary red flag. Faced with rising unemployment towards the end of the Weimar Republic, the communists held more and more sway in Wedding. At the parliamentary elections held in 1928, they gained more votes than the Social Democrats and, for the first time, became the strongest political party.

BELOW: entrance to the AEG plant.

At the turn of the 20th century Berlin was the largest industrial city in continental Europe. When the engineering and electrical industries moved in to north Berlin towards the end of the 19th century, at the time of rapid industrial expansion, thousands of workers were attracted to Gesundbrunnen and Wedding. Both districts had been part of Berlin since 1861, but now building land was in short supply. When pharmacist Ernst Schering bought a piece of land for his future factory on Müllerstrasse in 1858 it was still surrounded by fields and the last two windmills. Soon this was to change dramatically. Five-storey tenement blocks with dark inner courtyards shot up out of the ground, unbearably close to each other.

In the 1920s, more than 250,000 people lived packed together in the district's 15 sq. km (6 sq. miles), most in damp, dingy apartments. Mass poverty and factory work – if you were lucky enough to have a

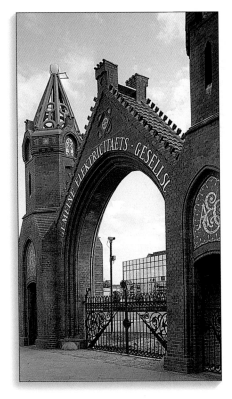

job at all – characterised the daily round in proletarian Wedding. In the wake of the industrialisation process, led by heavy and engineering industries (which were in Wedding represented by Wöhlert, Pflug, Egells and Schwartzkopff) other industries gradually developed. This was notably the chemical and electrical industries and also the food industry as Berlin's population crossed the million mark in 1877. The biggest of these in Wedding were AEG, Osram, Schering, Riedel, Essig-Kühne, Wittler-Brot, and the chocolate factory Hildebrandt. The chemical and pharmaceutical company Schering, originating from his "Grüne Apotheke" (Green Pharmacy) on Chausseestrasse, turned into an early multinational already before World War I.

The AEG plant

Wedding's industrial character has changed dramatically in the latter part of the 20th century. Nothing demonstrates this more clearly than the deserted AEG entrance in Brunnenstrasse, dating from 1891. One hundred years of Berlin industrial history came to an end when the electrical firm founded by Emil Rathenau in 1883 had to close its last production plant at Wedding in 1984.

Now the former "white-collar gate", a decorative neo-Gothic brick gateway, is reflected in the tinted glass of a state-of-the art office block. The computer firm Siemens-Nixdorf built a factory, employing 1,200 people, on the same site (No. 111). All around are the old AEG buildings, stretching as far as Ackerstrasse. The former light motor plant on Voltastrasse and the heavy machine plant on Hussitenstrasse, which was also known as the "cathedral of work", stand out as pioneering examples of industrial architecture. They were designed by architect Peter Behrens. Wedding's largest employer today is Schering AG.

The Zuckermuseum (Sugar Museum; Amrumer Strasse, Wedding) details the history of the sugar industry in Berlin. It is open Mon–Thurs 9am–4.30pm and Sun 11am–6pm.

LEFT:
Brunnenstrasse, Wedding.
RIGHT: exhibit in the Zuckermuseum.

About 5,000 people are employed at the extensive works on Weddingplatz and it employs 20,000 people worldwide, a fact it boasts with a 14-storey aluminium-clad headquarters. Together with the research centre, which is almost as high, it towers over the southwest corner of Wedding. Known mainly for the contraceptive pill and other special pharmaceutical products, Schering is the only international company to have retained its head office in West Berlin.

Map on page 194–95

Today, the area around **Ackerstrasse** is known as Silicone Wedding and the microchip age is evident in the AEG complex. On Gustav-Meyer-Allee are the offices of BIG, the Berliner Innovations und Gründerzentrum (Centre of Innovation and Business Start-ups). The Kunstquartier Ackerstrasse has established a new arts exhibition centre in one of the old factories. The environmental artist Ben Wargin uses the inner courtyard to show his highly original creations. Many of the Gewerbehöfe (inner courtyards of buildings, used for manufacturing and trade), restored or unrestored, have become the home for small new businesses in the IT and service sectors as, for example, on Gerichtstrasse.

The former assembly hall of the matchstick machine factory A.Roller on Osloer Strasse (No. 12) was turned into a cultural and local community centre in the early 1980s after production had stopped in 1977. "Fabrik Osloer Strasse" was a concept to counteract the economic and social decline of the district with cultural and social projects, a phenomenon mainly associated with Kreuzberg.

Wedding's parkland

A good one-fifth of the district, just over 297 hectares (734 acres), is parkland, located mainly around the man-made hill (87 metres/285 ft) at **Humboldthain**, the Schillerpark and Volkspark Rehberge – the latter famous for its open-air

BELOW: new industry in Wedding.

Map on page 194–95

summer theatre. Both banks of the river Panke, which rises in Pankow and flows through the district into the North Harbour, have been planted with trees and bushes to create an attractive riverside walk.

Compared to the 1920s, when Wedding was a burgeoning industrial district, its population has almost halved (161,000). At the same time the population density in the district (approximately 10,000 per sq. km/25,000 per sq. mile) is at least twice the average in Berlin. It also has the second highest share of foreigners (29 percent) after Kreuzberg. Wedding, like its eastern neighbour Prenzlauer Berg, is a working-class district, where you'll hear the thickest Berlin accents in the streets.

To appreciate how much the face of the district has changed since the war, take a walk through the redevelopment area on Brunnenstrasse, south of Gesundbrunnen S-Bahn station. The large area of new buildings was once a deplorable, poverty stricken slum. One of the most notorious examples was Meyer's Hof at Ackerstrasse 132–33, a run-down tenement with six courtyards. At one point up to 2,000 people lived here in just 230 tiny apartments with only outdoor toilets. In an attempt to rid itself once and for all of its grey stone boxes and squalid image, the district went in for demolition in a big way in the 1960s. The proletarian areas of old buildings on either side of Brunnenstrasse and Badstrasse were cleared away, together with their tenants, and the whole social and economic structure of the surrounding area changed.

From the start, the Social Democrats led the way in local politics. Wedding's first subsidised housing estates date from the time of the first SPD mayor, Carl Leid. In Kurt-Schumacher-Haus at Müllerstrasse 163 are the headquarters of the regional branch of the SPD. The Afrikanischesviertel (African Quarter) with its "living cubes" designed by Mies van der Rohe, is one example. Other famous Weimar architects such as Bruno Taut, Paul Emmerich and Paul Mebes responded to the degrading 19th-century tenements with their designs for apartments on the Friedrich-Ebert-Siedlung (housing estate) between Müllerstrasse and Rehberge.

Two neoclassical churches, the **Alte Nazareth Kirche** on Leopoldplatz and **St Paul's Kirche** at the corner of Bad Strasse and Pank Strasse in the Gesundbrunnen quarter are based on K.F. Schinkel's design and are among the oldest buildings in the district.

The Rudolf Virchow Hospital, named after its founder, stretches to the northern bank of the Berlin–Spandau Ship Canal. As a doctor and Progress Party member of the Reichstag, Virchow was committed to the building of a modern hospital in overpopulated North Berlin. It was opened in 1906 as a "garden city for the sick" with 57 pavilions, revolutionary for those times. Nature was to help heal the patients.

Nobel Prize winner Robert Koch (1843–1920), who discovered the cholera and tuberculosis bacilli, moved his Institute for Infectious Diseases from Charité to Wedding's north bank in 1900. Today, members of the Robert Koch Institute and their colleagues in the Federal Health Department are playing a key role in Aids research. ❏

BELOW: travelling along the Spree.
LEFT: *Molecule Man* sculpture in Treptow.

POTSDAM

*A visit to Potsdam is one of the most popular day trips from
Berlin; its highlights include Schloss Sanssouci,
Neuer Garten and Filmpark Babelsberg*

Map
on page
276

●Potsdam

Potsdam is an integral part of Berlin. Surrounded by lakes and fields, the town is easily accessible by train and bus. A trip to Potsdam should be part of every visitor's itinerary. Its attractions not only include the famous palaces and gardens of Sanssoouci, but also a remarkable old town whose streets and squares radiate a faded but brilliant charm.

Potsdam is an intriguing blend of a mighty Prussian garrison town and the splendour and elegance of a royal residence. The splendour is wearing thin here and there – more evidence of its changing history. Potsdam's fate was closely associated for centuries with the rise and fall of Prussia. Finally the destruction caused by World War II and the misjudged building concepts of the socialist period have left their mark. The new shopping centre tacked onto Potsdam-Stadt, the main station, is just one of the last projects in a long line of bright ideas which have changed the shape of this historic town in the past century.

Thousand-year history

In October 1990, Potsdam once again became the main city of the reformed Brandenburg *Land* or county. Before that, for almost 40 years it was the main city of the GDR area of Potsdam. In 1993 it celebrated its 1,000th anniversary: the date relates to records which come from the year 993, in which the place name "Poztupimi" (generally interpreted as Potsdam) was first mentioned.

Very little is known about Poztupimi's beginnings. It is known that it was inhabited by Slavs. German feudal lords conquered the area in the 12th century. The first official records mentioning Potsdam by name date from the 14th century. Its inhabitants lived by fishing and agriculture. The city played only a minor role economically as it lay outside the main trade routes. The situation changed dramatically in the second half of the 17th century when Elector Friedrich Wilhelm elevated Potsdam to be the Brandenburg-Prussian royal residence. "The entire eylan [*sic*] must be a paradise," he demanded of his architects. One can only guess as to why he chose this small city. Certainly the fact that the area was heavily forested must have played a part in his choice – it is well known that the Hohenzollerns were keen hunters.

A further reason may have been the town's lack of political and economic significance. A self-confident bourgeoisie who would show resistance to the absolute will of the elector would not be a problem here. As a result Potsdam's architecture was almost exclusively moulded by the ideas and tastes of royalty, and its economy developed according to the needs of the palaces and the garrison. A Prussian tradition, which is once more a welcome part of everyday life

PRECEDING PAGES:
facade carvings at
Schloss Sanssouci.
LEFT: statue
of Frederick the
Great at Schloss
Sanssouci.
BELOW: punting
on the Havel river.

here, is liberality towards different religious beliefs and acceptance of various ethnic groups. It began even before the promise given by Old Fritz (as Friedrich was known) that in his country everyone could worship according to their own beliefs. As early as 1685 the Great Elector issued an edict from Potsdam, an invitation to the Huguenots who were being persecuted in France, to build themselves a new home in the cultural and economic backwater of Prussia. In the event the Huguenots played a large part in the development of Prussia as a great European power.

This carried very little weight with the son of the Great Elector, Friedrich I (1688–1713). During his reign, Potsdam became an extravagant court in the style of Versailles. So that he might be comparable to the French Sun King Louis XIV, the Elector of Brandenburg bought himself, at great expense, the title "King in Prussia" from the emperor. His son was contemptuous of such vanities. Friedrich Wilhelm I despised the French court culture. He was the first European monarch always to wear uniform. The bourgeois-Protestant virtues which he drummed into his people, industriousness, duty, order, thrift, discipline and punctuality, enabled him to make unprecedented reforms.

The construction of a modern administrative state, compulsory school attendance, and the guarantee of religious freedom were all part of his initiative. The instrument used for the implementation of these swingeing reforms was the army, and it was the military who gave Friedrich Wilhelm I the nickname "Soldier King".

Under Friedrich Wilhelm I, Potsdam became a garrison town. In place of barracks he ordered houses to be built, in which he quartered the soldiers. During his long reign the city tripled in size, with the number of buildings growing

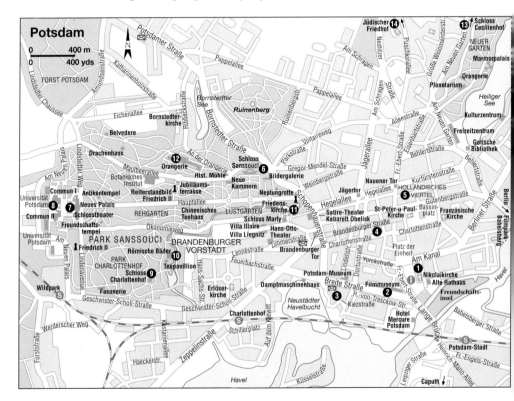

from 220 to 1,150. Friedrich Wilhelm I died in 1740. Under his son Friedrich II, Prussia developed into the most modern state in Europe. It gained respect as a great power after it won territory following the Silesian War (1740–42 and 1744–45) and because of its stance against stronger enemies during the Seven Years' War (1756–63).

Regarded with awe by the progressives in Europe and feared by the old powers, a legend in his own life time, Fredrich became known as "the Great".

This most popular of Prussian kings has to this day an aura of inapproachability, even though some 500,000 people a year are whisked through his pleasure palace of Sanssouci. Friedrich was a believer in the French Enlightenment. As a relaxation between slaughters he wrote French verse and sent them to Voltaire, a three-year resident in Potsdam, for correction. In Potsdam he surrounded himself with a circle of leading artists and intellectuals of whom the best, discouraged by the moodiness of the "hobby philosopher", avoided or secretly longed to escape.

Sans souci means without worries, and Schloss Sanssouci expressed the deep longing of the military leaders: the wish for a civilian life free from court etiquette and military drill, a life devoted to the arts and sciences, in perfect harmony with nature. If the Soldier King gave Potsdam its ground plan, Friedrich II gave it its characteristic appearance. Due to the new layout of the house facades, squares and arches, he gave the city a uniform appearance. The king sketched hundreds of facades himself, mostly in the Italian style. But behind the splendid Italianate facades the soldiers and workers lived, to a large extent, in modest apartments. After Friedrich the Great the realm declined as a result of the weakness of his successors. In 1806 the country

Map on page 276

BELOW: overview of Potsdam.

was overrun by Napoleon's troops. Potsdam was the main cavalry depot of the French army until 1808. After the occupation was overthrown the land was impoverished, the population in need.

In the 19th century Potsdam developed from a large barracks into a city, even if it still carried the military stamp of the Prussians. The authorities were prepared to go to great lengths to prevent the establishment of industries, so as to spare the king the sight of factory chimneys and emaciated workers. All around the baroque heart of the city stood the cultural landscape of Potsdam, an extensive civic work of art with fountains, lakes and gardens, parks and palaces. The great landscape designer Peter Joseph Lenné and the architect Karl Friedrich Schinkel were responsible for the design. Following the victorious end of the war against Austria in 1867, Berlin became the capital city of the North German federation and seat of the Reichstag. In 1871 Kaiser Wilhelm I finally made Berlin the capital of the German Empire. In 1895 the Wilhelminian Potsdam had 58,000 inhabitants, an eighth of whom belonged to the military.

The industrialisation which Berlin's foundation period set in motion circled Potsdam but did not include it and increasingly it became a retirement area for Prussian civil servants and military personnel. Only the annual spring parades pushed the city into the limelight for a few days. Even the Potsdam nobility seemed at this time to be almost paralysed, apart from the odd small scandal, which usually could be quickly hushed up.

As a result of Germany's defeat in World War I, Wilhelm II was forced to abdicate. The parks and palaces were handed over to the state, and the military nature of the city was lost. Potsdam remained a civil service city, however. Many government agencies, for example the Auditor General's office, were based there. Eventually the once proud city of Potsdam became a suburb of Berlin, a museum for the tourists and for those in the 1920s who still dreamt of the days of the Kaiser.

Weisse Flotte Potsdam (tel: 0331-275 9210 for details) operates boats on the Havel and the lakes around Potsdam.

BELOW:
Nikolaikirche.

Palaces and gardens

The oldest example of electoral architecture, the Potsdamer Stadtschloss (Potsdam City Palace) on **Alten Markt** (the Old Market), which dates from 1660, no longer exists. In April 1945 it was heavily damaged in the great air raid on the city. In 1961 the ruins were removed, a decision which is greatly criticised today. Since 1990, however, the possibility of reconstructing the original facade of the Stadtschloss, with a modern hotel or community institutions behind it, has been extensively discussed.

The two other buildings which dominate the appearance of the Alten Markt, the Alte Rathaus and the Nikolaikirche, were rebuilt in the 1960s and 1970s. The **Alte Rathaus**, whose tower with the gilded Atlas figure is visible from a long distance, was built by King Friedrich II in the style of an Italian palazzo. In the course of the reconstruction the architects linked the building with the adjoining **Knobelsdorffhaus**. Together they serve the city as a centre for culture and art. The **Nikolaikirche ❶** (St Nicholas' Church; open Mon 2–5pm, Tues–Sat 10am–5pm, Sun 11.30am–5pm) is regarded as one of the most significant buildings of the neoclassical period. The central building with cupola was built in the middle of the 19th century according to drawings made by Karl Friedrich Schinkel but purists have few good words for the restoration. The **Marstall** (Royal Stables, previously the Orangerie) of the Stadtschloss between Schloss Strasse and Breite Strasse received its present form from the architect Knobelsdorff in 1746. Today it houses the excellent **Filmmuseum ❷** (open Tues–Sun 10am–6pm; entrance fee) which comprehensively documents the history of German cinema from just before the start of the 20th century until 1980. The museum also details the history of the Babelsberg studios, which now house Filmpark Babelsberg *(see page 286 for details).*

Socialist memorials

Potsdam could well stand as a symbol of the contradictory traces of the Prussian tradition inherent in the foundation of the GDR state. This tradition, after all, symbolised military might, discipline and great power politics. Yet instead of a critical appraisal of these aspects of the national past, which might perhaps have proved useful, those in power simply used repression as their tool.

An example of this is the fate of the Potsdamer **Garnisonkirche** (Garrison Church), which was to be found in Breite Strasse on the corner of Dortustrasse. It was built in the 1830s by the architect Philip Gerlach and was regarded as a significant architectural achievement. The church attained regrettable notoriety on 21 March 1933, "Potsdam Day" when, within its walls, Hitler and Hindenberg agreed to the symbolic alliance between fascism and Prussian militarism. In 1945 the church was burnt down during a bombing raid. Only the tower was left standing. It was finally removed in 1968 despite the protests of many

Map on page 276

In 1991, after a break of 46 years, the recast bell from the demolished Garrison Church rang out again at its new location on the corner of Dortustrasse and Yorckstrasse.

BELOW:
Cecilienhof, the site of the Potsdam Conference of 1945.

Potsdam residents. In its place today stands the ugly Data Centre. Those who had fought for the preservation of the tower were reprimanded. The official line was that the removal of the tower represented a kind of exorcism of fascism and militarism, as if the spirit of these things lived in stone and brick and not in the hearts and heads of men. The approximate site of the former Garrison Church marks the Data Centre built between 1969 and 1972, on the corner of Breite Strasse. The 7-metre (8-yd) long mosaic on the ground floor is a kind of memorial to the GDR regime. It reads "Man conquers the cosmos".

The **Hiller-Brandtschen Häuser** (Hiller-Brandtschen Houses) opposite the Data Centre are named after their former residents. Soldiers were billeted in the narrow middle area. A model for these facades, paid for by the king, was a drawing of Whitehall Palace in London – an architectural sham, typical of the layout of the Frederican Potsdam. The facade-cult can be seen at its most extreme in Breite Strasse, looking from the palace towards Neustädter Tor.

Behind the Hiller-Brandtschen Häuser block and down as far as the Havel is **Kiezstrasse** ❸. There is nothing here to remind one of the former "Kiez", the fishing settlement by the gates of Potsdam. Thanks to the careful restoration of the two-storey rococo houses at the beginning of the 1980s, this is one of the loveliest streets in the city.

Until 1735 the northern city wall ran along the current Brandenburger Strasse. On the other side of this lies the "second baroque city expansion". This is bordered by Schopenhauerstrasse, Hegelallee, Hebbel and Charlottenstrasse. Work began on the area in 1734 during the reign of King Friedrich Wilhelm I. The Soldier King needed room for his Royal Guard, the "tall fellows" and other troops who were to be transferred to Potsdam. To this end he ordered the build-

BELOW: Hiller-Brandtschen-Häuser.

ing of two- and three- storeyed houses. Craftsmen and tradesmen from all over Europe came to work with the military, moved into the houses and rapidly turned the quarter into a multilingual, multicultural, melting pot. In the converted gables of the new houses the soldiers were quartered.

After the damage done to the old city in World War II, the area of "city expansion" was developed into the centre of Potsdam. The main shopping street of the quarter is **Brandenburger Strasse ❹**, which stretches from Brandenburger Tor to St Peter and Pauls Kirche. In the late 1970s, when there was a change of building policy, the street was lovingly restored and pedestrianised.

Map on page 276

The Holländisches Viertel (Dutch Quarter)

It was only after much protest at home and abroad that work slowly started on saving the unique **Holländisches Viertel ❺** (the Dutch quarter between Friedrich-Ebert and Hebbelstrasse) whose 134 redbrick houses formed an area of their own. Over the next couple of years, however, the rest of the area fell into ruin and many houses were pulled down. In Gutenbergstrasse and Hermann-Elflein-Strasse the gaps have been filled by modern timber constructions, which in height and form vaguely resemble the old building stock, but which in comparison appear plain and lacking in character.

An action group was only able to stop the demolition in the inner city after the political reunification. By then it was too late to save many houses. In 1945 there were 389 intact baroque houses in the city, but now there are fewer than 300. As late as August 1989 there was a great deal of protest about the demolition of the Theodor-Storm House, because it was in no way unsafe.

Friedrich Wilhelm I recruited Dutch workmen especially to build the squares in the correct style. They rammed entire oak forests into the boggy floor to create a solid foundation for the massive brick buildings. The king's intention to tempt large numbers of Dutch skilled workers to Potsdam was a failure. In 1742, the year of completion, only 22 Dutch families lived there. The remaining houses were given to soldiers and workers. Many of the artists who worked at Schloss Sanssouci had living quarters in the area. The sculptor Friedrich Christian Glume, creator of the figures on the garden facade of Schloss Sanssouci, lived at Mittelstrasse 25.

The **Holländischen Häuser** (Dutch houses) which stand at the end of Bassinplatz in the direction of **Brandenburger Tor** (Potsdam's own Brandenburg Gate precedes its more famous namesake by 21 years) were erected 30 years after the completion of the old Dutch quarter. In the house at Am Bassin 10 Mozart lived during his Potsdamer visit in May 1789. Mozart played many times for the king, but his hopes of becoming Kapellmeister were not fulfilled.

The restoration of classical statues is an ongoing process.

BELOW: Holländisches Viertel.

Schloss Sanssouci

The extensive grounds of Schloss Sanssouci with its palaces and historical buildings offer wonderful walks in all seasons. One can walk for hours through avenues and walkways, explore small paths, discover new views of foliage, sculptures, artificial ruins and splendid buildings. The special charm of the park is

the harmony of landscape and architecture which constantly presents a new and different aspect.

Sans souci (without care) is the name Friedrich II gave to the summer palace built by Knobelsdorff between 1745 and 1747. Here he wished not to entertain official guests but to enjoy life, to have a rural retreat where he could occupy himself with the arts and philosophise with intelligent companions. **Schloss Sanssouci** ➏ (open April–Oct 9am–5pm; Nov–March 9am–4pm; *see below for details;* guided tour; entrance fee) does indeed radiate a cheerful, rococo ease. This impression is amplified by the vineyard, the curved staircase, the trimmed hedges, the pergolas, goldfish ponds and the white marble statues, some of which, sadly, have suffered from the effects of pollution.

If you wish to see the inside of the palace, don't set out too late. The trust which runs the palace only allows 1,800 visitors a day. You must join a group of about 20–40 other people and wear the felt slippers provided. Tickets in the high season are usually sold out by lunch time. If possible, avoid Sanssouci at the weekend. The ticket office opens at 9am. Guided tours operate in summer until 5pm and in winter until 4pm. Competent members of staff are on hand to inform you about the various items of artistic and historical interest. The size of the palace is quite modest. The decoration is exquisite and happily free from exaggerated embellishment – the Stadtschloss fulfilled the function of representing the might of the Prussian court, and later the Neues Palais did the same, so it was thought not necessary to do so at Sanssouci.

The terraces, reminiscent of a vineyard with their warm, south-facing slopes, provide a fruit plantation all summer long. In glazed niches figs are grown and reseda vines grow along the rows, just as they did long ago. Flower and fruit

The park at Schloss Sanssouci is made up from a number of smaller gardens including the Lustgarten, the Dutch garden, the Marlygarten, and the Rehgarten.

BELOW: the rococo dome of Sanssouci.

ornaments are a speciality of Frederican rococo; look out for them as you go through the palace. You will see golden spiders on the ceilings and marble potatoes on the floors. In the parklands you will come across sculptures of Flora and Pomona, the flower and fruit goddesses.

It was on this terrace that Frederick had envisaged his own grave, but his successor and nephew, Frederick William II, considered such a resting place unworthy of a king and ordered that his coffin be put beside his father's in the Garrison Church. As the war was drawing to an end in 1945, his remains were whisked away to Swabia for safekeeping. In 1991, he was finally laid to rest on his beloved terrace, alongside his 11 favourite whippets (two more dogs are buried on the other side of the palace). The ceremony was a proud moment for those who still consider themselves to be Prussians. The coffins of Frederick and his father were brought from the Hohenzollern family home at Burg Hechingen near Stuttgart. Prussian flags accompanied the procession and the ceremony was attended by the German chancellor, Helmut Kohl. The solemnity of the occasion was disturbed, however, by a contingent of gay protesters who were intent on "outing" the great man, who enjoyed the company of his fellow men.

From the northern terrace you should be able to see the **Ruinenberg** (hill of ruins). The classical looking ruins appear to be from another period in history but they were deliberately so built by Friedrich II in 1754.

The main avenue from the large fountain going in the direction of the Neues Palais (New Palace) will take you past the **Chinesisches Teehaus** (Chinese Tea House; open mid-May–mid-Oct 10am–5pm; entrance fee) with its golden figures gleaming through the bushes and trees. Around 2 kg (5 lb) of gold leaf was used in the recent restoration work, which cost £750,000. The little round

Map on page 276

The Chinesisches Teehaus, designed by Johann Gottfried Bühring, was built between 1754 and 1756.

BELOW: the New Rooms in one of the buildings in the schloss park.

pavilion is an example of the fashion for all things Chinese which was popular in the 18th century European courts. The **Lustgarten** (pleasure gardens), largely the work of Knobelsdorff, end here with the geometrically styled hedges. The adjacent parkland was laid out by Peter Josef Lenné in the first half of the 19th century. The spacious lawns, groves and coppices appear to be natural rather than artificially designed. Lenné created individual gardens around the buildings to complement their respective architectural styles.

The building work on the **Neues Palais** ❼ (New Palace; open daily April–end October 9am–5pm; Nov–March 9am–4pm; closed Fri; entrance fee) began immediately after the Prussian victory in the Seven Years' War. Friedrich II, whose epithet "the Great" originates from this time, is said to have described the palace as a *fanfaronnade* (a show piece). The palace was intended to display to the world that, despite the heavy burdens of war, Prussian might was not diminished. The rooms of the 213-metre (232-yd) wide palace were equally splendid in layout. As in the building of Schloss Sanssouci, the king provided the drawings and followed the building process with great attention.

Once more he fell out with the pen pushing architects, who fled from Prussia soon after the building work began. When he was dissatisfied, the king was wont to throw his builders into a cell with only bread and water to eat for days, until they submitted to his will.

During the summer months when Friedrich II lived in the Neues Palais glittering parties were held in the splendid ballrooms. The family of the last Kaiser Wilhelm II celebrated Christmas Eve each year until 1917 in the beautiful Mussel Ballroom.

Behind the Neues Palais are the **Communs** ❽, two much more successful architectural pieces, designed by Carl von Gontard, which housed the royal household and the servants. In earlier times the meals were taken from the kitchen of the Communs to the Neues Palais via an underground passage. Today the buildings are used by the Brandenburgischen state high school, which was re-established in 1990. The buildings erected in the 19th century at Sanssouci are closely associated with the works of Karl Friedrich Schinkel and his pupils.

Schloss Charlottenhof ❾ (open mid-May–mid-Oct, Tues–Sun 10am–5pm; guided tour; entrance fee) was built like a Roman villa by Schinkel for Friedrich Wilhelm IV and is one of his masterpieces. The living rooms remain in their original state. They still convey a sense of the intimacy which was so valued by their royal inhabitant. One of the villa's highlights is the Humboldt Room which resembles a tent. The palace is surrounded by a park designed by Peter Joseph Lenné.

One feels transported to Italy in the **Römische Bäder** ❿ (Roman Baths; open mid-May–mid-Oct, Tues–Sun 10am–5pm; entrance fee), not far from the Maschineteich (Machine Pond). The southern character of the place owes much not only to the architectural details and the antique decoration but also to the fact that they were not erected according to one single preconceived idea. The individual pieces were added bit by bit. But the water-shy king never swam in them. The **Friedenskirche** ⓫ (Peace Church; open

A tour of the Neues Palais includes six of the most impressive of the palace's richly decorated 200 rooms.

BELOW:
Schloss Cecilienhof.

mid-May–mid-Oct, Tues–Sun 10am–5pm), at the eastern end, was built to resemble a Roman basilica and, in accordance with the wishes of Friedrich Wilhelm IV, replaced the garrison church of the Soldier King as the royal court's church. A 12th-century Italian mosaic was incorporated in the apse by the king. Under the altar lies the crypt which contains his coffin.

The **Orangerie** ⑫ (Orangery; open mid-May–mid-Oct, Tues–Sun 10am –5pm; entrance fee) is the most monumental building of the era. This creation of Friedrich Wilhelm IV can be seen as the Prussian equivalent of the over-the-top fairy-tale castle of King Ludwig II of Bavaria. The long side wings were intended to be winter quarters for the exotic plants which in summer, when they stand on the terraces, create the illusion that you are in Italy. In the middle section there is an art gallery for a collection of Raphael copies, and a guest room for the Russian Tsar Nikolaus I, the king's brother-in-law. Wilhelm IV went mad before the building was finished and therefore did not see the completion of his greatest achievement. The Orangerie's observation terrace, with views over Potsdam, is open Apr–mid-May at weekends; mid-May–mid-Oct Tues–Sun; entrance fee) and is well worth the climb.

Map on page 276

Statue in the grounds surrounding the Orangerie.

Schloss Cecilienhof and Neuer Garten

The only palace in Potsdam to have remained in the possession of the imperial family after 1918, and confiscated in 1945, is **Schloss Cecilienhof** ⑬ (open daily for guided tours except Mon; entrance fee) in Neuer Garten, the second largest parkland in the city, lying between Heiliger See and Jungfernsee. The palace was built for Crown Prince Wilhelm immediately before World War I. While people in the country starved and soldiers were dying at the front, the royal heir, who never came to the throne, allowed himself this luxury. Cecilienhof entered the world history books when in 1945 the heads of state of the three powers convened there to decide the future of con-quered Germany in the Potsdamer Abkommen (Pots-dam Agreement). The crown prince and his family fled the palace shortly before the Soviet troops marched in, taking all the furnishings with them. It was hastily refurbished to enable the delegation to carry out their task. You can visit the original confer-ence room with the famous round table, as well as the studies of Stalin, Churchill and Truman.

BELOW: marble statue in the grounds of Cecilienhof.

There are two goals worth remembering on your tour of the area around Neuer Garten. About a ten minute walk away, below the ruins of the Belvedere Schloss lies the **Jüdischer Friedhof** ⑭ (Jewish Cemetery) which was put at the disposal of the Jew-ish community during the reign of Friedrich the Great. It is the only remaining witness to Jewish culture in the area. East of Schloss Cecilienhof at the end of the Schwanenallee, the Glienicker Brücke (Glienick Bridge) is a reminder of the Cold War. Until the Wall came down it was a secretive place for the exchange of agents and the location for many films. The origi-nal wooden structure was replaced in 1905 with a steel construction which provided a suitable setting for the later operations of the secret service.

Potsdam has launched a campaign to encourage

Map on page 276

The 20-metre (65-ft) Einstein-Turm on Telegrafenberg was built in 1920.

BELOW: Glienicker Brücke, a symbol of the Cold War.
RIGHT: sunset at the Neues Palais.

tourism by bicycle or on foot to reduce the pressure on parking places in the town. Thanks to the area's lack of hills bicycles are a great way to see the sites *(contact the local tourist board for bike hire details)*. In a town centre the improved tram network, with its electronic scoreboard tram stops, aids the flow of human traffic but gives an odd 21st century edge to the old world feel of the place.

Filmpark-Babelsberg

Filmpark-Babelsberg (August-Bebel-Str. 26–53; open March–Oct, daily 10am–6pm; entrance fee), provides the visitor with yet another attraction. Once the largest film producers outside Hollywood, the Babelsberg Film Studios started out in 1912 as the home of the studio production company Bioscop. When the failing war effort in 1917 was attributed to poor propaganda, the Deutsche Bank stumped up the funds to aid the formation of Universum Film AG (UFA).

From 1921 the company transformed Babelsberg into its central film factory and continued to produce films – like *The Blue Angel* and *Metropolis* – until Soviet multiple rocket launchers rolled onto the site. Re-named Deutsche Film AG (DEFA) for its life in the GDR, many of its films didn't make it past one screening thanks to the watchful eye of the state. The fall of the Wall closed the studios but today they are again making films (although not to the same extent as in its heyday) and steering tourists round the plot which now doubles as a theme park. One of the theme park's highlights is the set of a Wild West town and visitors can also see some props from the studio's most well-known films.

Excursions into the countryside

If the hustle and bustle of Sanssouci and Nikolaikirche becomes too much for you, then make an excursion to the surrounding countryside of Potsdam. In the little village of **Caputh** Albert Einstein had a wooden house built in Waldstrasse 7, where he lived for three summers until his emigration in 1932. The modest dwelling has been used as a scientific meeting place and is only open to the public on Sunday morning. However, a detour is still worthwhile, the simplicity of the timber house and the choice of position on the edge of the woods with a view over the Templiner See tells us about the predilections of the great scientist and humanist.

From Caputh it's not far to **Werder**. The idyllic island city was, until World War II, the fruit cellar of Berlin. It was easy to ship the perishable fruits quickly to Berlin via the Havel lakes. The Berliners came in droves in the opposite direction to enjoy the fruits and their wines and the spring blossom festivals.

It is peaceful in the **Südwestfriedhof Stahnsdorf**, (Stahnsdorf Southwest Cemetery) 15 km (9 miles) east of Potsdam. The burial place is barely known despite its size of 200 hectares (500 acres). Here you will find the graves of many famous names: Lovis Corinth (painter), Friedrich Wilhelm Murnau (director of the film *Nosferatu*), Gustav Langenscheidt (publisher and language teacher), Werner von Siemans, Heinrich Zille and many others. ❏

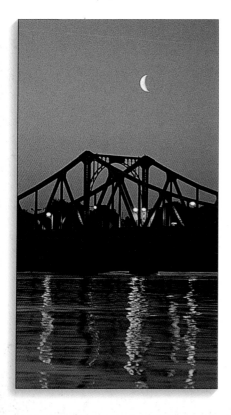

INSIGHT GUIDES
TRAVEL TIPS

Probably the <u>most</u> <u>important</u> TRAVEL TIP you will ever receive

Before you travel abroad, make sure that you and your family are protected from diseases that can cause serious health problems.

For instance, you can pick up *hepatitis A* which infects 10 million people worldwide every year (it's not just a disease of poorer countries) simply through consuming contaminated food or water!

What's more, in many countries if you have an accident needing medical treatment, or even dental treatment, you could also be at risk of infection from *hepatitis B* which is 100 times more infectious than AIDS, and can lead to liver cancer.

The good news is, you can be protected by vaccination against these and other serious diseases, such as *typhoid*, *meningitis* and *yellow fever*.

Travel safely! Check with your doctor at least 8 weeks before you go, to discover whether or not you need protection.

Consult your doctor before you go... not when you return!

SB
SmithKline Beecham
V A C C I N E S

Produced as a service to public health

CONTENTS

Getting Acquainted

The Place

Berlin, Germany's largest city, was re-established as the country's capital in September 1999 and is now fully operational as the seat of government and parliament.
Population: 3.4 million.
Language: German.
Religion: Mainly Protestant, 12 percent Catholic.
Area: 890 sq km (344 sq miles).
Highest point: Teufelsberg, 120 metres (394 ft).
Geography: Water, woods and meadows cover two-thirds of its area and there are 324km (201 miles) of paths beside its rivers and lakes. Over 900 bridges cross the waterways – more than in Venice.
Time zone: Central European time, one hour ahead of GMT, two hours ahead from April to September.
Currency: Deutsche Mark (DM), made up of 100 pfennigs (Pf). From 28 February 2002 the joint circulation of Marks and Euros will

Business Hours

Offices have flexible working hours between 7.30am and 5pm, on Fridays sometimes only to around 2pm. Business appointments are best made between 9 and 12am or 2 and 4pm.
Banks are usually open on weekdays 9am–4pm (lunch break possible), but are continually widening their services, at least in the city centres, so you may find some bank branches open for business on Saturday mornings.

come to an end. from then on the Euro (EUR), made up of 100 cents, will be the only currency.
Weights and measures: metric.
Electricity: 220 volts, two-pin plugs.
International dialling code: 49 (Germany) + 30 (Berlin).

Climate

The climate in Berlin is characterised by a mixture of ocean winds from the Atlantic and Continental air. During the winter it is sometimes very cold and in the summer months extremely high temperatures are rare. Nevertheless it is not unusual in January or February for temperatures occasionally to drop to –20°C (–4°F). The weather frequently remains quite cool until April. During the height of summer in July and August, temperatures may climb at times to 30°C (86°F) or higher. The summer months also often turn out to be the months with highest rainfall. In these months, hot, dry days can be interrupted by violent, heavy rainfall. The cooler temperatures of autumn come at the latest in the middle of October. Between November and March you may encounter snow.

Government

Berlin is one of the three city-states in the Federal Republic of Germany (the others are Hamburg and Bremen). It is situated in the middle of the German state called Brandenburg, of which Potsdam is the capital. The city is governed by the Senat (Senate), which sits in the Rotes Rathaus (red town hall).

On the 1 January 2001 Berlin's previous 23 administrative districts or Bezirke (boroughs) were reduced to just 12 after the majority of the districts were merged with their neighbours in order to cut administrative costs. Each is responsible for making local decisions and carrying out a wide variety of tasks. District authorities and mayors must answer to local district assemblies.

Public Holidays

Feiertagen (public holidays) are taken quite seriously in Berlin. Do all your shopping before the scheduled day of rest as only bars, restaurants, Turkish kiosks and supermarkets in the main stations will be open. Don't expect to find anyone in the office.
New Year's Day: 1 January
Good Friday: movable
Easter Monday: movable
May Day: 1 May
Christi Himmelfahrt (Ascension Day): movable
Whit Monday: movable
Day of German Reunification: 3 October
Christmas Day: 25 December
Boxing Day: 26 December

Economy

Berlin, once the largest industrial city in Germany, is now experiencing dynamic social and economic changes. Trade and services are taking precedence especially now that the city is once again the parliamentary seat and capital. The service industry, in particular, has expanded 50 percent since 1989. Large-scale manufacturing is also recovering after the stagnation of the last 60 years, with chemicals, textiles, pharmaceuticals and companies such as Siemens investing heavily. Through such institutions as Humboldt University the city is also considered the academic centre of Germany. The figures for tourism-related employment are 50,000 and rising.

Despite having one of the highest unemployment rates in Germany (16.5 percent compared with 9.3 percent nationally), Berlin, with its excellent infrastructure, access to East European markets and strong research and development capabilities, is expecting a bright future.

Planning the Trip

Visas & Passports

Visas are not required for EU citizens; a valid personal identification card or passport is enough to ensure entry and exit. Holders of Australian, Canadian, New Zealand, South American and US passports automatically get three-month permits on entering Germany but visas are required for longer stays. Visitors from many countries (particularly Asian countries) will need a visa.

Health & Insurance

You will find that health care in Germany meets high western standards. The doctors in Berlin are well educated and so there should be no complaints about the medical treatment. Phone the US or UK embassies *(see Embassies, Consulates and Missions)* for an extensive list of English-speaking doctors or call the International Emergency Hotline *(see below)*, to avoid a language problem during the consultation. Most medication can be found in the many pharmacists all over town. As name brands differ, people who need special medication should bring a sufficient supply or bring a list of the active ingredients.

No immunisation is currently needed for entry into Germany.

The national health insurance system completely covers doctors and hospital fees and only a token fee has to be paid for medication. All EU citizens will get the same treatment with an E111 form, but take care: it can only be used for emergencies. You may, therefore, wish to take out some private insurance before you go. All other foreign nationals should ensure, before leaving their home country, that they have adequate health insurance which covers them while they are abroad. Medical fees are very expensive in Germany and without insurance you will have to pay cash up front *(see Medical Treatment in the Practical Tips section)*.

Customs & Duty Free

For non-EU residents goods are tax-free up to the value of DM350. Gold, gold alloys and rolled gold, un-worked or semi-manufactured, e.g. cast bars, are an exception to this rule. If the goods are bought on the normal market in an EU country these restrictions do not apply. Apart from the normal prohibited articles, like weapons and endangered species, it is also not permitted to enter Germany carrying meat and meat products from countries included in the Commonwealth of Independent States, Portugal, Spain, Turkey and Africa and Asia.

Money Matters

The Deutsche Mark (DM) is a decimal currency made up of 100 pfennigs. Notes are issued in denominations of DM 1,000, 500, 200, 100, 50, 20 and 10, coins in denominations of DM 5, 2 and 1, and 50, 10, 5, 2 and 1 pfennigs (Pf). From 28 February 2002 the joint circulation of Marks and Euros will come to an end. From then, on the Euro (EUR), made up of 100 cents, will be the only currency.

There is no restriction on the quantity of money that may be imported.

All major credit cards are accepted in department stores and many high-quality shops, plus hotels, airlines, petrol stations and most restaurants. But there are still many occasions, especially in smaller shops and pubs, when credit cards are not accepted, so it is advisable to carry cash*. Credit cards give you access to cash from cash machines. Remember, though, that many banks charge a commission and fee every time you use your credit card abroad.

You'll find bank branches in department stores like the KaDeWe, in shopping malls like Potsdamer Platz Arkaden, and practically all over town. If you have an EC card you can get money from cash machines at bank branches city-wide. American Express has a Reiseland office in town where AmEx card holders can use their facilities: Bayreuther Str. 37, tel: 214 9830. For changing money and other services you should go to their office at Friedrichstrasse 172 (tel: 201 7400).

Bureaux de Change

Wechselstuben (exchange offices) have differing opening hours:
Bahnhof Zoo: daily 7am–1pm; tel: 881 7117.
Ostbahnhof: Mon–Fri 7am–10pm, all other days 8am–12pm, 12.30–4pm; tel: 296 4393.
Bahnhof Friedrichstrasse: Mon–Fri 7.30am–8pm, weekend 8am–8pm; tel: 2045 5096.
Tegel Airport: Mon–Sun 6am–10pm.
Tempelhof Airport: Mon–Fri 7am–10pm, Sat 7am–6pm, Sun 12.30–10pm.

There are also exchange offices in Bahnhof Alexanderplatz, Flughafen Schönefeld, Flughafen Tempelhof (Euro Change, tel: 6951 2850; Mon–Fri 7am–10pm, Sat 7am–6pm, Sun 12.30pm–10pm) and at Wechselstube (Joachimstaler Str. 1–3, Charlottenburg, tel: 882 1086, www.agw-berlin.de; Mon–Fri 9am–7pm, Sat 10am–3pm) at Bahnhof Zoo.

What to Pack

It is essential to take along warm clothing when travelling between October and April. In the summer you'll also be happy to have brought along a sweater or jacket. A lightweight raincoat and an umbrella will also stand you in good stead. With respect to the latest styles, just about everything and anything goes in Berlin; whether you attend the theatre dressed in an evening gown or jeans is entirely a matter of personal preference – whether you are admitted is up to the doorman. At clubs dress as you would for a night on the town at home.

National Tourist Offices Abroad

Australia: German National Tourist Office, c/o German-Australian Chamber of Industry and Commerce, P.O. Box A 980, Sydney South, N.S.W. 1235, tel: +61 (2) 9267 8148, fax: +61 (2) 9267 9035.
Canada: North Tower, Suite 604, 175 Bloor Street East, Toronto, ON M4W 3R8, tel: +1 (416) 968 1570, fax: +1 (416) 968 1986, email: germanto@idirect.com, www.germany-tourism.de.
UK: PO Box 2965, London, W1A 3TN, tel (brochure request): 0891-600100, tel (consumer info): +44 20-317 0908, tel (trade info): +44 20-495 0081, tel (press & admin): +44 20-495 0083, fax: +44 20-495 6129, email: German_National_Tourist_Office@compuserve.com.
US (New York): Chanin Building, 52nd Floor, 122 East 42nd Street, New York, NY 10168-0072, tel: +1 212-661 7200, fax: +1 212-661 7174, email: gntony@aol.com.
Chanin Building, 52nd Floor
US (Los Angeles): Post Office Box 641009, Los Angeles, CA 90064, USA, tel: +1 310-234 0250, fax: +1 310-474 1604, email: GNTOLAX@aol.com, www.germany-tourism.de.

German Embassies Abroad

Australia: 119 Empire Circuit, Yarralumla ACT 2600, Canberra, ACT. tel: 61/2 62 70 19 11 fax: 62 70 19 51.
Canada: 1 Waverley Street, Ottawa, Ontario K2P 0T8. tel: 613-232 1101 fax: 613-594 9330.

Getting There

BY AIR

Currently Berlin has three airports with regular scheduled flights: Tegel, Tempelhof and Schönefeld. Tegel, in the north, is the biggest of Berlin's airports and it is from here that most of the long-haul flights leave. Tempelhof, close to the city centre, is the airport for smaller carriers. But plans are in the works to remodel Schönefeld, which lies in the southeast corner of the city, into a major international airport by 2007. Tegel would then serve mainly domestic flights and the phasing out of Tempelhof would be completed.

There are direct flights from London-Heathrow, Birmingham and Manchester to Berlin-Tegel (TXL). AB Airlines operate between London Gatwick and Berlin-Schönefeld (SXF). Lufthansa flies once a week to Dublin. For ten years, there were no non-stop flights from the US to Berlin but now Lufthansa offers one to Washington DC. If you are flying with another airline or from another US city, there are good connections from Amsterdam, Paris and Frankfurt/Main.

Lufthansa Offices Abroad

UK: Tel: +49 0 69 696 0
US: Tel: 800 399 LUFT
Germany: 01 803 801 803

BY SEA

There are ferry connections from northern Germany (Hamburg and Rotterdam) with Scandinavia and the UK (Scandinavian Seaways

UK: 23 Belgrave Square, London SW1X 8PZ. tel: 020-7824 1300 fax: 020-7824 1435.
US: 4645 Reservoir Road NW, Washington DC 20007-1998. tel: 202-298 4000 fax: 202-298 4249 or 333 2653.

sailings on the Harwich Hamburg route). The port of Warnemünde has sailings to Trelleborg in Sweden.

From the Airport

Tegel and Tempelhof can be easily reached by regular public transport – Express Bus X9 runs from Tegel to Zoo station, where you can catch most bus and underground lines, and Tempelhof is close to the Platz der Luftbrücke underground station. The S9 and S45 underground lines run to Bahnhof Schönefeld, where you can catch a free shuttle to the airport itself.

BY RAIL

Through connections with Intercity and the ICE network, Berlin is quick and easy to reach by train.

At the moment there are two main stations in Berlin, the Ostbahnhof (East Station) and the Zoologischer Garten in the west of the city. Some trains stop at both stations, which can lead to confusion about departure times. Make sure you have the time for the station where you are actually boarding. Regional trains start in Bahnhof Lichtenberg, Alexanderplatz, and the Bahnhof Friedrichstrasse. You can purchase any type of train ticket at the Deutsche Bahn Reise Zentrum offices in all of these stations (Deutsche Bahn employees have a reputation for being unhelpful at times).

A huge new central station at Lehrter Bahnhof is being built near the new government buildings – it will act as a major European rail crossroads.

The Channel Tunnel is a quick way to get to Germany from the UK, but the Eurostar train, unless booked in advance, can be more costly than flying.

For information and reservations call: 01805-99 66 33 or on the web visit: www.deutschebahn.de.

BY ROAD

Germany's efficient motorway system is part of the European network. Berlin is surrounded by the Berliner Ring from where different motorways lead in all directions.

You can travel to Berlin on international bus lines. BerlinienBus (www.berlinienbus.de) has a daily bus running from London via Brussels to Berlin. Gullivers Reisen (www.gullivers.de) also has a daily bus directly from London. Both companies offer a variety of connections to and from Berlin with cheap prices and comfortable coaches that considerably breach the advantages of taking the train. You will arrive at the Omnibusbahnhof Funkturm, Radio Tower Bus Station on Masurenallee.

Travel Agents: Package and Other Tours

If you are thinking of taking a package vacation to Berlin, the best way to get information about different possibilities for your trip to Germany is to contact the German National Tourist Office. They have 26 foreign offices and sales agencies world wide, a large web site, www.germany-tourism.de, full of useful information, and a special site for Americans going to Germany www.visits-to-germany,com. You can either book your holiday through one of their offices or they can help you find a travel agent that will meet your needs.

Surf to www.deutschland-tourismus.de/e/1598.html to find the telephone number and location of a GNT Office in your country. The National Tourist Offices for Germany are on page 292.

Alternatively, take a look at what Eastline (www.eastline.com) have got to offer. They specialise in cultural and concert tours across Eastern Europe.

UK citizens can make use of DER travel service, Germany's largest travel agency on the internet. On www.dertravel.co.uk you can have a look at various package holidays, to suit your individual needs. You will find four-star hotels as well as pensions, you can go by air, by train or take your own car; you can arrange guided tours and collection from the airport if you want to. Bookings can be made by email: tours@dertravel.co.uk; by phone (reservation team tel: 020-7290 1111) or at your local travel agent.

If you chose not to book your holiday through a travel agent, have a look at the following website, either to have some idea about different accommodation possibilities and prices or to book on the internet. www.berlinfo.com offers lots of general information about Berlin, a long and varied list of hotels, hostels and camp sites in a wide price range. For people who are considering staying on in Berlin, Berlinfo even has information about renting or buying apartments.

FROM THE UK

Airtours Holidays, www.airtours.co.uk, tel (package): 0870-241 5299, tel(fly/drive): 0870-241 5400
British Airways Holidays, Astral Towers, Betts Way, London Road, Crawley, RH10 2XA, tel: 01293-723121, fax: 01293-722624.
DER Travel Service, www.dertravel.co.uk, tours@dertravel.co.uk, tel: 020-7290 1111.
Travel for the Arts, 117 Regent's Park Road, London, NW1 BUR, tel: 020-7483 4466, www.travelforthearts.co.uk, enquiries@travelforthearts.co.uk.

FROM IRELAND

Joe Walsh Tours, 8–11 Baggot St., Dublin, tel: 01-678 9555, fax: 676 6572, www.joewalshtours.ie, 31 Castle St, Belfast BT1 1GH, tel: 01232 241144.
Thomas Cook Overseas Ltd., 118 Grafton St, Dublin 2, tel: 01-677 1721, 11 Donegall Place, Belfast BT1 5AA, tel: 01232-240833.

FROM THE US

American Airlines Vacations, www.aavacations.com
EuroVacations.com
Go Ahead Vacations, www.goaheadvacations.com
Matterhorn Travel, 914 Bay Ridge Road, Annapolis, MD 21403, tel: 800-638 9150, fax: 410-266 3868, www.matterhorntravel.com

FROM AUSTRALIA AND NEW ZEALAND

Adventure World, 3rd Floor, 197 St Georges Terrace, North Sydney 2060, tel: 02-8913 0755, fax: 02-9956 7707.
73 Walker Street, Perth 6000, tel: 08-9226 4524, fax: 08-9281 3299, www.adventureworld.com.au
101, Great South Road, Auckland, tel: 09-524 5118, www.adventureworld.co.nz.
European Travel Office, 122 Rosslyn St, West Melbourne, tel: 03-9329 8844; 133 Castlereagh St, Sydney, tel: 02-9267 7727; 407 Great South Rd, Auckland, tel: 09-525 3074.

Specialist Holidays

The possibilities for specialist holidays, i.e. history, art and castles tours in Berlin is great or you can book different kinds of general guided tours once you're there. City Guide Berlin has tours on foot, by bike, car, tram or even by steamer or helicopter. Their website is at www.home.snafu.de/r.langer/ or you can call them on: 033-2961 4397, or fax: 033-2961 4415.

Practical Tips

International newspapers, magazines, city maps, etc. can be purchased after regular business hours from various stands at the Zoo, Alexanderplatz, Friedrichstrasse and Ostbahnhof stations, at the Ku'damm square, at Checkpoint Charlie (until 7pm) and in the Europa-Center (until 11pm).

NEWSPAPERS

In the middle of the 19th century Berlin developed into a significant media centre. Until 1929 it had 147 political newspapers and was the largest newspaper metropolis in the world. At the end of World War II, the allied powers occupying Berlin issued special licences for newspapers. After reunification the press experienced radical changes and increased their competitiveness.

Today the main competition is between the three major subscription daily papers. In order of circulation they are: *Berliner Zeitung* (with a total circulation of around 520,000) the *Berliner Morgenpost* and the *Tagesspiegel*. Published in Berlin but distributed nationwide are: *Die Welt*, to the right of centre; the *Neues Deutschland*, the former GDR official mass circulation daily, and the leftish, alternative paper *Tageszeitung (taz)*, which offers a change from the usual political monotony but is experiencing cash flow problems due to low circulation.

Although published regionally, the *Süddeutschezeitung* and the *Frankfurter Allegemeine* have sufficient circulation and content for them to be regarded as nationals.

Weeklies include the *Jungle World* and the culturally orientated *Freitag*. BZ and the *Berliner Kurier* are local tabloids, sold from newspaper stands. BILD, the broadsheet-cum-tabloid from the Axel Springer stable with various regional prints, is in the same vein.

At present the battle between publishers is intense. Some newspapers are handed out free of charge as early as three or four hours after publication.

MAGAZINES

The two twice-weekly magazines, *Tip* and *Zitty*, play an independent role in the Berlin media scene. Both cover local politics and cultural events and both have an extensive "What's on" listings section. All the important public events in Berlin from daily television and radio broadcasts to theatre productions, concerts, films, art exhibitions and panel discussions are listed here.

Monthly magazines include the lifestyle magazine, *Prinz*, and the tourist-oriented *Berlin Programm* which also has a "What's on" listings section and hotels, restaurants and tours listings. *Berlin: The Magazine*, a bilingual guide produced every four months, is published by Berlin Tourismus Marketing and is especially designed for tourists. Other titles from BTM include the annual *Berlin Moments* and *Event Flyer*.

RADIO AND TELEVISION

There are a great number of radio stations in Berlin. The broadcasting organisations SFB (Sender Freies Berlin) and ORB (Ostdeutscher Rundfunk Brandenburg) operate a number of different radio stations, from the all-news *Info-Radio* to *Fritz*, a youth station, and *Radio MultiKulti*. All the local stations provide regular local and international news bulletins. The BBC's World Service is on 90.2FM. English-language news from the USA can be heard on Rock Star FM at 87,9.

German television is divided into government-controlled television (*öffentlich-rechtliches Fernsehen*) and commercial TV stations, the most popular of which are SAT 1 and RTL. The state-run national TV stations are ZDF and ARD, with the latter providing a regional service. *Landesrundfunkanstalten* provide the so-called "third" programmes. Local channels that are easy to receive include Pro 7, ORB and TVB. With an electrically powered antenna you can receive BBC World and many households and hotels receive other international TV broadcasts from NBC, CNN via satellite or cable.

There are a handful of different websites on or about Berlin. The best for English speakers is **www.berlinfo.com** which has information on everything from applying for a residence permit to films showing in English. Berlin's official site, **www.berlin.de**, is a fairly comprehensive platform but pages in English are limited. At **www.berlin-info.de** is run by the Berlin Tourist and Marketing board and concentrates on their products.

INTERNET

The first thing most people do on holiday these days is email the friends they've left behind. A lot of bars have internet access as do many of the hostels. If you still can't find a computer, here is a small selection of web-cafes.
alpha Internet- and Computer Café, Dunckerstr. 72, Prenzlauer Berg, tel: 447 9067, www.alpha-icafe.de, daily 2pm–midnight. With a small bar, a range of small snacks and friendly, helpful staff, this small internet café

takes the stress out of cyber space. **Website – Internetcafé,** Joachimstaler Str. 41, Charlottenburg, tel: 8867 7360, daily 10–2am. Use one of the 40 terminals and sample something from the ample menu. **Webtimes – Internetcafé,** Chausseestr. 8, Mitte, tel: 2804 9890, Mon–Fri 9am–midnight, Sat–Sun 4pm–midnight. Costing between DM7 and DM9 per hour, the internet access here is some of the cheapest around. Patrons create the usual kind of webcafé atmosphere.

Postal Services

Postamt (Post offices) are usually open Mon–Fri 8am–6pm (with smaller ones closing at noon for lunch and some of the larger ones staying open until 6.30pm), and Sat 8am–1pm. You can have your mail sent care of an individual main post office provided it is marked "poste restante". Your mail will be left at the counter identified by the words *Postlagernde Sendungen*. Mail is best received at Postamt 120 (Zoo), Postlagernd, 10612 Berlin and Postlagernde Sendungen, Postamt Rathausstrasse, 10178 Berlin.

Briefkasten (local post boxes) are emptied at least once a day (late afternoon); those designated with a red point are emptied more frequently and later in the day. Ensure you post your mail in the correct slot. For mail leaving Berlin use the one marked "Andere Postleitzahlen", usually found on the left side. On weekends, however, there is a limited service.

When sending parcels, it is advisable to use the yellow "Pack-Sets" on sale at post offices. **Hotline postal customers:** 01802-3333; **Hotline business customers:** 01805-5555 If you want to send a telegram you can do so at the post office or use the freephone service: dial : 0180 5 12 10 for inland, or 0800 33 01133 for telegrams to foreign countries. **Post offices** are usually open Mon–Fri 8am–6pm, and on Sat 8am–noon. There are a few post offices with longer opening hours:

Main Post Office, Budapester Str. 42, Charlottenburg, tel: 2693 8831, Mon–Sat 8am–midnight, Sun 10am–midnight. Bahnhof Zoologischer Garten: Mon–Sat 6am–12am, Sun and holidays 8am–12am. Flughafen Tegel: daily 6.30am–9pm, Sat–Sun 8am–8pm. Flughafen Schönefeld: Mon–Fri 8am–7pm, Sat–Sun 8am–3pm. Bahnhof Friedrichstrasse, Georgenstr. 12: daily 8am–10pm.

Telecommunications

For most public pay phones you need a telephone card which can be purchased for DM12 in post offices or at newspaper stands. Some booths still take coins. For long-distance calls you can also dial direct from most public phone boxes or the operator at the post office will make a connection for you. Since the privatisation of German Telecom there has been competition from companies offering cheaper tariffs. You can make use of them in some "call cafés". Check the newspapers for the Vorwahl (low-tariff call pre-dials) – it can be much cheaper. This number should be dialled before any international or national codes.

Every place of reasonable size in Germany has its own dialling code, which is listed under the local network heading. Should you have a language problem, dial 11837 (inland directory enquiries in English) or 11834 (international directory enquiries). Phone calls from foreign countries to Germany must be preceded by 49, then the local dialling code without the 0. For Berlin the code is 49 followed by 30.

Local Tourist Offices

The main information office, located at the **Europa-Center** (Budapester Strasse entrance), is open Mon–Sat 8.30am–8.30pm, Sun 10am–6.30pm. Another information office is situated at the **Brandenburg Gate** and is open

daily 9.30am–6pm, and there are info points at **Tegel Airport** (main hall, opposite Pos. 0), open daily 5am–10.30pm, and in the **KaDeWe travel centre,** Mon–Fri 9.30am–8pm, Sat 9am–4pm.

Potsdam Information, Am Alten Markt, Friedrich-Ebert Str. 5, 14467 Potsdam, tel: 0331-27 55 80; fax: 275 5859. Hotel reservation, tel: 0331-275 58-55. Open: Mon–Fri 9am–8pm, weekends 9am–6pm.

Local Information

Deutsche Zentrale für Tourismus e.V. (DZT), Beethovenstr. 69, D-60325 Frankfurt am Main; tel: 069-97464, fax: 069-751903, www.deutschland-tourismus.de. **Berlin Tourismus Marketing GmbH (BTM),** Am Karlsbad 11, D-10785 Berlin; tel (reservation): 25 00 25, tel (info DM 2,90 per min): 0190-016 316, tel (from abroad): ++49 1805-75 40 40, email: information@btm.de. Provides help for travel preparations and will send brochures, hotel and shopping guides as well as a variety of other informative publications. You can also book hotel rooms by phone, post, fax or email.

Embassies, Consulates & Missions

European Community Commission: Press and information office, Unter den Linden 78, 10117 Berlin; tel: 22 80 20 00. **Australia:** Friedrichstr. 200, 10117 Berlin; tel: 88 0088-0, www.australian-embassy.de. **Canada:** Friedrichstr. 95, 10117 Berlin; tel: 20 31 20, www.kanada-info.de. **Ireland:** (Honorary Consul General) Ernst Reuter Platz, 1587 Berlin; tel: 3480 0822. **UK:** Wilhelmstr. 70–71; tel: 204 570, www.britischebotschaft.de. **US:** Neustädtische Kirchstr. 4–5; tel: 830 50, www.usembassy.de.

Women Travellers

Most women in Berlin say they feel safe alone on the streets at night. Rape and assault are rare occurrences. When out after hours by yourself, use your common sense. Avoid all parks, especially Tiergarten in the centre of town – it's not Central Park, but it is wise to be cautious. You can stop in for a nightcap at most bars in the city and be left in peace. If you do attract any unwanted attention, be straightforward and your suitor will get the message. Berlin women are known for being very vocal about what they want, so don't worry about being considered rude.

In the daytime, anything goes. You might get the odd catcall, but your best resource is to ignore it. If you want to read a book in a park or drink a coffee in a sidewalk cafe, no one will try to disturb you.

Public transport is safe, day or night. In stations and on lines in the far Eastern blocks of the city – areas you probably wouldn't frequent on your average visit – isolated incidents of racist violence have been a problem in the past. But most of the transport you would take during your stay is heavily trafficked and very safe.

In summer, women in Berlin will wear anything from a strappy tank top and short skirt to the Turkish head scarf. Wear whatever you feel comfortable in. On beaches and in parks, German women have absolutely no problem stripping down to their underwear or lounging around in the nude, whether they are escorted or not. If you want to take in some sun yourself, your best bet is to check if those around you are clothed or not before you strip completely. Some areas of swimming pools, beaches, and public parks are designated FKK (Frei Körper Kulture, or free body culture), in such cases you are expected to wear at least a bathing suit unless you are in the FKK section. If you are surrounded by nude bathers but would prefer to preserve your modesty, no one

would bat an eye. Berlin has a long tradition of influential woman, be it feminist or otherwise, and this is reflected in the number of institutions, services and clubs exclusively for women.

Helplines for Women

The **Frauenkrisentelefon** (tel: 615 4243, 615 7596; Mon and Thur 10am–12pm, Tues, Wed, Fri 10am–12pm, 7–9pm, Sat–Sun 5–7pm) offers advice and gives information on everything.
Notruf – Rape Crisis Phone Line (tel: 251 2828; Tues–Thur 6–9pm, Sun 12–2pm) is there to help in case of rape or sexual harassment and will help deal with all the relevant people.

ACTIVITIES

EWA **Frauenzentrum**
Prenzlauer Allee 6, Prenzlauer Berg; tel: 442 5542; Mon–Fri 10am–6pm; café and gallery Mon–Thur 6–11pm Standing for "Erster Weiblicher Aufbruch" or "first female awakening", the EWA offers counselling, advice, courses, discussions, readings and workshops for women. The first women's centre to open in the East after the Wall, it has all the facilities you could ever need.
Schoko-Fabrik
Mariannenstr. 6, Kreuzberg; tel: 615 2999, www.schokofabrik.de; Office hours – Mon–Thur 10am–2pm. In this renovated chocolate factory, women can take part in classes, courses and workshops and then take a plunge in the Turkish Bath.
Das Verborgene Museum – The Hidden Museum
Schlüterstr. 70, Charlottenburg; tel: 313 3656. In this museum dedicated to art by female artists, previously forgotten works are brought to the fore.
Hamam Turkish Bath
Schoko-Fabrik, Mariannenstr. 6, Kreuzberg; tel: 615 1464; Sept–June Mon–Sun 3–10pm. Located in the Schoko-Fabrik, this

women-only Turkish bath will help lift the woes of the world off your shoulders. Drink tea and head for the Finnish sauna with the ladies.
Seitenwechsel
Kulmer Str. 20a, Schöneberg; tel: 215 9000; Tues 5–7pm, Thur 4–6pm. If you would rather practise sport in a women-only environment, head for Seitenwechsel where you can take part in all kinds of sports.

OUT AND ABOUT

Compania
Anklamer Str. 38, Mitte; tel: 4435 8704, brigitta.schilk@berlin.de; Mon–Fri 11am–6pm
Berlin's first escort agency for lesbians and women runs Friday night tours of the city which take in bars, clubs and other cultural and historical places. You can pay to have a guide just to yourself.
Frauentouren
Sophienstr. 32, Mitte; tel: 281 0308, frauentouren@t-online.de, www.home.t-online.de/home/frauentouren Not just exclusively for women, these walking tours cover the last 700 years of women in history. Among the points of interest are buildings, streets and memorials, all linked intrinsically with the development of women in the city.
Frauen Unterwegs
Potsdamer Str. 139, Schöneberg; tel: 215 1022; Mon–Thur 10am–2pm, 5–7pm, Fri 10am–2pm

Accommodation

artemisia
Brandenburgische Str. 18, Wilmersdorf; tel: 873 8905, frauenhotel-berlin@t-online.de Opened in 1989, Berlin's first women-only hotel has conference room and welcomes groups and business travellers. Each room is dedicated to notable women of Berlin's past. **$$**
Intermezzo
Ander Kolonnade 14, Mitte; tel: 2248 9096
Friendly, inexpensive and bang in the centre of town.

The cultural tours organised by this women-only association cater for small groups. Some trips trace the achievements of notable women and meet up with locals. Walking and language based holidays are on offer as well as workshops.

Disabled Travellers

Although not the most wheelchair friendly city in Europe, Berlin is getting its act together. A lot of the U- and S-Bahn stations now have lifts for easier access but until all stations have them it makes travelling around a bit of a mixed bag. Check the transport network map inside the back cover of this book for details of disabled access. Where boarding the S- or U-Bahn is potentially difficult, the driver or platform controller will be glad to assist or provide you with a ramp – wait at the front of the train. More and more buses can now lower to street level to aid entry. The BVG also operates a taxi call service (Taxi-Ruf-System) for women and people with disabilities. To find out more about this service, which runs from 8pm until the network shuts down, just ask a BVG employee. The Telebus is another option for people with restricted mobility but, because

a pass must be issued beforehand, tourists have to contact the organisation in advance.
Telebus-Zentrale, Esplanade 17, Pankow; tel: 410 200; office open 7am–5pm.
Lazarus-Telebus Berlin Betriebsführung- und Trägergesellschaft Gmbh (Wendenschlossstr. 129, Köpenick; tel: 651 6642, fax: 651 6643, www.lazarus.de/berlin.htm, berlin@lazarus.de also provide a taxi service for people with restricted mobility.
Berlin Tourismus Marketing will be able to provide information on the hotels with the best access for the disabled or contact one of the following:
MOVADO e.V.
Langhanstr. 64, 13086 Berlin; tel: 471 5145, www.movado.de/indexe.html, info@movado.de
This non-profit organisation strives to break down barriers for people with restricted ability. Among the features on their website are wheelchair-friendly restaurants, hotels and restricted mobility activities for tourists.
Beschäftigungswerk des BBV (Berlin Centre for the Disabled) Bizetstr. 51–55, Weissensee; tel:

927 0360; open Mon–Fri 8am–4pm A transport service and travel information are among the many things on offer.
Touristik Union International (TUI) Kurfürstendamm 119; tel: 896 070; open Mon–Fri 9am–6pm but get in touch in advance for an appointment. Here you can find out about places to stay in Germany and ways to get there.

Religious Services

American Church in Berlin: tel: 813 20 21.
Anglican (Episcopal) Church of St George: tel: 304 12 80.
Berlin International Church (evangelical): tel: 3470 9176.
Christian Faith Fellowship (international, non-denominational): tel: 715 0777.
Friends of the Western Buddhist Order Berlin: tel: 28 59 81 39, www.fwob.org.
Jüdische Gemeinde zu Berlin (Berlin Jewish Community): Fasanenstr. 79/80, 10623 Berlin, tel: 880 28 0. For a list of **Islamic mosques** go to www.zentralrat.de and click "Moscheeadressen".

Medical Services

Nearly all the bigger hospitals maintain ambulances as well as emergency rooms. You can make emergency calls free of charge from any telephone booth.

If you should fall ill in Berlin take your insurance papers to the AOK Auslandersschalter (Foreign Section of the AOK, see below) before you go to the doctor. They will exchange it for a "Krankenschein" which you will need for a visit to the doctor or the hospital. Otherwise, check your insurance plan to see if you have to pay first and then make a claim for reimbursement or if your insurance will accept bills directly from the doctor. They will most likely require a translation of all documents you send to them.

Rettungswagen (Ambulance): 112
Polizei (Police): 110
Notzahnarzt (Emergency Dental): 89 00 43 33
They can generally speak English
Notarzt (Emergency Doctor): 310031 or 19720 – they speak English
Apotheken-Notdienst (Emergency Medications): 01189
Gesundheitslotsendienst (International Emergency Hotline): 31003-222 or 31003-243
Berlin city service connecting visitors with doctors speaking their languages.
Poison: 19240
There are hospitals all over Berlin. You can find a full list in the

GelbeSeiten (yellow pages) under Krankenhäuser or Kliniken. The following two both have large, 24 hour emergency rooms:
Charité Hospital: 2802-0 Schumannstrasse 20–21 10117 Berlin, Mitte near U-bahn station Oranienburger Tor
Virchow-Klinikum: 450-50 Augustenburger Platz 1 13353 Berlin, Wedding.
The following doctors speak English:
Dr med. I. Ernst, Kalckreuthstr. 5, Schöneberg, tel: 218 3869.
Dr med. Lisa Liccini, Windscheidstr. 31 (entrance Pestalozzistr. 58), Charlottenburg, tel: 324 1887.

Chemists

Apotheken (Chemists): In Germany it is not permitted for places like supermarkets to sell even common drugs such as painkillers. There are therefore chemist shops all over town which can be recognised by a red "A" outside the door. Each chemist should have a list of the other chemists open late and on Sundays. The following chemists all have a night service except the one in Mitte which is open until 10pm.

Dorotheenstädtische Apotheke, Friedrichstr. 154, Mitte, tel: 204 4817.

Hardenberg-Apotheke, Knesebackstr. 93, Charlottenburg, tel: 313 4010.

Grünberger Apotheke, Grünberger Str. 43–45, Friedrichshain, tel: 293 3543.

Apotheke am Schlesischen Tor, Skalitzer Str. 73, Kreuzberg, tel: 612 6723.

Wissmanns's Apotheke, Paulstr. 23, Tiergarten, tel: 391 8613, night service.

Arnim-Apotheke, Seelower Str. 8, Prenzlauer Berg, tel: 445 8653.

Pommern-Apotheke, Haupstr. 152, Schöneberg, tel: 782 1145.

Security & Crime

As long as the Wall stood, West Berlin enjoyed the reputation of being one of the safest cities in Europe. Like everywhere else, things have changed and nowadays, particularly in crowds or while making use of public transport, it pays to keep a look out for pickpockets. Following the dismantling of the Wall, the number of assaults – which not infrequently are violent – is on the rise.

Lost & Found

BVG (public transport) Lost and Found: Potsdamer Str. 180–182, tel: 25 62 30 40.

Central Lost and Found: Platz der Luftbrücke 6; tel: 6995; closed Wed.

Mastercard/Visa: 0697-933 1910

Diners' Club: 069-260 3050

If you find yourself in a relatively unpopulated area at night, the wisest thing to do is call a taxi. Don't go too far to the East if you may be the target of a racial crime and avoid the U-8 underground line, especially around Kottbusser Tor, if you don't want to be hassled by drunks and the like.

Etiquette & Behaviour

In a city where service industries has been rapidly expanding in the last decade you'd expect most Berliners to welcome the chance to speak English to visitors. This isn't always the case. Although most young Germans speak impeccable English and are more than happy to work on their accent while helping you, you may find that some of the older generation are more reluctant to speak it. Even if you do try to be polite with your hosts and, for example, attempt to splutter out "Zwei Tageskarten" on boarding the bus you may be surprised. Although you think it should be perfectly clear what you want, confusion may follow. This does not mean, however, that it is in any way acceptable for you to be rude. If you encounter difficulties or rudeness, just say "thank you" and leave. Don't assume that just because you are a customer that you are automatically entitled to a smile. Here are a few tips on etiquette in everyday situations.

Useful Numbers

ACE Autoclub Europa Travel Assistance Service, tel: 01802-33 66 77.
Breakdown Service, tel: 01802-34 35 36, www.ace-online.de.
ADAC Travel Assistance Service, tel: 01805-10 11 12, **Breakdown Service**, tel: 1802-22 22 22, www.adac.de.
ADFC Lobby and Help for Cyclists, tel: 0421-34 62 90, www.adfc.de.
Airports Tegel, Tempelhof and Schönefeld all have the same information hotline, tel: 01805-00 01 86. The call costs 24 pf/min.
Berliner Behinderten Verband (help for the disabled), tel: 3 41 17 97.
Bus Station at the Radio Tower,

tel: 302 53 61.
BVG (public transport) Customer Service, tel: 194 49, www.bvg.de.
City Autodienst (Breakdown Service), tel: 896 09 70, Mon to Fri 8am–10pm, Sat and Sun 10am–5pm.
Emergency Hotline for Raped Women, tel: 251 28 28.
Gay Hotline (for victims of attack), tel: 216 33 36.
Lara Crisis and Counselling Centre for Raped Women, tel: 216 88 88.
Lesbian Hotline (for victims of attack), tel: 215 20 00.
Messe Berlin (trade shows), tel: 30 38 44 44.
Taxi, tel: 690 22, 26 10 26, 21 01 01, 21 02 02, 44 33 22 or 42 28 28 28.

Telegram Sending Service, tel: 0180-5 12 10 (inland), 0800-33 01133 (abroad).
Telephone
● **National Information**, tel: 11833, information in English, tel: 118 37.
● **International Information**, tel: 11834.
Time, (a recording in German) tel: 01191.
Train Information (German Rail), tel: 0 18 05 99 66 33.
Velo Taxi (rickshaws for hire), tel: 44 35 89 90.
Wake-up Service, tel: 01141.
Women's Information Centre, Mulackstrasse 31–32, Mitte, tel: 280 61 85.

GETTING STARTED

When deciding what to wear, it is best to dress with your host in mind. In summer, standards are quite casual but if you're socialising with the old school, its best to dress smart to casual.

ARRIVING AND GREETING

Germans are extremely punctual and will arrive at the stated time for social arrangements. When meeting people for the first time, a handshake is appropriate. Greetings and farewells in general rarely require anything more, unless you are very close. Only then would a kiss be acceptable. If invited for coffee or dinner, especially if it is for the first time, expect to be well catered for. In such cases, remember to take along a small gift as a gesture to your host.

If attending a birthday party, Germans sometimes like to celebrate birthdays the night before and give gifts on the stroke of midnight.

BREAKING THE ICE

You may find that your host asks you to remove your shoes when entering their house and in some cases they will provide you with a pair of house shoes. When settled it is extremely bad form to put your shoes on the seats although nobody seems to mind when it is your stocking soles – this also applies to everywhere in public.

For some people, surnames are the appropriate way to address others unless they are close friends. If you are unsure, stick to the formal approach of using surnames.

Convention, before plunging into your drink, is to look your company in the eye and proclaim "Prost".

AT THE TABLE

It is customary, before eating, for the person who has made the meal to wish their company "Guten Appetit". Contrary to popular (and Basil Fawlty's) belief, the war is not such a taboo subject as you'd think – just be sensitive. Further difficulties may arise if too much sarcasm is used. Germans are very matter-of-fact people – a spade is a spade. However, a joke will always be understood if it contains sexual innuendo. When smoking at the table, it is frowned upon to light your cigarette from a candle – legend has it that, each time it happens, a seaman dies.

Tipping

Restaurant bills always include a 15 percent service charge. But it is common to reward good service with a gratuity (5–10 percent). In taxis it is usual to round up to the next mark, or more for a high fare.

WINDING DOWN

If you are a person who finds it hard to choose a suitable time to leave, you will be in good hands. Gestures from your host such as yawning or enquiring after your route home are, generally, hints. You will then be fully aware when it is time to say your "thank-yous" before departing.

Getting Around

Public Transport

In Berlin the public transport system is so well developed that you can safely forget your car. The Berlin transport services (BVG) operate underground trains (U-Bahn), bus lines, tramlines, a well-organised network of buses running throughout the night and boat connections crossing the Havel River between Wannsee and Kladow.

Maps

You can pick up a copy of the transport network at any of the BVG or S-Bahn stations, on the bus or in the tram. For a city plan, it is best to buy the Falk Plan Berlin from newsagents, petrol stations, bookshops and other outlets.

BY U-BAHN AND S-BAHN

The quickest way of getting around the city is on the underground system's 10 different lines (see map inside back cover). This system (the largest in Germany) is augmented by an excellent and extensive fast train network (S-Bahn, operated by the German Rail). By taking advantage of the underground, the commuter transport network on the Ringbahn and smaller, connecting fast trains, you can travel beyond the city limits into the countryside surrounding Berlin. For example, on an inner-city fast train you can get to Potsdam, Werder, Nauen, Oranienburg, Bernau, Strausberg, Erkner, Fürstenwalde and Königs Wusterhausen.

BY BUS

The number 100 city bus provides a good, cheap sightseeing tour. It runs from Bahnhof Zoo to Alexanderplatz (and beyond to Prenzlauer Berg) passing the Tiergarten, Brandenburger Tor and Unter den Linden. The number 129 bus runs from Grunewald via Kurfürstendamm to Kreuzberg and Neukölln and back; it also gives a good overview of the city. Both lines are served by double deckers.

PUBLIC TRANSPORT MAPS

Ask for a free map showing all the BVG transport routes at any ticket booth, or buy the inexpensive map which shows all the BVG routes and has relevant schedule information. There is also free information about public transport at night, obtainable from the BVG-Pavillon at the Bahnhof Zoo, the U-Bahn-station Kleistpark or Turmstrasse.

FARES

Fares increase nearly every year. All underground and fast train stations have ticket machines. For the bus you may buy your ticket from the driver. There are also ticket machines on all trams. There are three tariff zones (ABC); AB is for inner-city, C for the surrounding areas. The "Kurzstrecke" costs DM2,50 and is valid only for one short distance – three stops on the S- or U-Bahn or six on the bus or tram. The normal ticket (2001: DM4,20) is valid for two hours and allows changing as often as you want using bus, underground, fast train or tram. If you want to ride more than once a day a "Tageskarte" used to be worth buying. Now standing at a whopping DM12,00, it seems the BVG want to promote the longer term Monatskarten (monthly tickets; DM110,00) or the "7-Tage-Karten" (seven day tickets; DM44,00). For travellers in Berlin for just a few

days there is the Berlin Welcome Card (DM32,00 until Dec 2001), especially designed for tourists. Valid for three days, it allows unlimited rides and includes discount tickets for theatres, museums, sightseeing and other attractions. It can be purchased in the BVG ticket offices, in many hotels and at the BTM tourist information centres. There you can also purchase day and weekly tickets. At time of press it was possible to buy "Gruppenkarten" (group tickets) but this may not be the case in future. Also available at time of press is the "Schönes-Wochenende-Ticket" (DM40,00). For a whole day, a family of two parents and any number of kids can travel on all forms of transport, be it Regional Express, S-Bahn or tram. This also applies for a group of five people with no age restrictions.

Further information is available from BVG Customer Services, tel: 194 49. The BVG Kundenbüro (customer office; Mon–Fri 6.30am–8.30pm, Sat 9am–3.30pm) can be found at U-Bhf Turmstrasse. The S-Bahn has its own information centres in stations like Bahnhof Zoo, Alexanderplatz and Ostbhanhof and the customer office (tel: 2971 9843) which is situated at S-Bhf Nordbahnhof is open Mon–Thur 8.30am–7pm, Fri 8am–4pm.

Private Transport

BY BIKE

Berlin has an adequate bike lane system which allows easy movement from A to B within the city. Although the Germans consider Berlin to have one of the most hostile relationships between car and bike, it is quite tame compared to the rest of the world. If you don't want to bring your own bike with you then you can hire one for around DM10 to DM15 per day. Here is a list of some of places to try:
Fahrradstation Hackesche Höfe, Mitte, tel: 28 38 48 48, Bahnhof Friedrichstrasse, tel: 20 45 45 00

Fahrradverleih, Uhlandstr. 106a, Wilmersdorf, tel: 861 5237, www.citybikeservice.de.
Bike City locations: near Zoo Station at Hardenberg Platz, Hertzallee or on Alexanderplatz near the Forum Hotel.
Bikes & Jeans, Reinhardtstr. 6, Mitte, tel: 447 6666.

By Taxi

There are thousands of taxis in Berlin and, as they can use the bus lanes, they are generally significantly quicker than private cars. If you hail one on the street. the fare for short distances of up to 2 km is DM5 – ask for a "Kurzstrecke" tariff before the journey starts. You can also go to a special taxi rank, or call from one of the taxi telephone posts located throughout the city. Taxis can also be ordered through radio dispatch services by calling one of the following numbers: 690 22, 26 10 26, 21 01 01, 21 02 02, 44 33 22 or 42 28 28 28.

If you want to be chauffeur driven around the city contact "City Chauffeur", tel: 341 08 53.

BY CAR

Parking

There are more than 1.2 million registered cars in Berlin so finding a parking place in the city is a real challenge. If you have to drive into the city, the best thing to do is to park your vehicle at one of the Park-and-Ride areas and take a bus or underground. Parking in the Berlin side streets shouldn't cost anything but as the number of cars increases so too does the number of parking meters. Throughout the city no-parking and no-stopping zones are strictly patrolled as well as the time-limited parking zones. At these zones you have either to set a parking disk or – more often – to pay for a ticket at a machine (coins only, no change) for a specified time in advance. Avoid abandoning your car – even for the shortest time. Expect to be heavily fined, clamped or towed away for any of the usual parking offences (crossings, bus lanes etc.) but be aware that parking your car on the pavement in even the quietest street can result in a visit to the depot as well. Take special care in streets with tram-lines. If your car is even 2mm too close, the whole traffic system gets clogged and the authorities will not be happy. If you car isn't there when you get back, contact the nearest police station. **Police Headquarters:** Platz der Luftbrücke 6, 12101 Berlin, tel: 6995.

Insurance

In Germany, the car must be insured, not the person. When hiring a car, this will be taken care of as part of the process. *Haftpflichtversicherung* (third party insurance) is mandatory, with *Kaskoversicherung* (fully comp.) optional. If you are driving someone else's car, make sure their insurance covers other drivers.

Speed Limits

In built-up areas the speed limit is 50 kph (30 mph), in some indicated areas 30 kph. Maximum speed limit on the inner-city motorways is 100 kph (55 mph).

Petrol Stations

Throughout the city there are many filling stations serving 24 hours. The following list mentions just a few in convenient locations. Shell (Kant-Garages): Kantstrasse 126, 10625 Berlin, tel: 313 60 71. Shell: Hohenzollerndamm 41–42, 10713 Berlin, tel: 873 17 74. Elf: Holzmarkstr. 37, 10243 Berlin, tel: 2 49 37 77. Elf: Chausseestr. 98, 10115 Berlin, tel: 2 82 77 13.

Car Hire

Avis Berlin, www.avis.de
Flughafen Tegel (tel: 4101 3148)
Flughafen Schönefeld (tel: 6091 5710)
Flughafen Tempelhof (tel: 6951 2340)
Budapester Str. 41 (tel: 2309 370)

Sixt (German branch of Hertz – 12 branches Berlin wide, www.e-sixt.com/main.html, Flughafen Tegel (tel: 4101 2886) Robben & Wientje, www.robben-wientjes.de Prinzenstr. 90–91, tel: 616 770.

Breakdown Services

City Autodienst, Seesener Str. 8, 10709 Berlin, tel: 8960 97-0.
ACE (**Auto-Club-Europa**), tel: 01802-34 35 36.
ADAC (**German Automobile Association**), tel: 1802-22 22 22. (0.12DM per minute, when calling with a cell phone you don't have to dial the pre-code.)
Reifen Köhrich (emergency tyre service), tel: 03328-474630.
Pladeck repairs for all types of cars, Wexstrasse 21, Wilmersdorf, tel: 853 10 17.

Road Etiquette

Although the roads are getting busier, driving in Berlin can be fairly rewarding. Apart from the areas where construction is underway, the streets are wide and fairly straight.

Germans drive on the right hand side of the road. Take particular care at crossroads with no traffic lights – you must always give way to the right. However, this does not apply when the junction is marked with a sign shaped like a yellow diamond. When turning right on the filter, always remember that the pedestrian also has a green light and that he has right of way. Cutting up a tram is a distinct no-no – always give them the right of way. Be aware of bicycles. Although there are many bike lanes in Berlin, they are not on every street and cyclists are often a law unto themselves.

Sightseeing Tours

The cheapest tour is to hop on any bus, tram or S-Bahn and ride from one end to the other. You can get a good look at much of the city

from the seat of a double-decker bus – the bus No. 100 takes in almost all of Berlin's great sights as it travels from Bahnhof Zoo to Alexanderplatz *(see Public Transport: By Bus)*.

In summer excursion steamboats and other boats belonging to the Stern und Kreis Schiffahrt depart from various places in the city. The tours offered range from a two hour inner-city trip to whole day excursions in and around Berlin. The schedule can be obtained from **Stern und Kreis Schiffahrt**, Puschkinallee 15, 12435 Berlin, tel: 536360-0. **Reederei Bruno Winkler**, tel: 349 9595, www.reederei-h-triebler.de is another option as is **Weisse Flotte Potsdam**, tel: 0331-275 9210 in Potsdam.

GUIDED CITY TOURS

Art: Berlin. Guided tours of galleries and exhibitions and city tours on various subjects (architecture, Jewish life), tel: 28 09 63 90.
Berliner Geschichtswerkstatt. In summer, city tours by ship, only available in English for larger groups. Golzstrasse 49, (Schöneberg), 10781 Berlin, tel: 215 4450.
The Original Berlin Walks. Upbeat walking tours in English on various subjects. Meeting point is at the taxi stand outside the Bahnhof Zoologischer Garten. tel: 301 91 94, www.berlinwalks.com.
Insider Tour. Walking tours in English on various subjects, meeting point is at the McDonald's outside the Bahnhof Zoologischer Garten. The route is a bit different from that of the Berlin Walks, but otherwise the two companies offer fairly similar deals – although they would probably tell you differently. Insider Tour also offers a four-hour-long bike tour, with a lunch break, that covers all the sights on their regular tour and then some. Tel: 692 31 49, www.insidertour.de.
Brewer's (aka Top Hat Terry's) Berlin. A 4–5 hour tour stuffed with information and humour. The

founder lived through many of the events that the tour covers when he was stationed in Berlin with the British navy and diplomatic service. The meeting point is outside the New Synagogue at 10.30am or 1pm (10.30 only in winter). Tel: 28 09 79 79, www.hostel-berlin.de. **Blickwinkel.** Four different guided city tours: the new Potsdamer Platz; a look in the courtyards around Hackescher Markt with emphasis on Jewish life in Berlin; Berlin's roots and an architectural tour.

Kultur Büro Berlin. Zeit für Kunst e.V. Guided city tours with emphasis on the history of art. They only offer English tours at a fixed price for groups. Greifenhagener Str. 60, 10437 Berlin, tel: 444 09 36, www.stadtverfuehrung.de.

Schöne Künste: Kulturhistorische Stadtrundfahrten. The "Music and Theatre City Berlin" bus tour with sound clips is only available for groups by prior arrangement. Tel: 782 1202.

StattReisen Berlin. City walks with social history and political emphasis, also in English, French and Italian. Wide range of different subjects. Malplaquetstr. 5, 13347 Berlin, tel: 455 3028.

Velotaxi. One of the best ways to see the city is on an organised sightseeing tour by bicycle. Tours are available from April to October. Tel: 4435 8990.

Bus Tours

All of the companies below organise daily tours of Berlin. Tickets can be bought on the bus.

Berliner Bären Stadtrundfahrt (BBS): Alexanderplatz, c/o Forum Hotel, 10178 Berlin, tel: 3519 5270. Departure point: corner Rankestr. and Kurfürstendamm opposite memorial church and Alexanderplatz and the Forum Hotel. They also offer a Kombitour, where the bus turns into a boat halfway through.

Excursions

Spreewald

Spreewald Information, Ehm-Welk-Str. 15, 03222 Lubbenau; tel: 03542 3668; April–Oct daily 9am–4pm, Nov–March Mon–Fri 9am–4pm.

Extremely popular with day-trippers, the Spree Forest's network of small rivers, streams and canals can be busy with boaters in high season. The area, which was declared a "Biosphere Reserve" by UNESCO in 1990 – hence the ban on motorboats – is made up of around 400 km (249 miles) of waterways separated by farmland and deciduous forest. Spreewald is split into two sections by the river Spree around 100 km (62 miles) to the southeast of Berlin. In the upper part, Oberspreewald, you can go punting, take numerous hiking or nature trails or simply relax with a spot of fishing. The best starting point for a day's activities is the small town of Lübbenau. The town of Lübben in Lower (Unter) Spreewald is rich in architecture.

How to get there: Lübbenau: A Regional Express train leaves hourly from Berlin-Lichtenberg. It should take around 50 minutes to get to Lübben, and an hour to Lübbenau.

Sachsenhausen Concentration Camp

Strasse der Nationen 22, 16515 Oranienburg; tel (switchboard):

Berolina Stadtrundfahrten: Meinekestrasse 3, 10719 Berlin, tel: 8856 8030. Departure point: corner Meinekestr.1 and Kurfürsten-damm.

Busverkehr Berlin (BVB): Kurfürsten-damm 229, 10719 Berlin, tel: 885 9880. Departure point: Kurfürstendamm 225, opposite Café Kranzler.

Severin und Kühn Berliner Stadt-rundfahrten: Kurfürstendamm 216, 10719 Berlin, tel: 880 4190. Departure point: corner Fasanenstr. and Kurfürstendamm.

03301-2000, tel (visitor information): 03301-200 200; entry free; Tues–Sun 8.30am–4pm.

In 1936, a month before the start of the Berlin Olympics, a concentration camp opened its doors 35 km (22 miles) north of Berlin. Around half of the 220,000 men interned saw beyond the gates again. Its reopening in 1961 as a memorial and museum against fascism may have been understandable but it wasn't until after the fall of the Wall that its role after the war was fully realised. Between 1945 and 1950 another 60,000 ideologically unsound prisoners were brought in to "Special Camp 7" – more than 10,000 of them lie in the nearby mass graves. Nowadays, you'll find that a lot of the buildings still remain and within them is housed an extremely informative museum which traces the history of both anti-Semitism and the camp itself.

How to get there: Either take the S1 to Oranienburg, the RB (Regional Bahn) from Berlin-Charlottenburg (1h) or the RE (Regional Express) from Berlin-Lichtenburg (30 mins). From the station it is a 20 minutes signposted walk but you can also take bus 804 or 805 to the corner of Bernauer Strasse and Strasse der Einheit.

Kloster Chorin (Chorin Monastery) Amt Chorin 11, 16230 Chorin; tel: 033366-70377, fax: 033366-70378; April–Oct 9am–6pm, Nov–March 9am–4pm.

The Chorin Monastery is considered one of north Germany's most impressive pieces of red-brick Gothic architecture. The village Chorin was founded in 1273 by a band of Cistercian monks who then took it upon themselves to erect a church on the granite base – it took more than 450 of them over 60 years to build. A special summer music festival – Choriner Musiksommer (Schicklerstr. 5, 16225, Eberswalde, tel: 03334-657310) – which takes place at the church between June and August. Bus tours from Berlin to this event

Holiday villas beyond indulgence.

BALEARICS ~ CARIBBEAN ~ FRANCE ~ GREECE ~ ITALY ~ MAURITIUS
MOROCCO ~ PORTUGAL ~ SCOTLAND ~ SPAIN

If you enjoy the really good things in life, we offer the highest quality holiday villas with the utmost privacy, style and true luxury. You'll find each with maid service and most have swimming pools.

For 18 years, we've gone to great lengths to select the very best villas at all of our locations around the world.

Contact us for a brochure on the destination of your choice and experience what most only dream of.

INTERNATIONAL
CHAPTERS

Toll Free: 1 866 493 8340
International Chapters, 47-51 St. John's Wood High Street, London NW8 7NJ. Telephone: +44(0)20 7722 0722
email: info@villa-rentals.com   www.villa-rentals.com

can be booked through Regio Natour GmbH (Kietz 2, 16356 Blumberg bei Berlin, tel: 033394 56222, mail@regio-natour.de). For further information contact the Hotel Haus Chorin – tel: 033366 500, hotel@chorin.de.

How to get there: Take a one hour-long Regional Express journey from Berlin-Lichtenberg. The monastery is half an hour away on foot.

Schiffshebewerk Niederfinow (Niederfinow Ship Lift)

Oder River/Oder-Havel Canal, May–Sept 9am–6pm, otherwise until 4pm.

About 10 km (6 miles) southeast of Chorin at the Oder–Havel Canal lies quite a spectacular piece of machinery – the Niederfinow Ship Lift. Completed in 1934, the spectacular feat of engineering lifts huge cargo tankers from the Oder River to the canal approximately 36 meters (118 ft) above in a large, water filled cradle. Visitors can pay a nominal fee to stand on the viewing platform and witness the 10-minute-long process.

How to get there: One hour train journey from Berlin-Lichtenberg, change in Eberswalde. From the station at Niederfinow the lift is a 2 km walk to the north.

Buckow

Surrounded by five lakes, Buckow came to the public's attention in the 1950s when Bertholdt Brecht and his wife, Helene Weigel, used the place as a summer holiday destination – you can visit their summer house (Bertholdt-Brecht-Str. 29; open Wed–Fri, off season Wed–Fri afternoons only). The town is described as the "pearl of the Märkische Schweiz", the 205 sq. km (79 sq. miles) natural park made up of hills, lakes and streams. Friedrich Wilhelm IV's physician recommended it to his monarch as a place to improve his health. The area is also extremely popular with hikers and walkers who pound the numerous marked trails. At the tourist office (Buckower Fremdenverkehrsamt, Wriezener Str., tel: 033433-57500 or 65981)

you can buy maps with suitable routes. On Schermützelsee there's a pool, rowing boats and an opportunity to go on a small cruise, possible Tues–Sun, 10am–5pm.

How to get there: Take the Regional Bahn (RB) from Berlin-Lichtenberg to Müncheberg then change for Buckow. It should take about 50 minutes.

Rheinsberg

90 km (56 miles) to the north of Berlin you'll find the town of Rheinsberg. Known best for its castle on Grienerickesee, elsewhere in the area it is possible to go on lake and river cruises, rent horses or hire out kayaks – get in touch with the tourist information centre in the Kavalierhaus (tel: 033931-2059) at the "Markt" in the centre of town for information. The original castle, used in the Middle Ages to protect the March of Brandenburg from the savages of Mecklenburg, was rebuilt in 1566 in the Renaissance style. When Friedrich Wilhelm I bought it in 1734 as a grooming ground for his son, the Crown Prince Friedrich, he commissioned Messrs Kemmenter and Knobelsdorff to improve the castle. Used as an art treasure store during WWII, it was looted in 1945 and turned into a sanatorium by the Communists in 1953. Allowed to fall into a state of disrepair, the Schloss is now looking much better after continued renovation.

How to get there: Changing in Oranienburg, you can take a 2 hour 15 minute train journey from Berlin to Rheinsberg every two hours. The centre of town is a 1 km walk to the south east.

Where to Stay

How to Choose

Guests visiting Berlin will find over 50,000 beds in about 460 hotels and pensions to choose from. In times of huge trade shows like the ITB (International Tourist Fair) in March or the *Internationale Funkausstellung* (consumer electronics, communications, electronics) every two years in August, just about every bed in the city is booked solid and the prices are at their highest. At any other time you may have a good choice.

Compared with other European capitals' hotel prices in Berlin are still quite reasonable. The average price for a hotel room is DM150, but of course the range varies from about DM25 for a bed in a youth hostel up to some DM1,000 for a presidential suite in one of the luxury hotels. It is possible to stay in B&B establishments (Pensions). Through the Mitwohn-Zentralen (housing agencies that arrange private accommodation – look in the Yellow Pages under "Wohnungs- und Zimmervermittlung") it may be possible to rent an entire apartment which has been temporarily vacated by its usual occupants. Rooms in some pensions, in most private homes and many youth hostels have shared bathroom only.

The following list includes only a small selection of hotels available in Berlin. Although telephone numbers are given, it may prove easier to make a room reservation through the Berlin Tourismus Marketing GmbH (BTM) – see *Practical Tips: Tourist Offices* – which represents more than 250 partner hotels. Only through the BTM can you book a weekend-special which applies to guests arriving on Friday and departing on Monday (three nights). The prices for weekend-specials always include breakfast. There are other packages, for example a cultural package offered year round by BTM.

There are also private hotel booking services, including "Berlin Direkt" which offers a wide range of hotels for special rates. Call for information and reservation free of charge (inside Germany), tel: 7 87 77 70, or you can book online at nethotels.com. You will also find a hotel reservation office located in the Bahnhof Zoo, specialising in cheaper accommodation.

Luxury Hotels

These offer exquisite service to the point of pampering. They pride themselves on their attention to pricey details, from marble bathrooms to fruit and champagne greetings in the rooms. Of course, these touches will differ from hotel to hotel, but you can always expect a swimming pool, sauna, business centre, laundry service, a gourmet restaurant, and room service among the amenities.

MITTE

Hotel Adlon
Unter den Linden 77, 10117 Berlin
Tel: 22610
Fax: 22612222
Reservations: 2261 1111
www.hotel-adlon.de
Modern and luxurious, but in the legendary tradition of the original Adlon where emperors and movie stars met. Right at the Brandenburger Tor. Gourmet cuisine. **$$$$**

Hotel Four Seasons
Charlottenstrasse 49, 10117 Berlin
Tel: 20338
Fax: 2033 6166
www.fourseasons.com/berlin/index.html
Most rooms have a view to the Gendarmenmarkt in this renowned

luxury. Personalised service as well as a good restaurant. **$$$$**

The Westin Grand Berlin
Friedrichstrasse 158–164,
10117 Berlin
Tel: 2027 34 20
Fax: 2027 34 19
www.westin-grand.com
At the corner of the famous Boulevard Unter den Linden. Old fashioned elegance with indoor pool and fitness club. Garden courtyard. Several restaurants. The Golden Gans restaurant serves specialities of Thuringia. **$$$$**

WILMERSDORF

Hotel Brandenburger Hof,
Eislebener Str. 14, 10789 Berlin
Tel: 214050
Fax: 2140 5100
www.brandenburger-hof.com
Modern luxury in a lovely historical townhouse. Beautiful Japanese-style *Wintergarten*. Walking distance to the Europa Centre. **$$$$**

Kempinski Hotel Bristol Berlin,
Kurfürstendamm 27, 10719 Berlin
Tel: 88434-0
Fax: 883 60 75
www.kempinski-bristol.de
The essence of traditional luxury on the Kurfürstendamm, but is well due for some decorative updates. The "Berliner Brunch" is served Sundays with delicacies of Berlin and Brandenburg. **$$$$**

Schlosshotel Ritz-Carlton,
Brahmsstrasse 6–10, 14193 Berlin
Tel: 895840
Fax: 895800
www.ritzcarlton.com
Karl Lagerfeld designed this exclusive hotel in the quiet residential area Grunewald. The former palais is surrounded by a beautiful park. Elegant indoor pool and fitness area. Gourmet restaurant Vivaldi. **$$$$**

TIERGARTEN

Grand Hotel Esplanade
Lützowufer 15, 10785 Berlin
Tel: 254780
Fax: 265 1171.

www.esplanade.de
Modern, luxuriously designed Hotel at the Landwehrkanal with own boat for fun and dinner cruises. Works of Berlin artists give a special touch. Try the gourmet restaurant Harlekin and the famous Harry's New York Bar for the overloading Sunday brunch. **$$$$**

Grand Hyatt Berlin
Marlene-Dietrich-Platz 2
Tel: 2553 1234
Fax: 2553 1235
www.berlin.hyatt.com
Berlin's newest five-star hotel right at the Potsdamer Platz, surrounded by musical theatre, the Philharmonie and the Kulturforum, is the first Grand Hyatt in Europe. With all grand comforts and latest communication technology. **$$$$**

Inter-Continental
Budapester Strasse 2
Tel: 2602-0
Fax: 2602 2600
One of the oldest hotels in town, still exquisite. Everything's a bit over-sized but famous for its luxury. **$$$$**

Expensive Hotels

Hotels in this category usually cost less than luxury hotels, but they won't pamper you quite as much.

MITTE

Albrechtshof
Albrechtstrasse 8, 10117 Berlin
Tel: 308860
Fax: 30886100
www.hotel-albrechtshof.de
A friendly and quiet place next to the theatre district and the Friedrichstrasse. **$$$**

Art'otel Berlin Mitte
Wallstr. 70–73, 10179 Berlin
Tel: 240620
Fax: 2406 2222
www.artotel.de/berlin.html
Dedicated to and decorated with works of the German artist Georg Baselitz. Integrated in the modern building is the Ermeler House, a well-restored city *palais*, which houses the restaurant. **$$$**

Berlin Hilton

Mohrenstrasse 30
Tel: 20230
Fax: 20234 69
www.hliton.com
New hotel in the historical
Gendarmenmarkt, with a whiff of
the old-style Berlin luxury. **$$$$**

WILMERSDORF

Artemisia
Brandenburgische Strasse 18,
10707 Berlin
Tel: 873 8905
Fax: 873 6373
For women only. Friendly rooms on
the top floor of a residential
building. Rooftop terrace. Close to
the Kudamm. **$$$**
Avantgarde
Kurfürstendamm 15, 10719 Berlin
Tel: 882 6466
Fax: 882 4011
www.hotel-vantgarde.com
Neo-baroque hotel built in 1989
with huge stucco-decorated rooms.
$$$
Mondial
Kurfürstendamm 47, 10707 Berlin
Tel: 884110
Fax: 8841 1150
www.hotel-mondial.com
Huge rooms. The hotel was designed
to cater for disabled guests. **$$$**

TIERGARTEN

Hotel Berlin
Lützowplatz 17, 10785 Berlin
Tel: 2605-0
Fax: 2605 2716
Lovely and very spacious hotel with
lots of extras. **$$$**
SORAT Hotel Spree-Bogen
Alt-Moabit 99, 10559 Berlin
Tel: 399200
Fax: 39920999
www.sorat-hotels.com/spree-bogen/index.htm
Postmodern building integrating an
old milk trading post ("Meierei") as
dining hall. Close to the government
buildings. **$$$–$**
Steigenberger
Tiergarten, Los-Angeles-Platz 1
Tel: 21270
Fax: 2127117
www.berlinsteigenberger.com

Elegant furnishings and
occasionally a famous face or two.
$$$$

Price Guide

Prices are for a double room
$$$$ = over DM350
$$$ = DM350–DM200
$$ = DM200–DM100
$ = less than DM100

CHARLOTTENBURG

Hotel Bleibtreu
Bleibtreustrasse 31, 10707
Berlin
Tel: 884740
Fax: 88474444
www.bleibtreu.com
Well-designed small rooms in a
Savoy hotel. Nice courtyard. Good
cuisine. **$$$**
Hotel Palace
Im Europa-Center, 10789 Berlin
Tel: 25020
Fax: 2502 1197
www.palace.de
Right in the centre of the west city.
Renowned for its excellent
service. The restaurant First Floor
(see Where to Eat: Haute Cuisine)
is one of the best in Berlin.
Guests can use the spa amenities
in the Europa Center for free.
$$$$
Residenz
Meinekestrasse 9, 10719 Berlin
Tel: 88443-0
Fax 8824 726
www.hotel-residenz.com
Beautiful *belle époque* style with
intimate atmosphere, although the
rooms are a bit stark. First-class
service. **$$–$$$**
Savoy
Fasanenstrasse 9–10, 10623
Berlin
Tel: 31103-0
Fax 3110 3333
www.hotel-savoy.com
Comfortable and modern in the
heart of the city, former haunt of
Thomas Mann. **$$$$**
Seehof am Lietzensee
Lietzenseeufer 11, 14057 Berlin
Tel: 32002-0
Fax: 3200 2251

Idyllic location by the Lietzensee.
$$$–$
SORAT Art'otel
Joachimstaler Str. 29, 10719
Berlin
Tel: 88447-0
Fax: 88447-700
www.sorat-hotels.com/artotel-berlin/foto10a.htm
Paintings from the owner's
collection of works by Berlin artist
Wolf Vostell smatter the lobby and
rooms, but it has changed little
since it was avant-garde in the
1980s. **$$$–$**

PRENZLAUER BERG

Holiday Inn Berlin City Centre East
Prenzlauer Allee 169, 10409
Tel: 030-446610
Fax: 030-4466 1661
www. basshotels.com/holiday-inn?
franchisee=BERPA
Probably the best of Berlin's
Holiday Inns. It offers comfortable
rooms and a great buffet
breakfast, and has good, friendly
staff. **$$$**
SORAT Hotel Gustavo
Prenzlauer Allee 169, 10409 Berlin
Tel: 446610
Fax: 44661 661
Spanish painter Gustavo gives this
trendy place colour, fun and *joie de
vivre*. **$$$**

TEGEL

SORAT Hotel Humboldt-Mühle
An der Mühle 5, 13507 Berlin
Tel: 439040
Fax: 43904 444
www.sorat-hotels.com/humboldt-
muehle/index.htm
An old mill transformed into an
elegant and cosy hotel, with lots of
wooden paneling incorporated into
the decor. In the north, outside the
city centre. **$$$**

Moderately Priced Hotels & Guest Houses

WILMERSDORF

Hotel Albatros
Rudolstädter Str. 42, 10713 Berlin
Tel: 897830
Fax: 8978 3100
www.albatros-hotel.de
Friendly hotel, small rooms with a good standard. Not far from the convention centre and the Kudamm, but a short walk is necessary to the nearest U- and S-Bahn station. **$$**

Alpina
Trabener Strasse 3, 14193 Berlin
Tel: 8916090
Small villa with garden near Grunewald S-Bahn station. **$–$$**

Dittberner
Wielandstrasse 26, 10707 Berlin
Tel: 8846950
Individually furnished rooms, arranged by an artist's hand.
$–$$

Savoy
Meinekestrasse 4
Tel: 881 3700
Fax: 882 3746
Small but nice. **$–$$**

CHARLOTTENBURG

Art-Hotel Charlottenburger Hof
Stuttgarter Platz 14, 10627 Berlin
Tel: 329070
Fax: 323 3723
www.charlottenburger-hof.de
Bright colours and a friendly atmosphere. **$$**

Hotel am Park
Sophie-Charlotten-Straße 57–58,
14057 Berlin
Tel: 321 3485
Fax: 321 3485
Charming turn of the century pension, toilets are in the hallway but breakfast is part of the deal. **$$**

Hotel-Pension Imperator
Meinekestrasse 5, 10719 Berlin
Tel: 881 4181
Fax: 885 1919
John Cage liked the style in this place. One wall is dedicated to pictures of other musicians and artists who stayed here. **$$**

NEUKÖLN

Estrel Residence and Congress Hotel
Sonnenallee 225, 12057 Berlin
Tel: 6831 22522
Fax: 6831 2346
www.estrel.com
Germany's largest hotel (more than 1,000 rooms). Outside the centre but with good connections (S-Bahn: 10 minutes to Alexanderplatz). Comfortable, reasonably priced. Own variety theatre with kitsch Las Vegas-style shows. **$$–$$$$**

Price Guide

Prices are for a double room
$$$$ = over DM350
$$$ = DM350–DM200
$$ = DM200–DM100
$ = less than DM100

MITTE

Discount Hotel Aacron
am Alexanderplatz, Rathausstrasse 5, 10178 Berlin, and Friedrichstrasse 124
Tel: 282 9352
Double rooms start at DM50 (£18), breakfast from DM5 (£1.80). **$**

Hotel Künstlerheim Luise
Luisenstrasse 19, 10117 Berlin
Tel: 284 48 0
Fax: 2844 8448
www.kuenstlerheim-luise.de
Individual artists designed all the rooms with taste and flair. Breakfast is included in the price. **$$–$$$**

Honigmond Pension
Borsigstrasse 28, 10115 Berlin
Tel: 284 455-0
Fax: 284 455-11
Simple, cosy pension with wooden floors and white walls. **$–$$**

mitArt Pension
Friedrichstrasse 127, 10117 Berlin
Tel: 2839 04-30
Fax: 2839 04-32
Across from the eclectic cultural centre Tacheles, this pension was designed by artists with the same idea in mind. The rooms double as galleries. An organic breakfast is included. **$$**

KREUZBERG

Am Anhalter Bahnhof
Stresemannstrasse 36, Kreuzberg 10963
Tel: 030-251 0342
Fax: 251 4897
hotel-aab@t-online.de, www.hotel-anhalter-bahnhof.de
A short walk to the impressive ruined entrance of the Anhalter Bahnhof railway station, and Checkpoint Charlie. 24 hour check in. **$$**

Die Fabrik
Schlesische Strasse 18, 10997 Berlin
Tel: 611 71 16 / 617 51 04
Fax: 618 29 74
www.diefabrik.com/seiten/e_fr_ent.html
This converted factory is one of Berlin's biggest hotel-hostels. Bathrooms are in the hallway. **$**

Transit
Hagelberger Strasse 53–54
Tel: 789 047-0
Fax: 789 047-77
www.hotel-transit.de
Popular hotel for young people, with a good atmosphere. **$–$$**

PRENZLAUER BERG

Pension Acksel Haus
Belforter Straße 21, 10405 Berlin
Tel: 44 33 76 33
Fax: 441 61 16
Seven self-service apartments with a garden. You can negotiate the number of people per room, but book in advance. **$$**

Budget Hotels

MITTE

Circus The Hostel
Rosa Luxemburg Straße 39–41, 10118 Berlin
Tel: 2839 1433
Fax: 2839 1484
This popular hostel has everything the backpacker could ask for: central location, great service, clean atmosphere and guests can go on their city tours for free. Single sex rooms are available. **$**

The Clubhouse Hostel

Kalkscheunenstr. 2, 10117 Berlin
Tel: 28 09 79 79
Fax: 28 09 79 77
Upstairs there's a Biergarten, downstairs there's a club, and in between there's a friendly staff who offer you a free beer on arrival. **$**

Lette'm Sleep Hostel
Lettestrasse 7, 10437 Berlin
Tel: 44 73 36 23
Fax: 44 73 36 25
www.backpackers.de
Australian-run hostel in a great location. **$**

Mitte's Backpacker Hostel
Chausseestrasse 105, 10115 Berlin
Tel: 283 909 65
Fax: 283 909 35
www.backpacker.de/english/home.htm
Berlin's oldest hostel (opened 1994). Past guests have done the decorating in this renovated factory. Bike rental, walking tours and a bar with happy hour await you. **$**

FRIEDRICHSHAIN

The Odyssee Hostel
Grünbergerstr. 23, 10243 Berlin
Tel: 29 00 00 81
Fax: 29 00 33 11
www.hostel-berlin.de
Lots of extras, including bike rental and a bar. **$**

The Sunflower Hostel
Helsingforser Str, 17, 10243 Berlin
Tel: 4404 4250
Fax: 5779 6550
www.sunflower-berlin.de
Sister hostel of The Odyssee Hostel, with all the same extras but award winning decorations. **$**

Hotels in Potsdam

The Potsdam dialling code is 0331.

Arkona Hotel Voltaire
Friedrich-Ebert-Strasse 88, 14467 Potsdam
Tel: 23170
Fax: 231 7100
www.hotelvoltaire.potsdam.de
Modern elegant rooms in a former *palais*. Near the Dutch quarter. **$$**

Art'otel Potsdam
Zeppelinstr. 136

Tel: 98150
Fax: 9815555
www.artotel.de/potsdam.html
Cool modern design in an old storehouse conversion near the Sanssouci palace. Excellent restaurant. **$$$**

Filmhotel & Restaurant "Lili Marleen"
Grossbeerenstrasse 75, 14482 Potsdam-Babelsberg
Tel: 743200
Fax: 743 2018
www.filmhotel.potsdam.de
An ideal place for cinema lovers because the decor is inspired by movies. Filmpark Babelsberg is nearby. **$$**

Hotel Babelsberg, Stahnsdorfer Str. 68
Tel: 749010
Fax: 707668
Close to the film studios in a nice, quiet residential area. **$–$**

Hotel Bayrisches Haus
Im Wildpark 1
Tel: 963790
Fax: 972329
Bavarian style, outside the city in green surroundings. **$$**

Hotel-Café Reinhold
Dortustr. 10
Tel: 28499-0
Fax: 284 9930
www.hotel-reinhold.de
In the historic centre. Bike rental. The restaurant serves local cuisine at reasonable prices. **$$**

Hotel Mercure
Lange Brücke
Tel: 2722
Fax: 293496
High-rise building by the Havel River where the view is much better from the inside than it is from outside. **$$**

Schlosshotel Cecilienhof
Im Neuen Garten, 14469 Potsdam
Tel: 3705-0
Fax: 292498
www.castle-cecilienhof.com
This English country-style palace was the home of the last German emperor's son. Churchill, Stalin, Attlee and Truman signed the "Potsdamer Abkommen" here after World War II. Beautifully located in the "Neue Garten". The kitchen offers Brandenburg specialities. **$$$–$$$$**

Where to Eat

What to Eat

It can't really be said that Berlin has an indigenous cuisine, but this doesn't mean that there aren't a number of Berlin specialities. Over the course of the past few decades, the restaurants where you can have an authentic Berlin meal have been getting harder and harder to find. As everywhere else, restaurants serve what their clients like and this is food from all over the world. Yet there is also a trend to modernise the traditional regional recipes, most of which were originally developed for the poor man's table.

One of the traditional dishes is *Aal grün*, otherwise known as Havel eel in a herb sauce. Various types of freshwater fish including *Hecht* (sturgeon), *Barsch* (perch), and *Welse* (catfish) are also caught in local waters and sometimes served at waterside restaurants. The main fish from the river Havel is *Zander* (pike-perch).

An "Alt-Berliner Buffet" is sometimes arranged for parties, including quite large gatherings. Guests will stand in line for *Schusterjungs mit Schmalz* (rye rolls with dripping), *Kartoffelpuffer mit Apfelmus* (a kind of potato pancake served with apple sauce), *Bouletten mit Mostrich* (a type of croquette made from meat and served with mustard), sweet "Berliners" (the pastries filled with plum marmalade that taste a lot like American jelly do-nuts), *Rollmops* (herring marinated in vinegar) and *sauere Gurken* (pickled gherkins).

Various cafés throughout the city will sometimes offer what's called a *Katerfrühstück* (hangover breakfast), which always includes herring prepared in various ways. It is a culinary offence not to serve *Matjeshering* (young herring) with apples, onions and gherkins in cream. You can make your own from the cheap *Sahne hering* in any grocery store and some extra onions and apples. Another herring speciality is *Matjes-hering* served with green beans and potatoes boiled in their jackets; the *Matjes* fillets nestle between ice cubes, accompanied by butter.

There are still a few places left in Berlin (and among them are some classy restaurants) where the Berlin speciality *Eisbein* (pork knuckles) is prepared. Its popularity has declined, perhaps because nowadays many people are becoming more conscious of their fat intake and would rather eat *schnitzel* (veal or pork cutlets) instead. It's said that true *Eisbein* experts just lay the fat aside anyway and go directly to the lean, inner meat. The dish, served with sauerkraut and green-pea purée, is usually accompanied by beer and ice-cold Schnapps.

Finding a good *Kartoffelsalat* (potato salad) or *Berliner Bouletten* is a matter of luck. In bad restaurants, ready-made *Kartoffelsalat* is just slapped onto a plate out of a plastic bucket and the *Bouletten* often have too much bread dough in them. Because of this, they're often mockingly referred to as *verzauberte Schrippen* (bewitched buns).

Another dish you may want to try in Berlin is *Kasseler*, or cured spare ribs, chops, or belly of pork. It also comes prepared as a *Rolle*, which is made of pressed meat rolled up. Freshly roasted and accompanied by a tasty sauce, this dish is the real solution to what to serve at a family party. It's also quite delicious eaten cold, cut in slices and served with *Berliner Kartoffelsalat* prepared with either mayonnaise, or oil and vinegar. Either way, plenty of finely chopped onions are absolutely crucial to its success.

You'll find *Königsberger Klopse* appearing regularly both on restaurant menus and on dinner tables in private houses. They contain about the same quantity of meat as *Bouletten*, but are boiled rather than baked; the optimal mixture of meat is one part ground beef to one part minced meat. A light-coloured caper sauce is then made out of the broth. Potato soup, prepared with pieces of fried bacon or sausage and fresh parsley, is another Berlin speciality. Roasted joints of wild pork can be ordered in some restaurants; the best is served at the Forsthaus Paulsborn Restaurant, situated not too far from the hunting grounds in Grunewald.

Boiled potatoes accompanied by *Quark* (a kind of soft curd cheese) with *Spreewälder* linseed oil is a dish that only Berliners seem to appreciate. A fine hollow is made in the *Quark* and filled with the oil.

Where to Eat

There are countless restaurants in Berlin, from speciality restaurants serving dishes from all corners of the world to simple inns, and from sophisticated dining establishments right down to the numerous snack bars and sausage stands, the most famous of which is "Konnopke", located at the Eberswalder Strasse underground station.

If you include pubs, beer taverns and bars, the total number of premises in the city serving meals comes to a whopping 7,000. Every hungry visitor is sure to find something to satisfy his or her palette, be it "New German Cuisine", specialities from Copenhagen or Bombay, good old home cooking, or a juicy *Currywurst* (curried sausage). If you feel overwhelmed by the culinary variety, it may not be a bad idea to have a look at the gastronomic sections of the city magazines *(see Practical Tips: Media)* which has a smaller range of reviewed restaurants and eateries in the city.

HAUTE CUISINE

Altes Zollhaus
Carl-Herz Ufer 30, Kreuzberg
Tel: 692 3300
Revised German cooking in an old toll house on the banks of the Landwehrkanal. Perfect location on a summer evening. **$$$**

Bamberger Reiter
Regensburger Strasse 7, Schöneberg
Tel: 218 4282
Tues–Sat 6pm–1am. One of the best restaurants of the city (close to the Kudamm) with a rustic atmosphere. Intimacy and old-fashioned atmosphere combined with New German-style cuisine. Dishes are usually seasonal. **$$$**

First Floor
in the Palace Hotel
Europa-Center, Budapester Strasse 42, Charlottenburg
Tel: 2502 1020
Sun–Fri noon–3.30pm, daily 6–10.30pm. Excellent cuisine,

What to Drink

Beer is the most typical of all beverages served in Berlin. Around the turn of the 20th century, more than 100 breweries were producing approximately 5 million hectolitres (110 million gallons) of beer. Since that time, breweries have merged with one another or disappeared, until today there are only a few well-known brands: *Schultheiss, Engelhardt, Rex, Berliner Kindl* and *Hochschul-Brauerei. Berliner Weisse* (a type of light, fizzy beer made using top-fermentation yeast) is referred to as the "champagne of the north" and can be traced back to the Huguenots. As the local beers were too bitter for their taste, the Huguenots began, at about the end of the 17th century, to brew the very first top-fermented *Weissbier*. The special flavour is the result of a shot of raspberry or woodruff syrup, which lends the beer its singular taste and its red or greenish colour.

elegant surroundings and wonderful service. **$$$**

Harlekin
im Grand Hotel Esplanade,
Lützowufer 15, Tiergarten
Tel: 25478858
Tues–Sat 6.30pm–11pm. Creative new cuisine in a modern elegant atmosphere. The food is inspired by German, Franch and Mediterranean styles. **$$$**

Margaux
Unter den Linden 78, Mitte
Tel: 22 65 26 11
Situated in the middle of the new governmental district, this restaurant obviously caters to the international ambassador-type clientele. Very chic decor, this is the perfect choice for vegetarians and organic food lovers with a taste for the finer things. **$$$**

Portalis
Kronenstrsse 55–58, Mitte
Tel: 20 45 54
A relative newcomer to Berlin's gourmet scene. Chef Volker Drkosch serves bold nouveau cuisine, giving the fairy godmother treatment to common ingredients. **$$$**

Rockendorfs Restaurant
Passauer Str. 5–7, Tiergarten
Tel: 2199 2170
Daily noon–2pm, 7–10pm.
Rockendorf was one of the most respected chefs in Berlin until he died in 2001. His restaurants still serves his signature dishes lighter takes on Berlin originals. **$$$**

VAU
Jägerstrasse 54–55
Tel: 202 9730
Mon–Sat noon–2.30pm,
7–10.30pm.
Close to Gendarmenmarkt, a gourmet restaurant with an inviting, elegant atmosphere. It is a hang-out of Chancellor Gerhard Schröder. **$$$**

CHINESE

Ming's Garden
Tauentzienstr. 16, Schöneberg
Tel: 211 8728
www.mingsgraden.com

Open noon–midnight. The Cantonese food is both Peking and Shanghai, the atmosphere very elegant. Private rooms can be booked. **$$$**

FRENCH

Borchardt
Französische Str. 47, Mitte
Tel: 2038 7110
Daily 11.30–1am. Elegant old building integrated in the Neue Hofgarten near the marvellous Gendarmenmarkt square. Fine French cuisine. This is one of the "in" restaurants of the rich and beautiful. **$$$**

Ty Breizh (Savoir Rire)
Kantstr. 75. Charlottenburg
Tel: 323 9932
Open Mon–Fri 5pm–3am, Sat 6pm–3am (food is served until 1am). Know how to laugh is the name of the restaurant, and the host takes the motto to heart – he has earned a reputation for singing when he's in a good mood. The cooking will make you want to join him. **$$$**

GERMAN

Goldene Gans im Hotel Westin Grand
Friedrichstr. 158–162, Mitte
Tel: 2027-0
On the corner of Unter den Linden, this restaurant offers the fine cuisine of Thuringia. **$$$**

Kaiserstuben, Am Kupfergraben 6a, Mitte
Tel: 2045 2980
Mon–Sat 6–10pm. Good food and wines in a well-restored historical building right in front of the Pergamon Museum. German and some continental cuisine is on the menu. **$$$**

GREEK

Fofi's Estatorio
Rathausstr. 25, Mitte
Tel: 242 3435
Open 12.30pm–midnight.

Fofi's Estatorio
Fasanenstr. 70, Wilmersdorf
Tel: 881 8785
Berlin's classy Greek restaurants, are a meeting place for the rich and beautiful. **$$$**.

Price Guide

Prices are approximate per head for a main course
$$$ = over DM35
$$ = less than DM35
$ = less than DM20 for a simple one course meal

ITALIAN

Ana e Bruno
Sophie-Charlottenstr. 101
Tel: 325 7110
Open Tues–Sat 6pm–midnight. Classic Italian cuisine with an ambitious modern touch. The menu reflects the best of the seasons's offerings in unusual but impressive combinations. **$$$**

Ponte Vecchio
Spielhagenstr. 3, Charlottenburg
Tel: 342 1999
Specialises in first-class food from northern Italy. Closed Tuesday. **$$$**.

JAPANESE

Sabu
Damaschketestr. 31, Wilmersdorf
Tel: 327 4488
Mon–Fri noon–1am, Sat from 6pm. Recognised as one of the best Japanese restaurants in town with a superb menu. Expensive but good food. **$$$**

TURKISH

Istanbul
Knesebeckstr. 77, Charlottenburg
Tel: 883 2777
Open noon–midnight, all cards accepted. A traditional place, one of the oldest Turkish restaurants in Berlin, popular with Germans and tourists. Friday and Saturday bellydancing. **$$$**

OTHER

E.T.A. Hoffmann
Yorckstr. 83, Kreuzberg
Tel: 7809 8809
Mon–Sat from 6pm. International
cuisine by people who have respect
for the food they prepare. **$$$**

Mensa
Lützowplatz 5, Tiergarten
Tel: 2579 9333
Mon–Sat 5.30pm–1am. Well
thought out international cuisine.
$$$

Reinhard's
Poststr. 28, Mitte
Tel: 242 52 95
Open daily 9am–1am. A bit of the
1920s in old Nikolaiviertel, very
grand with an international cuisine.
A branch is on Kurfürstendamm
/Schlüterstrasse. **$$$**

AMERICAN

Andy's Bar and Diner
Potsdamer Str. 1, Mitte
Tel: 2300 4990
Daily 9–3am. The American
memorabilia makes this place feel
tacky but the food is generally
excellent. **$$**

Hard Rock Café
Meinekestr. 21, Wilmersdorf
Tel: 884 62-0
Open noon–2am
If you can stand the marketing
concept, you might just get a good
hamburger. **$$**

Jimmy's Diner
Pariser Str. 41, Wilmersdorf
Tel; 886 06 07
Open noon–2am (weekends 5am).
1950s style American and Tex-Mex
cooking that will please fans of red
meat but disappoint the
vegetarians. **$$**

Mexico Lindo
Kantstrasse 134, Charlottenburg
Tel: 312 82 18
Authentic Mexican cooking with a
friendly atmosphere. **$$**

Mississippi
Mehringdamm 45, Kreuzberg
Tel: 693 3659
Southern cooking; dinner and live
music. **$$**

Planet Hollywood
Mohrenstr. 68/Quartier 205
Tel: 2094 5820
Upmarket burgers in movie-theme
chain. **$$**

Tres Kilos
Marheinekeplatz 3, Kreuzberg
Tel: 693 6044
Open 6pm–2am. The best
Margaritas in town; Mexican
style cooking and young clientele.
$$

Price Guide

Prices are approximate per head
for a main course
$$$ = over DM35
$$ = less than DM35
$ = less than DM20 for a simple
one course meal

AUSTRIAN

Austria
Bergmannstr. 30, 10961 Berlin
Tel: 694 44 40
Open 6pm–1am. Their Schnitzel
knocks 'em dead. **$$**

Cafe Einstein
Kurfürstenstr. 58, Schöneberg
Tel: 261 5096
Daily 9am–2am. Peoplewatch in
the former villa of screen star
Henny Porten. as you take your
pick from the large array of snacks
and meals. Pleasant summer
garden. **$**

Exil
Paul-Lincke-Ufer 44a, Kreuzberg
Tel: 612 7037
Daily 7pm–1am. Arty Austrian pub
on the Landwehrkanal. **$–$$**

Offenbach Stuben
Stubbenkammerstrasse 8,
Prenzlauer Berg
Tel: 4458502
Nostalgic atmosphere, German-
Austrian food, huge portions. **$$**

CHINESE

Lon Men
Bamberger Str. 30, Schöneberg
Tel: 8545356
Intimate atmosphere, not a place
for large parties. **$$–$$$**

Perle
Schönhauser Allee 61, Prenzlauer
Berg
Tel: 444 72 70
Open 11.30am–11.30pm. The
oldest Chinese restaurant in
Prenzlauer Berg, Perle serves great
dim sum. **$$**

Petit Chinois
Spandauer Damm 82,
Charlottenburg
Tel: 3225157
Open noon–3.30pm, 6–11pm
Mon–Fri. Indonesian and Chinese
cooking, cleverly mixed, fresh and
delicious. **$$–$$$**

EAST EUROPEAN

Gorki Park
Weinbergsweg 25
Tel: 4 48 72 86
Open 10am–1am. This Russian run
locale sometimes poses as a bar,
sometimes as a café, and
sometimes as a restaurant, but it's
almost always full. You could go
there several times and never
notice that they serve fabulous blini
and pierogi and also have a
Russian Sunday brunch. **$$**

Marjellchen
Mommsenstr. 9, Charlottenburg
Tel: 883 2676
Open 5pm–1am. East Prussian,
Pomeranian and Silesian food in an
atmosphere which foreigners tend
to think of as *gemutlichkeit* (tidy
and cosy). **$$**

Pasternak
Knaackstr. 22–24, Prenzlauer Berg
Tel: 441 3399
Daily 10–2am. Russian food
inspired by the famous poet. **$$**

FRENCH

Bovril
Kurfürstendamm 184, Wilmersdorf
Tel: 8818461
Mon–Sat noon–2am. German and
French cooking on Ku'damm where
business people and the
intelligentsia meet in pleasant
surroundings. The speciality of the
house is veal in breadcrumbs.
$$–$$$

Chez Maurice
Bötzowstr. 39, Prenzlauer Berg
Tel: 4280 4723
Tues–Fri 11.30am–midnight,
Sat–Mon 6pm–midnight. The
shelves on the walls are filled with
wine bottles – delightful French
ambience. **$$**
Cour Carrée
Savignyplatz 5, Charlottenburg
Tel: 312 5238
Noon–1am, Sat–Sun 10am–1am.
Nice garden, attractive interior and
very acceptable food and prices. **$$**
Paris-Bar
Kantstr. 152, Charlottenburg
Tel: 313 8052
Open noon–1am daily. Famous
bistro always in the news as people
from the film industry hang out
here. Worth trying to get a table
during the Film Festival. **$$–$$$**
Storch
Wartburgstr. 54, Schöneberg
Tel: 784 2059
Open 6pm–1am. Wonderful Alsatian
cuisine. **$$–$$$**

Local Sausages

There is a wide range of local
sausages worth trying:
*Bockwurst mit Kartoffelsalat,
Jagdwurst, Bierwurst, Bratwurst
and Currywurst.*

GERMAN/BERLIN

Opernpalais Unter den Linden
Unter den Linden 5 (next to the
Staatsoper)
Tel: 20 26 83
Combines five different restaurants
as well as a terrace café and a self-
service outdoor eatery. You can take
your pick from the options below.
Operncafé serves lovely cakes, tarts
and light meals in a beautiful setting,
also a delicious breakfast buffet
daily; the elegant **Restaurant Königin
Luise** is famous for its classy
German cuisine, while **Fridericus**
stays with traditional specialities
from Berlin and Brandenburg. In the
rustic **Opernschänke** you can sample
a real Alt-Berliner Buffet; in the
Weinkeller the wine is accompanied
by oysters and cheese. **$$–$$$**.

Diekmann
Meinekestr. 7, Charlottenburg
Tel: 883 3321
Mon–Sat noon–1am, Sun
6pm–1am. Peaceful restaurant
where the French-German cuisine
adds to the mood. **$$–$$$**
Florian
Grolmannstr. 52, Charlottenburg
Tel: 313 9184
Open 6pm–3am. The food is south
German but served with French
panache which the clients seem to
enjoy. **$$**
Forsthaus Paulsborn
Hüttenweg 90, Grunewald
Tel: 818191-0
This is a nice rustic *Gasthaus* in the
woods, serving game as their
speciality. **$$**
Marjellchen
Mommsenstr. 9, Charlottenburg
Tel: 883 2676
Mon–Sat 5–11.30pm. East Prussian,
Pomeranian and Silesian dishes are
served in a cosy atmosphere. Bring
your appetite as the food is filling. **$$**
Offenbach Stuben,
Stubbenkammerstr. 8, Prenzlauer
Berg
Tel: 445 8502
Daily from 6pm. Big portions of
German and international cuisine
are served up with 1950s
nostalgia. It is now popular with
Berlin's gay scene. **$$**
Olive
Tegeler Weg 97, Charlottenburg
Tel: 344 33 96
Daily 11.30–1am. Traditional Berlin
dishes and a nice atmosphere. **$$**
Reinhard's
Poststr. 28, Mitte
Tel: 242 5295
Daily 9–1am. A bit of the 1920s in
the Nikolaiviertel. International
dishes and glazed duck feature in
this grand establishment. **$$**

GREEK

Skales
Rosenthaler Str. 13, Mitte
Tel: 283 30 06
Open 5pm–4am. In the middle of
the historic Scheunenviertel. Not
haute cuisine but the atmosphere is
the liveliest around. **$$**

Berlin Specialities

As **Hauptgericht** (main course
dishes) **Erbsensuppe mit Speck**
(pea soup with bacon), **Eisbein**
(pig's trotters) or **Berliner
Bierhähnchen** (loosely
translated "beer chicken") count
among the classics of Berlin
cuisine. Among **Nachtisch**
(desserts) can be found
Apfelkuchen (apple cake),
Pfannkuchen (the kind of
doughnut which, known outside
Berlin as a "Berliner", JFK
named himself during his
speech at Rathaus Schöneberg
in 1963) and the delicious **Rote
Grütze** (mixed soft, and often
alcoholic, berries eaten hot or
cold with vanilla sauce).

INDIAN

Kashmir Palace
Marburger Str. 14, Charlottenburg
Tel: 214 2840
Mon–Fri 12–3pm and
6pm–midnight, Sat–Sun
noon–midnight. You may pay more
money than in other Indian
restaurants but you can be assured
that every dish has an individual
taste. **$$–$$$**
Namaskar
Pariser Str. 56–57, Wilmersdorf
Tel: 8868 0648
Thur–Sun noon–midnight, Mon
5pm–midnight. One of the best
Indian restaurants around. **$$**

ITALIAN

Bar Centrale
Yorckstr. 82
Tel: 786 2989
Italian meals served in an unstuffy
pub atmosphere. Open daily from
midday to 2am (3am at the
weekend). **$$**
Hostaria del Monte Croce
Mittenwalder Str. 6, Kreuzberg
Tel: 694 3968
Opens Tues–Sat 7.30pm. There is
one menu only, which changes
daily. Wine included in fixed price.
Bring an empty stomach and a lot

of time – you've got eight (albeit small) courses to plough through. **$$**

Marcellino
Poststr. 28, Mitte
Tel: 242 7371
Open noon–midnight. Wonderful variety, a place where business people like to meet. **$$**

Osteria No 1
Kreuzbergstr. 71, Kreuzberg
Tel: 786 9162
Open noon–1am. The most fashionable Italian restaurant of all. It is both elegant and rustic. **$$–$$$**

Petite Europe
Langenscheidtstrasse 1, Schöneberg
Tel: 781 2964
Daily 5pm–1am, no CCs. Very busy and popular place which gets stars for service rather than gourmet quality. After the meal a grappa will be served on the house. **$$**

Rosmini Pastamanufaktur
Invalidenstr. 151, Mitte
Tel: 2809 6844
Mon–Sat noon–midnight. Nothing tastes like freshly made real pasta – here it is made fresh every day. **$$**

Trattoria Paparazzi
Husenmannstr. 35, Prenzlauer Berg
Tel: 440 7333
Daily 6pm–midnight, no credit cards. This highly rated restaurant is very good value for money. A good selection of wine accompanies the food. **$$–$$$**

Mexican Restaurants

Joe Penas Cantina y Bar
Marheinekeplatz 3, Kreuzberg
Tel: 693 6044
Daily 5pm–1am, weekends until 2am. Sup the best Margaritas in town as you listen to pianist during the happy hour, 5–8pm. Mexican style cooking with good vegetarian options. **$$**

Mexico Lindo
Kantstr. 134, Charlottenburg
Tel: 312 8218
Authentic Mexican cooking with a friendly atmosphere. **$$**

JAPANESE

Edogawa
Lepsiusstr. 36, Steglitz
Tel: 7970 6240
Mon–Fri noon–3pm 6pm–midnight, Sat–Sun noon–midnight. Light-hearted restaurant but they take the food seriously. **$$**

Kabuki
Olivaer Pltz 10, Wilmersdorf
Tel: 8862 8136
Daily noon–midnight, Sun from 1pm. Ambience, quality, price and uniqueness are the watch words of this Sushi establishment. **$$–$$$**

Kyoto
Wilmersdorferstr. 94, Charlottenburg
Tel: 883 27 33
Open 5pm–midnight but not on Mondays. Much loved by Japanese and lovers of Japanese food, who can witness the chef at work. **$$–$$$**

Sachiko Sushi
Grolmanstrasse 47, Charlottenburg, Tel: 313 2282,
Mon–Sat noon–midnight, Sun 4pm–midnight. Generally accepted as one of Berlin's best sushi bars, the food here comes to you on little boats. **$$**

Udagawa
Feuerbachstr. 24, Steglitz
Tel: 792 23 73
Open Wed–Mon 5.30pm–11.30pm. Very fine, very expensive; off the tourist track. **$$–$$$**

TURKISH

Merhaba
Hasenheide 39, Kreuzberg
Tel: 692 1713
Open noon–midnight, AmEx and Visa. The *nouvelle cuisine* of Turkey is served here with style. Light, friendly atmosphere and a young clientele. Great menu for vegetarians. **$$**

OTHER

Azul
Skalituer Str. 64, Kreuzberg
Tel: 618 3021

Mon–Fri 12.30pm–1am. Pseudo trendy hangout with a wonderfully international menu – great for lunch. **$$**

Dressler
Kurfürstendamm 207
Tel: 883 3530
Daily 8–1am, and
Unter den Linden 39
Tel: 204 4402.
On both main boulevards, a nice place for coffee, breakfast, lunch, or dinner. They always pay good attention to detail. **$$–$$$**

Edd's
Lützowstr. 81, Tiergarten
Tel: 215 5294
Tues–Fri 6pm–midnight, Sat–Sun 2pm–midnight. Thai cuisine for connoisseurs. **$$**

Best Vegetarian

Abendmahl
Muskauer Str. 9, Kreuzberg
Tel: 612 5170
Daily 6pm–1am. Absorb the laid-back atmosphere and sample some of the best vegetarian cooking in Berlin. **$$**

Hackescher Hof
Rosenthaler Strasse 40–41
Tel: 283 5293
Daily 7–3am. At the main entrance to the Hackesche Höfe, this is a place to see and be seen. **$$**.

Hakuin
Martin-Luther-Str. 1, Schöneberg
Tel: 218 2027
Tues–Sat 5pm–midnight, Sun noon–11pm. Not only vegetarian cuisine but Buddhist style too. **$$**

Jules Verne
Schlüterstr. 61, Charlottenburg
Tel: 3180 9410
Sun–Thur 8–1am, Fri–Sat 8–2am. The lunch buffet is a must and the relaxation will follow. **$$**

Lutter & Wegner
Schlüterstrasse 55, Charlottenburg
Tel: 881 3440, and
Charlottenstrasse 56, Mitte
Tel: 2029540,
www.restaurantlutterundwegner.de
Daily 6pm–2am. There are two restaurant-wineries with the same

name. The first has been serving for many good years in the west-city; the second, new and modern designed one is decorated by artists. Right at the Gendarmenmarkt. **$$–$$$**

Modellhut
Alte Schönhauser Strasse 28, Mitte
Tel: 283 5511
6.30pm–2am. Creative cuisine in an ex-hat shop. A minimalist cross between French and German cuisine is to be enjoyed. **$$**

Thymian (formerly Thürnagel)
Gneisenaustr. 57, Kreuzberg
Tel: 6981 5206
Daily 5pm–midnight. The name and the landlord have changed but the idea hasn't – beautiful vegetarian and seafood dishes. **$$**

Inexpensive

AMERICAN

Mississippi
Mehrungdamm 45, Kreuzberg
Tel: 693 3659
Daily 11.30–2am. Southern cooking; dinner and live music. **$–$$**

Tim's Canadian Deli
Maassenstr. 14, Schöneberg
Tel: 2175 6960
Self-explanatory north American style hangout. **$–$$**

GERMAN

Café Adler
Friedrichstr. 206, Kreuzberg
Tel: 251 8965
Daily till midnight, Sun till 7pm. Snacks, meals and great soups are all available opposite Checkpoint Charlie. **$**

Forsthaus Paulsborn
Huttenweg 90, Grunewald
Tel: 818 1910
Tues–Sun 11am–11pm. Barbecued game is the house speciality of this atmospheric old hunting lodge in the woods. **$**

Georgbräu
Spreeufer 4, Nikolaiviertel
Tel: 242 4244
Popular with tourists who like to order beer by the metre with their traditional Berlin food. **$**

Grossbeerenkeller
Grossbeerenstr, 90, Kreuzberg
Tel: 251 3064
Weekdays 4pm–1am, Sat 6pm–1am. Traditional food and a familiar atmosphere. **$**

Hardtke
Meinekestr. 27, Wilmersdorf
Tel: 881 9827
Open noon–midnight. A huge restaurant off Ku'damm with its own butchery. Berlin cuisine with mountains of meat such as *Eisbein* (pork knuckles). **$**

Price Guide

Prices are approximate per head for a main course
$$$ = over DM35
$$ = less than DM35
$ = less than DM20 for a simple one course meal

Henne
Leuschnerdamm 25, Kreuzberg
Tel: 614 77 30
Open Wed–Sun 7pm–3am. Serves only freshly baked chicken (with some side dishes), but the best ones you ever tried. **$**

Storch
Wartburgstr. 54, Schöneberg
tel: 784 2059
www.storch-berlin.de
Daily 6pm–1am. Book in advance for the wonderful hospitality. The Alsatian food is served at communal tables. **$–$$**

Zur Letzten Instanz
Waisenstr. 14–16, Mitte
Tel: 242 55 28
Open noon–1am. Berlin's oldest pub in the oldest part of the city, next to the Nikolaiviertel. The dishes also come from old Berlin and they include *Bouletten*, *Roulade* and *Eisbein*. Gorebachev and Napoleon have eaten here. **$**

GREEK

Terzo Mondo
Grolmannstr. 28, Charlottenburg
Tel: 881 5261
Open 6pm–2am. Frequented by Berliners as well as tourists. It is

owned by a Greek actor and frequented by celebrities and activists. **$**

INDIAN

Amrit
Oranienstr 202–203, Kreuzberg
Tel: 612 5550
Sun–Thur noon–1am, Fri–Sat noon–2pm. Extremely popular Indian restaurant where the food is definitely up to standard. **$**

Suriya Kanthi
Knaackstr. 4, Prenzlauer Berg
Tel: 442 5301
Daily noon–1am. Everything made here is from eco-products. Look out for their east-west breakfast buffet on Sundays. **$$**

ITALIAN

Frantoio Trattoria Bar
Zossenerstr. 15, Kreuzberg
Tel: 6950 9416
Mon–Sun noon–1am. Among the inexpensive offerings are pizzas baked in wood-fuelled brick ovens. **$–$$**

Osteria Romana
Uhlandstr. 43–44, Wilmersdorf
Tel: 883 8385
Mon–Sat from noon. Authentic atmosphere and food to match. **$**

Pasta e Basta
Knesebeckstr. 94, Charlottenburg
Tel: 312 5982
Open Monday–Friday noon–midnight. Pasta is cooked in every way for a young and unpretentious crowd. **$–$$**

Pizzeria Amigo
Joachimstaler Str. 39–40
Tel: 882 2549
Sun–Thur 11–1am, Fri–Sat 11–2am. Popular venue with a selection of pizzas and pasta dishes. Menu in English. **$**

Restaurante Bonfini Pastabar
Münzstrasse 20, Mitte
Tel: 2472 6670
Interesting Italian dishes at reasonable prices served up in the heart of Mitte. Open Mon–Fri noon–midnight, Sat–Sun 5pm–1am. **$–$$**

JAPANESE

Mäcky Messer
Mulackstr. 29, Mitte
Tel: 283 4942
No credit cards. The man wielding the knife in this establishment is actually German. There is, however, no need to be afraid as his soups, salads and dishes served from this hole in the wall are first class. **$–$$**

MEXICAN

Viva Mexico!
Chauseestraße 36, Mitte
Tel: 280 78 65
Open noon–11pm Mon–Fri, 2pm–midnight Sun. A Mexican family makes the best salsa and guacamole in town with authentic dishes to go with it. **$**

Price Guide

Prices are approximate per head for a main course
$$$ = over DM35
$$ = less than DM35
$ = less than DM20 for a simple one course meal

SWISS

Marché-Möwenpick,
Kufurstendamm 14
Tel: 882 7578
Daily 8am–midnight. Buffet style fast food including salads, noodles, meat and sweets. The atmosphere is not much to write home about. **$**

TURKISH

Bagdad
Schlesische Str. 2, Kreuzberg
Tel: 612 6962
Open 12pm–1am. The Near East in deepest Kreuzberg. A kitsch garden where half Berlin meets on summer nights to eat Turkish specialities. **$–$$**

Hitit
Knobelsdorffstr. 35, Charlottenburg
Tel: 322 4557
Open noon–1am. Stylish dishes, a bohemian atmosphere and a waterfall. Here you can get a huge selection of food – vegetarians won't be stuck for choice either. **$–$$**

OTHER

Alte Welt
Wissmannstr. 44, Neukölln
Tel: 6270 8262
Mon–Sat 4pm–midnight, Sun 11am–midnight. If you wake up one morning and crave for something from Denmark, head down to Alte Welt where the food is prepared by a real Dane. **$**

Dietrich's
Marlene-Dietrich-Platz 2, Tiergarten
Tel: 2553 1768
Daily 11–1am. The DM20 Business Lunch is a favourite at this yuppie stop off.

Mapati
Gneisenaustr. 4, Kreuzberg
Tel: 6950 8055
Mon–Sat 4pm–midnight, Sun 3pm–midnight. Highly recommended restaurant Brazilian style. **$**

Marché
Kurfürstendamm 14
Tel: 882 7578
Buffet style "fast food" with salads, noodles, meat and sweets. **$**

Monsieur Vuong
Gipsstr. 3, Mitte
Tel: 3087 2643
Mon–Fri noon–midnight, Sat 2pm–midnight, Sun closed. Vietnamese noodles and soups are their speciality. **$**

PI
Gabriel-Max_Str. 17, Friedrichshain
Tel: 0170 527 5882
Mon–Sat noon–midnight, Sun from 10am. Restaurant that prepares fish and vegetables, but be patient – these things take time.

Schwejk
Ansbacher Str. 4, Schöneberg
Tel: 2137 892
Open daily 6pm–1am. In this Prague-style bistro the food will fill you up more than delight the eye. **$–$$**

Wellenstein
Kurfürstendamm 190, Charlottenburg
Tel: 881 7850
Daily 9–3am. Surprisingly good prices for good food; nice atmosphere. **$–$$**

WKG – Wir kochen Gemüse
Kollwitzstr. 90, Prenzlauer Berg
Tel: 4405 6444
Sun–Fri noon–11.30pm. Translated as "We cook vegetables", this is a great little vegetarian restaurant. **$**

Cafés

Some are called cafés, others café bars. Some even say bistro. Whatever banner they come under, it is not very difficult to find somewhere for a coffee and a light snack. The list below is a brief compilation of recommendable cafés designed to aid the tourist who is short of ideas in a part of town they don't know.

100 Wasser
Simon-Dach-Str. 39, Friedrichshain
Tel: 2900 1356
Daily from 10am. Breakfast is available until 4pm.

aché
Wühlischstr. 29, Friedrichshain
Tel: 2966 6257
Daily 10–2am. The wide menu includes an English breakfast.

Bateau Ivre
Oranienstr. 18, Kreuzberg
Tel: 6140 3659
Daily 9–3am. Although it is meant to be French it doesn't come across that way. It is good, though.

Belmundo
Winterfeldstr. 36, Schöneberg
Tel: 215 2070
Mon–Sat 9–1am, Sun 10am–midnight. Nicely located on Winterfeldplatz, this no messing street café will hit the spot.

brennBar
Axel-Springer-Str. 40–41, Kreuzberg
Tel: 2539 9260
Mon–Fri 10am–6pm, Sun 10am–3pm. Mediterranean foodstuffs and a wide range of snacks. Sunday's breakfast buffet is nice.

Café Adler
Friedrichstr. 206, Kreuzberg
Tel: 251 8965
Open 10am–1am. Once the

foremost outpost of the West, directly opposite Checkpoint Charlie, now an historical city centre pub.

Café am Neuen See
Lichtensteinallee 2, Tiergarten
Tel: 254 4930
Daily 10am–11pm. The novelty of this waterside café wears off when it's full. try to get there early in the day.

Café am See
Mohriner Allee 145, Neukölln
Tel: 703 6087
Mon–Sat 10am–7pm, Sun 9.30am–7pm. Right on the lake, this is good place for day-trippers.

Café Cralle
Hochstädter Str. 10a, Wedding
Tel: 455 3001
Tues–Fri 11–2am, Sat–Sun 9–2am, Mon 8pm–2am. Extremely popular local café. Monday night is Games Night.

Café Einstein
Kurfüstenstr. 58, Schöneberg
Tel: 261 5096
Open 10am–2am. Vienna coffee-house atmosphere transplanted to Berlin in the former villa of the silent screen star Henny Porten.

Café in der Schwartz'schen Villa
Grunewaldstr. 54–55, Steglitz
Tel: 793 7970
Daily 10am–midnight. Beautifully set in the green south west.

Café Nord
Schulstr. 28, Pankow
Tel: 0173 986 2774
Daily 8–3am. It's also possible to find a good coffee in Pankow.

Café Olé
Viktoriastr. 10–18, Templehof
Tel: 7550 3120
Daily from 10am. Excellent selection of breakfasts and a great salad bar are the features.

Café Rix
Karl-Marx-Str. 141. Neukölln
Tel: 686 9020
Daily 10–1am. Legendary menu from sausages to Turkish yoghurt soup.

Café R.Z.
Grosse Hamburger Str. 15–16, Mitte
Tel: 282 7657
Mon–Sat 8–2am. Comfortable and popular, it is here that you can find some home-made goulash or Schnitzel.

Chicago Coffee Company
Berliner Str. 27, Reinickendorf
Tel: 4303 5242
Mon–Fri 8am–9pm, Sat 8am–5pm. Good service and great coffee.

Eckstein
Pappelallee 73, Prenzlauer Berg
Tel: 441 9960
Sun–Thur 9–2am, Fri–Sat 9–3am. Light café built across the corner of a building. Sadly, it faces the wrong way for the sunset.

Elsenstein
Elsenstr. 7–8, Treptow
Tel: 5343 3636
Mon–Fri 8am–8pm. At least when you find yourself this far down the river you have a place to try out.

Knobelsdorff
Knobelsdorffstr. 38, Charlottenburg
Tel: 322 5093
Daily 8am–midnight. Great for a half hour when you're reading your paper.

Möhring
Charlottenstr. 55, Mitte
Tel: 20309 2240
Daily 8am–midnight. Try the special tarts and ice cream in this traditional coffee house.

Strandbad Mitte
Kleine Hamburger Str. 16, Mitte
Tel: 280 8403
Mon–Sat 9–2am. Quiet and secluded, this nice café thinks it's a beach swimming pool.

Uebereck
Prenzlauer Allee 47, Prenzlauer Berg
Tel: 442 8077
Daily 9–2am. Nicely laid out café where nobody seems to worry about the time.

Van Loon
im Urbanhafen, Höhe Carl-Herz-Ufer 5–7, Kreuzberg
Tel: 692 6293
Daily 10–1am. It's on a boat – fantastic when the sun shines.

Village Voice
Ackerstr. 1a, Mitte
Tel: 282 4550
Mon–Fri 11–2am, Sat–Sun from noon. Rarely used by tourists, this café cum bookshop is perfect for a relaxing drink.

Zucca
Am Zwirngraben 11–12, Mitte
Tel: 2472 1212
Mon–Fri 9–3am, Sat–Sun 10–3am. Under the S-Bahn arches at Hackescher Markt, you can enjoy the coffee in the spacious interior or outside in the sun.

Fast Food

Those not wanting to sit down and take part in formalities will head straight for the Imbiss. Although incorrectly associated with Turkish kebab stalls the word "Imbiss" actually goes for any place where the food is fast and there is no table service. This can mean a stand up sausage bar or a shop selling bagels. The following selection of places is intended to give an idea of the type of establishment on offer in Berlin – it is by no means an exhaustive list.

Bagdad
Schlesische Str. 2, Kreuzberg
Tel: 612 6962
Attached to the restaurant of the same name, the Bagdad is famed for excellent Döner and chicken kebabs. They're even better when you chat with the friendly staff.

Bagels and Bialys
Rosenthaler Str. 46748, Mitte
Tel: 283 65 46
Open 7am–5am. This stand up cafe imports the bagels from New York and is perfectly located for late night munchies on a night out. Beware: the plain bagel is smaller than the special ones, but costs the same. Their *Schawarmas* are fairly good. **$**

Fish and Chips
Yorckstr. 15, Kreuzberg
Tel: 0173-801 3855
Daily noon–1am. The name hints at what they sell and it won't disappoint the British expats either.

Habibi
Goltzstr. 24, Schöneberg
Tel: 01781-215 3332
Daily 11am–late. Falafels are only a small part of what you can eat here. Middle Eastern food presented in that Middle Eastern way. Other branches are: Akanzienstr. 9,

Schöneberg and Körtestr. 35,
Kreuzberg.
Hot Dog Laden
Goltzstr. 15, Schöneberg
Tel: 215 6932
Daily 11am–midnight. It has been
known for people to fly over two
continents to sample these hot
dogs.
Klemkes
Wein- and Spezialitäteneck,
Mommsenstr. 9, Charlottenburg
Tel: 8855 1260
Mon–Fri 8am–4.30pm. Quick
service and lunch-time snacks.
Konnopke's Imbiss
under the U-Bahn tracks, corner
Danzigerstr. and Schönhauser Allee
Mon–Sat 5am–7pm. The Berlin
Imbiss of Imbisse, the sausages
here are home made. The stand
has been under the same family
management since 1930.
Le Marais
Linienstr. 153, Mitte
Tel: 281 0715
Mon noon–7pm, Tues–Fri
11am–7pm, Sat 10am–4pm. Fine
cheese and wine in the upright
position.
Maitre Vite
Potsdamer Str. 96, Tiergarten
Tel: 261 5060
Mon–Fri 7am–5pm. Homesick
French should not be able to
complain about the standard of
baking available here.
Marcann's
Invalidenstr, 112, Mitte
Tel: 2832 8388
Mon–Fri 7am–6pm, Sat 10am–4pm,
Sun till 1am. Over lunch hour
Marcann's is packed out with
people waiting for a selection of
delicious panini or sandwiches –
highly recommended.
Piccola Romantica
Oranienstr. 33, Kreuzberg
Tel: 6140 3011
Sun–Thur 11–2am, Fri–Sat until
3am. Italian Imbiss and restaurant
for when the hunger is big and the
pocket is nearly empty.
Soup Kultur
Kurfürdtendamm 224,
Charlottenburg
Tel: 8862 9282
Mon–Fri noon–8pm, Sat noon–4pm.
Soup is served in small paper cups.

Viva Vie
Immanuelkirchstr. 3–4, Prenzlauer
Berg
Tel: 4401 0477
Mon–Fri 10am–7pm. Fresh
vegetarian fare with a light hearted
approach.

Restaurants in Potsdam

The dialing code for Potsdam is
0331.

Havelgarten
14471, Auf dem Kiewitt 30
Tel: 972316
Open daily 11.30am–midnight, Sun
10am–midnight. Eat in summer on
a terrace overlooking the River
Havel. **$$–$$$**
Hofgarten Voltaire
Hotel Voltaire, Friedrich Ebert Str.
88
Tel: 31231 7610
www.hotelvoltaire.potsdam.de
Regional dishes with an
international touch are served in
the hotel restaurant. **$$–$$$**
Le Bistro Dorint
Jägerallee
Tel: 312740
www.dorint.de/potsdam
In this à la carte restaurant you will
sample some fine German cuisine
and a range of top wines. **$$–$$$**
Restaurant Juliette
Jägerstr. 39
Tel: 270 1791
Daily noon–11pm. French cuisine.
$$–$$$
Restaurant Schloss Cecilienhof
14469, Neuer Garten
Tel: 37050
www.castle-cecilienhof.com
Daily 7am–10.30pm. Sophisticated
regional specialities. Romantic,
historic ambience. During the
Potsdam Conference Stalin,
Churchill and Truman ate here. **$$$**
Ristorante Villa Kellermann
14467, Mangerstr. 34–36
Tel: 291572
Mon–Thur 4pm–midnight, Fri–Sun
noon–midnight. Over-praised for its
quality and service, but much loved
Italian restaurant with terrace on
the Heiligen See. **$$$**

Moderate

Aqua art'otel
Zeppelin Str. 136
Tel: 951 0585
www.artotel.de/potsdam.html
This hotel restaurant prides itself
on its seafood specialities.
Gastmahl des Meeres
14467, Brandenburger Str. 72
Tel: 291854
Open daily 11am–11pm.
International fish specialities.
Maison Charlotte
Charlottenstr. 13
Tel: 280 5450
Daily 10am–9pm. After trying the
regional French cuisine, sample
something from the tempting
patisserie. **$$**
Restaurant Bayrisches Haus
14471, Im Wildpark 1
Tel: 973192
Open daily 7am–11pm.
International cuisine with local and
Bavarian specialities. **$$**
Restaurant Kleines Schloss
14482, Im Park Babelsberg
Tel: 705156
Open daily 11am–7pm, in winter
until 6pm. Popular "day out"
restaurant with good food. **$$**
Restorante Zum Starstecher
Leibestr. 12
Tel: 270 1991
Daily noon–midnight. Experience
the flair and taste of the Italians.
$$
Rote Villa
14467, Berliner Str. 133
Tel: 294607
Open daily noon–midnight, Friday
until 3pm. German cuisine. **$$**
Terrassenrestaurant Minsk
14473, Max-Planck-Str. 10
Tel: 293636
Open Mon, Tues and Thur
noon–11.30pm, Wed and Sat
noon–2pm, Sun noon–11.30pm.

Good food, bar and weekend dancing for the older generation. **$$**

Zum Garde-Ulanen
Jägerallee 13
Tel: 291 261
Sun–Thur 8am–10pm, Fri–Sat till midnight. Traditional local dishes.

Inexpensive

Charlottenhof
14471, Geschwister-Scholl-Str. 34
Tel: 901 064
Open daily 11.30am–9pm.
Bavarian specialities in a beer garden. **$–$$**

Crepie La Madeleine
Lindenstr. 9
Tel: 270 5400
Daily noon–10pm. For Normandy crêpes look no further. **$**

Froschkasten
14467, Kiezstr. 4
Tel: 291315
Open Mon–Sat noon–midnight, Sun noon–10pm. Good food served in a relaxed setting. **$–$$**

Historischer Bacchuskeller im Alten Rathaus
14467, Am Alten Markt 9
Tel: 293135
Open Mon–Sat 6pm–midnight. Wine bar with good cooking. **$–$$**

Klosterkeller
14467, Friedrich-Ebert-Str. 94
Tel: 291 218
Open daily 8am–midnight.
International cooking with a hint of local solidity; Prussian specialities. Costume events are the norm. **$–$$**

Luise
Luisenplatz 6
Tel: 903663
Nice and friendly restaurant right in centre and close to the entrance of Park Sanssouci. Good food, good prices. **$**

Preussischer Hof
14467, Charlottenstr. 11
Tel: 270 0762
Open Tues–Sun noon–midnight.
German cuisine. Speciality is "cabbage soup à la Soldier King". **$–$$**

Ratskeller Babelsberg, 14482, Karl-Liebknecht-Str. 135
Tel: 707426

Open Mon–Thur 8am–midnight, Fri 8am–3pm, Sun noon–midnight. Good solid food. **$–$$**

Restaurant Börse
14467, Brandenburger Str. 35–36
Tel: 280 0164
Open daily 11am–midnight. Local cuisine. **$–$$**

Restaurant-Cafe Drachenhaus
Maulbeerallee 4a
Tel: 505 3808
Daily 11am–7pm (6pm in winter). If you are hungry while visiting Sanssouci, this café is set in the beautiful, historic Chinoiserie pagoda in the park. **$**

Restaurant Die Tenne
Potsdamer Str. 95
Tel: 504 800
www.restaurant-die-tenne.de
Daily from 11.30am. The landlord of this mock rustic establishment claims that every meal is made especially for each guest and that all ingredients are fresh – good for him. **$**

Restaurant Pegasus
14467, Schlossstr. 14
Tel: 291506
Open daily noon–3pm, 6–11pm, noon–4pm Sunday. Youthful atmosphere. **$–$$**

Waage
Am Neuen Markt 12
Tel: 2709675
German, Italian and French cuisine in the recently renovated historical scales. **$**

Cafés in Potsdam

Potsdam is really turning up the heat for the tourists and now has plenty of cafés and ice cream shops. Here are but a few.

Artur Café und Antiquariat
14467, Dorfustr. 16
Tel: 280 0087

Bowling-Center Babelsberg,
14482, Grossbeerenstr. 123
Tel: 0331-748 2689

Café im Filmmuseum
14467, Schlossstr. 1
Tel: 0331-270 2041

Café Herbst, 14467, Friedrich-Ebert-Str. 114a
Tel: 0331-293 063
www.cafe-herbst.de

Daily 11am–8pm. On Fridays and Saturdays the restaurant is open from 8pm.

Café Radio Eins
14467, Friedrich-Ebert-Str. 118
Tel: 0331-270 0642
Open daily 3pm–1am. Very young crowd.

Café Reinhold
14467, Dortustr. 10
Tel: 0331-284 990

Café-Restaurant Babette
14467, Brandenburger Str. 71
Tel: 0331-291648
Open daily 9am–10pm. Typical street café in Potsdam's shopping street.

Eiscafé Venezia
Brandenburger Str. 28a
Tel: 0331-270 1930.
Coffee and ice cream with that Venetian touch.

Internetcafé
14467, Am Alten Markt 10
Tel: 0331-280 0555
Where the Potsdamers come to check their mail.

Culture

Information Sources

The best way to get a feel for what is going on in Berlin is to take a look at one of the fortnightly city magazines *Tip* or *Zitty*. You will find current events and performances listed under the headings Theatre, Dance, Music, Film, Cabaret, Fine Arts, etc. Daily papers have daily tips and include a weekly preview on Wednesday *(Tagesspiegel)*, Thursday *(Berliner Zeitung)* and Friday *(Berliner Morgenpost)*. There are also the monthly magazines *Prinz* and *Berlin Programm*, and a lot of brochures and flyers. The free distributed *030* magazine is mainly addressed to young people looking for the party scene but you may find *Flyer*, the pocket-sized monthly freebie, easier to use. These all serve as trusty guides in helping to decide where to go and what to do.

Finally there are posters in all underground stations and last but not least, the big, round freestanding pillars pasted over with posters and situated on pavements throughout the city are another good source of information.

You can go directly to the box office of the theatre or concert hall you want to visit or phone to reserve tickets. You can also order tickets in one of the centrally located box offices which sell tickets for all events (*see Box Offices* at the end of this section for addresses). Be aware that they add an extra service charge.

For many selected events you can easily book tickets through Berlin Tourismus Marketing GmbH (BTM) – *see Practical Tips: Tourist Offices.* There are several festivals – Berliner Festwochen, Jazzfest, International Berlin Film Festival

and Theatertreffen (Theatre Meeting) organised by the Berliner Festspiele GmbH. Information and tickets can be obtained by writing to the Kartenbüro der Berliner Festspiele (Ticket Office), 10787 Berlin, Budapester Str. 50, or tel: 030-254890, fax: 25489 155, www.berliner-festspiele.de.

Further information, tickets (also for other events), books, posters and brochures for various cultural events and performances are available from Fullhouse Service, Budapester Str. 48, tel: 25489254. Open Monday–Friday 10am–6pm, Saturday 10am–2pm. Other options include KoKa36, Oranienstr. 29, Kreuzberg; tel: 615 8818, www.icf.de/koka36; where you can get tickets for just about anything, or the ticket booth in Bahnhof Friedrichstrasse.

Cultural Centres

Amerika Haus Berlin: Hardenbergstr. 22–24; tel: 311 07406.
Amerika-Gedenk-Bibliothek: (library with extensive collection of English language books and videos. You have to prove you live in Berlin to check anything out.) Blücherplatz, Kreuzberg, Zentral- und Landesbibliothek Berlin; tel: 902 26 0. www.zlb.de
Aspen Institut Berlin: Inselstr. 10; tel: 80 48 90-0.
The British Council – The British Centre Berlin: Hackescher Markt 1, Mitte; tel: 31 10 99-10, www.britcoun.de/infocent.html

Live Performance

There is a good choice of theatre, concerts, ballet and opera for all tastes. Some of the main venues are listed below.

CONCERTS

Philharmonie, Herbert-von-Karajan Str. 1, Tiergarten; tel: 2548 8232, www.berlin-philharmonic.com. Home of the world renowned Berlin

Philharmonia. Simon Rattle's arrival in 2002 should further strengthen the reputation of one of Berlin's greatest orchestras.
Konzerthaus, Gendarmemarkt 2, Mitte; tel: 2030 92101, www.konzerthaus.de. The Grosser Konzertsaal plays host to big orchestral works while the Kleiner Saal is better suited to chamber music in what used to be known as the Schauspielhaus. Enjoy some classical music in fine style.

OPERA

Deutsche Oper, Bismark Str. 35, Charlottenburg; tel: 341 0249, tickets: 343 8401, www.deutsche-oper-berlin.de. Home of the Berlin orchestra. Perforances are mostly classical although contemporary works are also featured.
Komische Oper, Behrenstr. 55–57, Mitte; tel: 202 600, tickets: 4799 7400, www.komische-oper-berlin.de. Not as grand as the Deutsche or Staatsoper, the Komische Oper is a reliable venue for comic opera.
Neuköllner Oper, Karl-Marx-Strasse 131–133, Neukölln; tel: 688 9070, box office: 688 90777. In this venue for innovative opera, Neuköllners and visitors alike enjoy low cost and high entertainment opera.
Staatsoper Unter den Linden, Unter den Linden 7; tel: 2035 4555, program info: 2035 4438, www.staatsoper-berlin.org. Originally Prussia's Royal Court Opera House, the Staatsoper is one of the two best operatic houses in Berlin. Occasionally, really big names play here.

THEATRE

Berliner Ensemble (Theater am Schiffbauerdamm), Bertoldt-Brecht-Platz 1; tel: 282 3160, tickets: 2840 8155, www.berliner-ensemble.de. Still named after the ensemble that no longer exists, the "house that Brecht built" is still a big favourite with theatre buffs.

Deutsches Theater, Schumman Str. 13a, Mitte; tickets: 2844 1225, info: 2844 1222, www.deutsches-theater.berlin.net. Still one of the most respected theatres in Berlin, it continues to present classic German and international productions.

Friedrichdstadtpalast, Friedrichstr. 107, Mitte; tel: 2326 2326, www.friedrichstadtpalast.de. Although usually performing its brand of glitzy juggling/dancing entertainment, this razmatazz memorial of the former GDR still takes itself very seriously.

Hebbel-Theater, Stresemannstr. 29, Kreuzberg; tickets: 2590 0427, www.hebbel-theater.de. Stages productions of international avant-garde productions continue to produce challenging performances for the upper echelon of theatre goers.

Komödie, Kurfürstendamm 206, Charlottenburg; tel: 4799 74 30–40, www.komoedie-berlin.de. Acting, laughter and song is on offer at this long established theatre.

Maxim Gorki Theater, Am Festungsgraben 2, Mitte; tel: 2022 1129, tickets: 2022 1115, www.gorki.de. For classics and contemporary drama, the Maxim Gorki is a sure bet.

Schaubühne am Lehniner Platz, Kurfürstendamm 153, Wilmersdorf; tickets: 890023, tickets info: 8900 2777, www.schaubuehne.de. Has played host to some of the German greats but rumours are always circulating about its imminent downfall – all, until now, wrong.

Theater am Kurfürstendamm, Kurfürstendamm 203–206; tickets: 4799 7440, info: 885 9110, www.theater-am-kurfuerstendamm.de. Popular with aging German tourists, the farcical comedy on offer is often played by TV stars better known in Germany than abroad.

Theater des Westens, Kantstr. 12; tel: 319 030, tickets: 0180-599 8999, www.theater-des-westens.de. Musicals are the mainstay of this house which used to be the Städtische Oper. Usually the first stop for those in the know about these things.

Volksbühne, Rosa-Luxemburg-Platz; tel: 247 6772, visitor service: 247 7694, www.volksbuehne-berlin.de. Always packed to the rafters, this theatre prides itself on controversy and new interpretation.

FRINGE THEATRE

Berliner Grundtheater tel: 782 7700, www.thebgt.de. British fringe theatre performed by a German and British cast. Once or twice a year they perform a classic.

Friends of Italian Opera (Freunde der italienischen Oper), Fidicinstr. 40, Kreuzberg; tel: 693 5692, tickets: 691 1211, www.thefriends.de.

Grips-Theater, Altonaerstr. 22, Tiergarten; tel: 397 4740, tickets: 3974 7477, www.grips-theater.de. Berlin's best loved English speaking theatre is still a big hit with kids.

STÜKKE (in der Palisa.de) Palisadenstr. 48, Mitte; tel: 4202 818, www.stuekke.de. Currently residing in the Kulturhaus Palisadenstrasse, this fringe theatre stages contemporary plays of young international playwrights.

Tacheles, Oranienburger Str. 54–56a; tel: 282 6185, www.tacheles.de. Experimentation, alternative theatre and solo performances are only part of what you expect here. Performances sometimes in English.

Tanzfabrik Berlin (Centre for contemporary dance), Möckernstrasse 68, Kreuzberg; tel: 786 58 61, www.tanzfabrik-berlin.de. Innovative dance theatre.

Theater am Halleschen Ufer Hallesches Ufer 32, Kreuzberg; tel: 2510941, www.thub.de. Home to innovative "free" theatre groups – occasionally in English.

Theater Zerbrochene Fenster, Fidicinstr. 3, Kreuzberg; tel: 694 2400, tickets: 691 2932, www.tzf-berlin.de. Fringe theatre atop a converted warehouse in Kreuzberg. Local English-speaking theatre companies take it in turn with German ones to present some interesting stuff.

Vagantenbühne, Kantstr. 12a, Charlottenburg; tel: 312 4529, www.vaganten.de. One of the oldest private theatres in Berlin, the company is said to be less experimental than when it was established.

Museums

Berlin has about 160 museums (it is popularly said that there are "more museums than rainy days in Berlin"). The collections include fine art, archaeology, ethnography, history, technology, natural history and much more. The most important museums are located at four centres: the Museumsinsel in Mitte, the Kulturforum in Tiergarten, near the Schloss Charlottenburg, and in Dahlem (see relevant Places chapters)

Entrance Fees
Most Berlin museums are owned and operated by the *Staatliche Museen zu Berlin Stiftung Preussischer Kulturbesitz* (the Stately Museums of Berlin Institute of Prussian Cultural Possessions).

The entrance fees are 4DM (reductions 2DM) for single tickets, DM8 (reductions DM4) for day tickets, valid for every permanent exhibit of the *Staatliche Museen*. The following museums sell day tickets only: Pergamonmuseum, Hamburger Bahnhof, Sammlung Berggruen, Ägyptisches Museum, Antikensammlung, Altes Museum, Neue Nationalgalerie and Gemäldegalerie. There is free entry the first Sunday of the month. For temporary exhibitions there are different fees, normally DM12.

The BTM offers a 3-day ticket for DM15, which entitles you to unrestricted admission to the permanent exhibits in all of Berlin's state museums.

Cinema

Berlin is a fantastic city for filmgoers, and not only during the annual International Film Festival in February. Numerous film production studios have their headquarters here and much up-and-coming talent is cultivated at the Deutsche Film und Fernsehakademie Berlin (DFFB) (the German Film and Television Academy in Berlin), Potsdamer Str. 2, 10785 Berlin, tel: 257 590, www.dffb.de.

In addition to these, the huge DEFA production studios (formerly called the UFA), are located in Babelsberg, near Potsdam.

There is a huge cinema complex at Potsdamer Platz. The **CinemaxX** combines 19 screens with seats for 3,500 people. Some cinemas are dedicated to movie classics and to un-dubbed films. Many other cinemas are concentrated in the area between the Europa-Centre and Uhlandstrasse but films shown here are usually in German. In addition to these huge complexes, there are many smaller, more independent cinemas which emphasise a selection of avant-garde, political, experimental, classical and exotic films. Many of these small cinemas can be found on a joint website at: www.independents.de. A list of all films playing in English in Berlin is updated every week at

www.berlinfo.com/freetime/Film-Theatre/Film/program/index.htm. Otherwise, turn to the listings magazines, *Tip* and *Zitty*, for what's on in the cinema. The initials OV next to a film means that it is in original version and OmU means original with subtitles. Don't assume that the film will be in English – the langauage will be of country that the film comes from. Worth mentioning here is the **Arsenal**, Potsdamerstrasse 2, tel: 2695 5100. The **Freunde der Kinemathek** cinema offers a programme of retrospective movies dealing with historical film topics. Consult their instructive monthly calendar at www.fdk-berlin.de/arsenal/calub.html for more information.

At the **Odeon**, Schöneberger Hauptstrasse 116, tel: 7815667, English-language films are shown in the original. Other cinemas showing original versions are (among others) **ufa-Arthouse die Kurbel**, Giesebrechtstr. 4, tel: 883 5325, **Tacheles**, Oranienburger Str. 54, tel: 283 1498, the **Village Cinemas Kulturbrauerei**, Schönhauser Alle 36–39, tel: 4435 4422 and **Babylon**, Dresdender Str. 126, tel: 6160 9693. The private **Berliner Kinomuseum** in Kreuzberg, Grossbeerenstrasse 57, scarcely larger than a living room, is devoted to the preservation of old films and projectors. There are presentations

at 8.30 and 10.30pm on Tuesday, Wednesday, Friday and Saturday, also at 6pm on Saturday.

Likewise the **Zeughaus-Kino** in the German History Museum on Unter den Linden shows historical productions.

Alternative Berlin

The "alternative" scene has taken root in Berlin as nowhere else in Germany, or even Europe. Evidence of this can be seen in the existence of numerous alternative cultural centres and institutions. You can tap into this scene by hanging out in various pubs, but to really get to know the city's alternative culture go and visit the centres themselves.

The largest collection of projects is to be found in the **Mehringhof**, Gneisenaustrasse 2, Kreuzberg – over 30 groups have made this building their headquarters.

On the basis of its sheer size and infrastructure, the **ufa Fabrik**, **ufa Factory**, Viktoriastr. 10–18, Templehof, tel: 75 50 30, www.ufafabrik.de for culture, sports and craft workshops, is practically a village in itself. The **Kunsthaus Tacheles**, Oranienburger Str. 54–56, tel: 2809 6123, is also large. A lively, varied programme including concerts and films, as well as a café (Café Zapata), are to be found in the now renovated shell of what was once the Friedrichstadt Passagen.

Other places are the **Haus der Kulturen der Welt**, John Foster Dulles Allee 10, Tiergarten, tel: 3978 7175, which has an interesting programme of exhibitions, theatre productions and discussions on literature and film, the **Werkstatt der Kulturen**, Wissmannstr. 32, Neukölln, tel: 622 2024, the **Kulturbrauerei**, Knaackstr. 95, tel: 44192 69/70, www.kulturbrauerei.de, and the **Tempodrom**, Askanischer Platz 4, Kreuzberg, tel: 263 9980, www.tempodrom.de. In Mitte the **Acud**, cultural centre, Veterananatr. 21, tel (club): 4435 9499, tel (gallery): 449 1067 has a cinema, two clubs and an art gallery and often puts on

Literary Berlin

The great era of the Romanische Café, which was located just across from the memorial church in the Ku'damm, has long since passed. But literary Berlin has taken on another face and its focal point remains predominantly in Charlottenburg. **The Literaturhaus**, in a tastefully renovated city villa at Fasanenstrasse 23 (tel: 882 6552) is the centre for all manner of literary events and performances. The centre includes three lecture rooms, a café with garden, the Tucholsky

Memorial and a book store in the basement. A calendar of events is available; for further information tel: 882 6552.

Other places where literary folk congregate are the **Akademie der Künste**, Hanseatenweg 10; tel: 390760 or Pariser Platz 4, www.adk.de/e_index.html, the **Literarische Colloquium Berlin**, Am Sandwerder 5, Wannsee; tel: 8169960, www.lcb.de and the **Literaturwerkstatt**, Majakowskiring 46–48; tel: 485 2450, www.literaturwerkstatt.org in Pankow's Majakowskiring.

special events. A popular place for women to meet is in the neighbourhood cultural centre **Begine**, Potsdamer Str. 139, tel: 215 4325 or in the **Schoko-Fabrik**, Mariannenstr. 6, tel: 615 2999 in Kreuzberg.

Art Galleries

Art galleries take various different forms in Berlin. If you are looking for classical pieces of work by the great masters and their contemporaries, there are the big (and often state run) museums and galleries. In Charlottenburg and the West you can find works by high profile artists in the private galleries. For the new wave of artists, look no further than Mitte. In the 1990s, behind the walls and in the cellars of the damp, crumbling and run-down buildings of the Scheunenviertel, young contemporary artists were finding their feet. Semi-illegal bars, clubs and galleries started to appear and became popular with the underground. Word spread about these ambassadors and people flocked to see their brand of visual media, which was often in collaboration with DJs and other people on the scene.

As the property developers began to move in the walls of buildings were painted, central heating was installed and running water was connected in the rundown studios. An air of professionalism took hold of the young art scene. The move seems to have been well received and the streets of Mitte are now awash with fashionable art galleries, particularly around Hackescher Markt, August Strasse and Sophien Strasse.

Whether art has suffered is for the individual to decide but a good way to assess what's going on is to go on a *Rundgang* (walk around). Often on the first Saturday of the month, a *Rundgang* evening is arranged when most of the galleries in Mitte are open so you can take in a handful of them at your leisure.

Art Festivals

Berlin has two big art events – the annual **Art Forum**, held at the end of September or in early October and the **Biennale** (Berlin Film Festival) which takes place in February.

MITTE AND THE EAST

aktions galerie, August Str. 20, Mitte; tel: 2859 9650, www.aktionsgalerie.de; Tues–Sat 2–7pm. Many hoped that this established name on the Berlin scene could have held out against the gentrification trend in Mitte but it was not to be. Light and video installations are their favourite media.

Asian Fine Arts, Sophien Str. 18, Mitte; tel: 2839 1387, www.asianfinearts.de; Tues–Fri 2–7pm, Sat 11am–5pm. A fine selection of Asian art has been on display here since 1997.

Contemporary Fine Arts, Sophien Str. 21, Mitte; tel: 288 7870, www.cfa-berlin.de; Tues–Fri 10am–6pm, Sat 11am–6pm. Here you'll mostly find the British art scene featuring ironic and conceptual works.

Galerie Arndt + Partner, Auguststr. 35, Mitte; tel: 280 8123, www.arndt-partner.de; Tues–Sat noon–6pm. Recently moved north from Stadtmitte into the trendy Scheunenvietel in Mitte, A+P was established in 1994 by Matthias Arndt. Shows international contemporary art.

Galerie Barbara Thumm, Dircksenstr. 41, Mitte; tel: 28391387; Tues–Fri 1–4pm, Sat 1–5pm. This gallery focuses on a high standard British and Berlin art.

Galerie Berlin, Kunsthof, Oranienburgerstr. 27, Mitte; tel: 2514420; Tues–Fri 1–7pm, Sat 1–6pm. Before November 1990 this was the former GDR's official art house. Although it turned into a thriving new private venture, they still concentrate on eastern German expressive painting. You will also find a large collection of German works from the early 20th century.

Galerie Eigen + Art, Auguststr. 26, Mitte; tel: 280 6605, www.eigen-art.com; Tues–Sat 11am–6pm. The exhibitions feature contemporary art from all over the world. The owner is known for his big and tireless contribution to the promotion of young, modern artists from the former eastern Germany.

Galerie Wohnmachine, Tucholskystr. 35, Mitte; tel: 3087 2015; Tues–Sat 11am–6pm. This important experimental art-gallery borrowed its name from Le Courbusier's *machine à habiter* (living with art and in art). It was set up in 1988 in the owner's apartment and was one of the first of its kind.

Gallery Guides

Those seeking more information on the art world can pick up free copies of the *Mitte Gallery Guide* or *Berliner Gallerien* in most galleries. The *Berlin Artery* covers all galleries and is published every two months. Containing reviews in both English and German, it can be picked up at major galleries and tourist information points.

Kuckei Kuckei, Linienstr. 158, Mitte; tel: 883 4354; Tues–Fri 11am–6pm, Sat 11am–5pm. In the summer of 1998 this gallery moved from Wilmersdorf to the freshly renovated courtyards on Linienstrasse. Exhibits young art from the 1990s.

Kunst-Werke Berlin, Auguststr. 69, Mitte; tel: 243 459-0 www.kw-berlin.de; Tues–Sun noon–6pm. The owner of this gallery was one of the pioneers of the art scene in Mitte. Lots of young and emerging contemporary artists are drawn to this place. There is a café pavilion in the building where you can enjoy the art over a drink.

Neue Berliner Kunstverein, Chausseestr. 128–129, Mitte; tel: 280 7020-2, www.nbk.org; Tues, Thur, Fri noon–7pm, Sat noon–4pm. This well-funded art gallery is located in a building that looks as if it could be a bank. The exhibitions consist mainly of contemporary Berlin art, international, modern photography and video art.

CHARLOTTENBURG AND THE WEST

Akademie der Künste, Hanseatenweg 10, Tiergarten; tel: 390760, www.adk.de; Tues–Sun 10am–7pm, Mon 1–7pm. In 1696 the Akademie was founded by Preussian prince Friedrich III, which makes it one of the oldest cultural institutions in Berlin. At the end of the 1930s it lost its importance when the Nazis sent most of its prominent members into exile. Since its re-establishment in 1954 it houses free jazz concerts, films and poetry readings next to the exhibitions.

Galerie Anselm Dreher, Pfalzburger Str. 80, Wilmersdorf; tel: 883 5249, www.galerie-anselm-dreher.com; Tues–Fri 2am–6.30pm, Sat 11am–2pm. About 30 years ago this gallery started the promotion of concrete, minimal and conceptual contemporary art. They were the first to do so and were followed by others about a decade later.

Galerie Franck + Schulte, Mommenstr.56, Charlottenburg; tel: 3240 0440; Mon–Fri 11am–6pm, Sat 11am–3pm. This is one of Berlin's main upmarket galleries. You will mostly find work of famous American artists, although different art forms are exhibited.

Galerie Springer + Winkler, Fasanenstr. 13, Charlottenburg; tel: 315 7220, www.springer-winckler.de; Tues–Fri 10am–1pm and 2.30pm–7pm, Sat 11am–3pm. Located in Hamburg until 1998 before moving to Berlin, this gallery now focuses on contemporary and post-war German art. The program features painting as well as photography, film and sculpture.

Haus am Waldsee, Argentinische Allee 30, Zehlendorf; tel: 801

8935; Tues–Sun noon–8pm. In the 1950s this gallery exhibited art that had been banned by the Nazis. In the 1980s they supported neo-Expressionists and it now houses some important works of contemporary art.

Haus der Kulturen der Welt, John-Foster-Dulles-Allee 10, Tiergarten; tel: 3978 7175; Tues–Sun 10am–9 pm. The 'House of world cultures' was set up in 1989 to promote artists from developing countries. It is located in a congress centre shaped like an oyster – America's first cultural contribution to Berlin. They feature large and varied exhibitions. Ask for a programme of film festivals, lectures, panel discussions, dance performances.

Hochschule der Künste, Hardenbergstr. 33, Charlottenberg; tel: 3185-0, www.hdk-berlin.de; Mon–Sat 6am–12pm. The school's gallery features work from students or teachers of the HdK resulting in a colourful and very diverse exhibition.

Künstlerhaus Bethanien, Mariannenplatz 2, Kreuzberg; tel: 616 9030; Wed–Sun 2–7pm. In the 1970s the old hospital buildings, in which this gallery is now housed, were squatted and used as an alternative art gallery and theatre. Nowadays it consists of three large galleries and studio residencies, which are inhabited by artists from all over the world. Artists from Sweden and Australia have permanent studio exhibitions.

Raab Galerie, Potsdammer Str. 58, Tiergarden; tel: 2619217, www.raab-galerie.de; Mon–Fri 10am–7pm, Sat 10am–4pm. Here the emphasis lies on the expressive and figurative painting once associated with Berlin.

Sammlung Berggruen, Schlossstr. 1, Charlottenberg; tel: 209 055-55, www.smpk.de; Tues–Fri 10am–6pm, Sat–Sun 11am–6pm. On display here you will find Erika and Rolf Hoffmann's private collection of contemporary art, including a large collection of Picassos.

JANUARY

Lange Nacht der Museen – Long Night of the Museums (Saturday in the last weeks of January & August) Museums all over town. Info: 2839 7444, www.lange-nacht-der-museen.de. Berlin's civic museums stay open late and extra performances and events are staged. Special buses are put on to ferry visitors about.
Internationale Grüne Woche – Green Week (1 week in January) Messedamm 22. Info: 30380, www.gruenewoche.com. Disguised as an annual farming and agriculture show, the Grüne Woche is just a good excuse to eat and drink speciality foods from Germany and around the globe.

FEBRUARY

Berlinale – Berlin International Film Festival (12 days in February) Main locations: Berlinale Palast and around Potsdamer Platz. Info: www.berlinale.de. One of the world's best film festivals. Tickets can be obtained at the Arkaden am Potsdamer Platz, Kino International and the Europa Center.
Transmediale (during the Berlinale) Podewil, Kloster Str. 68–70. Showcasing forms of visual media using video, TV, computers and the internet.

MARCH

Musik Biennale Berlin (2003, then every other year in March) Berliner Festspiele, Budapester Strasse 50 This 12-day contemporary music festival attracts many musicians.

JUNE

Karneval der Kulturen – Carnival of Cultures (Whit weekend, June) Kreuzberg. Info: 622 4232, www.karneval-berlin.de. Berlin celebrates its multicultural diversity in a parade consisting of drum beats and bright costumes.

La Fête de la Musique – World Music Day (21 June) Throughout Berlin. The joys of music are celebrated as Berlin heralds the official arrival of summer. DJs, bands, singers and musicians take part in a multitude of musical events.

Berlin Philharmonie at the Waldbühne (June) Waldbühne, Glokenturm Strasse, Charlottenburg, tel: 2308 8230. Annual end of season concert.

Schwullesbisches Strassenfest – Gay and Lesbian Street Party (second or third week in June) Nollendorfplatz, Schöneberg. Info: 216 8008. Nollendorfplatz and the surrounding area is transformed into a two day street festival for both gay and straight communities. DJs, performers and numerous stalls provide the entertainment.

Christopher Street Day Parade (Saturday at the end of June) Ku'damm to the Grossen Stern, parties at various venues. Berlin's most colourful street parade commemorates the turning point of gay liberation at the Stonewall riots in 1969.

JULY–AUGUST

Love Parade (first or second Saturday in July) Strasse des 17.Juni (barring a change of plans). This is the event that everybody is waiting for. Up to 2 million people hit the Tiergarten to take part in the biggest dance music party/parade in the world. Its future is unsure.

Alternative Parade (same day as Love Parade) Usual starting point: Bunker, Reinhardt Strasse. The counter demonstration of those disillusioned with the Love Parade.

Hanfparade – Hemp Parade (end of August) Alex to Brandenburg Gate (routes can change). Info: 2472 0233. Parade for those still striving for the total legalisation of hemp.

Internationales Bierfest – International Beerfestival (first weekend in August) Strausberger Allee – Frankfurter Tor. Info: 508 6822. Karl Marx Allee is the venue for this beer festival which showcases all sorts of Germany's favourite lubricant.

Heimatklänge (Sounds Like Home) World Music Festival (July through August) Tempodrom, Askanischer Platz 4. Info: 263 9980. For Berlin's biggest world music event.

Hofkonzerte – Courtyard Concerts (every weekend in July and August) In the courtyard at Podewil. European jazz and classical music feature in a series of concerts.

Classic Open Air (4 days in July) Gendarmemarkt, Mitte. Tel: 315 7540. Big voices, big entertainment and big names are all part of a four day classic/popular opera event.

SEPTEMBER–OCTOBER

Berliner Festwochen (September) Info: Berliner Festspiele, Budapester Str. 50, tel: 254 890.

Marking the end of the culturally rich summer, a festival of classical music, theatre and other events and exhibitions is put on across Berlin. **Art Forum Berlin** (end of Sept/early Oct) Messedamm 22. Tel: 8855 1643. The world of art converges on Berlin to sell and be seen.

NOVEMBER

JazzFest Berlin (November) Haus der Kulturen der Welt, John-Foster-Dulles Allee 10, tel: 3978 7175, www.berlinerfestspiele.de/jazzfest. Started in 1964, this highly regarded festival recently welcomed a new musical director.

Jüdische Kulturtage – Jewish Culture Days (November) All around the city. Contact: Jüdisches Gemeindehaus, Fasanenstr. 79–80, tel: 880 280, www.herden.de/jkt/ During this Jewish awareness festival lasting two to three weeks Berlin is treated to a wide range of theatrical, film and dance events as well as forums and workshops. With a different theme each year, it has attracted some big names from Jewish society to take part.

Christmas Markets (November–Christmas) Alexanderplatz, Breitscheidplatz, Opera House, Altstadt Spandau. Germans love Christmas markets. *Glühwein* and chestnuts are consumed and decorations and other home-made gifts are sold from little huts.

DECEMBER

German Tattoo Convention (3/4 days in December) Columbiahalle, Columbiadamm 13–21, tel: 698 0908, www.tattoo-convention.de/english/home.htm The convention welcomes enthusiasts to take part in one of the world's largest tattoo events.

Silvester – New Year's Eve (31st December) Germans like to welcome in the new year with fireworks and rockets.

Trade Fairs

Internationale Tourismus Börse – International Trade Fair (Early March) Messedamm 26. Info: Exhibitors from the international, regional and local tourist industries come together for this event.

Internationale Funkausstellung – International Electronics Exhibition (end of August 2003 then every second year) Messegelände, Messedamm 22. Info: 3038 2274, www.ifa-berlin.com.

Check out all the latest gadgets in the world of electronica and communications.

AAA – The Berlin Motor Show (1 week in Oct/Nov every even year) Messedamm, Charlottenburg. Info: tel: 3038 2014, www.aaa-berlin.de, Every two years the motor industry gets its chance to showcase all its latest cars, gadgets and accessories. For the public, the fair also has a range of activities to take part in.

Nightlife

Where to Go

When does the evening start? At 8pm, when plays, concerts and other cultural events usually begin? Or at midnight, when all the beautiful people emerge into party land? Whatever your taste, Berlin caters for you throughout the night.

In other areas of the city, locals and tourists often enjoy a late-night stroll and a drink or a meal in one of the many pubs, restaurants or bars. In what was once West Berlin, the hotspots are in Charlottenburg around Savigny-Platz, Wilmersdorf (south of the Ku'damm), Schöneberg (near Winterfeldtplatz) and Goltzstrasse. Legendary Kreuzberg has two main meeting points: around Bergmannstrasse and Marheinekeplatz or in Oranienstrasse near Mariannenplatz.

Some areas of the former East Berlin are booming. The crowds tend to meet in Mitte, mainly along Oranienburger Strasse, around the Tacheles Cultural Centre and the stylishly restored Hackesche Höfe. The social scene in Prenzlauer Berg around Kollwitzplatz and Kastanienallee is more relaxed and diverse. Here you will find students, artists, tourists and locals all having a good time. Friedrichshain has its own Oranienburger Strasse of sorts. In Simon-Dach-Strasse you'll find lots of bars, most with tables and chairs outside in summer, and a clientele which isn't so touristy.

Bars and Pubs

MITTE

Oranienburger Str. and the Scheunenviertel

When in swinging Mitte, most fun seekers head straight for Oranienburger Strasse. After the Wende, the first signs of social activity were initiated by squatters and alternative types but the potential sound of cash registers proved too much of a temptation and the developers moved in. Now mostly under the umbrella of one property developer, each café bar has tried to stamp its own identity on the proceedings. Some pass the test but in others leave you with the impression that your money is just contributing to a laboured formula. In sunny weather, most places put chairs and tables on the pavement and a nice atmosphere is often created. The nearby backstreets of August Strasse and Sophien Str don't operate quite so much with the tourist trade and tend to be rather bland.

Bar Lounge 808
Oranienburger Str. 42–43
Tel: 2804 6727
Open daily 10am–3pm. Hip fashion and self-consciousness prevail in this trendy bar.

Café Zapata – Tacheles
Oranienburger Str. 53–56
Tel: 283 1498
Here tourists and locals alike knock back all sorts and swap their life stories. Live music often accompanies the goings-on.

Keyser Soze
Tucholsky Str. 33, Mitte
Tel: 2859 9489
Daily 10–3am. Pleasant corner bar.

Obst and Gemüse
Oranienburger Str. 48
Open daily from 12pm. Benefiting from its position near the start of Oranienburger Strasse, this pleasant enough establishment is self-service. Although not earth shattering, it serves as a good starting point for the evening.

Irish Pubs

There are 47 Irish pubs in Berlin where you can expect to pay from DM10 for a shepherds' pie to DM25 for a sirloin. The average for a half litre of draught beer is between DM6 and DM7. A whisky will set you back DM5 and although the Guinness is okay, please remember that you're not in Dublin.

The Irish Harp
Giesebrechtstr. 15, Charlottenburg
Tel: 882 7739
Sun–Mon 11–1.30am, Tues, Wed, Thur 11–2am, Fri–Sat 11–3am.
This pub provides a calming break from the bustle of the Ku'damm.

An ample kitchen and drinks card should satisfy all palates.

The Old Emerald Isle
Erkelenzdamm 49, Kreuzberg
Tel: 615 6917
On a quiet, leafy corner of Kreuzberg not far from Kotbusser Tor stands a little piece of Ireland that is to many the best Irish pub of the lot. Go in, have a beer and order some of the finest food to be had in any pub.

The Oscar Wilde
Friedrichstr. 112a, Mitte
Tel: 282 8166
Daily 4pm–late, w/e lunch till late.
The Oscar Wilde has a history and an atmosphere unequalled by any

other Irish pub in town. The back bar has live music, karaoke and a large screen for the big match. There is even Irish dancing if you're so inclined. The bill of fare is standard Irish pub fare and the staff are welcoming.

The Sean Og
Schönhauser Allee 6–7, Mitte
Tel: 440 6030
Open daily. With seating for 600 the Sean Og is big. There is a full menu with particularly popular home-made burgers which can be washed down with a cold beer from the well-maintained taps. The Dolmen Club below has Britpop sounds and a cocktail bar.

Silberstein
Oranienburger Str. 27, Mitte
Tel: 2812095
Open from 10am until all hours, weekends from noon. Avant-garde art and scene people from the Oranienburgerstr., the noisy night club district in Berlin's centre.

Zosch
Tucholsky Str. 30
Tel: 280 7664
Open daily. This bar hidden up Tucholsky Str. has lots of character. Downstairs in the cellar, the live music ranges from beats to jazz.

Elsewhere in Mitte

Bar 37 im Forum Hotel
Alexanderplatz, 37th Floor of Forum Hotel, Mitte
Yes, on the 37th floor of the Forum you can lose some money in the casino – but only if you're over 18 and have a jacket and tie.

Broker Bier Börse
Schiffbauerdamm 8
Tel: 3087 2293
Open daily 8–3am, stock market from 5pm. After 5pm in this bar the prices of drinks are determined by demand and are displayed on the wall on an electronic scoreboard.

lore.berlin
Neue Schönhaiser Str. 20, Mitte
Tel: 2804 5134
Mon–Fri 5pm–4am, Sat–Sun 9pm–4am. Stylish scene bar at Hackescher Markt.

Kaffe Burger
Torstr. 60, Mitte
Tel: 2804 6495
Daily from 6pm. Former brothel decked out in kitsch style.

Reingold
Novalisstr. 11
Tel: 2838 7676
Daily from 6pm. To see how far Mitte has developed in the last couple of years, see if you can make it past the doorman into this vision of future socialising.

Roberta
Zionskirchstr. 7, Mitte
Tel: 4405 5580
Mon–Sat 6pm–4am, Sun 10–4am. Popular bar for hip youngsters but it's too cramped to be much fun.

Ständige Vertretung
Schiffbauerdamm 9
Tel: 2859 8725
Open daily 11–1am. The name of this bar/restaurant refers to the West German non-embassy in East Berlin. The memorabilia on the walls reflects this.

PRENZLAUER BERG

If you can't decide where to go in Prenzlauer Berg, the best places to start are at the Kollwitzplatz, along Kastanienallee or further north around the Helmholtzplatz and Stargarder Strasse.

An einem Sonntag im August
Kastanienallee 103
Tel: 4405 1228
Open daily till late. Slightly grungy and often frequented by over-exuberant youths with guitars, this café hang out has an all-day, eat-all-you-want buffet for around DM 5.

(The former) Café Schliemann
Schliemann Str. 21
Open daily until late. This is one of Prenzlauer Berg's last bastions of bohemian socialising.

Noxz
Lychener Str. 67
Tel: 4473 6989
Open daily 11am–2am. The regulars are usually fans of electronic music.

Restauration 1900
Husemannstr.1, Schöneberg
Tel: 4494052
Open 6pm–2am. This Prenzlauer Berg bar is one of the few that was privately ran under the GDR. Now a much appreciated meeting place.

Schwarz Sauer
Kastanienallee 13–14
Sunglasses and shopping bags are essential accessories at this café bar for the hip kids. When the weather is good, the tables on the pavement outside catch the sun beautifully.

Wohnzimmer
Lettestr. 6
Tel: 445 5458
Open daily 10am–aprrox. 4am. Having survived the clean up on the Helmholtzplatz, this makeshift but refined café bar has kept much of its original charm.

FRIEDRICHSHAIN

Simon-Dach-Str. is most people's destination in Friedrichshain. In summer, most bars will have tables and chairs out on the pavement.

Astro-Bar
Simon-Dach-Str. 40
Tel: 2966 1615
Daily from 6pm. Drink in a bar with a 1960's feel.

Ex
Rigaer Str. 25
Tel: 4208 7444
Daily from 5.30pm. With 156 different cocktails and a collection of Latin and Salsa CDs, this place is only to some people's taste.

Queen Vic Public House
Samariterstr. 35
Tel: 4201 2904
Wed–Mon from 5pm. An authentic British pub. Wednesday is fish and chips day and you will find an in-house shop that sells English foodstuffs .

U5-Club-Cocktailbar
Frankfurter Tor 9
Tel: 0172-384 3846
Daily from 7pm. Cocktails like you've never had them before.

Weinsalon
Schreinerstr. 59
Tel: 4201 9408
Daily from 7pm. Relaxed wine bar with that living room feel.

SCHÖNEBERG

Bar Am Lützowplatz
Lützowufer 7, Schöneberg
Tel: 262 6870
Open 3pm–3am. At 16 metres (50 ft), the bar is the longest in Berlin, with the nicest barkeepers and gorgeous cocktails.

Café M
Goltzstr. 33
Tel: 216 7092
Mon–Thur 8–2am, Fri 8–3am, Sat 9–3am, Sun 9–2am. A Schöneberg institution that serves muffins and bagels and acts as a trendy meeting point.

Destillery-Scottish Pub
Eisenacher Str. 64
Tel: 784 5010
Mon–Sat from 7pm. Take your pick

from as many as 650 different malts and blends of Scottish whisky.

Hudson Bar
Elssholzstr. 10
Fri and Sat 9pm–3am. Exclusive bar where they take care over your drinks.

Leuchtturm
Crellestr. 41, Schöneberg
Tel: 781 8519
Daily 4pm–3am. This traditional Berlin pub has been in existence for over 100 years.

Zoulou-Bar
Hauptstr. 4
Tel: 784 6894
Sun–Thur 9pm–4am, Fri–Sat 9pm–7am. Mixed crowd and friendly waiters.

TIERGARTEN

Caroshi Bar
Linkstr. 7
Tel: 2529 3352
Daily from 10am. *Caroshi* is the Japanese word for suicide due to over work. Situated at Potsdamer Platz, this bar for the upwardly mobile can relieve that stress with an after-work partyheld every Thursday.

Harry's New York Bar
in Grand Hotel Esplanade,
Lützowufer 15, Tiergarten
Tel: 2547 8821
Open from noon. One of the nicest bars in Berlin; it has a sophisticated atmosphere and portraits of American presidents on the walls.

Insel
Gotzkowkystr. 23
Tel: 3910 2344
Mon–Fri 9–1am, Sat–Sun 2pm–1am. Everyone gets served in this pub where there is a selection of over 200 whiskies.

Kumpelnest 3000
Lützowstr. 23
Tel: 261 6918
Sun–Thur 5pm–5am, Fri–Sat from 5pm. This former brothel is popular among many younger Berliners who like to stay out until late.

Trompete
Lützowplatz 9
Tel: 2300 4794

Sun–Thur 9pm–3am, Fri–Sat from 10pm. Owned by German actor Ben Becker, this fashionable bar has live music at the weekend.

CHARLOTTENBURG

Wherever possible, try and avoid the bars directly on the Ku'damm. Take a stroll down the side streets or head for Savignyplatz where there are plenty of places to visit.

Barbar Bar
Krumme Str. 41
Tel: 313 3808
Daily 10–2am. A nice atmosphere in which to wind down after an evening at the nearby Kant cinema.

Champussy
Uhlandstr. 171, Charlottenburg
Tel: 881 2220
Open 3pm–3am. Good live music in a sophisticated bar.

Diener
Grolmannstr. 47, Charlottenburg
Tel: 881 5329
Open 6pm–2am
Inoffensive 1950s atmosphere in the once famous Boxer's Diener.

Gainsbourg – Bar américain
Savignyplatz 5
Tel: 313 7464
Daily 5pm–4am. The relaxed and somewhat sophisticated atmosphere is enhanced in summer when you can sit outside.

Schwarzes Café
Kantstr. 148, Charlottenburg
Tel: 313 8038
Open almost around the clock except Tuesday. Breakfast or after-hours bar depending on time of day. For years the focal point of the Charlottenburg scene.

Times Bar
Hotel Savoy, Fasanenstrasse 9, Charlottenburg
Like in good old England. You can read English papers with your whisky.

KREUZBERG

The best places to try out are along Oranienstrasse, around U-Bhf Mehringdamm and along the Landwehrkanal at Paul-Linke-Ufer.

Bar
Skalitzer Str. 64
Tel: 612 4388
Mon–Fri 10–3am, Sun from 11am, Sat–Sun until 4am. No hiding behind names, this establishment has been in business since 1989.

Bellman Bar
Reichenberger Str. 103
Tel: 6128 0334
Daily from 5pm. This is the kind of place you don't want to tell anyone else about – quiet, laid back and an absolute gem.

Golgatha
Auf dem Kreuzberg, Dudenstr. 48–64, Kreuzberg
Tel: 785 2453
Open 10–6am. Huge garden pub on the Kreuzberg with disco dancing until the early hours.

Konrad Tönz
Falckensteinstr. 30
Tel: 612 3252
Tues–Sun from 5pm. Get on down with the retro kids.

Madonna
Wiener Str. 22
Tel: 611 6943
Daily 3pm–3am. Recently done up, this Kreuzberg rock institution caters for long hair and its sympathisers.

Max und Moritz
Oranienstr. 162
Tel: 614 1045
Daily 4pm–1am. Traditional Berlin pub with wood floors and tables.

Milchbar
Mantueffelstr. 40–41
Tel: 611 7006
Sun–Thur 5pm–4am, Fri–Sat 5pm–6am. Former squat that is popular with the locals. It does sell beer despite the name.

ELSEWHERE

Anker-Klause
Kottbusser Damm 104/Corner Maybachufer, Neukölln
Tel: 693 5649
Mon from 4pm, Tues–Sun from 10am. Young and studenty crowd.

Luise, Königin-Luise-Str. 40, Dahlem, Zehlendorf
Tel: 841 8880
Open 10am–1am. Frequented by students and other university folk

who like to drink under the spread of old chestnuts.

Live Music

Because the jazz, rock and pop music scene in Berlin is constantly changing, it is always difficult to know what's going on where. In this Live Music section, we have attempted to represent the choice of music in Berlin. As clubs and bars come and go quite quickly so the best thing to do is to check out the listings magazines *Tip* and *Zitty* for up-to-date information.

CONCERT VENUES

Here are a few places which are considered to be classic venues for live music. The best way to buy tickets for concerts is to phone the ticket agency on the advertisement, to get in touch with the venue of the concert or to try one of the many tickets agencies across the city *(see sources of information)*.
Arena, Eichenstr. 4, Treptow, tel: 533 7333, www.arena-berlin.de. One of Berlin's biggest venues, it has played host to names such as Lauryn Hill and Massive Attack. It also doubles up as a venue for big name DJs.
Columbiahalle, Columbiadamm 13–21, Templehof, tel: 698 0980. Berlin's second largest rock/pop venue. Having hosted concerts of Beck and Iggy Pop in the past, it constantly stages concerts for most mid-range music celebrities on tour in Europe.
Columbiafritz, Columbiadamm 9–11, Templehof, tel: 6981 2828. The Columbiahalle's little sibling caters for acts who either can't or don't want to fill a bigger venue.
Max-Schmeling-Halle, Am Falkplatz, Prenzlauer Berg, tel: 44 30 45, www.velodrom.de. If you want to see superstars, most of whom are past their best, then the Max-Schmeling-Halle is the place to see them.
Velodrom, by S-Bahnhof Landsberger Allee, tel: 44 30 45, www.velodrom.de. The Max-

Schmeling-Halle's sister venue is much in the same vein, just a different shape.
Waldbühne, Am Glockenturm, Charlottenburg. This outdoor stage in Grunewald has been trodden on by Michael Jackson and the Rolling Stones but is equally at home with classical concerts, oldie parties and film screenings.
Wuhlheide, Eichgestell 30, Oberschöneweide. Way out East in the middle of the woods, this large venue has seen some big names and some serious oldie parties.

Other smaller, less brash and, probably more enjoyable, venues for music include **Maria am Ostbahnhof**, Strasse der Pariser Kommune 8–10, Friedrichshain, tel: 2900 6198. **Bastard@Prater**, Kastanienallee 7–9, Prenzlauer Berg, tel: 0177-641 1424. The **Knaack-Club**, Greifswalder Strasse 224, Prenzlauer Berg, tel: 4427061. **SO36**, Oranienstr. 190, Kreuzberg, tel: 6140 1306-7 and **Insel**, Alt-Treptow 6, Treptow, tel: 5360 8020.

Jazz Clubs

In addition to the Jazz Festival in November and the "Jazz Across the Border" festival that takes place each summer in the Haus der Kulturen der Welt, jazz fans will find a number of interesting jazz venues in Berlin.

For starters, try the **A-trane**, Pestalozzistr. 105, Charlottenburg, tel: 3132550, www.a-trane.de; which features modern jazz and avant-garde.**b-flat**, Rosenthalerstr. 13, Mitte, tel: 2806349. Live jazz in every style. The **Junction Bar**, Gneisenauerstr. 18, Kreutberg, tel: 694 6602; open from 8pm, you should be sure of hearing all kinds of music from jazz to jazz; or the **Tränenpalast**, Reichstagsufer 17, tel: 2061 0011; where cabaret, comedy and other music is also performed .

At **Quasimodo**, Kantstrasse 12a, Charlottenburg, tel: 312 8086, www.quastmodo.de; you can hear famous jazz as well as rock and blues musicians at work. Listen to

jazz, rock and other genres at the **Podewil**, Klosterstrasse 68–70, tel: 247 496. **Passionskirche**, Marheinekeplatz 1–2, Kreuzberg, tel: 6940 1241 and in the cellar at **Zosch**, Tucholskystr. 30, tel: 280 7664.

The **Blue Café**, Holsteinische Str. 1a, Wilmersdorf, tel: 86 4555 specialises in jazz and blues as does **Vollmond**, Oranienstr. 60, tel: 614 292 which has been making a name for itself. **Salsa**, Wielandstrasse 13, Charlottenburg, tel: 324 1642 is the place to head to for Latin American sounds and Irish folk-music fans should seek out **Shannon**, Apostel-Paulus-Strasse 34, Schöneberg, tel: 781 8676 or head for any of the Irish pubs – most should have some sort of live music at the weekends.

You can sip the first beer of the day while hearing live music in the little **Yorck Castle** (Yorck Strasse 15, Kreuzberg, tel: 215 8070); where there is a live band playing every Sunday from 2pm.

Cabaret/Revue/Variety

Bar Jeder Vernunft, Schaperstrasse 24, Wilmersdorf, tel: 883 1582, www.bar-jeder-vernunft.de. Daily shows at 8.30pm; piano bar 11.30pm. The modern "mirror tent" is the perfect place for intimate shows, such as music, cabaret, *chansons* and comedy. Some names, such as Meret Becker, Georgette Dee, Tim Fischer, Max Raabe, Geschwister Pfister, attract a full house. Late-night shows on Friday and Saturday at 11.30pm are normally free.
BKA, Mehringdamm 32–34, Kreuzberg, tel: 2022 007. The Berliner Kabarett Anstalt presents comedy, *chansons*, cabaret, variety and a lot of trash. They used to perform in a tent which had to be moved from the Kulturforum to Schlossplatz.
Chamäleon Varieté, Rosenthaler Strasse 40–41, Mitte (Hackesche Höfe), tel: 2827118, www.chamaeleonberlin.de. The younger and rebellious sister of the Wintergarten. The fabulous shows include singers and acrobats,

comedians and dancers. Midnight performances on Friday and Saturday nights.

Die Distel, Friedrichstrasse 101, Mitte, tel: 204 4704, www.die-distel.berlin.de. The former East Berlin equivalent of the Stachelschweine.

Die Stachelschweine, Europa-Center, Charlottenburg, tel: 261 4795, www.die-stachelschweine.de. Classic German *Kabarett*. Now perhaps a little old-fashioned but still entertaining, if you understand enough German.

Estrel Festival Center, Hotel Estrel, Sonnenallee 225, Neukölln, tel: 6831 6831, www.stars-in-concert.com. Daily except Tues at 8.30pm; Sat and Sun at 5pm. "Stars in concert" is the title of this Las Vegas import, with singers and dancers imitating stars like Elvis Presley, Tina Turner and Michael Jackson.

Friedrichstadtpalast, Friedrichstrasse 107, Mitte, tel: 232 62326, www.friedrichstadtpalast.de. Everything is vast in Europe's largest revue theatre: it has space for 2,000 visitors; the stage – with every imaginable technical gadget at its disposal – can be used for sumptuous events. The dancing girls here, it is said, have the longest legs in the world. There is a small intimate theatre (Kleine Bühne) adjacent with shows at 11.30pm.

La Vie en Rose, Tempelhof airport, Tempelhof, tel: 6951 3000, www.revuetheater.de. Tues–Sun at 9pm. Dancing girls, erotic shows and busloads of Germans. Tackety-tack.

Ufa Fabrik, Viktoriastrasse 10, Tempelhof, tel: 755030, www.ufafabrik.de. Diverse programme, including children's events during the day. One of the oldest alternative theatre and variety groups in the city. There is a school for acrobats.

Wintergarten – das Varieté, Potsdamer Strasse 96, Tiergarten, tel: 250 0880, tickets: 2500 8888, www.variete-online.de/wintergarten. In the nostalgic style of the golden 1920s. The constantly changing programme is a mixture of variety, cabaret and music with top artists. Dinner or snacks are served before the show.

Discos & Dance Clubs

In Berlin there are hundreds of clubs and locations where you can hear all the latest in funk, soul, hip-hop, techno, metal or world music. The scene is changing rapidly, but there are some venues that have been in existence for nearly 10 years. Details of events are usually passed on by flyers distributed outside clubs. Some are only open from Thursday to Saturday, but some hold gigs on Monday too. Berlin also has many traditional style discos.

For nightclubs, there are two main options. The night spots in Mitte, which although popular, tend to be newer, glitzier and more contrived. Mühlen Strasse, in Friedrichshain, is Berlin's clubbing mile. From Ostbahnhof until past the Warschauer Brücke there are a multitude of possibilities but you may want to check where you are going before you set out as some entrances are concealed. It is always best to consult the listings magazines beforehand. If you want to ensure a good night out, try and avoid anything too near the Ku'damm.

The following is just a small selection, but bear in mind that it is fashionable for some clubs to change location occasionally.

MITTE

Delicious Doughnuts, Rosenthaler Str. 9, tel: 283 3021, daily from 11pm. Highly overrated and quite small, it still manages to attract a crowd.

Dolmen Club, Schönhauser Allee 6–7, tel: 440 6026, Fri–Sat from 10pm. Looking for a typically British club experience? Look no further. Blur and co. are going strong in this club located at the Sean Og pub.

Grüner Salon, Rosa-Luxemburg-Platz 2, tel: 2859 8936. Attached to the Volkbühne theatre, the nights range from tango dancing to good old student favourites.

Kalscheune, Johannisstr. 2, Mitte, tel: 2839 0065, Sun 11.30–4pm,

Mon–Sat depending on events. Cultural institution that has Tango dancing to House music.

Oxymoron, Hackesche Höfe, Rosenthaler Strasse 40–41, tel: 2839 1885, daily. The "in" venue for a variety of events from jazz to "pasta operas".

Pfefferbank, Pfefferberg, Subground, Schönhauser Allee 176, tel: 4438 3110. www.pfefferbank.de, www.pfefferberg.de, www.subground.de. A trio of three venues which feature beats, eclectic fayre and more beats respectively.

Sage-Club, Köpenicker Str. 78, tel: 278 5052, www.sage-club.de. Not as unrefined as some of the older clubs in Berlin – this is house and all the trappings. Try the hedonistic gay night on Sunday.

Tresor and Globus, Leipziger Strasse 126 A, tel: 229 0611, www.tresor-berlin.de. Wed, Fri and Sat from 11pm. One of the originals and still the best for techno. Softer music sometimes features. Its future at this location is uncertain.

WMF, Ziegelstr. 23, tel: 2887 8890. Now in its fifth location, WMF considers itself to be one of Berlin's best clubs. The week starts on Thursday night with mixed DJs and continues with beats and house on Friday and Saturday. Sunday is the famed Gay Tea Dance.

FRIEDRICHSHAIN

Maria am Ostbahnhof, Strasse der Pariser Kommune 8–10, tel: 2900 6198, at least every Fri and Sat. Still considered the best all round club in Berlin, the music here is usually electronic although some big bands have played here too.

Matrix, Warschauer Platz 18, tel: 2949 1047, www.matrix-berlin.de. Hang out for the young electronic music fan. Thursdays are more for those of a student rock ilk.

Nontox, Mühlenstr. 12, tel: 2966 7206. Techno and crossover venue where the youngsters sometimes get out of hand.

Ostgut, Mühlenstr. 26–30, no phone, www.ostgut.de. One of the best techno clubs in Berlin. The mixed gay and straight crowd are sensible about their clubbing. Check press details as the occasional men only Snax club is not for the weak.

PRENZLAUER BERG

Bastard Club @ Prater, Kastanienallee 7–9, tel: 247 6772. Small and hip venue where the music is quite diverse.
Duncker, Dunckerstrasse 64, Prenzlauer Berg, tel: 4459509. Small independent club music venue.
Icon, Cantianstr. 15/Milastr., tel: 6128 7545. Underground and drum 'n' bass derived music. The entrance is through a car lot.
Knaack Klub, Greifswalder Strasse 224, Prenzlauer Berg, tel: 442 7060.
Monday karaoke, Wednesday hiphop from 11pm, Friday and Saturday disco from 9pm. Live gigs, discos and billiards situated on three levels.

ELSEWHERE

90 Grad, Dennewitzstr. 37, Schöneberg, tel: 262 8984, Tues, Fri and Sat. Trendy club where the trendy go to look trendy.
Big Eden, Kurfürstendamm 202, Charlottenburg, tel: 882 6120, www.big-eden.de, daily from 9pm. Sat from 10pm. Pop, dance, funk and soul in a plush setting. A disco for many years. Very popular with tourists, but the locals are extremely wary of it.
El Barrio, Potsdamer Strasse 84, Tiergarten, tel: 262 1853.
DJs and live gigs, daily from 9pm. *Salsateca* and a popular meeting-place for Latino fans.
Huxley's Neue Welt, Hasenheide 108–114, Kreuzberg, tel: 627 9320. Saturday dance parties.
SO36, Kreuzberg *(see Gay Scene)*.

Berlin has one of the most vibrant gay and lesbian scenes in the world. Most of the proceedings centre on and around

Nollendorfplatz so a general wander in this area should lead to some sort of night out. In Prenzlauer Berg things happen on Greifenhagnerstrasse and further north. There are also some places around Oranienstrasse in Kreuzberg. Alternatively, check out the two monthly freebie listings magazines, *Siegesäule* and *Sergej*, to see what's happening in general. Both have information on cafés, clubs, services and are to be found in all of the cafés and bars – not just the gay ones.

To recognise a gay friendly establishment look for the multi-coloured flag or sticker at the door.

CAFÉ/BARS

Schöneberg
Café Berio, Maassenstr. 7, Schöneberg, tel: 216 1946, daily 8–1am. Mixed bar at Nollendorfplatz which acts as a springboard for the night ahead.
Hafen, Motzstrasse 19, tel: 211 4118. Traditional gay/lesbian meeting place.
Tom's Bar, Motzstr. 19, tel: 2134570. Very lively and intense gay bar.
Windows Café, Martin Luther Str. 22, tel: 214 2384, daily 4pm–4am, Sun 3pm–4am. Watch the crowd go by through the huge windows of this gay/lesbian bar.

Kreuzberg
Café Anal, Muskauer Str. 15, tel: 6107 3030, Mon–Thur from 7pm, Fri–Sat 9pm, Sun 4pm. Rougher looking end of the scale – Monday is women only.
Melitta Sundström, Mehringdamm 61, tel: 692 4414, sundstroem@crosswinds.net, daily from 9am. Typical Berlin gay café with shelves of books in French, German and English.
Roses Bar, Oranienstr. 187, tel: 615 6570, daily 9.30pm–5am. Kitschy gay/lesbian bar that acts as a stop off before or after SO36.
Schoko-Café, Mariannenstr. 6, tel: 615 1561, daily from 5pm. Long established women's café bar.

Prenzlauer Berg
Oxen Magenta Restaurant-Café, Greifenhagnerstr. 58, tel: 4473 6482, daily from 10am. Great food, nice people and tasteful decor but a poor location behind a shopping mall.
Romeo Nightbar, Greifenhagner Str. 16, tel: 447 6789, nightly 11pm–past 8am. A place for insomniacs to while the night away.
Schall & Rauch, Gleim Str. 23, tel: 448 0770, daily 10–3am. Stylish mixed café bar where the Sunday breakfasts are a hit.
Sonntags-Club, Greifenhagner Str. 28, tel: 449 7590, www.sonntagsclub.de, Mon–Sun 5pm–midnight. Former GDR underground gay café-cum-community centre with a bar and lots of other resourses.

Elsewhere
Arc, Fasanenstr. 81, Charlottenburg, tel: 313 2625, Mon–Fri 11–1am, Sat–Sun 10–1am. Nicely fitted out gay place with a good menu.
Kleine Philharmonie, Schaperstrasse 4, Wilmersdorf, tel: 883 1102, Sat 5pm–3am, otherwise 8pm–3am. Here you will find a slightly older gay crowd.
Offenbar, Schreinerstr. 5, Friedrichshain, tel: 426 0930, daily 10–4am. Eclectic bar where the service is friendly and the crowd is mixed.

CLUBS

Die Busche, Mühlenstrasse 11, Mitte, tel: 296 0880. Kitsch club for fancy gays and lesbians.
Connection, Fuggerstr. 33, Schöneberg, tel: 218 1432. Fridays and Saturdays go to the sound of techno.
KitKat-Club, Bessemerstr. 4, Schöneberg. Third generation of this institution where everything goes.
lab.oratory, Mühlenstr. 26–30, Friedrichshain. Mud, nudity, sex and hedonism.
Metropol, Nollendorfplatz 5, Schöneberg, tel: 217 3680. Former home of the KitKat, it nowadays hosts an eclectic mix of nights.

Schwuz, Mehringdamm 61, Kreuzberg, tel: 693 7025, www.schwuz.de, check press. The oldest gay club in Berlin, the music here ranges from latin to House. **SO36**, Oranienstr. 190, Kreuzberg, tel: 6140 1306, www.so36.de. From gay techno on Mondays to the gay Turkish party every fourth Saturday, there is always something here to see – not exclusively gay. **WMF/GMF**, Ziegelstr. 23, Mitte, tel: 2887 8890. Sun from 10pm. A Sunday night institution, GayMF is listed as a tea dance although it bounces to the beat of House.

Sport

Participant Sports

Sporting activities are available on almost every green space in Berlin. The forest paths around the Grunewald lake and through the Tiergarten are nearly invisible thanks to the crowds of joggers there. In summer months the Wannsee and Havel River are full of sailing boats. Even downhill skiing is possible on the Teufelsberg. Each city district has one or more sport fields and swimming pools, both indoor and outdoor, which are open to the public when they are not being used by sport clubs or schools.

For information about sports in Berlin contact:
Landessportbund Berlin (Regional Sports Union), Jesse Owens-Allee 1–2, Charlottenburg, tel: 300020.

GOLF

Golfers have two choices within the city limits:
Golf- und Land-Club Berlin-Wannsee, Am Golfweg 22, tel: 805 5075.
Berliner Golf Club Gatow, Kladowerdamm 182, tel: 365 7660 Outside Berlin, the **Golfclub Schloss Wilkendorf e.V**, Am Weiher 1, OT Wilkendorf 15345 Gielsdorf, tel: 03341-330 960, has an 18 and a 9 hole course but you'll have to have your golfing certificate to play.

CYCLING

Popular with many is to put the bike on the S-Bahn and go and discover the surrounding countryside. For a guide of all the best cycle routes go to the **Fahrradstation** at Bahnhof

Friedrichstrasse and pick up a free copy of their booklet. Otherwise, the various parks across town provide ample track to get some exercise.

HORSE RIDING

Many opportunities are available in Berlin for horse riding. The open greenness of Reinickendorf and Grunewald make them perfect for a bit of trotting and cantering. Most clubs expect you to have your own horse but if you take lessons at some of the riding schools you can go on a trek through Grunewald. Some places to try are:
Reitsportschule Onkel Toms Hütte, Onkel-Tom-Str. 172, tel: 813 2081
Reitschule Stall-Schmitz, Hennigsdorfer Str. 162, Berlin-Heiligensee, tel: 431 9393
Ponyhof Pelludat, Wilduferweg 37, Neukölln, tel: 604 4059

JOGGING

Thanks to the many parks and green spaces in Berlin jogging is an extremely popular pastime.
One place to note if you are a fanatic is **Laufstrecke Schlachtensee**, Am Schlachtensee, Zehlendorf, where the conditions are just perfect.

If you need a little company on the run, try and meet up with the chaps at **Lauftreff Grunewald** who meet on Wednesday evenings at 6pm at the Mommensenstadion, Waldschulallee 34, reinald.roessler@gmx.de. Visitors are always welcome but drop them a line by email to inform them that you are coming.

SKATING

At **Rollerhouse**, Mieraustr. 2, Reinickendorf, tel: 8356631, there is in-line skating and rollerskating. Skates are available to hire at **Boarderline**, Köpenicker Str. 9, tel: 611 6484
Roadworx, Motzstr.9, tel: 2175 2005 and, in Grunewald,

Skatecity, Hohenzollerndamm 143, tel: 8972 2394 Among the many places where the skate kids meet are **Volkspark Friedrichshain** (two half-pipes and a track), **Böcklerpark**, Prinzenstr. (half-pipe) and **Winterfeldplatz** in Schöneberg.

Tennis

There are tennis courts in every area. The most elegant, both for members and tournaments, is the **Tennis-Club Rot-Weiss** in Wilmersdorfer Stadtteil Grunewald, Gottfried-von-Cramm-Weg 47–55, tel: 8957 5520. To find out more get in touch with the **Tennis Verband Berlin-Brandenburg**, Auerbacher Strasse 19, Charlottenburg, tel: 825 5311.

TO THE WATER

Cruising down the Spree is very popular. **Stern und Kreisschiffahrt GmbH**, Puschkinallee 15, tel: 536 3600, do tours down the river and have various get-on and get-off points along the route. If you want to sail then the many waterways (especially in the south west at Wannsee) are the place to go. Boats and lessons are available at the **Segelschule Hering**, Bielefelder Str. 15, tel: 861 0701, but to make sure you are qualified and to find out about more water sport venues call the **Berliner Segler-Verband**, Bismarckallee 2, tel: 893 8490.

Diary of Sporting Events

German Open, Berlin (third week in May) LTTC "Rot-Weiss" e.V. Tennis Club, Gottfried-von-Cramm-Weg 47–55, Grunewald, www.german-open-berlin.de The elite of the women's tennis world arrive in Berlin to contest one of the top events in the tour calendar.
Deutsche Pokalendspiele – German Cup Final (end of the German football season) Olympic Stadium, Charlottenburg.

SWIMMING

For mermaids and "mermen" there is plenty on offer – wave pools, sauna, sunbathing areas and other pleasures.
Blub, Badeparadies, Buschkrugallee 64, Neukölln, tel: 606 6060. Fun in the water with 120-metre (395-ft) slide and waterfall. Admission is expensive.
Sport und Erholungszentrum SEZ, Friedrichshain, Landsberger Allee 77, tel: 421 820.
Sport- und Lehrschwimmhalle, Schöneberg, Sachsendamm 11, tel: 780 9830.
Call the **Berliner Schwimm-Verband**, swimming federation; Landsberger Allee 203, tel: 971 0150, to find out the closest swimming pool to you. Also try calling the **Berlin Bäder Betrieb**, tel: 2312 1332.

OUTDOOR SWIMMING

The best swimming in summer is the **Strandbad Wannsee** on the Wannsee-lake, with beach chairs and promenades. This is in Zehlendorf south of the Schwanenwerder Island, Am Wannseebadweg, tel: 8035612. Two more alternatives include **Strandbad Müggelsee**, Fürstenwader Damm 838 in Köpenick, tel: 648 7777 and the extremely popular **Sommerbad Kreuzberg**, Prinzenstr. 113–119, tel: 616 1080. Before you dive in, make sure you know what you're getting yourself into: Normale Bäder

Germany's answer to the F.A. Cup is played before a capacity crowd.
ISTAF Athletics (end of August) Olympia Stadion, Olympischer Platz 3. Tickets tel: 313 4554. A large and famous entry list of athletes is assured.
Berlin Marathon (last Sunday in September). Contact: Waldschulallee 34, tel: 302 5370, www.berlin-marathon.com/world. The world's third largest marathon.

are pools at a temperature of 26ºC or just below. Warmbauder are 27ºC or above. There are other lakes good for swimming like Plötzensee (in Wedding), Halensee (Wilmersdorf) or Schlachtensee (Zehlendorf) and on the many lakes in surrounding Brandenburg. Test the water beforehand.

Spectator Sports

Berlin plays host now and then to some rather large sporting events. At the **Olympia-Stadion**, Olympischer Platz, Charlottenburg, tel: 300633, Berlin's Bundesliga team Hertha BSC battle it out every second weekend. Every year the ISTAF Golden League athletics meeting (www.istaf.de/en) takes place here too. German basketball masters **Alba Berlin** play at home in the **Max-Schmeling-Halle**, Am Falkplatz, Prenzlauer Berg, tel: 443 04430 and **Berlin Thunder**, www.berlin-thunder.de, Berlin's representatives in the World Bowl American Football league play next door in the **Friedrich-Jahn-Sportpark**, Cantianstr. 24, 10437, tel: 3110 2222. The **Velodrom** (Landsberger Allee, Prenzlauer Berg, tel: 443045) is home to various sporting events from show jumping to indoor cycling. One half of Berlin's ice hockey rivalry, the **Berlin Capitals**, ply their trade in the **Eissporthalle**, Jaffestr, Charlottenburg, tel: 3038 4387, www.berlin-capitals.com) and their sworn enemies, the **EHC Eisbären Berlin**, do their stuff at the **Sportforum**, Steffenstrasse, tel: 971 8400, tickets 9718 4040, www.eisbaeren.de.

Equestrian and horse racing fans can find their pleasure at the following venues:
Galopprennbahn Hoppegarten, 15366 Dahlwitz-Hoppgarten, Goetheallee 1, tel: 03342-38930.
Trabrennbahn Karlshorst, Lichtenberg, Hermann-Duncker-Str. 129, tel: 50017-0.
Trabrennbahn Mariendorf, Mariendorf, Mariendorfer Damn 212, tel: 7401-1.

Shopping

Where to Shop

Shopping in Berlin is yet another pastime that has been altered by the long presence and sudden departure of the Wall. Berlin retailers would like nothing better than a centrally located pedestrian district like you'll find in many other German cities. But, today, the lack of any district that has either of the two advantages to offer has kept the city from developing into a place where you can spend a decadent day wandering from one store to the next.

THE KU'DAMM

The **Ku'damm** used to be the closest thing to a city centre that West Berlin had to offer and major boutiques lined the boulevard. But when consumer focus underwent a massive shift towards the former East throughout the 1990s, the Ku'damm suffered more than anywhere else in the city.

Today, if you can ignore the heavy traffic on the street and the shabby looking post-war construction, this is the best place in Berlin for a solid day of brand name shopping, with the occasional bargain thrown in. Every major label in Berlin has an affiliate somewhere along this street, including H&M, the German designer store that has thousands of fabulous bargains on hip clothes, Germany's largest Benetton, Esprit, and The Gap. Crowning the Tauentzienstr. at the end of the boulevard like the diamond on a society dame's brooch is the KaDeWe (Kaufhaus des Westens), the up-market German department store where you'll find the best designer quality on every type of

merchandise imaginable, for a price. The best experience the KaDeWe has to offer is the huge gourmet grocery store on the 6th floor, where food lovers can spend hours ogling artfully organised fresh fish displays, surprisingly affordable slices of mouth-watering chocolate cake, lunch counters where chefs prepare their specialities in front of you, and probably the best selection of chocolates and candies in the city.

The smaller streets along the western side of the Ku'damm, near Savigny Platz, have developed an atmosphere that is much more conducive to relaxed strolling with a break for lunch. Exclusive designers like Prada and Escada adorn the main drag. If you slip into Bleibtreustr. and Fasanenstr. you'll find some of the city's best designer shops.

POTSDAMER PLATZ

One of Berlin's newest attractions, the shopping arcade at newly developed Potsdamer Platz which has more than 100 shops from a cheap supermarket to high-quality clothing, is not proving to be a favourite of the locals. Saying that, it does attract a lot of tourists but most go to see the layout and not to fill their wardrobes like they do when they visit the Ku'damm.

FRIEDRICHSTRASSE

Friedrichstrasse in the East is meanwhile rivaling the Ku'damm for its place in the heart of Berlin consumers. Here you will find a few branches of the same European shopping mall standards that are also on the Ku'damm, along with exclusive designers like Hermes, Gucci, or DKNY. The Berlin Branch of the Galeries Lafayette sells French clothing in the Parisian style, with an equally Parisian food hall in the basement. Smattered in between these larger stores are independent designers who have been successful enough to pay the rent.

MITTE

If you have the patience to hunt down the perfect find from the mesh of less established designers who have camped out in the new quarters of the city, there is no better place to start your stalking than in Mitte. You won't find the worry free one-stop-shop, but you will be rewarded with high quality creations direct from the heart of Berlin's burgeoning fashion scene. In the Hackesche Höfe, the Heckemann Höfe and the streets around them, up-and-coming designers have opened combination workshops and show rooms. You will also come across various art galleries and individual shops selling art books and antiques.

Further afield, places like Marheinekeplatz, Chamissoplatz and Bergmannstrasse in the district of Kreuzberg are interesting shopping destinations, as are Winterfeldtplatz and Goltzstrasse in Schöneberg.

Opening Times

Strict laws on shop opening hours are set to change and you may soon be able to shop in Berlin until 10pm or even midnight, and on Sundays too. Occasionally shops stay open on Saturdays until midnight but this is an exception that happens every few months. Shop owners are currently allowed to keep their doors open until 8pm. While in smaller towns many shops still close at 6pm, as was usual for many years, in Berlin you can easily continue shopping until 8pm. All department stores and shopping malls remain open until 8pm, as do most shops in the city centre.

Morning opening times vary from shop to shop. Some open at 9, others at 10, but smaller, independent stores tend to wait until around 10 or 11am. Bakeries start selling fresh bread and rolls and news-stands sell the papers of the day at around 6 or 7am. Only very small places close for lunch.

On Saturdays small shops normally open from 8am to 1 or

2pm; department stores close at 4pm. On the four Saturdays before Christmas, shops stay open until 6pm. Normally there is no trading on Sundays with the exceptions of bakeries, news- and flower-stands, souvenir shops and some others, usually run by Turkish people. For late needs you can always find a *Tankstelle* (petrol station). Officially only allowed to meet "travel needs", they actually offer a wide variety of goods from food to cosmetics – for somewhat higher prices than supermarkets. Shops located at airports and railway stations like Ostbahnhof and Friedrichstrasse also usually have late shopping hours, as do some Metro stands in underground stations (for example, Kurfürstendamm, Fehrbelliner Platz, Schloss Strasse in Steglitz, Osloer Strasse in Wedding).

During big touristic events (sports and trade shows) longer opening hours are possible in that particular area. The Kulturkaufhaus Dussmann at Friedrichstrasse, which mainly sells books, newspapers and CDs, is open Monday–Saturday 10am–10pm.

Markets

If you are in Berlin at the weekend, check out some of the city's fabulous open-air markets. From flea to food, Berliners are great adherers to the old fashion tradition of getting what they need in markets, which are open all year round.

FOOD

The cheapest place to get all varieties of fresh produce and one of the best crash courses on all the different subcultures living in Berlin, the **Turkish market** on Maybachufer in Kreuzberg (open Tuesday and Friday) is an absolute must for any visit to the city, even if you don't plan on making a purchase. For a more upscale food market, try the Winterfeldplatz on Saturday or Wednesday. For some eco-friendly

food go to Lausitzer Platz in Kreuzberg on a Friday. From around 11am until about 5pm a small Ökomarkt (bio-market) is open.

FLEA MARKETS

There's no telling what you might find at a Berlin flea market. Sunday afternoon flea market shopping is a favourite pastime in Berlin, and the best way to find souvenirs that really say something about the city. The market on **Strasse des 17 Juni** (Sat, Sun 11am–5pm) is an antique dealer hang-out. You're likely to make some nice finds here, but less likely to find a real bargain than some of the markets where anyone can rent a stall for the day. The market at **Arkonaplatz** in Mitte (Sun, 10am to 6pm) is always full of hip young Berliners with correspondingly artistic tastes. At **Moritzplatz** on Saturday and Sunday between 8am and 4pm you'll find plenty of junk in a market that seems to have strayed from the concept. Avoid the cheap, and often new, electrical appliances and mobile phone covers and head straight for the tent where you'll find ridiculously large mountains of marvellous second-hand clothes.

What to Buy

FASHION

International designer boutiques including Versace, Armani, Escada, Gucci, Jil Sander, Gaultier, Yves St. Laurent and others are lined on Ku'damm between Bleibtreustrasse and Olivaer Platz. The numerous little side streets in its vicinity also offer a wide selection of shops and boutiques. The boutiques in Fasanenstrasse and the shops along Uhlandstrasse are especially elegant. If second-hand clothing is more your style, go to Mommsen Strasse in Charlottenburg, Prinzenallee in Wedding or the Mehringdamm area in Kreuzberg.

BOOKS

Berlin has dozens of bookstores. At **Bücherbogen**, Kochstr. 19, Kreuzberg, tel: 251 13 45, you will find a good selection of maps and travel guides. **Marga Schoeller**'s, Knesebeckstr. 33, tel: 881 11 12/22, has an assortment of English literature. **Kiepert**, Hardenberstr. 45, Charlottenburg, tel: 311880, www.kirpert.de have a large English section which specialises in history and story **Village Voice**, Ackerstr. 1A, Mitte, tel: 282 4550, an American bookshop, also has a café (open daily 11am–2am, book sales to 8pm). English and American literature can also be found at **Books in Berlin**, Goethestr. 69, Charlottenburg, tel: 313 12 33.

For German books, the **Karl-Marx Bookstore**, Karl-Marx Allee 78–84, tel: 293 3370, www.kmbuch.de, is well worth taking a peek into and at **Hügeldubel**, Friedrichstr. 83, Tauentzienstr. 13, you should be

Antiques

Berlin is a real paradise for antique lovers. There is a high concentration of good – and extremely expensive – antique shops along Keithstrasse and in that general area, between Eisenacher and Motz Strasse, as well as on Fasanenstrasse and Kurfürstendamm. Another place you may want to try antique hunting is Suarezstrasse in Charlottenburg.

The junk shops in Nollendorfstrasse, in Kreuzberg around Bergmannstrasse and in Neuköllner Flughafenstrasse may not be as exclusive as the above, but they are without a doubt much cheaper. In addition to all these, try the Berliner Antik & Flohmarkt in the S-Bahn arches at Friedrichstrasse station (daily except Sunday from 10am–6pm), and the flea markets on Strasse des 17. Juni and near the Bodemuseum (Sundays).

able to find what you are looking for here. For second-hand books, try the large stall in front of the Humboldt or saunter down either Knesebeckstrasse in Charlottenburg, Winterfeldtstrasse in Schöneberg or Husenmannstrasse and Kollwitzstrasse in Prenzlauer Berg.

Arts and Crafts

Around Auguststrasse, a gallery scene has developed which specialises in avant-garde art. Here you can find small handmade bits and pieces in the small shops. At the Kunst und Nostagie Markt, Museuminsel, next to the Zeughaus, Mitte, tel: 03341-309 411 (Mon, Wed–Sun) you will not only find a section given to modern arts and crafts but also GDR memorabilia.

JEWELLERY

If you have money burning a hole in your pocket and are searching for something extra special, you might want to pay a visit to some of Berlin's jewellery shops. As ever, the best places to go are the Ku'damm and the adjacent Fasanenstrasse where there is also a tiny shop packed out with second hand *Schmuck*, as it is known in German. Friedrichstrasse, south of Unter den Linden, also has good jewellery shops.

PHOTOGRAPHIC AND ELECTRICAL EQUIPMENT

For reasonably priced photographic equipment and supplies, visit one of the electronics markets, Media Markt, Pro Markt or Saturn, which are located in shopping malls (Potsdamer Platz, Alexanderplatz or at Kurfürstendamm in the Ku'damm Karree).

SOUVENIRS

The central Tourist Information Office has its own, well-stocked

souvenir shop (entrance on Budapester Strasse). The wide range of items takes in books on Berlin, videos and elegant vases and plates from KPM. The Nikolaiviertel, the oldest part of the city, is developing into a tourist district with souvenir shops.

Whatever you do, don't leave Berlin without the *Berliner Bär* (Berlin Bear); this typical Berlin souvenir continues to sell like hot cakes. There are over 60 variations of the *Berliner Bär* – for example, book ends, ornaments with a crown, and of course cuddly toys in all sizes.

Germans love marzipan, and you'll know why once you take a bite of the German version of the finely ground almond sweet. A box of **Lubecker marzipan**, made in a Northern town on the Baltic sea, is certain to show friends at home how much you care.

Leydicker, the chocolate chain with a store on Friedrichstr. and one in the Tegel airport, makes incredibly delicate concoctions, and while you're in the Friedrichstr. store you can take a look at their chocolate model of the Brandenburg Gate. Confectionery is also available at Fassbender und Rausch on the Gendarmemarkt.

Germans are rightly proud of their dense, grainy **brown bread**. A loaf of it, freshly baked at any bakery, makes a perfect, customs-safe gift for the health-conscious folks back home.

A **Stövchen**, an apparatus that is designed to keep a pot of tea warm for hours on end with the help of a single tea candle, is a triumph of German engineering, and makes a wonderfully practical souvenir. They come in cute ceramic models, metal, or glass and range in price anywhere between DM11 and DM80. Although they can be tricky to find, if you ask at the KaDeWe, In Bestform on Bergmannstr. in Kreuzberg, or any department store that sells kitchenware, someone will take you right to them.

The company that owns the U-Bahn, buses, and trams (the BVG) has recently been privy to marketing

genius. A couple of students from a Berlin University designed a series of **BVG underwear,** and the company had the good sense to start selling the models in all of the BVG information shops in the U-Bahn stations. The underwear comes in a selection of men's and women's models, each one adorned with a clever pun borrowed from a Berlin U-Bahn station name. The women's *Gleisdreieck* translates as track triangle, *Jungfernheide* is maiden heath, the bra *Schöneberg* is pretty mountains and the men's *Krumme Lanke* means crooked pipe.

Since reunification, Berliners have developed a keen fondness for the **Ampel Menschen**, the crosswalk signs designed exclusively by the East German government, and only to be found in the former Eastern sector of the city. If you look closely at the green one, you'll notice that the attraction seems to be mutual. You can pick up Ampel Menchen key chains, coffee cups, T-shirts, magnets, and any other souvenir item imaginable in any shop that sells souvenirs in the city.

For original GDR era souvenirs, go to the Mitropa store on Ehrenbergstr. across from the East Side Gallery. Here you won't find any mass-manufactured trinkets, but you will find all sorts of interesting merchandise left over from Eastern Germany, all at reasonable prices.

Tax

If you are visiting Berlin from outside the EU it is possible for you to receive your tax back. To do so you must have shopped in a place that displays the Global Refund "TAX FREE SHOPPING" sign. For more information pick up the booklet at the travel information office or any of these places: Tegel Airport, Schönefeld Airport, Tempelhof Airport, Bahnhof Zoo, Ostbahnhof and the KaDeWe.

Children

Playgrounds

There are playgrounds for children all over Berlin. At many adventure playgrounds kids are allowed to build, saw and hammer. The **Jugendfarm Lübars**, Quickborner Strasse, Reinickendorf, tel: 415 7027. Open Tues–Fri, Sun 9am–7pm; entry free, offers numerous opportunities for various kinds of play and sports activities. There is also a young people's farm, where visitors can see the handmade items once produced and used in the countryside. The following adventure playgrounds (Abenteuerspielplätze) may also come in handy:
Abenteuerspielplatz Marie, Marienburger Str. 42–46, Prenzl Berg, tel: 440 6032.
Kolle 37, Kollwitzstr. 35–37, tel: 4428 122. Open Mon–Fri 1–6.30pm. A whole day can be spent in the FEZ **Freizeit- und Erholungszentrum Wuhlheide**, Eichgestell, Köpenick, tel: 5307 1146, www.fez-berlin.de. Open Tues–Sun 10am–6pm, later during the school term, Sat from 1pm; where children can participate in a variety of organised activities or just play by themselves. The **Spreepark Berlin**, im Plänterwald, Treptow, entrance Neue Krugallee, DM28/26, groups over 20 – DM20, tel: 5333 5260, is a summer-long amusement and leisure park.

Farms

The following farms – complete with resident animals – are designed for kids in inner-city districts. Large and small visitors are welcome:
Weddinger Kinderfarm, Wedding, Luxemburger Strasse 25, tel: 462 1092. Open Tuesday–Sunday 10am–6pm.
Kinderbauernhof Am Mauerplatz e.V., Leuschnerdamm 9, Kreuzberg tel: 615 8149. Open weekdays except Wed 10am–7pm.

Children's Theatre

There are several performance stages in Berlin which cater specifically to children. The best-known productions are those put on by the "**Grips**" theatre, Altonaer Strasse 22, Tiergarten, tel: 3974 7477, www.grips-theater.de. "**Klecks**"-**Kindertheater with puppets**, Schinkestr. 8, Neukölln, tel: 6937731 and the **Berliner Figuren Theater**, Yorckstrasse 59, Kreuzberg, tel: 786 9815; DM10/6.50; Mon–Fri 10am, Sun 11am & 4pm, offer programmes that are suitable for younger children. Look in the city magazines or dailies for programmes. Perhaps better for the tourist is the **Hackesches Hof Theater** in Mitte, Rosenthaler Str., 40–41, tel: 283 2587; where at 10am on Sundays you can enjoy brunch and then a puppet and clown show. There are always plenty of theatrical events for kids going on. To find out more call: 2500 3322

Museums for Children

There are also plenty of exciting things for children to explore in Berlin's museums. Especially interesting are the **Ethnologisches Museum** (Museum of Ethnology), Lansstrasse 8, Dahlem; closed Mondays. The **Deutsche Technik Museum**, Trebbiner Strasse 9, Kreuzberg 10963; tel: 254 84284; closed Mondays. The **Museum für Naturkunde**, Invalidenstr. 43, Mitte; tel: 2093 8951, closed Mondays and the **Museum Europäischer Kulturen** (Folklore Museum or Museum of European Cultures), Im Winkel 6–8, Dahlem; www.smb.spk-berlin.de/mek/e/i.html; closed Mondays. If your kids want to see how fortunate they are, try **the Museum Kindheit und Jugend des Stadtmuseums Berlin** (Berlin Museum of Youth and Childhood), Wallstrasse 32; tel: 275 0383; open Tues–Fri; entrance fee. There you will find not only toys of yesteryear but also artefacts from classrooms of the Weimar, Nazi and GDR eras. More of a village museum is **Domäne Dahlem**, Königin-Luise-Str. 49; tel: 832 5000; open Wed–Mon 10am–6pm; free entry for kids, where you can see a working 17th-century farm with carpenters, blacksmiths and other guild members. An alternative is **Museumdorf Düppel**, Clauertstr. 11, Zehlendorf; tel: 802 6671; open mid-April–mid-Oct, Thur 3–7pm, Sun and holidays 10am–5pm; entrance fee. Where a 14th-century village has been reconstructed from archaeological excavations. There you can take a ride in a oxen cart. There are also

Travelling with Children

Berlin is extremely accommodating to children. All forms of transport have wide doors and spaces for prams and push-chairs, and on trams and buses there is a button you can press to tell the driver that you need more time to get in or out. Kids under six years of age accompanied by an adult with a valid ticket can travel for free on all BVG and S-Bahn modes of transport i.e. bus, tram, U-Bahn and S-Bahn. If staircases are proving to be too much of a problem don't be afraid to ask a stranger for help – they're usually more than happy to lend a hand. On ferries, there is a limit of three children.

There is a fairly relaxed attitude towards children in bars and restaurants. If in doubt, ask if it's okay to bring them in. The numerous beer gardens and outdoor terraces are perfect for kids, too. And don't worry about museums – entry for children to most places is either reduced or free – they are more than welcome.

an aquarium and two zoos in Berlin. The **Zoologischer Garten** on Budapester Strasse has plenty of outdoor enclosures, a tropical and nocturnal house, pony and carriage rides, as well as a section where you can stroke and pet all the animals. It stays open daily until around 6pm or dusk. The ex-eastern alternative is the **Tierpark Friedrichsfelde**, Am Tierpark 125; tel: 515 310; open 9–5 daily. Three museums are especially designed for children and young people. The **Labyrinth Kindermuseum**, Osloer Str. 12, Wedding, tel. 4930 8901, www.kinder-museum-labyrinth.de, has an exhibition demonstrating the five senses. The **Kinder & Jugend Museum Prenzlauer Berg**, Prenzlauer Allee 75, tel: 7477 8200, has changing exhibitions and projects, and the **Jugendmuseum Schöneberg**, Hauptstrasse 40–42, tel: 78762234, has treasures and miracles to explore.

Babysitters

The Free University's "Heinzel-männchen" (open 7.30am–5pm; tel: 831 6071) and the Technical University's TUSMA (open 7am–6pm; tel: 315 9340) both arrange babysitters at an hourly rate. Hotels also can arrange for babysitting, as can the last-minute ticket office Hekticket.

General

Nachbarschaft- und Selbsthilfe Zentrum e.V., Viktoriastrasse 13–18, Berlin-Tempelhof; Children's Farm, open Mon–Fri 10am–6pm in summer, 10am–5pm in winter, weekends 12pm–3pm; tel: 7517244; General Enquiries: 7550 3125. is one of Berlin's best-known self-help projects, which has been developed on the grounds of the former UFA film studios. There are regularly scheduled theatre, music and circus performances for children.

Language

General

German is the native language of about 100 million people, but not all of them live in continental Europe. As well as Germany, Austria, parts of Switzerland and some small German enclaves in eastern Europe, there are also German-speaking communities in North America, South America and South Africa.

In terms of language groups, German and English are both part of the West Germanic languages, together with Dutch, Frisian, Flemish and Afrikaans, but while a Dutchman and a German may be able to communicate quite effectively, an Englishman and a German are unlikely to make much progress, despite the many similarities between the two languages. A glance at the numbers from one to ten (see end of this section) will prove that point.

Anyone who learnt Latin at school will be familiar with some of the difficulties that the German language presents to foreigners: nouns have three genders and four cases, verbs are conjugated, pronouns are followed by one of three cases, the word order in sentences is governed by some complicated rules and there are five different ways that you can say "the". The only compensation is that pronunciation is always perfectly consistent with the spelling.

Pronunciation

Most consonants are pronounced as in English with the following exceptions: g as in "get", ch as in

the German composer Bach or the Scottish "loch", j is like "y", k is pronounced even before an "n", v is more like an "f", w is pronounced like the English "v" and z is pronounced as "ts". The *scharfes* S or ß is sometimes used to replace "ss".

Vowels and vowels with umlauts are not so straightforward:
a   as in bad
e   as in hay
i   as in seek
o   as in note (Scottish accent)
u   as in boot
ä   is a combination of "a" and "e" and pronounced like the "e" in get
ö   combines "o" and "e" like the "er" in Bert (English accent)
ü   combine "u" and "e" as in true.

Plus there are dipthong sounds:
ai as in tie
au as in sauerkraut
ie as in thief
ei as in wine
eu as in boil

The Alphabet

Learning the pronunciation of the German alphabet is a good idea. You will find it helpful to be able to spell your name.
a = ah
b = bay
c = tsay
d = day
e = eh
f = eff
g = gay
h = har
i = ee
j = yot
k = kar
l = ell
m = emm
n = enn
o = oh
p = pay
q = koo
r = air
s = ess
t = tay
u = oo
v = fow
w = vay
x = icks
y = upsilon
z = tset

On the Telephone

I must make a phone call *Ich muss telefonieren*
Can I use your phone? *Kann ich Ihr Telefon benutzen?*
Can I dial direct? *Kann ich direkt wählen?*
Please connect me to... *Bitte verbinden Sie mich mit...*
What is the code for Great Britain? *Was is das Vorwahl für Grossbritannien?*
Who is speaking? *Wer spricht da?*
The line is engaged *Die Leitung ist besetzt*
A reversed charges call, please *Ein R-Gespräch, bitte*
I'll call again later *Ich rufe später wieder an*

Words & Phrases

GENERAL

Good morning *Guten Morgen*
Good afternoon *Guten Tag*
Good evening *Guten Abend*
Good night *Gute Nacht*
Goodbye *Auf Wiedersehen*
Goodbye *Tschüs* (informal)
Do you speak English? *Sprechen Sie Englisch?*
I do not understand *Ich verstehe nicht*
Could you please speak more slowly? *Könnten Sie bitte etwas langsamer sprechen?*
Can you help me? *Können Sie mir helfen?*
Yes/No *Ja/Nein*
Please/Thank you *Bitte/Danke*
Sorry *Entschuldigung*
How are you? *Wie geht's?*
Excuse me *Entschuldigung Sie, bitte*
You're welcome *Bitte schön*
It doesn't matter *(Es) macht nichts*
OK *Alles klar*
Pity *Schade*
Thank you for your help *Besten Dank für Ihre Hilfe*
See you later *Bis später*
See you tomorrow *Bis morgen*
What time is it? *Wie spät ist es?*
10 o'clock *zehn Uhr*

Half past ten *halb elf*
This morning *heute Morgen*
This afternoon *heute Nachmittag*
This evening *heute Abend*
Let's go! *Los!*
Leave me alone *Lass mich in Ruhe*
Clear off *Hau ab*
Where are the toilets? *Wo sind die Toiletten?*
large/small *gross/klein*
more/less *mehr/weniger*
now *jetzt*
later *später*
here *hier*
there *dort*

ON ARRIVAL

Station *Bahnhof*
Bus station *Busbahnhof*
Bus stop *Bushaltestelle*
Will you tell me when to get off the bus? *Können Sie mir Sagen, wann ich aussteigen muss?*
Where can I get the bus to the Adler Hotel? *Wo kann ich den Bus zum Hotel Adler nehmen?*
Does this bus go to the town centre? *Fährt dieser Bus zur Stadtmitte?*
Which street is this? *Welche Strasse ist das?*
How far is it the station? *Wie weit ist es zum Bahnhof?*
Do you have a single room? *Haben Sie ein Einzelzimmer?*
Do you have a double room? *Haben Sie ein Doppelzimmer?*
Do you have a room with a private bath? *Haben Sie ein Zimmer mit Bad?*
How much is it? *Wieviel kostet das?*

Emergencies

Help *Hilfe!* **Stop** *Halt!*
Please call a doctor *Holen Sie einen Arzt*
Please call an ambulance *Rufen Sie einen Krankenwagen*
Please call the fire-brigade *Rufen Sie die Feuerwehr*
Where is the nearest telephone box? *Wo ist die nächste Telefonzelle?*

How much is a room with full board? *Wieviel kostet ein Zimmer mit Vollpension?*
Please show me another room *Bitte zeigen Sie mir ein anderes Zimmer*
We'll (I'll) be staying for one night *Wir bleiben (Ich bleibe) eine Nacht*
When is breakfast? *Wann gibt es Frühstück?*
Where is the toilet? *Wo ist die Toilette?*
Where is the bathroom? *Wo ist das Badezimmer?*
Where is the next hotel? *Wo ist das nächste Hotel?*

TRAVELLING

Where is the post office? *Wo ist das Postamt?*
Where is the nearest bank? *Wo ist die nächste Bank?*
Where can I change money? *Wo kann ich Geld wechseln?*
Where is the pharmacy? *Wo ist die Apotheke?*
What time do they close? *Wann schliessen sie?*
open/closed *geöffnet/geschlossen*
close/far *nah/weit*
cheap, expensive *billig, teuer*
free (of charge) *kostenlos*
price *Preis*
change *Wechselgeld*
Have you got any change? *Können Sie Geld wechseln?*
telephone booth *Telefonzelle*
Is this the way to the station? *Ist das der Weg zum Bahnhof?*
Where is platform one? *Wo ist Gleis eins?*
Where is the airport? *Wo ist der Flughafen?*

I am ill *Ich bin krank*
I have lost my wallet/hand-bag *Ich habe meine Geldtasche/Handtasche verloren*
Where is the nearest hospital? *Wo ist das nächste Krankenhaus?*
Where is the police station? *Wo ist die Polizeiwache?*
Where is the British consulate? *Wo ist die britische Konsulat?*

Can you call me a taxi? *Können Sie mir ein Taxi rufen?*
Can you take me to the airport? *Können Sie mich zum Flughafen fahren?*
Where do I get a ticket? *Wo kann ich eine Fahrkarte kaufen?*
departure, arrival *Abfahrt, Ankunft*
When is the next flight/train to ...? *Wann geht der nächste Flug/Zug nach ...?*
to change (flights/trains) *umsteigen*
Have you anything to declare? *Haben Sie etwas zu verzollen?*
bridge *Brücke*
customs *Zoll*
entrance *Eingang, Einfahrt*
exit *Ausgang, Ausfahrt*
fee *Gebühr*
ferry *Fähre*
gas (petrol) station *Tankstelle*
height/width/length *Höhe/Breite/Länge*
hospital *Krankenhaus*
no stopping *Halten verboten*
one-way street *Einbahnstrasse*
picnic area *Rastplatz*
travel agency *Reisebüro*

Days of the Week

Monday *Montag*
Tuesday *Dienstag*
Wednesday *Mittwoch*
Thursday *Donnerstag*
Friday *Freitag*
Saturday *Samstag, Sonnabend*
Sunday *Sonntag*

ON THE ROAD

I have run out of petrol *Ich habe kein Benzin mehr*
My car has broken down *Ich habe eine Autopanne*
Could you give me a push/tow? *Könnten Sie mich bitte anschieben/abschleppen?*
Can you take me to the nearest garage? *Können Sie mich zur nächsten Werkstatt bringen?*
Can you find out what the trouble is? *Können Sie feststellen, was das Problem ist?*
Can you repair it? *Können Sie es reparieren?*
The road to...? *Die Strasse nach...?*

left *links*
right *rechts*
straight on *geradeaus*
opposite *gegenüber*
beside *nebenan*
Where is the nearest car-park? *Wo ist der nächste parkplatz, bitte?*
over there *da drüben*
on foot *zu Fuss*
Turn left/right after the bridge *Biegen Sie hinter der Brücke links/rechts ab*
Here is my driving licence *Da ist mein Führerschein*
Here are my insurance documents *Hier sind meine Versicherungsunterlagen*
brakes *Bremsen*
bulb *Glühbirne*
by car *mit dem Auto*
dead end *Sackgasse*
diesel *Diesel*
give way *Vorfahrt beachten*
headlights *Scheinwerfer*
jack *Wagenheber*
map *Strassenkarte*
no parking *Parken verboten*
one-way street *Einbahnstrasse*
petrol *Benzin*
road/street *Strasse*
slow/fast *langsam/schnell*
square *Platz*
unleaded *bleifrei*
water/oil *Wasser/Öl*
windscreen wipers *Scheibenwischer*

Numbers

0	*null*	80	*achtzig*
1	*eins*	90	*neunzig*
2	*zwei*	100	*hundert*
3	*drei*	200	*zweihundert*
4	*vier*	1,000	*tausend*
5	*fünf*	2,000	*zweitausend*
6	*sechs*	1,000,000	*eine Million*
7	*sieben*		
8	*acht*	1st	*erste(r)*
9	*neun*	2nd	*zweite(r)*
10	*zehn*	3rd	*dritte(r)*
11	*elf*	4th	*vierte(r)*
12	*zwölf*	5th	*fünfte(r)*
13	*dreizehn*	6th	*sechste(r)*
14	*vierzehn*	7th	*siebte(r)*
15	*fünfzehn*	8th	*achte(r)*
16	*sechzehn*	9th	*neunte(r)*
17	*siebzehn*	10th	*zehnte(r)*
18	*achtzehn*	11th	*elfte(r)*
19	*neunzehn*	12th	*zwölfte(r)*
20	*zwanzig*	13th	*dreizehnte(r)*
30	*dreissig*	20th	*zwanzigste(r)*
40	*vierzig*	21st	*einund*
50	*fünfzig*		*zwanzigste(r)*
60	*sechzig*	100th	*hundertste(r)*
70	*siebzig*	1000th	*tausendste(r)*

SHOPPING

Where is the nearest post-office? *Wo ist die nächste Post?*
I'd like ... *Ich hätte gern...*
How much is this? *Was kostet das?*
Do you take credit cards? *Akzeptieren Sie Kreditkarten?*
I'm just looking *Ich sehe mich nur um*
Do you have ...? *Haben Sie ...?*
That'll be fine. I'll take it. *In Ordnung. Ich nehme es.*
No, that is too expensive *Nein, das ist zu teuer*
Can I try it on? *Kann ich es anprobieren?*
Do you have anything cheaper? *Haben Sie etwas Billigeres?*

open/closed
geöffnet/geschlossen
bookshop Buchhandlung
butcher's Metzgerei
cake shop Konditorei
cash desk Kasse
confectionery, sweets Süsswaren
department Abteilung
department store Kaufhaus
drugstore, chemist (not
medications) Drogerie
fashion Mode
food Lebensmittel
fresh every day täglich frisch
ladies' clothing Damenkleidung
launderette Wäscherei
magazines Zeitschriften
newspapers Zeitungen
self-service Selbstbedienung
shoes Schuhe
special offer Sonderangebot
stationery Schreibwaren
travel agent Reisebüro

Months

January Januar
February Februar
March März
April April
May Mai
June Juni
July Juli
August August
September September
October Oktober
November November
December Dezember

SIGHTSEEING

Where is the tourist office? Wo ist
das Fremdenverkehrsbüro?
Is there a bus to the centre? Gibt
es einen Bus ins Stadtzentrum?
Is there a guided sightseeing tour?
Werden geführte
Besichtigungstouren durchgeführt?
When is the museum open? Wann
ist das Museum geöffnet?
How much does it cost to go in?
Was kostet der Eintritt?
Where can I buy souvenirs? Wo
kann ich Souvenirs kaufen?
art gallery Kunstgalerie
castle Schloss
cathedral Dom
church Kirche

exhibition Ausstellung
memorial Denkmal
old part of town Altstadtviertel
tower Turm
town hall Rathaus
walk Spaziergang
Roman Römisch
Romanesque Romanisch
Gothic Gotisch
open daily täglich
open all year ganzjährig
swimming pool Hallenbad (indoor),
Freibad (open-air)

DINING OUT

Do you know a good restaurant?
Kennen Sie ein gutes
Restaurant?
A table for one/two/three Ein
Tisch für eine Person/zwei/drei
Personen, bitte
Could we order a meal, please?
Können wir bitte bestellen?
Can we have the bill, please?
Können wir bitte bezahlen?
beer, wine Bier/Wein
bread Brot
bread roll Brötchen
butter Butter
cake Kuchen
children's portion Kinderteller
coffee Kaffee
complain sich beschweren
dessert Nachspeise
dry/sweet trocken/süss
egg Ei
evening meal Abendessen
jam Konfitüre
knife/fork/spoon
Messer/Gabel/Löffel
lunch Mittagessen
main course Hauptgericht
menu Speisekarte
milk Milch
mineral water Mineralwasser
mustard Senf
pay bezahlen
potatoes Kartoffeln
rice Reis
salt/pepper Salz/Pfeffer
snack Imbiss
soup/starter Suppe/Vorspeise
sugar Zucker
tea Tee
tip Trinkgeld
tomato sauce Ketchup
wine list Weinkarte

Table Talk

I am a vegetarian Ich bin
Vegetarier(in)
I am on a special diet Ich halte
Diät
What do you recommend? Was
würden Sie empfehlen?
I am ready to order Ich möchte
bestellen
Enjoy your meal Guten Appetit
What would you like to drink? Was
möchten Sie trinken?
Did you enjoy your meal? Hat es
Ihnen geschmeckt?
Cheers Prost

Markets and Delis

Can I taste it? Kann ich einmal
probieren?
That is very nice. I'll take some.
Das schmeckt sehr gut. Davon
nehme ich etwas.
What's the price per kilo? Was
kostet es pro Kilo?
About 200g ham please Etwa
Zweihundert Gramm Schinken,
bitte
A piece of that cheese, please
Ich hätte gern ein Stück von dem
Käse

Frühstück/Breakfast

Brot bread
Brötchen roll
Eier eggs
Fruchtsaft fruit juice
hartgekochtes Ei hard-boiled egg
heiss hot
kalt cold
Marmelade Konfitüre jam
Orangensaft orange juice
Pumpernickel black rye bread
Rühreier scrambled egg
Schinken ham
Schwarzbrot brown rye bread
Speck bacon
Weissbrot white bread

Suppen/Soups

Eintopf thick soup
Erbsensuppe pea soup
Flädlesuppe consommé with strips
of pancake
Gemüsesuppe vegetable soup
Griessnockerlsuppe semolina
dumpling soup
Hühnersuppe chicken soup

Kartoffelsuppe **potato soup**
Kraftbrühe **bouillon**
Leberknödelsuppe **liver dumpling soup**
Linsensuppe **lentil soup**
Nudelsuppe **noodle soup**
Ochsenschwanzsuppe **oxtail soup**
Pilzsuppe **mushroom soup**
Spargelcremesuppe **cream of asparagus soup**
Zwiebelsuppe **onion soup**

Vorspeisen/Starters
Austern **oysters**
Froschschenkel **frogs' legs**
Gänseleberpastete **pâté de foie gras**
Geeiste Melone **iced melon**
Rollmops **rolled-up pickled herring**
Schnecken **snails**
Spargelspitzen **asparagus tips**
Strammer Max **ham and fried egg on bread**
Wurstplatte **assorted cooked meats**

Saying the Date

on the 20th October 1999
am zwanzigsten Oktober, neunzehnhundertneunundneunzig
yesterday *gestern*
today *heute*
tomorrow *morgen*
last week *letzte Woche*
next week *nächste Woche*

Fleischgerichte/Meat Courses
Backhuhn **roast chicken**
Blutwurst **black pudding**
Bockwurst **large frankfurter**
Bouletten **meatballs**
Brathuhn **roast chicken**
Bratwurst **fried sausage**
Currywurst **pork sausage with curry powder**
Deutsches Beefsteak **minced beef/hamburger**
Eisbein **knuckle of pork**
Ente **duck**
Fasan **pheasant**
Fleischklösschen **meatballs**
Gans **goose**
Gulasch **goulash**
Hackbraten **meatloaf**
Hähnchen/Huhn **chicken**
Hammelbraten **roast mutton**
Herzragout **heart stew**
Hühnerfrikassee **chicken fricassee**

Jägerschnitzel **cutlet with mushrooms**
Kalbsbries **veal sweetbreads**
Kalbsbrust **breast of veal**
Kalbshaxe **roast knuckle of veal**
Kalbskoteletts **veal cutlets/chops**
Kaninchen **rabbit**
Kasseler Rippchen **smoked pork chop**
Lamm am Spiess **lamb on the spit**
Lammbraten **roast lamb**
Lammskeule **roast leg of lamb**
Leberknödel **liver dumplings**
Leberwurst **liver sausage**
Nieren **kidneys**
Ochsenschwanz **oxtail**
Pichelsteinertopf **vegetable stew with beef**
Pute **turkey**
Räucherschinken **cured ham**
Rehrücken **saddle of deer**
Rheinischer Sauerbraten **braised beef**
Rind **beef**
Rinderbraten **roast beef**
Rinderfilet **fillet of beef**
Rinderroulade **stuffed beef roll**
Rinderschmorbraten **braised beef**
Sauerbraten **braised pickled beef**
Schinken **ham**
Schlachtplate **mixed cold meat**
Schweinebauch **belly of pork**
Schweinebraten **roast pork**
Schweinefilet **loin of pork**
Schweinefleisch **pork**
Serbisches Reisfleisch **diced pork, onions, tomatoes and rice**
Spanferkel **sucking pig**
Speck **bacon**
Speckknödel **bacon dumplings**
Sülze **brawn**
Szegediner Gulasch **goulash with pickled cabbage**
Tafelspitz **boiled rump**
Taube **pigeon**
Truthahn **turkey**
Ungarischer Gulasch **Hungarian goulash**
Wiener Schnitzel **breaded escalope of veal**
Zigeunerschnitzel **veal with peppers and relishes**
Zunge **tongue**

Fisch/Fish
Aal **eel**
Austern **oysters**
Barbe **mullet**

Bismarckhering **filleted pickled herring**
Fischfrikadellen **fishcakes**
Flunder **flounder**
Flusskrebs **crayfish**
Forelle **trout**
Garnelen **prawns**
Hecht **pike**
Heilbutt **halibut**
Heringstopf **pickled herrings in sauce**
Hummer **lobster**
Jakobsmuscheln **scallops**
Kabeljau **cod**
Karpfen **carp**
Krabbe **shrimps**
Lachs **salmon**
Languste **spiny lobster**
Makrele **mackerel**
Matjes **young herring**
Miesmuscheln **cockles**
Muscheln **mussels**
Renke **whitefish**
Rotbarsch **red sea bass**
Sardinen **sardines**
Schellfisch **haddock**
Scholle **plaice**
Schwertfisch **swordfish**
Seebarsch **sea bass**
Seezunge **sole**
Steinbutt **turbot**
Süsswasserfische **freshwater fish**
Thunfisch **tuna**
Tintenfisch **squid**
Zander **pike-perch, zander**

Seasons

spring *Frühling*
summer *Sommer*
autumn *Herbst*
winter *Winter*

Knödel/Dumplings and Noodles
Kartoffelklösse **potato dumplings**
Klösse **dumplings**
Leberknödel **liver dumplings**
Maultasche **Swabian ravioli**
Nudeln **noodles**
Spätzle **grated pasta**

Eier/Eggs
Bauernomelett **omelette with diced bacon and onion**
gekochtes Ei **boiled egg**
hartgekochtes Ei **hard-boiled egg**
Rührei **scrambled eggs**

Russische Eier **hard-boiled eggs
with caviar, capers and mayonnaise**
Spiegeleier **fried eggs**
verlorene Eier **poached eggs**

Vorbereitung/Preparation

am Spiess **on the spit**
blau blue **boiled in salt and vinegar**
durchgebraten **well-done**
eingelegt **pickled**
flambiert **flambée**
fritiert **deep-fried**
gebacken **baked**
gebeizt **marinated**
gebraten **fried**
gedämpft **steamed**
gedünstet **steamed**
gefüllt **stuffed**
gekocht **boiled**
gepökelt **salted**
geräuchert **smoked**
geschmort **braised**
Geschnetzeltes **strips of meat in a
sauce**
gratiniert **au gratin**
halbdurch **medium**
Hausmacher Art **home-made**
mariniert **marinated**
nach Hausfrauenart **home-made**
nach Jägerart **sautéed with
mushrooms**
paniert **breaded**
pikant **spicy**
pochiert **poached**
roh **raw**
rosa **rare to medium**
rot **rare**
süss-sauer **sweet and sour**
überbacken **au gratin**
vom Grill **grilled**

Gemüse/Vegetables

Blumenkohl **cauliflower**
Bohnen **beans**
Bratkartoffeln **fried potatoes**
Brunnenkresse **watercress**
Champignons **mushrooms**
Dicke Bohnen **broad beans**
Erbsen **peas**
Feldsalat **lamb's lettuce**
Fenchel **fennel**
Grüne Bohnen **green beans**
Grünkohl **curly kale**
Gurke **cucumber**
Kapern **capers**
Karotten **carrots**
Kartoffeln **potatoes**
Kartoffelpuree **creamed potatoes**
Kartoffelsalat **potato salad**
Knoblauch **garlic**
Kohl **cabbage**
Kopfsalat **lettuce**
Kürbis **pumpkin**
Lauch **leek**
Linsen **lentils**
Maiskolben **sweetcorn**
Meerrettich **horseradish**
Paprika **peppers**
Pellkartoffeln **jacket potatoes**
Pfifferlinge **chanterelle
mushrooms**
Pilze **mushrooms**
Pommes (frites) **chips/French fries**
Prinzessbohnen **unsliced runner
beans**
Reis **rice**
Rettich **radish**
Risi-Pisi **rice and peas**
Rosenkohl **Brussel sprouts**
Rote Beet **beetroot**
Rotkraut/Rotkohl **red cabbage**

Salat **salad**
Salzkartoffeln **boiled potatoes**
Sauerkraut **pickled cabbage**
Sellerie **celery**
Spargel **asparagus**
Spinat **spinach**
Tomaten **tomatoes**
Weisskohl **cabbage**
Wirsing **savoy cabbage**
Zwiebeln **onions**

Nachspeisen/Desserts

Apfelkuchen **apple cake**
Apfelstrudel **flaky pastry stuffed
with apple**
Auflauf **soufflé**
Bienenstich **honey-almond cake**
Eis **ice cream**
Eisbecher **ice cream with fresh fruit**
Fruchttörtchen **fruit tartlet**
Gebäck **pastries**
Kaiserschmarrn **sugared pancake
with raisins**
Käsetorte **cheesecake**
Kompott **fruit stew**
Krapfen **doughnuts**
Linzer Torte **cake spread with jam
and topped with cream**
Mandelkuchen **almond cake**
Mohnkuchen **poppyseed cake**
Obstkuchen **fruit tart**
Rote Grütze **raspberries or
redcurrants cooked with semolina**
Sacher Torte **chocolate cake with
jam and chocolate icing**
Schlagsahne **whipped cream**
Schwarzwälder Kirschtorte **Black
Forest gateau**
Streuselkuchen **cake with crumble
topping**

In the Café

café *ein Café, ein Gasthaus*
waiter/waitress *Herr
Ober/Fräulein*
What would you like to drink?
Was möchten Sie trinken?
cup of coffee *eine Tasse Kaffee*
with milk/sugar *mit Milch/Zucker*
decaffeinated coffee
Haag/koffeinfrei
black *schwarz*
milk *Milch*
mineral water *Mineralwasser,
Sprudel, Selters*
still/fizzy *ohne/mit Kohlensäure*
tea *Tee*

lemon tea *Zitronentee*
iced tea *Eistee*
hot chocolate *(heisse)
Schokolade*
lemonade *Limonade*
apple juice *Apfelsaft*
orange juice *Orangensaft*
cola *Cola*
a beer, please *ein Bier, bitte*
a small beer *ein kleines Bier*
a large beer *ein grosses Bier*
another beer, please *noch ein
Bier, bitte*
a lager *ein Pils, ein Pilsener*
draught *vom Fass*

dark beer *ein Altbier*
cider *Apfelwein*
shandy *ein Radler*
non-alcoholic *alkoholfrei*
a glass of white wine, please *ein
Glas Weisswein, bitte*
a glass of red wine, please *ein
Glas Rotwein, bitte*
a sparkling wine *ein Sekt*
liqueur *Likör*
hot rum *Grog*
mulled wine *Glühwein*
sweet/dry *süss/trocken*
the bill, please *Zahlen, bitte*

Früchte/Fruit

Apfel **apple**
Apfelsine **orange**
Aprikose **apricot**
Backpflaumen **prunes**
Banane **bananas**
Birne **pears**
Blaubeere **bilberries/blueberries**
Brombeere **blackberries**
Erdbeere **strawberries**
Himbeere **raspberries**
Kirsche **cherries**
Melone **melons**
Pampelmuse **grapefruit**
Pfirsich **peach**
Pflaumen **plums**
Preiselbeere **cranberries**
Reineclauden **greengages**
Rosine **raisins**
Rote Johannisbeere **redcurrants**
Schwarze Johannisbeere
blackcurrants
Stachelbeere **gooseberries**
Weintraube **grapes**
Zitrone **lemon**
Zwetschen **plums**

Further Reading

History and Society

Ardagh, John, **Germany and the Germans**, Penguin US 1996. Respected, canny and incisive insight into the German culture and society.

Craig, Gordon, **The Germans**, Meridian 1996. More for the academically minded but, nevertheless, a reasonably comprehensive view of the socio-political make-up of the Germans and their institutions.

Erikson John, **The Road to Berlin**. Yale Univ Pr, 1999. Comprehensive but possibly over-indulgent study of the Soviet advance to the roof of the Reichstag. Extremely meaty.

Garton Ash, Timothy, **We Are The People**, Penguin 1999. An account of not only the 1989 revolution in Berlin but also those witnessed in Warsaw, Budapest and Prague.

Gordon Mel, **Voluptuous Panic: The Erotic World of Weima Berlin**, Feral House, 2000. Photos, theatre programs, special guidebooks, magazines, personal memoirs, interviews and sociological accounts - slide into the debauched world of pre-Nazi Berlin and get a taste of what decadence was all about.

Hertz Deborah, **Jewish High Society in Old Regime Berlin**, Yale University Press, 1988. Think of the Jews in Germany and you think of the Holocaust but it wasn't always hardship and suffering. This book takes a look at some of the more privileged lifestyles before the oppression started.

Holborn, Hajo, **A History of Modern Germany: 1840–1945**, Princetown UP 1992. A standard university text covering German history from ca 1000 until 1945. Comes as three former titles combined into one.

Jelavich, Peter, **Berlin Cabaret (Studies in Cultural History)**, Harvard UP 1996. A magnifying glass on German society and culture between the 1920s and the Nazi era in the early 1903s. Each chapter concentrates on a different cabaret, for example, *Sound and Smoke.*

Kettenacker, Lothar, **Germany since 1945**, Oxford University Press 1997. Although containing lots of useful information, maps chronologies and biographies Kettenacker's book has been accused of being slightly over political.

Kitchen Martin, **Cambridge Illustrated History of Germany**, Cambridge UP 2000. In answering the questions – "Who is a German?" and "Where is Germany" – Kitchen manages to provide an interpretive account of political structures from the Holy Roman Empire to the reunified state.

MacDonogh, Giles, **Berlin**, Griffin 1999. Thematically arranged impressions of Berlin's people, which concentrates more on the spirit of the city than its chronological make-up.

Millar, Peter, **Tomorrow Belongs To Me**, Bloomsbury 1992. An account of life in East Berlin both before and after the Wall came down.

Read, Anthony and Fisher, David **Berlin, the Biography of a City**, Pimlico 1994. A social history of Berlin from its beginnings to the modern day.

Read Anthony and Fisher David, **The Fall of Berlin**, William s Konecky Assoc, 2001. Apocalyptic portrait of the last days of the Third Reich which also delves into Hitler's relationship with his devastated capital.

Richie, Alexandra, **Faust's Metropolis – A History of Berlin**, HarperCollins 1999. An audacious, but spirited, attempt to chronicle the complete history of one of the most tempestuous metropolises on earth. This popular 1000 page tome continues to be well received.

Taylor Ronald, **Berlin and Its Culture: A Historical Portrait**, Yale University Press, 1997. Here, Ronald Taylor maps the various areas of Berlin's society while paying attention to the writers, actors, designers and filmmakers

who made the city so culturally rich.
Shirer, William, **This is Berlin**,
Arrow 2001. After stints in Europe,
Africa and the Middle East Iowa
born reporter William Shirer found
himself in Berlin in the mid-1930s.
This book of his radio scripts not
only describes the significant
events in Germany's run-up to the
war but also acts as a good primary
source for the opinions and feelings
of the time within Germany.

Fiction

Benjamin, Walter, **One Way Street**,
Verso Books 1997. Contains the
essay "A Berlin Childhood", an
acessible text by the influential
philosopher.
Le Carré, John, **The Spy Who Came
in from The Cold**, Sceptre 1999.
Kalashnikovs and alsatians on the
bridge at Wansee – vintage cold-war
spy novel.
Döblin, Alfred, **Berlin
Alexanderplatz**, Continuum
Publishing Group 1994. The story
of Franz Biberkopf, flawed lover and
ex-con. Döblin's novel of small-time
gangsters in 1930s Berlin was
brilliantly filmed by Rainer Werner
Fassbinder in a seven-part TV epic.
Fontaine, Theodore, **Effi Briest**,
Penguin Books 2000. The tragic
story of a young woman's struggle
with aristocratic family duties.
Grass, Gunther, **Too Far Afield**,
Faber and Faber 2000. This oblique
and controversial novel, four years
in the translation, is the Nobel
Laureate's confrontation with the
East–West divide.
Hensher, Philip, **Pleasured**, Chatto
and Windus 1998. A plot to
destabilise the GDR through a
saturation of ecstasy pills, among
other things.
Isherwood, Christopher, **Goodbye to
Berlin**, Minerva 1989. The classic
expat novel – Isherwood's
patchwork narrative of pleasure
seekers whose fun is just about to
be ruined by the Nazis.
Kerr, Phillip, **Berlin Noir**, Penguin
Books 1993. Hard-boiled Berlin
detective causes problems for the
corrupt Nazi regime – a trilogy.
Schneider, Peter, **The Wall Jumper**,

University of Chicago Press 1998.
Narratives of Berliners linked and
divided by the wall.
Stuart, Francis, **Black List, Section
H**, The Lilliput Press 1995. This
autobiographical novel by the 'black
listed' Irish writer whose career was
blighted for alleged cooperation with
Lord Haw Haw is an existentialist
masterpiece.

Other Insight Guides

Insight Guide Germany takes the
reader through every region of the
country and explains what makes
this contradictory country tick.

Insight Pocket Guides

Insight Pocket Guides are designed
for short-stay travellers who need to
get the best out of their destination
in a short time. The authors have
local knowledge which they use to
take you on the best tailor-made
tours and show you places both on
and off the beaten track.

Insight Pocket Guide Bavaria covers
the soaring mountains, deep pine
forests and fairy-tale castles of this
magical region.

Compact Guides

These handy guides are in essence
mini-encyclopedias. They provide all
the on-the-spot information you
need to find your way round a
destination. *Compact Guide:
Munich* is a culture-based guide for
a culture-based destination that
reveals all the splendours of this
beautiful city.

Feedback

We do our best to ensure the information in our books is as accurate and
up-to-date as possible. The books are updated on a regular basis, using
local contacts, who painstakingly add, amend and correct as required.
However, some mistakes and omissions are inevitable and we are
ultimately reliant on our readers to put us in the picture.

We would welcome your feedback on any details related to your
experiences using the book "on the road". Maybe we recommended a hotel
that you liked (or another that you didn't), as well as interesting new
attractions, or facts and figures you have found out about the country itself.
The more details you can give us (particularly with regard to addresses,
e-mails and telephone numbers), the better.

We will acknowledge all contributions, and we'll
offer an Insight Guide to the best letters received.
Please write to us at:

**Insight Guides
PO Box 7910
London SE1 1WE
United Kingdom**
Or send e-mail to: **insight@apaguide.demon.co.uk**

ART & PHOTO CREDITS

AKG London 31, 32, 36, 42, 45, 57
Archive for Art & History, Berlin 16/17, 20, 22, 23, 24, 26, 27, 28, 37, 39L/R, 40, 41, 76/77, 165
Archive Jürgens, Cologne 54, 114, 122, 209, 210/211, 279
Archive of Prussian Cultural Possessions, Berlin 30, 35
David Baltzer 71, 85
Bauhaus-Archiv Museum 4R, 144T
Schloss Charlottenburg, Berlin 18
Günter Breithaupt 84
Checkpoint Charlie Publishers 49
Wolfgang Fritz 52/53
Max Galli/Look 10/11
Wieland Giebel 87, 124, 213, 286T
Frances Gransden/Apa back cover right, left & bottom, spine top & bottom, front & back flap, 21, 129T, 145, 147, 160, 164T, 165T, 220T, 239, 242L/R, 245T, 246T, 255, 256T, 258, 260, 261, 263T, 269T, 248, 248T, 282T, 282
Frances Gransden/Mark Read/Apa 120T, 130T, 133, 135, 138, 138T, 139, 146, 155, 155T, 176, 243T
Annette Hauschild/Ostkreuz 191
Harold Hauswald 106/107, 188, 221
Blaine Harrington 6/7, 8/9, 19, 60/61, 64, 94, 98/99, 102/103,

112, 113, 118, 121, 128, 129, 154, 179, 180/181
Brigitte Hiss/Ostkreuz 67
Michael Jenner 4L, 96, 114T, 117T, 130, 161, 182
A. Kamper/Ostkreuz 204
R. Kiedrowski 200
Benno Kraehahn 234
Karl-Heinz & Sabine Kraemer 171, 198, 218, 219, 220, 247
Ute Mahler/Ostkreuz 62, 70, 78, 140
Rainer Martini/Look 112T
Andreas Muhs/Ostkreuz 241
Kal-Ullrich Müller 214, 287
John D. Norman 5B, 88/89, 141, 163T, 164, 170, 272/273
Erhard Pansegrau 1, 4/5, 14, 68, 73, 79, 80, 81, 82, 90, 91, 92, 93, 97, 100/101, 111, 116T, 116, 117, 119, 126, 127, 132, 136, 142, 144, 152, 157, 158/159, 162, 163, 166, 167, 172, 173, 174, 175, 177, 179T, 183, 184, 187, 187T, 190, 192/193, 196, 203, 205, 206, 207, 212, 215, 216, 217, 222, 230, 231, 233, 236, 237, 239T, 240, 243, 244, 245, 246, 250T, 250, 251, 252/253, 256, 257, 259, 262, 263, 264, 265, 266, 267, 267T, 268L/R, 269, 270, 271, 274, 275, 277T, 277, 278T, 278, 280, 281T,

281, 283, 285T, 285, 286, 288
Lesley Player 2B, 56, 59, 74, 120, 123, 131, 175T, 284
Julian Roder/Ostkreuz 185
Stefan Maria Rother 199, 201
Jens Rötzsch/Ostkreuz 12/13, 65
Thomas Sandberg 202
Jordis Antonia Schlösser/Ostkreuz 2/3, 58, 63, 75, 189
S. Schönharting/Ostkreuz 223
Günter Schneider back cover top right, 55, 66, 69, 72, 148/149, 150, 151, 178, 208, 226/227, 228, 229, 235, 249
Jonathan Smith 145T
Spandau Press Office 254
Staatliche Museen zu Berlin 145, 145T
State Picture Library, Berlin 34, 38, 44, 46, 47, 48, 50, 51, 137, 156
Rolf Steinberg 25, 29, 33, 43, 238
Michael Trippel 86
Jörn Vanhöfen/Ostkreuz 204T
Maurice Weiss/Ostkreuz 83, 104, 224, 225
Heinz Wohner/Look 168/169
Konrad Wothe/Look 95, 186

Map Production Colin Earl
© 2001 Apa Publications GmbH & Co.
Verlag KG (Singapore branch)

INSIGHT GUIDE
BERLIN

Cartographic Editor **Zoë Goodwin**
Production **Linton Donaldson**
Art Director **Carlotta Junger**
Picture Research
Hilary Genin, Britta Jaschinski

Index